DOLLS STUDIES

mediated youth

Sharon R. Mazzarella
General Editor

Vol. 19

The Mediated Youth series is part of the Peter Lang Media and Communication list.
Every volume is peer reviewed and meets
the highest quality standards for content and production.

PETER LANG
New York • Bern • Frankfurt • Berlin
Brussels • Vienna • Oxford • Warsaw

DOLLS STUDIES

The Many Meanings of Girls' Toys and Play

Edited by Miriam Forman-Brunell
and Jennifer Dawn Whitney

PETER LANG
New York • Bern • Frankfurt • Berlin
Brussels • Vienna • Oxford • Warsaw

Library of Congress Cataloging-in-Publication Data

Dolls studies: the many meanings of girls' toys and play /
edited by Miriam Forman-Brunell, Jennifer Dawn Whitney.
pages cm. — (Mediated youth; vol. 19)
Includes bibliographical references and index.
1. Dolls—Social aspects. 2. Toys—Social aspects.
3. Games for girls. 4. Gender identity.
I. Forman-Brunell, Miriam. II. Whitney, Jennifer Dawn.
GN455.D64D65   688.7'221—dc23   2014012236
ISBN 978-1-4331-2070-1 (hardcover)
ISBN 978-1-4331-2069-5 (paperback)
ISBN 978-1-4539-1364-2 (e-book)
ISSN 1555-1814

Bibliographic information published by **Die Deutsche Nationalbibliothek**.
Die Deutsche Nationalbibliothek lists this publication in the "Deutsche
Nationalbibliografie"; detailed bibliographic data are available
on the Internet at http://dnb.d-nb.de/.

The paper in this book meets the guidelines for permanence and durability
of the Committee on Production Guidelines for Book Longevity
of the Council of Library Resources.

© 2015 Peter Lang Publishing, Inc., New York
29 Broadway, 18th floor, New York, NY 10006
www.peterlang.com

Printed in the United States of America

Table of Contents

Acknowledgments

The dolls I played with in my girlhood stirred feelings I can still summon today after all these many years. Yet it was my encounter with Victorian dolls during my senior year of college that inspired my scholarly interests. Not only did the bisque dolls seem so very different from the Thumbelina and Ginny dolls of my girlhood but also they seemed to "say something" about girls, women, and gender I could not comprehend. Relentless curiosity fueled the research that led to the publication of my dissertation, *Made to Play House: Dolls and the Commercialization of American Girlhood, 1830-1930* (1993; 1998). Two decades later, as guest editor of the doll-themed issue of *Girlhood Studies: An Interdisciplinary Journal*, I took up the task to reexamine the state of doll research in the twenty-first century. The new research methods, theoretical applications, subjects and subjectivities examined by a new generation of young outstanding scholars contributed to the publication of the Journal issue that inspired this collection. Among them, Jennifer Dawn Whitney stood out as a gifted young scholar.

At Peter Lang, Mary Savigar and Sharon Mazzarella, saw in this project something worth pursuing and publishing. Their understanding of the significance of girls' culture is unmatched in the publishing field. Bernadette Shade and Phyllis Korper carefully groomed the manuscript making it fit for publication. Many thanks to the outstanding scholars who shared their research featured in this collection. I owe all of you—and my dear co-editor, Jennifer Dawn Whitney—my sincere appreciation for your patience, understanding, and support during the unexpected events that interrupted my life and interfered with the book's production schedule.

For their expertise and encouragement, I thank Drs. Alexander Swistell and Anne Moore, Drs. Amy Rabe, James Coster, Amie Jew, and the team of outstanding chemotherapy and radiology nurses. Many thanks as well to my department. John Herron not only negotiated my leave during my treatment but also paid for the lion's share of the indexing and the permission for the book cover illustration. Amy Brost expertly formatted, printed, copied, forwarded, and figured out all things technological. Melissa Morris skillfully indexed the manuscript.

Thank you David and Ellen Formanek, Susan Medyn, and Colette Brunell for being there; Ruth Formanek and Perry Brunell for helping me *every* step of the way; and Hagrid Meriweather Brunell for never leaving my side. This book is most lovingly dedicated to Claude Brunell, the dearest of husbands, and Max, the dearest of cats.

Miriam Forman-Brunell
Kansas City, MO

My affection for dolls—the Barbie doll, in particular—is inseparable from my friendship with Tiffany Parilla. I am forever grateful to her, and to my sister, Rachel Whitney-Boulanger, for filling my life with the sparkle that inspired not only years of fun in "Barbie World," but also eventually my doctoral dissertation, *Playing With Barbie: Doll-like Femininity in the Contemporary West* (2013).

I am indebted to my PhD supervisor, Jane Moore, for believing in the academic merit of researching and writing about girlhood, material and popular cultures, and doll studies, and for encouraging me to start publishing my work. She, as well as, Neil Badmington, Becky Munford, Melanie Waters, and Chris Weedon have been the most supportive of mentors.

Miriam Forman-Brunell saw in me a potential at a time when I needed it most, and she nurtured it with the opportunity to co-edit this collection. Her kindness and wisdom have been absolutely invaluable.

This collection would not be possible without the contributors' hard work, commitment, and enthusiasm for the project. And, thanks are also due to the experts at Peter Lang, especially Bernadette Shade, for her patience and assistance.

For their love and support, I would like to thank my parents, Leslie and Don Whitney. And, lastly, thank you to my husband and champion, Rhys Tranter.

Jennifer Dawn Whitney
Cardiff, Wales

Introduction

MIRIAM FORMAN-BRUNELL AND JENNIFER DAWN WHITNEY

In a 2015 exposé about "the secret world" of animated doll videos, the BBC re-counts how "young women are using the age-old technique of stop motion ani-mation to bring their dolls to life."[1] Many of these video-makers feel a need to keep their identities under wraps, fearing criticism that they are long past their doll-playing years. Well, incognito animators, you are not alone in your enthusi-asm. In 2014, viewers watched such videos more than 33 million times, starring American Girl dolls in a multitude of scenarios—from high school prom and the first day of school to the confrontation of bullies. Likewise, homemade videos featuring the antics of Barbie and her friends amassed millions more viewers on the YouTube video-sharing website. As girls grow into adulthood, many continue to play with dolls, collect, and curate, as well as research and write about them. Examining the meanings of dolls as well as girls' play practices and productions is the focus of this collection, the first to identify Dolls Studies as an interdisciplinary subject of scholarly inquiry.

The foundation of Dolls Studies dates to the end of the twentieth century when Miriam Forman-Brunell, Karen Calvert, and other scholars influenced by the Second Wave of feminism, the emergence of the "new" women's history, and the increasing legitimacy of material culture methods, analyzed dolls as historical texts.[2] Placing dolls at the center of inquiry, *Made to Play House: Dolls and the Commercialization of American Girlhood, 1830–1930* (Yale UP, 1993) challenged a dominant assumption that dolls conveyed patriarchal ideals to docile girls. This study brought to light dolls' varied meanings among American businessmen, women designers, and girls who competed to define girlhood.

The influence of postmodern theory, Black Studies and Women's Studies interdisciplinarity and multiculturalism, the rise of the girl power ethos, and the proliferation of the Barbie brand and the American Girl doll line, led Ann DuCille, Elizabeth Chin, Mary Rogers, Erica Rand, Sherrie A. Inness, and others in departments of history, English, anthropology and programs in Women's Studies, Black Studies, and American Studies, to study dolls. [3] Interest in the impact of mass-produced and -marketed dolls, scholars, cultural theorists, critics, and activists studied the racialization, socialization, sexualization, commodification, exoticization, commercialization, and essentialization of girlhood.[4]

Building on more than a quarter of a century's worth of research, and the doll-themed issue of *Girlhood Studies: An Interdisciplinary Journal* that inspired this collection,[5] *Dolls Studies: The Many Meanings of Girls' Toys and Play* features the work of established scholars, Catharine Driscoll and Elizabeth Chin, recent pioneers, such as, Robin Bernstein, along with emergent GenX and Millennial researchers. Together, those conducting doll research today see dolls as dynamic texts that represent layered versions of realities, mediated by the often-contradictory ideologies, values, or worldviews of doll creators, producers, consumers, and players. Consequently, their work reveals the complexities and contending elements embodied in these objects as well as the conflicts embedded in the sub/cultures that produce and play with dolls. Their scholarship utilizes a variety of critical practices in order to analyze the textuality of dolls and to interpret the ambivalence and/or agency that dolls generate in girls and young women. Locating novel doll play in new spaces and sites where doll performances take place, they unpack dolls' and doll players' potentiality to construct and disrupt, mediate and contest, perform and rescript girlhoods.

The contributors to this collection are representative of Dolls Studies scholars who are everywhere in the academy in the US and across the globe. Greater flexibility within traditional fields and fluidity across disciplinary borders has enabled Lisa Marcus, a professor at Pacific Lutheran University, to make use of prose and poetry along with photographs and dolls in her study of Jewish American girlhood. Professor of Education Vanessa Rutherford studies doll houses as discursive "technologies of power" in nineteenth-century Ireland. Juliette Peers, a Senior Lecturer in the School of Architecture and Design and the School of Fashion and Textiles, RMIT University, Melbourne, is a historian of art, design, and culture who examines French female doll producers in her study on modernity.

New scholarly fields (most prominently Cultural Studies and Girls' Studies) and innovative programs shaped by historical forces from the Civil Rights movement and feminism to post-colonialism, have produced a number of young contributors to this collection. The several scholars who earned their doctorates in

Visual Studies at the University of California, Irvine, are representative of Dolls Studies scholars in cross- and post-disciplinary programs. In fact, the co-editor of this collection, Jennifer Dawn Whitney, recently earned her doctorate at the Centre for Critical and Cultural Theory at Cardiff University in Wales. This more multi-, inter-, and post-disciplinary generation of doll scholars draws upon museum studies, memory studies, performance studies, material culture, visual culture, and object studies. The changing academic landscape makes it possible for researchers to intermingle disciplinary specializations. Challenging established approaches, dominant interpretations, and familiar critiques, they are leading scholarly conversations about dolls in new directions.

As both a subject of study and as bodies of evidence, Dolls Studies provides insight into changes and continuities in the construction of dolls, the conditions of play, and the making—and undoing—of imaginations, ideologies, and identities. By constituting "dolls" broadly, scholars are not only uncovering new sources, sites of play, and players but also revising understandings of what or *who* is a doll. Researchers who move beyond the proverbial doll corner to more public locales are also remapping the changing boundaries of dollhood. By examining the many doll-related products girls make, investigators are finding more evidence of on-going battles over long-standing beliefs. In her chapter, Jennifer Dawn Whitney argues that hip hop artist Nicki Minaj playfully subverts the iconic Barbie doll through her lyrical and visual performances. Film studies scholars Diana Anselmo and Meghan Chandler interpret the destruction and appropriation of dolls by Riot Grrrls in music videos, stage performances, and on album covers. By dollifying their bodies, these performers establish a means for self-fashioning female agency, sexuality, and identity.

Examining dolls across time and place further than others, this newest wave of scholars reveals Dolls Studies to be an international and interdisciplinary endeavor. New research on topics from fashion to fascism utilizes innovative methodologies and research designs. Many make use of material culture methods in order to "read" encoded ideals that also serve as "scripts" designating "a set of invitations or prompts" (p. 8, this volume). In combination with material culture methods Dolls Studies scholars also use textual and visual strategies to illuminate a broad spectrum of dolls and forms of play. Interrogating dolls and investigating their production, consumption, representation, and reception, the authors shed collective light on the many meanings of dolls that continue to serve centrally as objects through which girlhoods are constructed and reimagined, mediated and contested, played and performed.

In order to ground understandings of seemingly unimportant artifacts (dolls) and activities (doll play) in broader cultural contexts (e.g., children's culture; girls' culture; dominant culture), Dolls Studies research often blends post-structuralist theoretical perspectives with feminist epistemologies. Contemporary feminist and post-structuralist theories provide critical Dolls Studies research with new frameworks for understanding how dolls and related texts (books about dolls) function culturally, socially, politically, and psychologically. Based on the understanding that notions and narratives appear in a wide variety of literary and non-literary forms of expression, Robin Bernstein utilizes *performance theory* to investigate the performance of race in her study of canonical children's books and dolls like Raggedy Ann as well as girls' doll play. Alexandra Lloyd's study of dolls and girlhood during the Third Reich is informed by Carlo Ginzburg's theory of "conjectural knowledge" and Annette Kuhn's theoretical writing about *memory work* (Kuhn, 2007, p. 283). And, co-authors Naghmeh Nouri Esfahani and Victoria Carrington utilize *post-phenomenological theory* (Verbeek, 2005; 2006; 2007) in their study of how diasporic Iranian girls in Australia modify and rescript their Bratz dolls.

The five-part organizational framework of this collection emphasizes the similarities as well as the differences between and among the different research studies summarized below. Those chapters included in Part 1 share a similarity in regard to objects, narratives, and issues of historical memory. The chapters in Part 2 address a variety of different discourses, performances, and the formation of identities. Part 3 focuses specifically on two different mediating contexts of girls' doll play. The essays in Part 4 explore the origins of modernism and processes of modernization at different times and in different places of the globe. The three chapters that complete Part 5 investigate the many ways in which dolls have commodified multiculturalism, nationalism, racism, and girlhood.

OBJECTS, NARRATIVES, AND HISTORICAL MEMORY

Among some Dolls Studies scholars there are those who "read" doll artifacts as they do stories that, ranging from fiction to life writings, illuminate vexed issues about race and ethnicity. In her essay, "Children's Books, Dolls, and the Performance of Race; or, the Possibility of Children's Literature," elaborated upon in her recent book, *Racial Innocence: Performing American Childhood from Slavery to Civil Rights*, Robin Bernstein examines nineteenth-century children's literature manufactured alongside dolls and the performances they scripted for children—largely girls—who enacted often disturbing stories about race. Bernstein explores how and why "racial and racist fantasies emerged through doll-play" (p. 4, this volume), and interrogates how these texts were often designed, produced, and marketed to convey conventional notions about femininity and race.

In "Dolling Up History: Fictions of Jewish American Girlhood," Lisa Marcus explores a dominant version of Jewish American girlhood embodied by the Jewish American Girl doll, Rebecca Rubin, and how this is encoded in a variety of printed texts. Although the Rebecca Rubin doll seemed to signal a progressive version of Jewish American girlhood, Marcus argues that the doll and the box-set of books about Rebecca's life merely repackaged a narrative in which America figures as "benevolent sanctuary" (p. 27, this volume), while the Holocaust, American anti-Semitism, and the costs of assimilation were "elided and smoothed away" (pp. 16–17, this volume). Marcus traces the origins of this "triumphalist story" (p. 27, this volume) to the postwar period, when Americanized Anne Frank became the inspiring icon of Jewish girlhood. Marcus details how Sydney Taylor's *All of a Kind Family* series of children's books similarly provided "dolled-up" versions of a darker history, while contrasting these with the more accurate retellings of Anzia Yezierska in her autobiographical fiction and Adrienne Rich in her poetry.

Rather than eliding the past, dolls speak volumes about Nazi Europe in "Dolls and Play: Material Culture and Memories of Girlhood in Germany, 1933–45." Alexandra Lloyd, a lecturer in German, Magdalen College and St. Edmund Hall at Oxford University, reads dolls as objects of memory and historical narrative alongside memoirs that contextualize their meanings. Drawing on a range of material from German-language dolls studies research, English- and German-language memory texts, including autobiographical accounts, and collections of oral testimony, Lloyd explores the role of dolls in girls' lives during the Third Reich and World War II. By examining "the complex relationships between girls and their dolls and the place of dolls in memory" (p. 36, this volume), this chapter sheds light on the meaning of dolls in girls' lives during this troubled period of German history.

DISCOURSES, PERFORMANCES, AND IDENTITIES

Discourses are fundamental in defining girls, dolls, and the role dolls should play in making girls into women. Discourses about girlhood and dollhood are laid bare when girls and young women play with, and play at, dolls in ways that often unsettle conventions. How the Riot Grrrls of the 1990s radically altered the meanings of dolls is the subject Meghan Chandler and Diana Anselmo-Sequeira's co-authored essay, "The 'Dollification' of Riot Grrrls: Self-Fashioning Alternative Identities." Their critical examination details the ways in which reappropriated dolls can subvert gendered expectations. Utilizing press interviews, music videos, and the bodies of high-profile musicians as texts, the chapter traces an intercontinental dialogue between feminist bricoleurs who "gleefully embraced the process of 'dollification'" (p. 64), in order to tailor their public images and to refashion empowered female identities into the semblance of dolls. This willing process of "dollification" turned upside down influential psychological theories that had long associated doll-like femininity with beauty, modesty, and passivity and instead "rehearsed a much darker, sexualized play with dolls" (p. 64, this volume). American and British girl singers who sported ripped baby-doll dresses, smeared makeup, tangled hair, and combat boots, "dollified" themselves as an act of feminist rebellion and agency that continues to ripple through girls' culture today.

Similarly, in "'It's Barbie, Bitch': Re-reading the Doll Through Nicki Minaj and Harajuku Barbie," Jennifer Dawn Whitney explores the public persona of hip hop artist Nicki Minaj, and her appropriation of the iconic Barbie doll. Although Minaj's image has drawn criticism from critics and peers alike, it has, nonetheless, inspired a creative fan following. Through lyrical and visual analysis, Whitney argues that Nicki Minaj's co-opting of Barbie can be read as a playful subversion of the doll's fifty-year history and worldwide brand status. With reference to Lady Gaga, contemporary feminist theory, and recent trends in post-structuralist thought, Whitney suggests the ways in which Minaj and her fans find "pleasure in the fragmentation and hyperbole" (p. 99) of the postmodern and, thus, liberate and pluralize how we think about Barbie, race, and idealized femininity in the West.

In "Technologies of Gender: Doll Discourses in Ireland, 1801–1909," Vanessa Rutherford, a professor in the School of Education at University College Cork, Ireland, critically evaluates the power of doll discourses in sculpting gender identities and performances in Ireland during the "long" nineteenth-century. Drawing on nineteenth-century Irish periodicals and newspapers, religious tracts, political articles, and medical treatises, Rutherford examines the doll discourses that defined ways of knowing, valuing, and experiencing the world. Applying the interdisciplinary methodology of critical discourse analysis and drawing on Foucault's insights into discourse and the instrumentality of power, the chapter demonstrates how doll discourses were "designed to alter and mold behaviors" (p. 104, this volume), thus shaping and reshaping gender categories, understandings, and negotiations.

MEDIATING CONTEXTS OF PLAY

What dolls are designed to do is not always what they end up doing, and everyday sites of play—across diverse cultural settings—can often contribute to new meanings for dolls and their players. Co-authors Naghmeh Nouri Esfahani and Victoria Carrington are concerned with this notion of the everyday and how it emerges between human actions and the mass-produced artifact of the doll. Their chapter, "Rescripting, Modifying and Mediating Artifacts: Bratz Dolls and Diasporic Iranian Girls in Australia," addresses the cross-cultural play narratives of two young girls from immigrant Iranian families living in Australia in order to assess how girls interact with the heavily "scripted artifact" (p. 130, this volume) of the Bratz fashion doll. Esfahani and Carrington suggest ways in which Bratz dolls are used to mediate a range of cross-cultural and social contexts, negotiate cultural boundaries, and organize identities.

Girls have long drawn upon various materials from cloth to cardboard to negotiate meanings in their doll play. The recent accessibility of video cameras (especially by way of camera phones), the fostering of technology by girls and the rise of social media each provide new tools, as well as new sites, to create and communicate narratives of doll play.[6] In "Barbie Sex Videos: Making Sense of Children's Media-Making," Elizabeth Chin provides a model analysis of doll play that mediates online spaces and engages with online audiences. The chapter begins by questioning the assumptions around normative consumption practices and the presumed influences of the Barbie doll. Chin's close analysis of the YouTube video *Barbie Sex life*—created by children in the middle childhood age range— reveals how girls invent sophisticated narratives that "explore a range of complex territories having to do with romance, power, gender, and sexuality" (p. 133, this volume). She concludes that such videos and such play cannot be reduced to simple readings, and instead insists that we must ask "sincere questions" (p. 151, this volume) about how doll play is mediated in order to push our scholarship further.

MODERNISM AND MODERNIZATION

Moving away from the post-1945 era of plastics and mass retail, the essays in Part 4, explore an equally complex period in doll production that addresses issues of modernism and modernization. In "Adelaide Huret and the Nineteenth-Century French Fashion Doll: Constructing Dolls/Constructing the Modern," Juliette Peers looks at the rise of the French luxury doll trade in mid-nineteenth century Paris. Peers begins her chapter by taking to task traditional scholarship on the making of the modern public sphere in France. Masculinist in its focus upon modern art, design and consumerism, Peers describes how this traditional reading "rendered women invisible" (p. 158). Disputing this narrow interpretation, Peers goes on to explain how female dollmakers, dressmakers, designers, and retailers, including Adelaide Huret, contributed to the modern urban experience in both design and lifestyle. This chapter not only locates dollmaking alongside, and in conversation with, the emergence of modern art, design, and consumerism but also identifies dollmaking's influential role in defining modern life.

Like Peers, Catherine Driscoll, in her chapter "The Doll-Machine: Dolls, Modernism, Experience," also articulates the doll's significant role in our understanding of modernism and modernization. Stating emphatically that the "modern doll is something quite different than the dolls that preceded it" (p. 185, this volume), Driscoll goes on to consider a range of doll-figures, including Robot-Maria from Fritz Lang's *Metropolis*, Hans Bellmer's puppet and doll works, and Mikhail

Fokine and Igor Stravinsky's ballet *Petrushka*. Putting these dolls in dialogue with the Barbie doll, which Driscoll suggests shares in the same modernizing history, she then explores each doll's role in understanding "modernism as an experience of technology" (p. 201, this volume). This chapter not only reflects on how the modern, technologized doll occupies the liminal space between subject and object—and the cultural meanings that this might signify—but also suggests how this space is complexly and irrefutably gendered.

COMMODIFYING MULTICULTURALISM, NATIONALISM, RACISM, AND GIRLHOODS

The ways in which dolls call attention to the tensions between the subject and the object, the self and the other, can also be explored through the embodied notions of race, nationalism, and multiculturalism. How these ideas are codified and commodified in dolls is the focus of the last group of essays. In "Girls' Day for Umé: Western Perceptions of the Hina Matsuri, 1874-1937," Judy Shoaf examines the role of doll play in the Japanese Doll Festival in the last quarter of the nineteenth and the beginning of the twentieth centuries. As very little scholarship has been undertaken on this topic, Shoaf sets out to define it for her readers. With precision, she explains the components of the Doll Festival, examines Western attempts to understand (or ignore) it, and outlines the "strategies of various writers for making the festival into some kind of mirror for the doll culture of American readers" (p. 208, this volume). Significantly, Shoaf's chapter considers how cross-cultural readings of the Doll Festival complicate understandings of who plays with dolls, how dolls are used in play, and, indeed, if such play might redefine what is meant by the figure of the doll.

In "The Secret Sex Lives of Native American Barbies, from the Mysteries of Motherhood to the Magic of Colonialism," Erich Fox Tree also examines the dominant cultural readings that are ascribed to the figure of the doll. In this chapter, Fox Tree is particularly concerned with marketing strategies deployed in the retailing of Native American Barbie dolls. These Barbie dolls, he details, are often sold with babies in tow—an unusual phenomenon given that conventional commercial narratives promote the original white Barbie doll as a single and childless young woman. Fox Tree convincingly argues how this marketing strategy "naturalizes" (p. 251, this volume) imperialist fantasies and perpetuates colonial ideologies about Native American women and suggests the ways in which it also reiterates the dangerous trope of the miscegenating "Indian Princess."

The final chapter in this collection, Amanda Murphyao and Anne Trépanier's "Canadian 'Maplelea' Girl Dolls: The Commodification of Difference," examines the nationalistic significance of the Maplelea doll. It is through these dolls, Murphyao and Trépanier assert, that examples of "large-scale political and rhetorical concerns around the Canadian federal policy of multiculturalism" are enacted (p. 275, this volume). By focusing on how the Maplelea Girl dolls engage with diversity and multiculturalism in the context of English-language merchandise, the co-authors attest to how difference is only accommodated when it is both "celebratory" and "commercially viable" (Ibid.). Engaging with its American, British ("My London"), Australian, and Jewish ("Gali") Girl doll counterparts, the co-authors conclude that the Canadian Maplelea doll, too, troublingly promotes a kind of playful patriotism.

Dolls Studies is a subject of inquiry that is not only interdisciplinary and international but also intergenerational. By engaging a wide variety of new interdisciplinary fields, this collection aims to meet the needs of students and instructors in courses on: girls' studies, childhood studies, women's studies, popular culture, visual studies, cultural studies, and material culture. In addition to students in humanities and social science departments, this book aims to reach future teachers enrolled in schools of education where courses on early childhood and play are standard offerings. Whether conducting original research on dolls specifically or toys, consumer culture, play, girls, children, and/or women and gender more generally, students as well as scholars are likely to find this collection especially valuable. By presenting a broad range of methodological, theoretical, and conceptual approaches to doll research, we seek to provide a useful context in which to better understand debates about dolls in academic monographs, the traditional media, and on the web.

This work aims to reach a broad audience—from students to scholars and curators to collectors. Whether mounting an exhibition, publishing a catalogue, cataloging artifacts, or archiving documents, curators of museums and historical societies often hanker for more interpretive understandings of dolls than the factual information typically provided by price guides or included in works largely written for collectors. It is our hope that public historians, collectors, and especially young women professionals-in-the-making will find in *Dolls Studies* useful models and methods for examining dolls' many meanings.

NOTES

1 http://www.bbc.com/news/blogs-trending-32130050
2 Formanek-Brunell [Forman-Brunell], Miriam. 1993. *Made to Play House: Dolls and the Commercialization of American Girlhood, 1830–1930* (Yale University Press); Calvert, Karen. 1994. *Children in the House: The Material Culture of Early Childhood, 1600–1900* (Northeastern University Press).
3 DuCille, Ann. 1996. "Toy Theory: Black Barbie and the Deep Play of Difference." In *Skin trade*. (Harvard University Press); DuCille, Ann. 1994. "Dyes and Dolls: Multicultural Barbie and the Merchandising of Difference." In *Differences* 6 (1), 46–68; Rand, Erica. 1995. *Barbie's Queer Accessories*. (Duke University Press); Rogers, Mary F. 1999. *Barbie Culture*. (Sage); Wood, Gaby.

2003. *Living Dolls: A Magical History of the Quest for Mechanical Life*. (Faber and Faber); Inness, Sherrie A. (1998). "'Anti-Barbies': The American Girls Collection and Political Ideologies." In *Delinquents and Debutantes: Twentieth Century American Girls' Cultures*. Ed. Sherrie A. Inness. Pp. 164–183. (New York University Press).

4 Peers, Juliette. 2004. *The Fashion Doll: From Bébé Jumeau to Barbie*. (Berg); Driscoll, Catherine. 2005. "Girl-Doll: Barbie as Puberty Manual." In *Seven Going on Seventeen*. Eds. Claudia Mitchell and Jacqueline Reid-Walsh. Pp. 217–233. (Peter Lang); Eds. Claudia Mitchell and Jacqueline Reid-Walsh. *Girls: Feminine Adolescence in Popular Culture and Critical Theory*. (Columbia University Press).

5 Forman-Brunell, Miriam, Guest Editor. (2012)*Girlhood Studies: An Interdisciplinary Journal 5* (1) Summer.

6 Kearney, Mary Celeste. 2006. *Girls Make Media*. (Routledge).

Part I: Objects, Narratives, Historical Memory

Children's Books, Dolls, AND THE Performance OF Race; OR, THE Possibility OF Children's Literature

ROBIN BERNSTEIN

In about 1855, more than three decades before Frances Hodgson Burnett wrote the bestselling children's books *The Secret Garden* and *Little Lord Fauntleroy*, she was a child, Frances Eliza Hodgson, and she read Harriet Beecher Stowe's *Uncle Tom's Cabin*.[1] The girl found Stowe's novel, like all stories she encountered, to be "unsatisfactory, filling her with vague, restless craving for greater completeness of form" (Burnett, 1893, p. 44). The form the girl craved—that is, the material by which to complete the narrative—was a black doll.[2] When Burnett obtained that doll, she named it Topsy and used it to "act" out the parts of the novel that she found most "thrilling" (p. 53). Casting a white doll she already owned as Little Eva, Burnett played out ever-repeating scenes of Eva laying hands on Topsy and thus awakening the hardened slave girl to Christian love. Burnett also kept the Eva doll "actively employed slowly fading away and dying," and in these scenes Burnett played the role of Uncle Tom (p. 57). At other times, Burnett performed the scene of Eva's death, casting the white doll as Eva and herself as "all the weeping slaves at once" (p. 58). And on at least one occasion, the girl re-designated the doll as Uncle Tom and cast herself as Simon Legree. For this play-scenario, the girl bound the doll to a candelabra stand. "[F]urious with insensate rage," she whipped her doll. Throughout the whipping, the doll maintained a "cheerfully hideous" grin, which suggested to the girl that Uncle Tom was "enjoying the situation" of being "brutally lashed" (pp. 56, 55).

Burnett was no outlier; many nineteenth-century white children—especially but not exclusively girls—read books about slavery and then used dolls to act out scenes of racialized violence and forced labor. Memoirist Georgianna Hamlen (1885) recalled that an antebellum childhood friend "who had been reading about Southern plantations and the negro slaves" procured six black china dolls, which she then configured as slaves to a white doll who "looked very Southern and very proud" (p. 227). Another girl, the future British American novelist Amelia Barr, read a school book that contained "a picture of a very black slave loaded with chains, toiling in the sugar field, and a tall, white overseer with a whip standing near." Inspired by this book, the white girl "very soon abstracted the steel chain that held my mother's bunch of keys, loaded my negro doll with chains, [and] selected a white doll to act as overseer" ("Dolls of Famous Women," 1889, p. 17).

These racial and racist fantasies emerged through doll-play, and not other means of representation such as drawing, because for Burnett, Barr, and many other children, literature and material culture appeared to invite engagement with each other. As Burnett (1893) wrote, stories in the absence of dolls were "imperfect," while dolls "seemed only things stuffed with sawdust" until "literature assisted imagination and gave them character" (p. 44). The commercial interdependence between children's literature and material culture dates from 1744, when British publisher and book vender John Newbery sold *A Little Pretty Pocket-Book* ensemble with balls and pincushions, and extends to the present-day American Girl series, in which books and dolls accessorize each other (Clark and Higonnet, 1999, p. 1). When Newbery paired books with toys, he not only sold an extraordinary quantity of merchandise, but also conceived of children as a market and children's books as a distinct literary category (Noblett, 1980). This accomplishment earned Newbery the honorific of the "father of children's literature" (Kidd, 2007, p. 171).

Children's literature as a genre, then, emerged in crucial part through the relationship between books and toys, and that connection has only expanded since the eighteenth century. This magnetism with the material culture of play distinguishes children's literature from other literatures. The actions of individual book publishers and children vary infinitely, but the pairing, through play, of children's literature and toys has persisted for three centuries. Even when manufacturers do not market books and dolls in pre-packaged combinations, many children invent their own, as Burnett did. And in recent years, many works of children's literature such as *Curious George* and *The Cat in the Hat*, which were not initially marketed with non-book consumer items, have been commodified through products ranging from dolls to stickers to pajamas. Books and toys jumble together in children's rooms, in their beds, and in their practices of play.

In contradiction to children's lived experiences, however, most scholars treat children's literature and material culture as separate discourses. Superb historians of play such as Karin Calvert, Howard Chudacoff, Gary Cross, and Miriam Forman-Brunell comment on literature mainly as a source or representation of ideology that concretizes in material culture. Meanwhile, leading scholars of children's literature, including U.C. Knoepflmacher, Seth Lerer, Perry Nodelman, and Maria Tatar, focus their core analyses on textual representation. Some scholars connect children's literature and toys by foregrounding their similarities: Anne Scott MacLeod, for example, reads books and toys together as meaning-making texts, while Philip Nel and Leonard Marcus historicize both books and playthings as consumer products. Lois Kuznets and Sharon Marcus examine representations of dolls and doll-play in literature. Even books that aim to study toys and children's literature simultaneously may draw the fields of inquiry toward each other rather than integrate them: for example, in Beverly Lyon Clark and Margaret R. Higonnet's (1999) foundational collection *Girls, Boys, Books, Toys: Gender in Children's Literature and Culture*, most essayists consider literature or material culture, but not both.[3]

Either to split or to lump children's literature and material culture, however, is to erase *representational play* as many children's lived connection between them. For Burnett, *Uncle Tom's Cabin* and a black doll were not two kinds of texts (literary and visual/material, respectively), nor were they two forms of material culture. Nor did Stowe's story provide a linear narrative that the girl simply imitated. To the contrary, Burnett's practices of play connected literature and material culture without eliding differences between the two forms: the girl perceived an absence in a text, she sought out the black doll that filled, in her view, Stowe's void, and she then used the doll along with her white doll to perform specific scenes that she chose among a panorama of possible scenarios from *Uncle Tom's Cabin*. Jacqueline Rose, in her 1984 field-defining book, *The Case of Peter Pan, or, The Impossibility of Children's Fiction*, called children's literature "impossible" because it is the only genre written by one group for another group; thus, the genre imagines the category of "child" through simultaneous description and hailing of a category that it is in fact creating. Rose argued that children's literature creates a dynamic in which the empowered "adult comes first (author, maker, giver)" and the disempowered, even colonized "child comes after (reader, product, receiver), but... neither of them enter the space in between" (Rose, 1984, pp. 1–2). In the past 3 years, scholars such as Marah Gubar, Kimberley Reynolds, and David Rudd have led a major reassessment of the "impossibility" of children's literature. Absent from this reassessment, however, is consideration of how the linked acts of reading and playing disrupt Rose's paradigm. This absence obscures the role of children's agency in the formation of race. Burnett and children like her did not passively receive works of literature. Rather, Burnett used dolls to reconfigure the stories she read. She entered Rose's "space in between" through play, through performance.

Representative play is performative in that it produces culture. As the Dutch historian Johan Huizinga argued in 1938, "culture arises in the form of play"; culture, including racial formation, "is played from the very beginning" (Huizinga, 1950, pp. 1, 46). Performance theorists have expanded upon Huizinga's arguments to understand play as a major mode of performance in everyday life and a crucial component in the construction of race, gender, and other categories of analysis (Goffman, 1959, Bial, 2007). Burnett's play did not represent some pre-existing racial or gendered essence, but instead constructed her whiteness and girlhood through alternating performances of debased blackness and iconic whiteness in men and girls. When Burnett played weeping slaves and vicious slaveowner against her dolls, or when, as puppeteer, she ventriloquized both Topsy and Eva through her dolls, Burnett performed race and gender as complexly as did the blackface minstrels who trod the boards in the same historical moment.

When scholars tear children's literature from material culture, despite the interweaving of fiction and playthings that has grown ever-denser since 1744, they create the appearance of an "impossible" top-down system in which adults produce and children receive culture. This paradigm erases the ways in which children's play-performances revise, rather than only reify, narratives. The stakes of this erasure become visible through a case study of the racial functions of black dolls and white children's performative doll-play during the second half of the nineteenth century.[4] Through these performances, nineteenth-century white children played at violence against African Americans exactly as abolition, Emancipation, and freedom eroded American white supremacy.

Animate dolls, in literature and play, raise slavery's most foundational, disturbing, and lingering question: what is a person? As Bill Brown (2006) has observed, this question has, from the antebellum period to the present, underlain anxieties so powerfully as to constitute the "American Uncanny." *Uncle Tom's Cabin* encapsulated and shaped this anxiety because, as Philip Fisher (1987) argued, the Emancipation Proclamation combined with the Union's military victory and "the cultural work of *Uncle Tom's Cabin*" to "redesign" the "boundary" between human and thing (Stowe acknowledged this project when she originally subtitled her novel "The man that was a thing" (Fisher, 1987, pp. 4, 100). In other words, slavery legally defined some humans as things, and Emancipation legally re-defined all humans as humans. Antebellum abolitionist culture, including *Uncle Tom's Cabin*, laid conceptual groundwork that made this legal change comprehensible and therefore possible. After Emancipation, however, "Lost Causers" and other white supremacists marshaled popular culture to undo this work and to re-design yet again the boundary between human and thing. This effort appeared especially clearly in the post-Emancipation effort by the Daughters of the Confederacy and other groups to freeze the imagined "faithful slave" in stone monuments (Savage, 1997, McElya, 2007, Blight, 2001).

The cultural effort to objectify and later re-objectify African Americans found rich potential in doll-play and doll literature, because all stories about sentient dolls re-organize the boundary between human and thing. As Kuznets (1994) observed, sentient dolls in literature "embody human anxieties about what it means to be 'real'—an independent subject or self rather than an object or other" (p. 2). Around the time of the American Civil War, books about sentient dolls increased in popularity (Formanek-Brunell, 1993, p. 23), and dolls in these books discuss their racial status, their duties to their owners, and even their relationship with enslaved people of African descent. The doll narrator of Julia Charlotte Maitland's *The Doll and Her Friends* (published in 1852, the same year as *Uncle Tom's Cabin*) describes dolls as "a race of mere dependents; some might even call us slaves" (p. 1). The narrator pointedly informs the reader, however, that she is "not a negro doll, with wide mouth and woolly hair" (p. 4). In this children's book and many others, dollness is itself as a racial category that denotes servitude. Stowe (1852, 1994) injected these anxieties about dolls and slaves, things and people, into *Uncle Tom's Cabin* by likening Topsy to a doll with eyes as "glittering as glass beads" (p. 206). Stowe is careful, however, to identify Topsy repeatedly as an "abused child" (209), even *the* abused child, as Richard Brodhead (1988, p. 85) argued. When Eva converts Topsy, the enslaved girl's formerly bead-like eyes become "overcast with tears" (p. 245); thus, Topsy's conversion alters the precise organ that previously constituted the character's doll-likeness. Stowe configured Topsy's conversion as one from superficial doll-likeness caused by slavery's pathology to the release of the Christian humanity; thus Stowe delivered one of her sharpest arguments against slavery (Brodhead, 1988, pp. 84–86).

When Burnett read *Uncle Tom's Cabin*, however, she was not filled with the impulse to engage in abolitionist activism, nor even to "feel right," but instead to reconstitute Topsy in doll form—that is, to reverse the trajectory that Stowe wrote for Topsy. Thus, Burnett resisted Stowe's narrative even as she enacted it. Burnett behaved as she did not only because of her individual psychology, but also, crucially, in response to two sets of external cues: Stowe's story and the doll's color and tough material composition.

Nineteenth-century doll manufacturers invited such enactments of racial violence when they built black dolls of materials, especially rubber and cloth that could withstand rough usage, that would destroy wax or ceramic dolls. Patent applications and advertisements often explicitly described soft black dolls as prompts toward violent play. From 1893–1894, for example, Arnold Print Works of Massachusetts (1893) advertised a black doll alternately called "Topsy" and "Pickaninny": "What child in America does not at some time want a cloth 'Nigger' dollie—one that can be petted or thrown about without harm to the doll or anything that it comes in contact with [?] 'Pickaninny' fills all the requirements"

(p. 550). This advertisement claimed that the doll, identified by a racial epithet, could and should be "thrown about" because it was black and of cloth, and that this abusability constituted its desirability. For the Massachusetts manufacturer that named its doll "Topsy," and for Burnett, soft black dolls combined with the narrative of *Uncle Tom's Cabin* to script performances of violent play.

The term *script* does not refer to compulsory behavior, but instead describes a set of invitations or prompts that by definition remain open to agency, resistance, and revision. Like theatrical practitioners, I understand a script as a dynamic substance that deeply influences but does not entirely determine live performances, which constantly change according to agential individuals' visions, impulses, and accidents. Items of material culture *script* in much the same sense that literary texts *mean*: neither a thing nor a poem (for example) is conscious or agential, but a thing can invite behaviors that its maker did and did not envision, and a poem may produce meanings that include and exceed a poet's intentions. To describe elements of material culture as "scripting" actions is not to suggest that things possess agency or that people lack it, but instead to propose that agency emerges through constant engagement with the stuff of our lives. In my book, I develop a method for reading the scripts co-produced through literature and material culture: I use archival evidence to determine the documented, probable, and possible uses of a category of object such as a doll.[5] This horizon of known and possible uses then informs a close reading of an individual artifact. The operative questions are: What historically located behaviors did this artifact invite? And what actions did it discourage? The goal is not to determine what any individual *did* do with an artifact, but rather to understand how a non-agential artifact, in its historical context, prompted or invited—scripted—actions of people who were agential and often resistant. That act of scripting, that issuing of a culturally specific invitation, was itself a historical event—one that can be recovered and then analyzed as a fresh source of evidence.

Toni Morrison (1970) fictively described the process of scripting, and its racial ramifications, in *The Bluest Eye*, set in 1941: her narrator, a black girl named Claudia, is given a white baby doll and wonders, "What was I supposed to do with it? Pretend I was its mother?" However, Claudia reads "[p]icture books" that are "full of little girls sleeping with their dolls"—that is, white girls and white dolls—and from these books "learn[s] quickly" that she is "expected" to "rock [the doll], fabricate storied situations around it, even sleep with it" (p. 20). The narratives in Claudia's picture books combine with the materiality of the doll—specifically, its blond hair and white skin—to tell Claudia what she is "supposed to do"; that is, children's literature together with the doll itself prompt tender bodily actions, and these actions interpellate Claudia into a racist ideology that Morrison's novel attacks.

Like the fictional Claudia, historical children of the nineteenth century absorbed prompts toward tender play with white dolls, but they also received the violent scripts co-produced by black dolls such as the Arnold Print Works' Topsy and the widespread, repetitious works of children's literature in which black dolls endured whipping, flogging, beating, drowning, shooting, burning, decapitation, and destruction from overwork (*Jimmy*, 1888, Trew, 1869, Fanny, 1870, E. L. E., 1879, Optic, 1863). Certainly, girls in literature and in life abused white dolls (Marcus, 2007, pp. 159–163, Formanek-Brunell, 1993, pp. 24–32)—but novels singled out black dolls for especial viciousness that was ritualistic and that took racially specific forms such as hanging. Mrs. D. P. Sanford's 1875 *Frisk and His Flock* provides one of many examples: in this novel, a white girl named Eva (a name that invokes Stowe's novel) hangs a black doll "for a *punish*"—a spectacle that causes other white children to laugh (Sanford, 1877, p. 110, original emphasis).

Many white children did perform the ritualistic violence that black dolls and children's literature co-scripted. In the magazine *Babyhood* in 1887, for example, one mother described her daughter's black rag doll, which endured a "gash in her throat" (English, 1887, p. 264). A decade later, psychologists G. Stanley Hall and A. Caswell Ellis (1897) observed white children in Worcester, Massachusetts, burning black dolls and using them to stage slave auctions (pp. 30, 34). And in 1898, a Minneapolis newspaper invited children to write letters describing their play with toys. Seven of the 40 published letters focused on black dolls, and most of these reported violence. A girl named Alice Leland announced that she "burned to death" a black doll, while Wm. Scholtz reported that he enjoyed pinching his "little black rubber doll named Tom," and that he allowed a cat to "bite Tom's toes and pull his hair," which provided "fun" for the cat. Scholtz declared that his Tom doll, like Burnett's rubber doll of the same name, "never complained." Harry Cass, too, enjoyed violence with his black doll: "Sometimes I would play I was hanging him" ("Toys," 1898, pp. 1, 6–7).

Harry Cass performed a lynching, but probably never witnessed one: no African Americans were hanged—legally or by mob—in Minnesota during the seventh-grader's lifetime (Bessler, 2003, pp. 104–105). And the Worcester children whom Hall and Ellis observed playing at "slave selling" in 1897 could not have witnessed those historical events. These children, like Burnett, Georgianna Hamlen's friend, and Amelia Barr, performed in response to narratives they read, saw, or heard, and to the materiality of dolls. Perhaps the slave-selling children of Worcester read *Uncle Tom's Cabin*. Cass, who named his doll Tom, may have read Stowe's novel, and perhaps he read *Frisk and His Flock* or one of the many other stories in which white children hanged black dolls. And he very likely observed the play practices of other children, including his Minneapolis neighbors who cheerfully reported destroying black dolls.

Literature and material culture, I have argued, co-scripted nineteenth-century practices of play, and white children like Burnett enacted—and thus revised—these scripts. Significantly, this process of reinvention, of repetition with differences, was collective. Nineteenth-century doll-play was not private; representational play occurred throughout the home and also outside, where it was witnessed by families, neighbors, and most importantly, other children. Children and former children described their practices of play in periodicals and books; thus they further transmitted practices child-to-child. Burnett took cues from Stowe's novel and a doll, but published accounts of her play then co-scripted other children's behaviors: in 1888, when Burnett was publicizing her novel *Little Lord Fauntleroy*, a girl approached the famous author to tell her that she had read about Burnett's whipping of her black doll, and that she had been inspired toward similar play with her own black doll ("A Pleasant Chat," 1888, p. 1). But we cannot tell exactly which of Burnett's practices the girl may have repeated or expanded, and which she refused. The script that literature, material culture, and children co-created remains productively legible even when an individual's response to the prompt slips through the cracks of the archive.

Since the eighteenth century, children's play has increasingly connected children's literature and material culture; and today, children's play, literature, and material culture are conjoined. Many observers decry these connections as the commercialism and dilution of literature. But it is precisely these connections that deliver children's literature beyond the paradigm of "impossibility." In the triangulation of play, literature, and material culture, the three categories of cultural actors are children, authors, and those who manufacture and sell playthings. In other words, children are co-producers within the play-book-toy formation from which children's literature is now inextricable. Some scholars may criticize the commodification of children's literary characters in everything from dolls to pajamas to keychains to sneakers, but as children play with, dream in, and unlock doors with the material inter-dependents of children's literature—as children literally walk in characters' shoes—they alter the landscape of children's literature, as Eliza Hodgson Burnett and Harry Cass did when they re-cast Topsy and Uncle Tom as things. *Pace* Rose, children do not only receive literature. Rather, children receive the co-scripts of narratives and material culture and then collectively forge a third prompt: play itself. The three prompts then entangle to script future play, which continues to change as children collectively exercise agency. The scripts that children co-create with authors and toymakers are inseparable from children's literature and are therefore a functional part of it. Performative play makes children's literature possible—all too possible, it turns out. The possibility of children's literature forces us to look anew at nineteenth-century white children and see not racist culture's reflectors, but its co-producers.

NOTES

The author thanks Colleen S. Boggs, Julie Buckler, Caroline Levander, Linda Schlossberg, and especially Ellen Gruber Garvey for their comments on this essay.

1. *Uncle Tom's Cabin* was widely read by or to children, starting with Stowe's own, to whom Stowe read her first draft (C. E. Stowe, 1890, pp. 148–149). On children's ability to define a work as "children's literature" by reading it, see Hunt (2001, pp. 2–4). Marah Gubar argued that defining children's literature as anything young people read is overly broad, but including children's acts of reading among qualities that constitute the "family resemblance" of children's literature grants the suppleness that the field requires. Barbara Hochman (2011) read *Uncle Tom's Cabin* as children's literature in *"Uncle Tom's Cabin" and the Reading Revolution: Race, Childhood, and Fiction-Reading 1851–1911*; Gubar, Marah. "On Not Defining Children's Literature." *PMLA* 126.1 (January 2011): 209–216.

2. "Black doll" is the term that people of diverse races used most consistently throughout the nineteenth and twentieth centuries to identify dolls that represent people of African descent.

3. Karen Sánchez-Eppler and Gillian Brown are among the few scholars who brilliantly analyze literature, material culture, and historical children's practices in complex relation to each other.

4. For analysis of the construction of gender and sexuality through literary representations of doll-play, see Sharon Marcus (2007, pp. 149–166). For analysis of African American children's practices with dolls, see Robin Bernstein (2011), *Racial Innocence: Performing American Childhood from Slavery to Civil Rights*. On representations of Japanese dolls, see Judy Shoaf.

5. See also Bernstein (2009).

REFERENCES

A pleasant chat with the gifted author of a children's classic. (1888, November 4). *The Daily Inter Ocean*, *224*, 17, column E.

Arnold Print Works. (1893, October 26). [Advertisement for doll]. *The Youth's Companion*, 550.

Bernstein, R. (2009). Dances with things: Material culture and the performance of race. *Social Text*, *101*, 67–94.

Bernstein, R. (2011). *Racial innocence: Performing American childhood from slavery to civil rights*. New York, NY: New York University Press.

Bessler, J. D. (2003). *Legacy of violence: Lynch mobs and executions in Minnesota*. Minneapolis, MN: University of Minnesota Press.

Bial, H. (2007). Play. In H. Bial (Ed.), *The performance studies reader* (2nd ed., pp. 115–116). London, England; New York, NY: Routledge.

Blight, D. W. (2001). *Race and reunion: The Civil War in American memory*. Cambridge, MA: The Belknap Press.

Brodhead, R. H. (1988). Sparing the rod: Discipline and fiction in antebellum America. *Representations*, *21*, 67–96.

Brown, B. (2006). Reification, reanimation, and the American uncanny. *Critical Inquiry*, *32*(2), 175–207.

Burnett, F. H. (1893). *From the one I knew the best of all: A memory of the mind of a child*. New York, NY: Charles Scribner's Sons.

Clark, B. L., & Higonnet, M. R. (Eds.). (1999). *Girls, boys, books, toys: Gender in children's literature and culture.* Baltimore, MD: The Johns Hopkins University Press.

Dolls of famous women: Miss Mary Wilkins, Miss Susan B. Anthony, Mrs. Kate Douglas Wiggin and others had them. (1899, April 16). *Portland Oregonian.*

E. L. E. (1879, May 8). Topsy. *The Youth's Companion. 52*(19), 159.

English, M. (1887, July). Home-made rag doll. In L. M. Yale (Ed.), *Babyhood: A monthly magazine for mothers devoted to the care of infants and young children, and the general interests of the nursery, 3*(32), 264. New York, NY: Babyhood Publishing Company.

Fanny, A. [France Elizabeth Barrow]. (1870). *The children's charity bazaar.* Edinburgh, Scotland: Edmonston and Douglas.

Fisher, P. (1987). *Hard facts: Setting and form in the American novel.* New York, NY: Oxford University Press.

Formanek-Brunell [Forman-Brunell], M. (1993). *Made to play house: Dolls and the commercialization of American girlhood, 1830–1930.* New Haven, CT; London, England: Yale University Press.

Goffman, E. (1959). *The presentation of self in everyday life.* Garden City, NY: Doubleday Anchor Books.

Hall, G. S., & Caswell Ellis, A. (1897). *A study of dolls.* New York, NY; Chicago, IL: E. L. Kellogg and Company.

Hamlen, G. (1885). *Chats: "Now talked of this and then of that."* Boston, MA: Lee & Shepard.

Hochman, B. (2011). *"Uncle Tom's cabin" and the reading revolution: Race, childhood, and fiction-reading 1851–1911.* Boston, MA: University of Massachusetts Press.

Huizinga, J. (1950). *Homo ludens: A study of the play element in culture* (J. Huizinga, Trans.). New York, NY: Roy.

Hunt, P. (2001). *Children's literature.* Malden, MA: Blackwell.

Jimmy: Scenes from the life of a black doll. Told by himself to J. G. Sowerby. (1888). London, England: George Routledge & Sons.

Kidd, K. B. (2007). Prizing children's literature: The case of Newbery Gold. *Children's Literature, 35,* 166–190.

Kuznets, L. (1994). *When toys come alive: Narratives of animation, metamorphosis, and development.* New Haven, CT: Yale University Press.

Maitland, J. C. (1852). *The doll and her friends; or, memoirs of the Lady Seraphina.* London, England: Grant and Griffith.

Marcus, S. (2007). *Between women: Friendship, desire, and marriage in Victorian England.* Princeton, NJ: Princeton University Press.

McElya, M. (2007). *Clinging to Mammy: The faithful slave in twentieth-century America.* Cambridge, MA: Harvard University Press.

Morrison, T. (1970). *The bluest eye.* New York, NY: Pocket Books.

Noblett, W. (1980). John Newbery: Publisher extraordinary. In S. Egoff, G. T. Stubbs, & L. F. Ashley (Eds.), *Only connect: Readings on children's literature* (pp. 28–38). Toronto, Canada; New York, NY: Oxford University Press.

Optic, O. (1863). *Dolly & I.* Boston, MA: Lee & Shepard.

Rose, J. (1984). *The case of Peter Pan, or, the impossibility of children's fiction.* Philadelphia, PA: University of Pennsylvania Press.

Sanford, D. P. (1877). *Frisk and his flock.* New York, NY: E. P. Dutton and Company.

Savage, K. (1997). *Standing soldiers, kneeling slaves: Race, war, and monument in nineteenth-century America.* Princeton, NJ: Princeton University Press.

Shoaf, J. (2010, February). Queer dress and biased eyes: The Japanese doll on the Western toyshelf. *Journal of Popular Culture, 43*(1), 176–194.

Stowe, C. E. (1890). *The life of Harriet Beecher Stowe.* Boston, MA: Houghton, Mifflin and Company. Retrieved from http://utc.iath.virginia.edu/index2f.html

Stowe, H. B. (1852). *Uncle Tom's cabin, or, life among the lowly.* In E. Ammons (Ed.). New York, NY: W.W. Norton.

Toys that made childhood sweet. (1898, December 17). *Minneapolis Journal*, Supplement, 1+.

Trew, G. (1869, September 9). Sweet-water. *The Youth's Companion, 42*(36), 284.

CHAPTER TWO

Dolling Up History: Fictions OF Jewish American Girlhood

LISA MARCUS

In the spring of 2009 the American Girl Company introduced Rebecca Rubin, a new Jewish American Girl historical doll (Fig. 1). Girls in Los Angeles lined up at 4 a.m. for her launch; New York families could coordinate their visit to meet the new doll with a tour of the Lower East Side Tenement Museum. Rebecca Rubin's debut was exuberantly welcomed by both the mainstream and Jewish press, with *The New York Times* running a detailed story about her origins and the extensive research that went into creating her. (Apparently, choosing hair color alone took years—it's "mid-tone brown" with "russet highlights"). The *Times* reporter subjected the doll to a vetting by Abraham Foxman, of the Anti-Defamation League, who confirmed that "most of the time these things fall into stereotypes which border on the offensive" (a fact evidenced by Foxman's own collection of Polish wooden dolls, depicting Jewish businessmen counting coins). The Rebecca Rubin doll, he was surprised to find, is a "sensitive" representation of Jewish girlhood (Salkin, 2009). Jewish cultural critic Daphne Merkin (2009) wrote in *Tablet Magazine* about "rush[ing] to order her, despite my advanced years," and Jewish mothers enthused on the American Girl website (2010) as they ordered dolls and accessories for Hanukkah. One lucky doll recipient gushed, "She is just like me with greenish eyes, brown, curly, shoulder length hair, being Jewish, and loving acting. She could be my twin! I love this doll!." Another wrote, "This is the best doll ever!!!! She is soooo cute!!! It is also cool that she is Jewish!!! That will be very educational for so many people!!!! She is beautiful!!!!!!" A father, signing in as "Papa Rosenbaum" raved, simply: "Mazel Tov AG!" Real American girls can buy Rebecca for $95.

They can also buy a Hanukkah set complete with a shiny menorah made in China, a Sabbath set that includes challah and shabbos candles, a school lunch kit that comes with a plastic bagel and the score for "You're A Grand Old Flag" (along with the flag itself), and a pricey bedroom ensemble accompanied by two kittens. Rebecca and her many accessories and outfits can all be had for the whopping sum of $901.95 before tax.

Figure 1. Rebecca Rubin doll and book. Photo courtesy of American Girl.

ANNE FRANK, AMERICAN GIRL

So what can a doll tell us about constructions of Jewish American girlhood? I want to contend that the eagerness and hunger with which girls—and their parents and grandparents—embraced Rebecca Rubin as an icon of Jewish American girlhood is significant, because the version of American history for sale in the Rebecca doll and the books that accompany her presents an idealized America in which anti-Semitism and anxieties about Jewish American identity are elided and smoothed away. One might counter, of course, that narratives for children quite appropriately offer gentler, more optimistic visions of history. And, indeed, the Rebecca Rubin books promote an affirmative vision of Jewish American identity that, as the website insists, offers a "girl-sized" view "of significant events that helped shape our country, and…bring history alive for millions of children" (American Girl, 2010). Yet the history represented in this work of children's literature is instructive precisely because it illustrates—and taps into—patterns of ideological desire that resonate more broadly throughout the Jewish American imagination: the desire for fictions of a tolerant and welcoming America, and of a Jewish American identity that fits comfortably within it.

To appreciate the significance of the appearance of a Jewish "American Girl" in our current moment, the importing and Americanizing of the tragically iconic Jewish girl Anne Frank can be instructive, for it reveals many of the same ideological pressures that shape the Rebecca Rubin version of American girlhood. Critics have ably outlined the troubling aspects of Anne Frank's reception in the United States. Cynthia Ozick (2000) has argued trenchantly that Anne Frank's story has "been bowdlerized, distorted, transmuted, traduced, reduced; it has been infantilized, Americanized, homogenized, sentimentalized; falsified, kitschified….A deeply truth-telling work has been turned into an instrument of partial truth, surrogate truth, or anti-truth" (pp. 77–78). She cautions that the diary is not "to be taken as a Holocaust document," and worried that it has "contributed to the subversion of history" (p. 78). Her particular quarrel is with the popular reduction of Anne into a sunny icon of hope most evident in the 1955 play and 1959 Hollywood film that rely too much on the optimistic spirit of Anne's oft-quoted statement (taken out of context from the diary) that "in spite of everything" she believes people are basically good at heart. This "Hollywood Anne," as Tim Cole (1999) has called her, is quintessentially hopeful; she "comforts us that people are still basically pretty decent, thus silencing any challenge that the Holocaust might make to our naïve optimism in human potential" (p. 77). As Bruno Bettelheim (2000) insists, the immense popularity of an idealized Anne stems from audiences' desire for a history that acknowledges the horror of genocide only to release us from the burden of its legacy:

> Her seeming survival through her moving statement about the goodness of men releases us effectively of the need to cope with the problems Auschwitz presents. That is why we are so relieved by her statement. It explains why millions loved the play and movie, because while it confronts us with the fact that Auschwitz existed, it encourages us at the same time to ignore any of its implications. If all men are good at heart, there never really was an Auschwitz. (p. 189)

Indeed, such audience desires directly shaped the construction of a "Hollywood Anne." As Ellen Feldman (2005) reports,

our need for a happy Anne, despite her profoundly unhappy ending, runs so deep that
when preview audiences saw the last scenes of the original cut of the movie, which
showed Anne at Auschwitz, they scrawled outrage on their opinion cards. This was
not the Anne they knew. (n.p.)

That scene was scrapped and replaced with the hopeful voiceover.

One of the reasons that Anne Frank's narrative is so popular in the American
imagination, these critics challenge, is that "Hollywood Anne" doesn't really die,
at least not in front of us. Lawrence Langer (2000a), arguing that "upbeat endings
seem to be de rigueur for the American imagination which traditionally buries its
tragedies and lets them fester in the shadow of forgetfulness" (p. 200), suggests that
"one appeal of the diary is that it shelters both students and teachers from the worst,
to say nothing of the unthinkable, making them feel they have encountered the
Holocaust without being threatened by intolerable images" (Langer, 2000b, p. 204).
Martha Ravits (1997) adds, "It has served like Perseus's shield as a polished mirror in
which a viewer can behold the face of atrocity without being paralyzed by it" (p. 18).

At stake in such critiques are important issues about the uses to which historical memory (or amnesia) are put. The Americanization of Anne Frank feeds a
desire for a flattering and exceptionalist American self-image: one of benevolence,
innocence, and affirmation of diversity. Mark Anderson (2007) writes provocatively that while child narratives such as Anne Frank's

> had the undeniable merit of winning the hearts of mainstream, non-Jewish audiences
> in the 1950s and 60s…they also set the terms for an Americanization of Holocaust
> memory that privatized and sentimentalized the historical event…they also depoliti-
> cized and sacralized the Holocaust, filed off the rough edges of the Jewish protagonists,
> and sought reconciliation rather than confrontation with the gentile world. (p. 19)

His worry, which I share, is that too often Anne Frank's story is embraced as a vehicle
for "teaching tolerance" and that this is frequently based on what he calls "no cost
multiculturalism," which "provides the illusion of diversity without requiring that
anything or anyone actually change" and "goes hand in hand with an almost complete
lack of historical perspective" (p. 17). Startling, then, if not wholly unsurprising, is the
fact reported by Francine Prose (2009) that while 50% of American schoolchildren
had studied Anne Frank in a classroom assignment in 2004, 25% of American teenagers in another study could not correctly identify Hitler (pp. 253–254).

That Anne Frank continues to be symbolically important to Americans can be
seen in the plan to plant at Ground Zero, in commemoration of the 9/11 attacks,
a sapling from the tree that Anne gazed at from her hidden attic in Amsterdam
("Rooted Remembrances," 2009). If such Americanization of Anne Frank weren't
troubling enough, her transformation into an American girl was almost completed
in 2004 when a Long Island congressman petitioned for her honorary U.S.

citizenship. Though the petition was not successful, Islip Town Council member Christopher Boykin regards "America as Anne Frank's natural home. Who better than this country to afford Anne Frank citizenship? It's been a place that has been safe for the Jews literally since day one" (Clyne, 2004). While history proves otherwise, it is compelling that an elected official, speaking on record, would hold to such a romantic view of Jewish American history. But that view is matched by many, including the American Girl Company.

HISTORY FOR SALE

Sue Fishkoff (2009), writing for *The Jerusalem Post*, asserts in her review of the Rebecca Rubin doll, "Jews love history, especially their own." She goes on to suggest that,

> Jewish parents hip to the American Girl formula of nicely-made dolls and well-written books about the period of American history they represent, wanted a piece of their own people's story to give their daughters. "This is our history, right here in this doll," says author Meredith Jacobs of Rockville, MD., host of The Modern Jewish Mom on The Jewish Channel.

Another mother, writing in to the American Girl website (2010), gushes: "I love that when you buy an AG historical doll—you are also buying a bit of the past!" I want to think here about what it means to "buy a piece of the past," particularly a piece of Jewish American history that has been sanitized and reconstructed in frilly white pajamas with two pet kittens. All of the American Girl historical dolls are created with a boxed-set of six books that lay out the girl's story in a particular year (always ending in 4) in American history. The books are researched, and include historical appendices that add authenticity to the fictional tales offered within the covers.[1] Rebecca Rubin's story is set in 1914, a shrewd choice that was evidently vetted with focus groups and historical research initiated by the American Girl marketing department. Setting the fictional Rebecca, who is 9 in the stories, in 1914 strategically enables the American Girl Company to present an upbeat Jewish American history that highlights "assimilation, blending in and becoming American," as the senior vice president for marketing, Shawn Dennis reported in a *Times* article (Salkin, 2009). And 1914 is safely far enough past the Triangle Shirtwaist Factory fire (1911), prior to the lynching of Leo Frank in Atlanta in 1915, and well in advance of the drastic restrictions of 1924 that effectively choked off immigration from Eastern Europe, as Nativist legislators sought to control the racial and ethnic make-up of the United States, sometimes explicitly stating that their efforts would curb Jewish migration. It also falls before the implementation of quotas limiting Jewish enrollment at elite universities, and, importantly, it allows for a pre-Holocaust Jewish America unscarred by the Nazi genocide.

Housed within the confines of this carefully selected historical moment, the Rebecca stories construct an idealized, triumphalist immigrant narrative of a welcoming America and a Jewish American girl whose potentially conflicting identities are happily fused and only minimally challenged. In the first book, the question of naming is easily resolved when cousin Moyshe Shereshevsky enthusiastically announces, "it's no more Moyshe Shereshevsky…I am Max Shepherd, if you please…an American name for an American actor" (Dembar Greene, 2009b, p. 8). While "Bubbie" grumbles that "you don't change a name like a dirty shirt" (p. 8), her Old World view is quickly swept aside as Max—seemingly with no effort—becomes a rich movie actor and contributes his first paycheck to help finance the passage for Rebecca's cousin's family to flee the pogroms of Russia just in time to avoid conscription in the war. Indeed, the Historical Notes to the Rebecca series feature a poster (on display at Ellis Island), which contrasts the anti-Semitic old world to the welcoming new world (see Figure 2).

Figure 2. 1919 Poster contrasting Old World and American possibility. Photo courtesy of Library of Congress and the Statute of Liberty National Monument.

In the second book in the series, when the cousin's family arrives, Max and Rebecca joyfully serenade the new immigrants with a loud rendition of "You're a Grand Old Flag," emphasizing "free" and "brave" in the lines, "You're the land I love, the home of the *free* and the *brave*" (Dembar Greene, 2009c, p. 5). Even Bubbie nods in time with the music while "Grandpa" (too assimilated, we assume, to be called Zadie) taps his foot. The thick patriotism of this narrative offers a syrupy version of easy assimilation, highlighted when newly arrived cousin Ana is featured in a duet with Rebecca singing George M. Cohan's lyrics at a school assembly to celebrate the arrival of a new flag for display. In the school auditorium, under the golden lettering of the "names of famous Americans: George Washington, Thomas Jefferson and Abraham Lincoln" (p. 66), the two Jewish girls belt out their patriotic song, pledging allegiance to a welcoming America in which new immigrants quickly lose their accents, assimilate, and move out of the tenements and into the American dream. This matters to American Girl marketers, because in order to sell this "bit of history" to moms like the ones cited above, Rebecca can't live in a tenement like the one Lewis W. Hine photographed in 1910 (Figure 3). Her bedroom set has to be cute enough for little girls to want to play house with (Figure 4), and should include matching pajamas for doll and girl.

Figure 3. Lewis Wickes Hine, tenement rear bedroom, circa 1910. Photography Collection, Miriam and Ira D. Wallach Division of Art, Prints and Photographs, The New York Public Library, Astor, Lenox and Tilden Foundations.

Figure 4. Rebecca Rubin bedroom collection (includes kittens, for $178). Photo courtesy of American Girl.

To be sure, these books chronicle Rebecca's struggles as well, but these are limited to incidents such as the anxiety she faces about having to make a Christmas centerpiece at school (because her teacher insists that Christmas is a national holiday, not a Christian one), and all such conflicts are easily dealt with: in this case, with Rebecca re-gifting the pine-scented masterpiece to the ailing Italian superintendant of her building. She manifests just enough nascent feminism to appeal to contemporary mothers, best evidenced when she grumbles about the gender-segregated synagogue in which her brother is bar mitzvahed. Scolded for her kvetching, Rebecca is reminded by Bubbie that, "to be a good Jewish wife and mother…you must keep the house kosher and observe the Sabbath every week. The men will do the Torah reading" (Dembar Greene, 2009d, p. 6). She later performs a daring rescue of her cousin who is stuck on a broken Ferris wheel in Coney Island, asserting her girl power without really challenging the patriarchal status quo.

Rebecca's chutzpah resurfaces in the final, and most politically radical, of the books when she becomes a veritable voice for the union after her uncle and cousin strike to protest the miserable conditions of garment workers. As Rebecca declaims from a platform on Labor Day, 1914, American Girl offers a nod to Jewish labor history, but it's all in the service of (Jewish) Hollywood. Rebecca's speech, we're told, is indicative of her acting talent; as Max heads west to the silver screen,

Rebecca's family learns that she's already been an extra in a film and has diva aspirations. It's "all good" for this (Jewish) American girl, because the book boxed-set ends with Rebecca feeling "like she could do just about anything" (Dembar Greene, 2009a, p. 70). Contemporary girls can help her along by buying her movie dress for $32 and her costume chest for a cool $100. Her soapbox and union activist outfit are not for sale, but maybe girls can make them if they buy Rebecca's Fashion Studio for $17.95.

ALL OF A KIND

If Rebecca Rubin and her family offer wholesome fare for twenty-first-century girls and their families eager to connect with fictions of Jewish American history, these characters find themselves in good company with a family of fictional girls that were introduced to a warmly welcoming public over half a century ago. The *All- of-a-Kind Family* books, written by Sydney Taylor and first published in 1951, are compelling precursor texts in that they, too, look back to the Lower East Side of 1912 as a paradigmatic moment for Jewish Americans.[2] Hasia Diner (2000) has explored how "[t]he Lower East Side has become fixed in American Jewish memory as the site from which a singular story has been told," a story of origins and "founding myth" that "bears a striking resemblance to the Pilgrims' tale" (p. 7). She notes that it

> has all the markings of an apocryphal tale: a people persecuted in the "Old World" picked up their featherbeds, Sabbath candlesticks, and samovars and fled to Atlantic ports. They never looked back as they traveled in steerage across the ocean to a land of freedom, their landing welcomed by a massive statue grasping the beacon of liberty. (p. 7)

While Diner is most interested in how the Lower East Side has been sacralized as a site of cultural memory, just as important as the geographic location is the time frame from which the originating tale springs. A generation after Jews began fleeing Eastern Europe en masse in 1880, just before World War I, and before the nativist immigration quotas imposed in 1924, the 1910s offer a powerful temporal locus for this "apocryphal" origin myth.[3] Unlike Jaqueline Dembar Greene, author of the American Girl Rebecca books, Taylor didn't need the likes of a marketing research team to locate the 1912 timeframe for her tale. (Nor, in 1951, could she have imagined "featherbeds, Sabbath candlesticks, and samovars" transformed into historical mementoes available for purchase to accessorize your historical doll.) She turned back to her own life growing up on the Lower East Side to provide fodder for bedtime stories created for her daughter, Jo, an only child. As June Cummins (2003) explains,

She always claimed that she wrote the *All-Of-A-Kind Family* stories for her daughter Jo, who asked "Mommy, why is it every time I read a book about children, it is always a Christian child? Why isn't there a book about a Jewish child?"….Taylor attempted to capture the past and present it to her daughter and other readers as personal and ethnic history. (pp. 325–326)

The *All-Of-a-Kind Family* books—revered by many, and still widely read by Jewish families—offer what Diner (2000) aptly terms "a hermetically sealed world of Jewishness and love," set in a Lower East Side where "families could be observant Jews and enthusiastic Americans at one and the same time" (p. 65). As Diner writes, "on Taylor's Lower East Side, American patriotism cozily existed side by side with Jewish life, uncontested by conflicting demands" (p. 65). This is particularly evident in a chapter on the Fourth of July. While Taylor is careful to alert readers to the patriotism of the neighborhood through the American flags that decorate the tenements, these flags are never presented as an oxymoron that puts into question the immigrants' loyalty or patriotism (as happens in the Rebecca book discussed above).[4] Taylor's books affirm Jewish Americanness as unproblematic and uncontested. Perhaps that is why they have been so adored. For example, the family celebrates Independence Day with potato kugel and firecrackers, exhilarating in the "crusty brown" deliciousness of the kugel and the sparkling firework display that follows. While the chapter is quick to affirm patriotic Americanness—"Everybody was expressing their joy in freedom today. From tenement house windows and from storefronts flew American flags of all sizes" (Taylor, 1989, p. 135)—it is tempered by a Jewish immigrant flavoring.

Cummins (2003) reports that Taylor's series, "read by Jews and non-Jews alike…lovingly describes Jewish rituals and holidays, simultaneously educating those readers unfamiliar with these traditions and affirming the experiences of children who know them already" (p. 324). For Jewish readers, like Taylor's daughter, Jo, the books "obviously validate Jewish observance and identity," as Cummins notes (p. 324). This is best evidenced in the way that the narrative of the first book is structured around the seasonal calendar of Jewish holidays. The "lovely feeling of peace and contentment" that suffuses the Sabbath chapter enables Taylor to serve up Jewish tradition and ritual along with gefullte fish and chicken soup (Taylor, 1989, p. 78). Rather than overwhelming readers with didactic religious instruction, Taylor instead presents Jewish ritual as warm and inviting, almost as local color.

Accordingly, Taylor's narrative simultaneously functions to introduce Jews and Jewishness to a larger American audience unfamiliar with Jewish tradition and religious practice. The *All-of-a-Kind* family seems carefully crafted to fulfill an intermediary or liminal role, bridging the Jewish and gentile worlds; they are "like" but "unlike" their Lower East Side neighbors, all-of-a-kind, but also all-American.[5] In the third chapter we move away from the domestic world of Mama and her girls, a world in which dusting (every day!) is made into a clever game in order to instruct the five daughters to be "the best little housekeepers in the whole world" (Taylor, 1989, p. 33), to the exterior landscape of the East Side, which "was not pretty" (p. 34). In a paragraph punctuated by negatives ("no grass," "no flowers," "no tall trees," "no running brook," p. 34), readers are stripped of any pastoral illusions that might accompany the quaint domesticity outlined earlier and reminded of the urban landscape that "smelt of fish, ships and garbage" (p. 34). We learn, importantly, that

> [l]ike many other families, Mama and Papa and their children lived in the crowded tenement house section of the lower east Side of New York City. But unlike most of these families, their home was a four-room apartment which occupied an entire floor in a two-storied private house. (p. 35)

The family's difference from their "not pretty" surroundings is highlighted by their spotlessly clean home, and though all five girls share one bedroom, their "all-of-a-kind" difference from the rest of the community is subtly noted when shopping for the Sabbath:

> Only one tongue was spoken here—Yiddish. It was like a foreign land right in the midst of America. In this foreign land, it was Mama's children who were the foreigners since they alone conversed in an alien tongue—English. (p. 72)

The girls' status as "like" but "unlike" their "foreign" neighbors makes them fitting guides for readers unfamiliar with this "foreign land right in the middle of America." Mama, too, proves a usefully liminal character in the figure she cuts:

> the children were very proud of Mama. Most of the other Jewish women in the neighborhood had such bumpy shapes. Their bodies looked like mattresses tied about in the middle. But not Mama. She was tall and slim and held herself proudly. Her face was proud too. (p. 65)

Mama's slender body, in contrast with her more lumpy peers, aligns her with the gentile "Library Lady" (described earlier in the book as "fresh and clean and crisp," slender, with light hair and clean nails) and marks her as a useful guide to help navigate readers through "the foreign land right in the middle of America."

That the all-of-a-kind family is positioned to make Lower East Side Jews accessible to a wider readership is evident in the way Taylor introduces gentile characters as surrogates for readers, and it is through these figures that many of the Jewish holidays are experienced. Because of their presence in key scenes, Taylor is able to offer a primer on Jewish Holidays (a kind of Jewish Holidays 101) without seeming to dumb down Judaism for the already initiated. More fundamentally, these surrogates serve to symbolize the relationship between Jews and gentiles, a relationship that in Taylor's depiction is both one of accessible and comfortable interaction, and yet one in which difference is maintained. Charlie, a beloved young peddler and frequenter of Papa's junk shop, "handsome, blond, and blue-eyed," and who we later learn has a WASP pedigree, a "wealthy family" and "fine education" (Taylor, 1989, p. 41), joins the family for many of their holiday gatherings, for "he was always at home in Mama's house, even when he was the only gentile present" (p. 101). Taylor, through Charlie, makes a wide readership "at home" amongst her Jewish family, instructing these readers in Jewish customs and traditions without becoming too anthropological. When eldest daughter Ella sings "a mournful Jewish melody" on Purim, Charlie's praise cements her crush on him. Yet, in a surprising plot twist, Charlie is revealed to be betrothed to none other than the girls' darling "Library Lady," whom he rediscovers in the all-of-a-kind family's Succah. We learn that Charlie's family had opposed their marriage because his sweetheart had "no family," that they had each (unbeknown to the other) fled to the Lower East Side, with Charlie shedding his name, career, and prospects in anger at his family. That both of these "orphaned" gentile figures find comfort among the all-of-a-kind family, and that they find each other during Succos in the temporary shelter erected by the Jewish family, enables Taylor to show that the benign Jewish family—while influencing and nourishing the gentiles with whom it has contact—will remain intact and all-of-a-kind together in their "hermetically sealed" world. The resolution of this romance plot affirms that Jews can be part of America while ethnic (and religious) differences are safely maintained. With Ella's crush dashed, and Charlie appropriately mated with one of his "kind," Taylor ensures that the only challenge to the family's of-a-kind-ness is the addition of a baby boy (named Charlie, of course) to the all-girl family at the end of the book.

While Cummins (2003) has argued convincingly that Taylor employs "strategies of assimilation" and Americanization in *All-of-a-Kind Family*, even though they are "not dealt with frankly" and seem to occur "at subtextual levels and even extranarratively"[6] (p. 326), it is still remarkable that Mama's quaint family never faces any overt conflict or tension around assimilation, a conflict that so often shapes immigrant narratives. As Diner (2000) noted,

> In at least this Jewish home of the Lower East Side, traditional practices, holidays and Sabbaths in particular, caused no one embarrassment. In no place did Mama, Papa, and the girls…suffer any personal inconveniences in order to fulfill ritual practice, nor did the demands of acceptance into the American mainstream rub up against the inherited, cherished ways. (p. 63)

Taylor's placid narrative, penned in the late 1940s and revised for publication in 1950, offers a romantic portrait absent of tension. Cummins (2003) notes a fascinating exchange between Taylor and her editor, Esther Meeks, who wrote to Taylor, "The family seems to live in a world of its own—the Lower East Side, not America. I have the feeling that these episodes were lived and wonder if this isolation really existed" (p. 334). Cummins contextualizes the editor's worries that "particularly today" "the family [needs to] show some signs of being American as well as Jewish" (p. 334), by reminding us that as Taylor was writing, the Rosenberg trial was stirring up suspicion against Jews.

Indeed, what is perhaps most striking about Taylor's placid narrative is its juxtaposition to the historical moment in which it was written. This period—as Americans came to grips with the Holocaust, Israel was founded, the Rosenbergs were arrested—was, after all, rife with tension and anxiety. And it was a period in which anti-Semitism remained pervasive, as has been freshly evidenced by a recently released questionnaire about attitudes toward Jews conducted by the U.S. military in 1947, which revealed a troubling anti-Semitism among the armed forces, with 86% of those surveyed agreeing that "there is nothing good about Jews" (ThinkProgress, 2010). It is thus understandable why the quaint and benign version of Jewish American history that Taylor constructs would be so desirable from the vantage point of 1950—when Jews were, as Karen Brodkin (1998) has argued, "not quite white" (p. 60). While the Rebecca Rubin narratives in one sense are more frankly assimilationist in their vision—think of cousin Moyshe Shereshevsky transformed into "Max Shepherd" heading off to Hollywood—in another sense what is most striking about these two narratives is their underlying similarity: the fact that, in 2010, fully 60 years after the first of Taylor's "all-of-a-kind" books appeared, there is still such an appetite to rehearse a nostalgic tale about the Lower East Side, circa 1910, a narrative in which America figures as benevolent sanctuary, a golden land in which the conflict and persecution of the old country is answered by an embracing and relatively harmonized America.

"PRETTY SENTIMENTS" OR "BLACK TRAGEDY"?

An alternative to this kind of triumphalist story can be seen in the writings of Anzia Yezierska, most famous for her 1925 novel *Bread Givers*, which follows its gritty protagonist Sara Smolinsky as she negotiates a much thornier path of Americanization. The context Yezierska offers for understanding the Jewish Lower East Side circa 1912–1914 is perhaps most poignantly rendered in her 1923 short story "Children of Loneliness." There, Cornell-educated protagonist Rachel Ravinsky is heart-achingly at odds with her Old World parents, whom she refers to as "lumps of ignorance and superstition," "ugly and gross and stupid," "wallow[ing] in dirt" (1991, p. 181). Her father curses her for "aping gentiles": "you think you got different skin from us because you went to college?....Pfui on all your American colleges! Pfui on the morals of America!" (p. 179). Bitterly denouncing the college-educated Rachel, he spits out:

This is our daughter, our pride, our hope, our pillow for our old age that we were dreaming about! This is our American *teacherin!* A Jew-hater, an Anti-Semite we brought into the world, a betrayer of our race who hates her own father and mother like the Russian Czar once hated a Jew. She makes herself so refined, she can't stand it when we use the knife or fork the wrong way; but her heart is that of a brutal Cossack, and she spills her own father's and mother's blood like water. (p. 182)

Later, Rachel cautions her privileged gentile boyfriend, Frank Baker (a budding sociologist), who sees poetry in the immigrant's struggles of the Lower East Side: "it's a black tragedy that boils there, not the pretty sentiments that you imagine" (p. 188). While I don't want to argue that the Jewish American immigrant story must be told as a "black tragedy," I do want to be cautious about the overuse of "pretty sentiments" in rendering the story of Jewish immigration and Americanization. Yezierska's Rachel ends in extreme ambivalence and anguished double-consciousness. Her aching finale includes this lament: "I can't live with the old world, and I'm yet too green for the new. I don't belong to those who gave me birth or to those with whom I was educated" (p. 188). There's no Hollywood ending for Yezierska's American girl.

HISTORY LESSONS

In "In the Wake of Home" Adrienne Rich (1993) wrote with unflinching clarity of the nostalgia that often shapes the stories we tell ourselves about the past. Her poem offers a tough-minded political critique of the seductive ideal of home while simultaneously expressing a compassionate appreciation for the human desire that craves it. Writing, knowingly,

> you will be drawn to places
> where generations lie
> side by side with each other:
> fathers, mothers and children
> in the family prayerbook
> or the country burying-ground

Rich acknowledged the longing for a coherent family history, a hope that

> once at least it was all in order
> and nobody came to grief. (p. 120)

Even as she articulates such desire, Rich portrays it as tied to romanticized ideas of a traditional past:

You imagine an alley   a little kingdom
Where the mother-tongue is spoken
a village of shelters   woven
or sewn of hides   in a long-ago way
or a shanty standing up
at the edge of sharecropped fields
a tenement where life is seized by the teeth
You imagine the people would all be there
Fathers mothers and children
the ones you were promised would all be there
eating   arguing   working
trying to get on with life
you imagine this used to be
for everyone   everywhere. (pp. 121–122)

Rich (1993) insists on exposing the "hole torn and patched over" (p. 121) in overly coherent narratives of the past. Such narratives, though seductive, are potentially dangerous in the way they romanticize history: "What if I told you your home / is this continent of the homeless / of children sold taken by force," "—this continent of changed names and mixed up blood," of "diasporas unrecorded," "underground railroads" and "trails of tears" (p. 122). Continuing in the wary mode of a conditional question, Rich suggests there is a freedom in getting beyond such romanticized ideals: "What if I tell you, you are not different / it's the family albums that lie," but then immediately she noted the imaginative and emotional hunger that persists despite or beyond such critical insights: "will any of this comfort you / and how should this comfort you?" (p. 122).

The tensions that Rich locates in the pull of "home" help illuminate the fictions of Jewish American girlhood I've explored here. On the one hand, it is quite understandable that the historical moment (circa 1912–1914) that both the Rebecca Rubin and *All-of-a-Kind Family* narratives re-write exerts a seductive pull on Jewish Americans, for it anchors a kind of authenticating narrative that is both positive and exemplary—where Jews become the quintessential American immigrants embracing and embraced in return by the nation. Like many American Jews, I too can trace a family history to the narrative encapsulated in this paradigmatic moment. My own grandmother came to the U.S. as a 3-year-old in 1914—a Russian Jewish immigrant from Soroki, Moldova, a town whose name translates literally as "poverty." She traveled to Ellis Island in steerage on the last sailing from Hamburg of the ship *The Pennsylvania* before the outbreak of World War I. Her name was Zlata Jampolski, the youngest child of Azreal and Shendel Jampolski, and their family of 10, who bypassed the Lower East Side and settled directly in Brooklyn. Captured in a Coney Island photograph from the mid-1920s (see Fig. 5), my grandmother is wearing a revealing bathing suit, leaning over her Old-World father, who is clad in suit and tie.

Figure 5. Azreal Jampolski at Coney Island with author's grandmother (private collection).

The iconography of this photograph, with the bespectacled, patriarchal Azrael surrounded by his scantily clad daughters, fits right into a classic immigrant myth—highlighting the contrast between the older generation, still dressed in traditional garb and ways, and their Americanized offspring. By the 1930 Census my grandmother had shed her identity as Zlata Jampolski, registering her name as "Jean Jay," and within several years she would be married, would give birth to my father (who would go on to an Ivy League education), would secure a foothold in the American dream. I am almost certain my grandmother would have endorsed this optimistic take on her life story; accordingly, I have little doubt that she would have celebrated the assimilationist, quintessentially American Rebecca Rubin, joining in spirit her peers on the American Girl website in cheering the arrival of this new version of American Girl(hood).

On the other hand, like Rich, I am also cognizant of the dangers of histories that idealize the past. Even the story I've told about my grandmother above—culled, as Rich depicts, from "old family albums / with their smiles"—leaves out, among other things, the "subtle but powerful" anti-Semitism of Princeton in the

1950s, well documented by Jerome Karabel (2005) and experienced by my father (p. 303). Just because I can tie my grandmother to what Hasia Diner calls the "apocryphal tale" of Jewish American origins, to the moment offered by American Girl Company as the touchstone of Jewish American history, doesn't mean that I must offer it only as a tale of "pretty sentiments" minus the "black tragedy" Yezierska so poignantly noted.

Narratives that stress immigrant assimilation and belonging not only promote a triumphalist or exceptionalist vision of America as benign, tolerant, and just; in their erasure of conflict, oppression, and resistance, they also fail to offer models for confronting injustice in a complex world. Elizabeth Marshall (2008/2009), writing of American Girl's Latina Josefina doll, argued that "the creators at American Girl favor a whitewashed...history" in which "issues such as racism, colonization, and war" are "presented as things that America has overcome," and that "avoids any lessons about social activism...to fight ongoing gender and/or racial discrimination." When I first presented a shorter version of this piece (at a Holocaust conference), a Historian colleague of mine provocatively advocated for "historical amnesia," arguing that children need narratives that stress harmony and tolerance, not ones that perpetuate conflict and division. Overlooking the chutzpah of invoking historical amnesia at a Holocaust conference, I would insist that children are ill-served by sanitized and overly cheerful fictional histories. As Sherrie Inness (1998) notes, "[p]eople often wish to view children's literature and children's culture as politically and ideologically neutral and naïve" (p. 170), yet the ideological tensions at play in the children's texts discussed above clearly suggest otherwise. Historian Lisa Gordon, interviewed about the American Girl series, critiques "the 'obvious dumbing-down' of complex topics. ...'It's a mistake to think that children don't like scary or painful things. ...If you think about fairy tales, they are often extremely scary or violent, and children love them for precisely that reason'" (Kinzer, 2003). Adrienne Rich (1986) provided a striking account of the "belated rage" that can emerge when young people who've been denied access to darker histories are confronted with them. In her essay "Split at the Root: An Essay on Jewish Identity" Rich chronicles a memory from 1946—of being 16 and viewing alone a newsreel of the Allied liberation of concentration camps. She laments that she had "nobody in my world with whom I could discuss those films," that she "had no language for anti-Semitism," no ability to even ask "are those men and women 'them' or 'us'?" (p. 107).

I am not advocating stories that dogmatically emphasize oppression and victimhood. American Girl has already ventured into that territory in its construction of the African American doll Addy (whose story begins in slavery), participating in the overwhelming tendency in American popular culture to portray African Americans as perpetual victims, pathologically impoverished, forever linked to slavery and its aftermath. Yet, as Jeanne Brady (1994) has argued, the "chocolate cake with Vitamins" approach to history peddled by American Girl, in which "history and politics are disguised in the image of nostalgia, innocence, and simplicity," deprives girls of the "opportunity to read and understand history in all its complex forms in order to help them problematize the past and begin to see themselves as historical beings who can challenge the present and create a more democratic future" (p. 5). The benefit of more historically complex fictions is not simply to teach children to see oppression in the past, but rather to acknowledge the structures of inequality and prejudice that call us to solidarity with others in the present. Narratives of Jewish American girlhood that more forthrightly acknowledge anti-Semitism, for instance, not only prepare young readers for a world in which the anti-Semitism prevalent in the 1920s and 1950s has not simply vanished, but equip them to understand contemporary iterations of nativist, anti-immigrant prejudices such as those undergirding recent immigration legislation.[7]

***

In *The Holocaust in American Life*, Peter Novick (1999) concludes,

> Along with most historians, I'm skeptical about the so-called lessons of history. I'm especially skeptical about the sort of pithy lessons that fit on a bumper sticker. If there is, to use a pretentious word, any wisdom to be acquired from contemplating an historical event, I would think it would derive from confronting it in all its complexity and its contradictions....If there are lessons to be extracted from encountering the past, that encounter has to be with the past in all its messiness; they're not likely to come from an encounter with a past that's been shaped and shaded so that inspiring lessons will emerge. (p. 261)

Jewish American girls—*all* girls—deserve a more complex history lesson, one that hasn't been simplified to bumper-sticker slogans purchase-able on a website or in a megastore. There may be reasons to celebrate this doll that's not Barbie, this doll that has chutzpah and performs tikkun olam,[8] but while the American Girl Company sold itself to Mattel some years back, we shouldn't sell ourselves short. Whether it's the problematic repackaging of Anne Frank's Holocaust experience, or the seemingly benign narrative of American Girl Rebecca Rubin, or even the beloved "All-of-a-Kind" family, we should be wary of the icons of Jewish American girlhood we buy into.

NOTES

1. For an excellent critique of the "feel-good, progress-oriented version of American history" offered by the American Girl historical fictions, see Hade (2000).

2. Jacqueline Dembar Greene (personal communication, 2010) commissioned author of the American Girl Rebecca books, claimed that, "she didn't read Sydney Taylor's once-popular book series." Interestingly, however, she noted that she "re-read *Rebecca of Sunnybrook Farm* so that my character, Rebecca, might relate to the spunky character in that book, which was quite popular in 1914."

3. For a more detailed discussion of this period in Jewish American history, see Sorin (1992).

4. In the scene where Rebecca and Ana sing "You're a Grand Old Flag" in the school auditorium, Rebecca worries whether her cousin, who barely speaks enough English to learn the lyrics, is indeed American enough to be authentically patriotic. Ana herself questions her loyalty to an America that has detained her brother Josef at Ellis Island. True to the optimistic formula of the series, the book ends with Josef's release and Ana "feeling *patriotic*" (Dembar Greene, 2009c, pp. 31–33, 70).

5. The family's "all-of-a-kind" designation ostensibly refers to the fact that, in the first book, the family is composed of all daughters. But the moniker clearly signifies much more, as my interpretation of Taylor's narrative suggests.

6. For instance, Cummins cited the fact that Yiddish terms are often translated into English, and that the romance between Charlie and the "Library Lady," Kathy, displaces the narrative focus away from the Jewish protagonists.

7. I am thinking, for example, of recent legislation in Arizona (see Archibold, 2010) and Alabama.

8. Tikkun olam translates from the Hebrew as "repairing the world," and usually calls for community service or activism.

REFERENCES

American Girl® Dolls: Rebecca doll & book. (2010, July 16). Retrieved from http://store.american girl.com/agshop/static/rebeccadoll.jsp

Anderson, M. (2007). The child victim as witness to the Holocaust: An American story? *Jewish Social Studies: History, Culture, Society, 14* (Fall), 1–22.

Archibold, R. (2010, April 23). Arizona enacts stringent law on immigration. *The New York Times.*

Bettelheim, B. (2000). The ignored lesson of Anne Frank. In A. E. Hyman & S. Solotaroff-Enzer (Eds.), *Anne Frank: Reflections on her life and legacy* (pp. 185–191). Urbana, IL: University of Illinois Press.

Brady, J. (1994). Reading the American dream: The history of the American Girl collection. *Teaching and Learning Literature* (Sept/Oct), 2–6.

Brodkin, K. (1998). *How Jews became white folks.* New Brunswick, NJ: Rutgers University Press.

Clyne, M. (2004, December 31). Anne Frank, an American citizen? A New Yorker's quest to make it so. *The New York Sun.*

Cole, T. (1999). *Selling the Holocaust: From Auschwitz to Schindler, how history is bought, packaged and sold.* New York, NY: Routledge.

Cummins, J. (2003). Becoming an "All-Of-A-Kind" American: Sydney Taylor and strategies of assimilation. *The Lion and the Unicorn, 27*(3), 324–343.

Dembar Greene, J. (2009a). *Changes for Rebecca.* Middleton, WI: American Girl.

Dembar Greene, J. (2009b). *Meet Rebecca.* Middleton, WI: American Girl.

Dembar Greene, J. (2009c). *Rebecca and Ana.* Middleton, WI: American Girl.

Dembar Greene, J. (2009d). *Rebecca to the rescue*. Middleton, WI: American Girl.

Diner, H. (2000). *Lower East Side memories: A Jewish place in America*. Princeton, NJ: Princeton University Press.

Feldman, E. (2005). Anne Frank in America. *American Heritage, 56*(1). Retrieved from http://www.americanheritage.com/content/anne-frank-america

Fishkoff, S. (2009, May 25). The new American Girl doll: She's Jewish and she's poor. *The Jerusalem Post*.

Hade, D. (2000). Lies my children's books taught me: History meets popular culture in "The American Girls Books." In R. McGillis (Ed.), *Voices of the other: Children's literature and the postcolonial context* (pp. 153–164). New York, NY: Routledge.

Inness, S. (1998). "Anti-Barbies": The American Girls collection and political ideologies. In S. Inness (Ed.), *Delinquents and debutantes: Twentieth-century American Girls' cultures* (pp. 164–183). New York, NY: NYU Press.

Karabel, J. (2005). *The chosen: The hidden history of admission and exclusion at Harvard, Yale, and Princeton*. Boston, MA: Houghton Mifflin.

Kinzer, S. (2003, November 6). Dolls as role models, neither Barbie nor Britney. *The New York Times*.

Langer, L. (2000a). The Americanization of the Holocaust on stage and screen. In A. E. Hyman & S. Solotaroff-Enzer (Eds.), *Anne Frank: Reflections on her life and legacy* (pp. 198–202). Urbana, IL: University of Illinois Press.

Langer, L. (2000b). The uses—and misuses—of a young girl's diary: "If Anne Frank could return from among the murdered she would be appalled." In A. E. Hyman & S. Solotaroff-Enzer (Eds.), *Anne Frank: Reflections on her life and legacy* (pp. 203–205). Urbana, IL: University of Illinois Press.

Marshall, E. (2008/2009). Marketing American girlhood. *Rethinking Schools Online, 23*(2). Retrieved from http://www.rethinkingschools.org

Merkin, D. (2009, December 16). Dolled up. *Tablet*. Retrieved from http://www.tabletmag.com/life-and-religion/22439/dolled-up

Novick, P. (1999). *The Holocaust in American life*. Boston, MA: Houghton Mifflin.

Ozick, C. (2000). Who owns Anne Frank? In *Quarrel and quandary* (pp. 74–102). New York, NY: Knopf.

Prose, F. (2009). *Anne Frank: The book, the life, the afterlife*. New York, NY: HarperCollins.

Ravits, M. (1997). To work in the world: Anne Frank and American literary history. *Women's Studies, 27*, 1–30.

Rich, A. (1993). In the wake of home. In B. Charlesworth Gelpi & A. Gelpi (Eds.), *Adrienne Rich's poetry and prose* (pp. 119–123). New York, NY: Norton.

Rich, A. (1986). Split at the root: An essay on Jewish identity. In *Blood, bread and poetry: Selected prose 1979–1985* (pp. 100–123). New York, NY: Norton.

Rooted remembrances: Tree that gave hope to Anne Frank to blossom wonderfully in U.S. (2009, April 17). *New York Daily News*.

Salkin, A. (2009, May 24). "American Girl's journey to the Lower East Side." *New York Times*, 24 May.

Sorin, Gerald. (1992). *A Time for Building: The Third Migration, 1880–1920*. Baltimore: Johns Hopkins University Press.

Taylor, S. (1989). *All-Of-A-Kind Family*. Follett, 1951. Reprint, New York: Yearling.

ThinkProgress, (2010). "Records Show Military Surveyed Troops' Attitudes Toward Jews in 1940s." Retrieved from http://thinkprogress.org/justice/2010/07/22/176892/exclusive-records-show-military-surveyed-troops-attitudes-towards-jews-in-1940s

Yezierska, A. (1991). Children of loneliness. In *How I found America: Collected stories of Anzia Yezierska* (pp. 178–190). New York, NY: Persea.

CHAPTER THREE

Dolls AND Play: Material Culture AND Memories OF Girlhood IN Germany, 1933–1945

ALEXANDRA LLOYD

My doll carriage with my doll Marlene stood nearby. Marlene sat like a princess on her throne, watching my every move. My doll had been a gift from Grandma for my second birthday. She must have felt lonely, since I was not paying much attention to her these days. (Auerbacher, 2009, p. 55)

This memory from Inge Auerbacher's girlhood in Kippenheim in the 1930s appears at first glance like so many other accounts of girls and their dolls. Yet only a few years later the Nazis would deport Auerbacher, a German Jew, to the Theresienstadt ghetto where, along with her doll Marlene, she would remain until the end of World War II. Her doll had been produced by the famous Schildkröt firm, an "Inge" doll, marketed to celebrate the 1936 Olympic Games in Berlin. It had blue eyes, blond hair done in an "Olympic Roll," (Auerbacher, 2009, p. 55) and reinforced Nazi racial stereotyping and gender roles. Auerbacher had named it Marlene after Marlene Dietrich who, she recalled, like the doll, had blond hair and blue eyes. That this doll, the epitome of Nazi racial profiling, helped "a Jewish [girl] with dark hair to survive the hell that was…Theresienstadt" is full of pathos (Ruder, 2006, p. 33).[1] Yet this story of the complex relationship between a girl and her doll and the National Socialist utilization of this child's toy raises a number of questions about dolls and their owners in the Third Reich.

Dolls tell the historical narrative of everyday life, of political and social attitudes, and of the role of the sexes. In Germany, dolls have historically played an important role, as items of material culture and industrial production, and as important recurring figures in the literary imagination. Yet despite the substantial amount of German-language research into Doll Studies, only a handful of critical texts discuss doll production and play under Nazism.[2] Those which do, focus primarily on the material culture and pedagogical aspects of dolls. This chapter therefore seeks to widen the debate by examining the meaning of dolls in the Third Reich—to the National Socialists who made use of their potential as propaganda tools, and to the many girls who played with them. It addresses the complex relationships between girls and their dolls and the place of dolls in memory. In doing so, it poses a number of questions. To what extent did dolls play into the Nazi conception and control of gender roles? To what extent do we find dolls recognizably codified as National Socialist, for example bearing Nazi insignia or dressed in Nazi uniforms? How did girls interact with their dolls? What do dolls signify, both to children at the time, and to women seeking to remember and recount their childhood? How do dolls feature as memory objects in texts and photographs?

A rich source of information about dolls and their meanings to girls and grownups are the many historical documents and studies upon which this chapter draws. An examination of the production of dolls in the period confirms established ideas about Nazi attitudes towards gender and education, but also about the problematic, often haphazard way in which Nazism implemented its totalitarian ideals in practice. The study of memory texts about girls and their dolls shows not only how important dolls were to girls at the time—as a source of comfort, for example—but also how important they remain in women's memories of girlhood. More than merely the accoutrement of childhood, they often figure as the only fellow witness of the horrors they endured. Furthermore, girls' relationships with their dolls can be traced across the full range of girlhoods in the Third Reich. There is diversity of experience among those who grew up under Nazism and the variety of memories and accounts reflects this.

I examine published autobiographical accounts in the form of memoirs, historical studies, and collections of oral testimony despite their potential problems: the unreliability of memory and the inevitable influence of the present on the way the past is viewed.[3] Other documentary evidence—dolls produced during the Third Reich in addition to photographs of girls in the period—corroborates autobiographical recollections about how girls viewed their dolls. This study is informed by recent theoretical writing about memory, in particular Annette Kuhn's (2002) application of memory work (pp. 3–10, 159–169) to read both visual and literary sources, and her adoption of an approach in line with Carlo Ginzburg's theory of "conjectural knowledge" within cultural memory (Kuhn, 2007, p. 283).[4] Conjectural knowledge requires an analysis of "expressions of memory," using them as a starting point from which to speculate on broader issues and the workings of cultural memory. It can be carried out using individual memories in the form of memoir, recollection, film and photographs, or with a collection of such examples. The texts and photographs analyzed in this chapter constitute part of the cultural memory of Fascism. They are both private, in that they narrate individual girls' experiences, and public, in that they are published and available in the public sphere. Thus they offer an account not only of how girls played with their dolls, but also of cultural memories of, and attitudes towards, doll play in the period.

My approach is also informed by Nicholas Stargardt's (2006) critically acclaimed study of children in the Third Reich and World War II, *Witnesses of War: Children's Lives Under the Nazis*, which was groundbreaking both in its focus on children's own expression of experiences and emotions during the period 1933–45, and in its discussion of perpetrators and victims simultaneously.[5] In this way, the current chapter seeks to contribute to a wider discourse about the experience and memory of childhood in the Third Reich. This three-part chapter begins with an exploration of the meaning of dolls in Germany, examining both the symbolism of dolls in the public imagination, and their significance as a girls' toy. Second, I explore doll production during the period 1933–45, including the kinds of dolls available to girls and the extent to which Nazism may be considered to have politicized these items of material culture. Finally, I examine the way dolls and doll play feature in written memories of childhood in the Third Reich.[6]

THE MANY MEANINGS OF DOLLS

As objects of girls' material culture, dolls possess different meanings amongst producers, the adults who purchase them, and the girls who receive them. Producers, parents, and the experts who advise them have long agreed that dolls are designed to provide an important focus for socialization and preparation for womanhood (Fooken, 2012, 73). However, intention and reception do not always correspond. Indeed, both Miriam Forman-Brunell (Forman-Brunell, 2011, pp. 222–241) and Jane Eva Baxter (Baxter, 2005, pp. 42–45) rightly pointed to the discrepancy between adults' intentions for dolls and the different ways in which girls play with them. Dolls can contribute to the construction of feminine identity, as girls simulate maternal actions, but they can also provide an outlet for anger and violence. As the educator Jürgen Fritz (1992) argued, girls can take out their anger on dolls, which come to suffer in their place (p. 24).

It is not only the use to which dolls are put that is of significance here, but also the way in which they are created. Sharon Brookshaw (2009) suggested that those theorizing about children's material culture in the museum context should differentiate between the material culture of childhood and that of children respectively. The material culture of *childhood* should be used to refer to objects made by adults for children, while the material culture of *children* should encompass "those items that children make themselves or adapt into their own culture from the adult world that have a different use to that intended by the adult manufacturer" (p. 381). This point is important to consider when exploring the potential extent to which National Socialism influenced girls through dolls and doll play. If Nazi educators furthered the production of dolls as tools of indoctrination, we must consider the extent to which real-life doll play corresponded to their intentions. This is, of course, extremely difficult to judge. And, following Brookshaw's model, we must consider the extent to which girls made dolls for themselves. This in itself is a well-documented phenomenon. For example, writing in 1932, Max von Boehn pointed out that children without a doll will use everyday materials to fashion one, and that it will be as real to them as if it were a living creature (p. 172).

Dolls can also be invested with a complex symbolic capital. In the popular adult imagination, dolls represent nostalgia for childhood, the world of the imagination, and joy, but at the same time can act as an embodiment of evil forces or fears. In the same way, the doll has a well-established meaning in German literature, where it appears in the literary texts of German Romanticism, in the works of authors such as E.T A. Hoffmann, Heinrich von Kleist, and Gottfried Keller, and in German Modernism, particularly in Rainer Maria Rilke's writing.[7] The recurring figure of the doll in such texts often embodies the uncanny: familiar yet somehow peculiar, inanimate objects are invested with life to unsettle those around them.[8]

Dolls also have the potential to embody the innocence associated not only with childhood, but—often more potently—with girlhood. Writing on the common association between innocence and girls, Renée R. Curry (1998) explained that, when deployed to refer to girls as a group, the term "innocence" "assumes a monolithic definitude. Girls equate with innocence, and innocence is equivalent with girls. This homology between girls and innocence deems young females to be blameless, faultless, virtuous, spotless, pure of heart, irreproachable" and much else in the same vein (p. 96). Likewise, dolls evoke the kind of innocence held in a Romantic vision of girlhood, one that focuses on the dual concepts of the child's innocence and association with the natural world.[9] In her study on the German child's perspective of Nazism in post-war German literature, Debbie Pinfold (2001) contended that "German writers, even those dealing with the Third Reich, are deeply saturated with the Romantic myth of childhood that has dominated German thinking on the subject for over two centuries" (p. 158). This association between Romantic innocence and dolls was perpetuated under Nazism through school books.[10] In the school primer *Die Fibel der Mark Brandenburg* (1943), for example, blond-haired, rosy-cheeked girls are depicted playing with their dolls in an idyllic domestic scene (Mansfeld, 1943).[11]

Heavily invested with Romantic notions of innocence, dolls today seem far removed from the world of the Nazi dictatorship. First, the political, nationalist, and militaristic intentions of the regime sit uneasily with the notion of childhood as a time of carefree innocence. The poet Yusef Komunyakaa (1979) succinctly captured this paradox in his poem "The Nazi Doll" in which he apparently regarded a doll from the Third Reich.[12] He wrote: "This precious, white / ceramic doll's brain / twisted out of a knob of tungsten. / …Its eyes an old lie" (p. 54). This "lie" is the undermining of innocence that the corrupted doll represents. It is a disturbing image: with its "bogus tongue" and "crooked smile" the doll is recognizable as the innocuous toy, and yet, at the same time, it is infused with the threat and horror of the Nazi dictatorship. It is such an arresting image precisely because it juxtaposes these two worlds.

Yet dolls can act as a source of childhood memory that proves problematic for those who grew up under Nazism and experienced its "poisonous pedagogy," a term coined by the Swiss psychoanalyst Alice Miller (quoted in Schaumann, 2008), in her study of harmful child-raising practices, and which has become synonymous with the kind of political indoctrination implemented by the Nazis (p. 30).[13] While those born in the late 1920s and early 1930s may mourn the passing of their childhood, it is more difficult for them to mourn the historical conditions in which they lived. Retrospective knowledge of Nazi crimes prevents them from remembering childhood during this era with the kind of legitimate sense of nostalgia permitted in writing about other, "normal" childhoods. While we might be reluctant to consider all children as implicated in the guilt of those responsible for crimes carried out during the Third Reich, nevertheless, history has complicated their position and past.

At the same time, while it might seem inappropriate to consider dolls alongside the horror of the Holocaust and its indiscriminate annihilation of children and others, historical research into children's play shows that games take place during even the direst circumstances.[14] A number of historical studies have engaged with this topic, including, most recently, Patricia Heberer's (2011) *Children During the Holocaust* and Nicholas Stargardt's (2006) *Witnesses of War*. In addition to scholarly studies, dolls are also mentioned in autobiographical and fictional accounts, for example Ursula Fuchs's (1979) *Emma or the Time of Anxiety* (*Emma oder Die unruhige Zeit*), and Yona Zeldis McDonough's (2005) *The Doll with the Yellow Star*. Claire A. Nivola's (1999) *Elisabeth: The True Story of a Doll* is based on her mother's experience, and tells the story of a Jewish girl who flees Germany in the 1930s with her family. She leaves her beloved doll behind, but they are reunited years later. In such works, the image of the doll as a symbol of childhood happiness jars when placed alongside representations of children suffering as a result of Nazi persecution.[15]

Despite the apparent incongruity between the image of the doll and the reality of girls' lives during this period, dolls undeniably constituted part of the material culture of their childhood. Indeed, photographs of the period bear this out and reflect the problematic juxtaposition of dolls and their owners under Nazism. For example, the Nazis disseminated hundreds of images of Hitler with children in order to reinforce the conceptual link between Nazism and the young. A collection of such photographs appeared in the December 6 issue of the American publication *LIFE* magazine in 1937. The article described Hitler's propagandist use of photographs depicting him with children, with one photograph showing Hitler acting as judge in a girls' doll contest (p. 6).

When viewing such images today, those that feature girls clutching a doll reinforce the idea of corrupted innocence thanks to the context and framing of the image. There are also a great number of images of Jewish girls with dolls, particularly of those travelling on the Kindertransports. In many of these images, girls clutch their dolls in a protective stance, or cling on to them as they might their mother. These images—both staged and spontaneous—are a powerful part of cultural memory, revealing a glimpse of the relationships between girls and their dolls.

DOLLS AND THEIR OWNERS, 1933–45

The historical, pedagogical, and social interest in Doll Studies in Germany stems from the long history of German doll manufacture that dates back to the Middle Ages.[16] Yet it was during the nineteenth century that the town of Sonneberg in Thuringia arguably became the major point of toy production in Europe (Ciesliks, 1979, p. 109). Between 1865 and 1880, the mass production of porcelain doll parts fueled the expansion of the German toy industry (Cieslik and Cieslik, 1979, p. 108), and by the beginning of the twentieth century approximately half of the world's production of dolls derived from Germany (Bachmann & Hansmann, 1973, p. 141). In the early 1900s in Germany, dolls sold better than any other toy (Hamlin, 2007, p. 53).

While the German doll industry never recovered its control over the foreign market after 1918, German companies continued to produce dolls throughout the twenties and during the Third Reich. Examples of such dolls, found in German toy and doll museums today, are a useful source of information about their ideological meanings and pedagogical purposes.[17] As a movement, National Socialism tapped into the energy and positive potential of young gentile children.[18] With the process of social and cultural consolidation ("Gleichschaltung") in 1933, the school became a primary locus of indoctrination. The revised curricula articulated Nazi racial, national, and political ideals; by 1938, official texts focused on these subjects more systematically.

In 1936, membership of the Hitler Youth became compulsory for all German youth aged 10 to 18. The Hitler Youth consisted of individual youth organizations segregated by gender, with the "Jungvolk" and Hitler Youth ("Hitlerjugend"; HJ) for boys, and the "Jungmädel" and League of German Girls ("Bund deutscher Mädel"; BDM) for girls. There was not always a clear differentiation in the way the organization of the groups was conducted (Kater, 2006, p. 73).[19] Because of the pressures of the war effort after 1939 it was necessary for girls to bolster production in a variety of ways (Kater, 2006, pp. 85–94). As a result, in many respects, girls' socialization during the Third Reich closely resembled that of their male contemporaries.

On the other hand, however, there was a marked difference in the activities of the two gender divisions, and in what was expected of their members. In line with National Socialist ideology and the perceived needs of the regime, BDM meetings consisted of primarily gender-specific activities, which placed emphasis on the importance of each girl's calling to become a mother and a "bearer" of German culture (Pine, 2010, p. 120).[20] Gender played a crucial role in National Socialist philosophy, which included clear ideas about girls' education and upbringing. In *Mein Kampf*, Hitler wrote that female education should, on the whole, be directed at producing the mothers of the future (Hitler, 1997, p. 377). As a result, female education in general placed emphasis on girls' responsibility when they became women "to serve as helpmates to the men, to bear them children and rear them according to Nazi values, and to be faithful homemakers" (Kater, 2006, p. 73). Indeed, from 1938, mothers with several children received the "Cross of Honor of the German Mother" ("Ehrenkreuz der Deutschen Mutter"), and the SS-run "Lebensborn" program encouraged young women and adolescent girls to "give a child to the Führer." [21] The influence and effects of National Socialism's gendered policies are also evidenced in many autobiographical accounts of girlhoods during the Third Reich.[22]

Control was thus exerted in the education system, in extra-curricular activities, and also in the gendered upbringing of children in the family home. Research has shown that gender ideals influenced the production of toys for children and the ways in which girls and boys played. In his theoretical study of play in the Third Reich the educationalist Ulrich Heimlich (2001) wrote that while boys "play at war" girls play with dolls and kitchenware (p. 124). As Heimlich pointed out, this is borne out in some children's books of the period. For example, the *Arithmetic Book of the Western Kurmark* (*Rechenbuch für die westliche Kurmark*), published in 1937, depicts a boy playing with toy soldiers and war apparatus, while a girl plays with dolls, and counts money in preparation for the role she will play as a mother in the domestic sphere (Lukasch, 2013).[23] Similarly, Richard Benzing (quoted in Bamler, Schönberger, & Wustmann, 2010), a National Socialist medic writing in 1941, observed two children playing: while little "Gretchen" plays with her dolls, "Hänschen" prepares to kill a sparrow with a rock. He commented that in this scene there could be found the future models of male and female, the homemaker and the defender of Germany (p. 36).

Toys based on warfare and combat were marketed for boys, and dolls for girls. The historian Mathias Rösch (2002) wrote of one toy manufacturer in Munich who advertised toys with a slogan promising that parents would do well to purchase military toys such as soldiers and knights for boys (p. 454).[24] While the National Socialists certainly utilized this gender differentiation, it was not their innovation: toy production had already assumed this strictly gendered position in the early twentieth century (Hamlin, 2007, pp. 53–55). As Hein Retter (1979) argued, while educators devoted little space to discussions about toys as "a means to educate the people" ("Volkserziehungsmittel") in the pedagogical literature of the period 1933–44, the two distinct groups of toys established technical, military-themed toys for boys, and "Aryan"-looking dolls for girls (p. 202).

During the period from 1933 to 1945, many doll designs reflected the racial ideals of Third Reich ideology. After 1934 the Schildkröt firm[25] produced a series of dolls bearing Germanic names such as Bärbel, Hans, and Inge, which—whether politically motivated or not—embodied the Aryan aesthetics favored by the Nazis (Dröse, 1996).[26] Schildkröt manufactured "Inge" dolls to celebrate the 1936 Olympics, an important national event. The Käthe-Kruse firm, established in 1912, produced dolls that proved equally popular in the Weimar Republic, Imperial Germany, and the Third Reich (Peers, 2004, p. 102). However, only the children of wealthy families had access to such dolls since they required a great deal of handcraft, which made them expensive (Vincenz, 1995, p. 16). Kruse was concerned above all that the dolls should resemble real children, thus encouraging girls to see themselves in the role of mother. Though not Kruse's original intention, this no doubt played into National Socialist policy of girls being raised to be mothers.[27]

Although manufacturing continued into the war years and constituted a crucially important industry in the Third Reich, it eventually stalled due to the lack of available workers as a result of conscription (Peers, 2008, p. 28). For manufacturers who continued to produce dolls the situation proved problematic. The Käthe-Kruse company, for example, had difficulty keeping up the rate of production, and in order to maintain it, required customers to send material to make the dolls' clothes, and locks of their own hair to make the dolls' wigs ("Käthe Kruse," 2013). Many toy companies ceased production, working instead to support the war effort (Wolf, 2010, p. 80).[28] For example, while the Engel-Puppen firm in Mönchröden, Coburg, exported a significant number of dolls throughout Europe before 1939, it suspended production during World War II and manufactured uniforms instead ("Die Geschichte der Engel-Puppen," 2013).[29] Consequently some adults and children made dolls when they could not afford to buy them, or when dolls were scarce. The Doll Museum in Coburg, for example, possesses cloth dolls with faces made of pressed cardboard, which families would have bought in order to fashion their own dolls. In addition, individuals built furniture for doll houses out of accessible materials such as cigarette cartons (Spiller, personal communication, 2013). Eventually, after 1943, toy production was prohibited (Malzahn, 2001, p. 190).

Research has shown that National Socialism played a role in the politicization of dolls. In fact, the "Nazification" of toys had begun as early as 1932. In Munich, for example, advertisements for explicitly National Socialist toys could be found in Nazi-Party publications (Rösch, 2002, p. 454) and toy manufacturers had to join state-controlled trade associations ("Berufsorganisationen") to be able to trade (Retter, 1979, p. 194). One advertisement for Käthe-Kruse dolls in the German Toy Magazine (*Deutsche Spielwarenzeitung*) in 1933 depicts a Friedebald doll, modeled on Kruse's son, dressed in a Hitler Youth uniform, and performing the Hitler salute (Retter, 1979, p. 196).[30] The doll could also be purchased wearing the uniforms of the SA ("Sturm Abteilung"), and the "Jungvolk" (Retter, 1979, p. 196).[31] However, objects codified as National Socialist—which bear Nazi symbols—remained relatively rare, and were certainly not representative of doll makers' output during the Third Reich.[32] Indeed, as Retter (1979) argued in his analysis of toy production during the period, National Socialism had an ambivalent attitude towards the toy industry, and it would be wrong to think that Nazism developed a clear pedagogy of toys (Retter, 1979, pp. 194–205). While doll manufacturers did mass-produce some miniature uniforms, others were homemade (Dröscher, personal communication, 2013). The Doll Museum in Falkenstein possesses two celluloid dolls made by the Schildkröt firm, one of which is dressed as a mountain rifleman ("Gebirgsjäger") with Nazi insignia (see Figure 1), and the other, clad in a BDM uniform. However, as Heimlich (2001) pointed out, it is ultimately difficult to establish what influence Nazi-approved dolls had on doll players.[33]

Figure 1: A mountain rifleman ("Gebirgsjäger") with Nazi insignia © Elke Dröscher-Puppenmuseum Falkenstein.

On one level, dolls that appear as explicitly National Socialist—through their appearance and manner of dress—create an unsettling image, whether mass-produced or home-made. A good example of this is a doll house from the 1930s in the permanent exhibition of the German Historical Museum in Berlin.[34] The doll house has a bedroom and sitting-room decorated in the style of a nineteenth-century interior. The kitchen, however, is wallpapered with a pattern that depicts groups of BDM girls engaged in activities such as cooking, drill, and dancing, while Hitler Youth boys participate in equivalent activities.[35] A photographic portrait of Hitler with Mussolini hangs on the far wall. From the Romantic perspective, a doll house, as a girls' toy, provides an image of childhood innocence. However, in this case, the National Socialist elements are effective symbols of the indoctrination and corruption of youth by the Nazi state.[36] Dolls dressed in Nazi uniform invite a similar response. In Germany today, where fascist symbols are banned by law,[37] the sight of objects bearing such marks has a very particular resonance, and again we see the effect of the incongruity between the sweet child depicted in the doll and the connotations of the Nazi symbols, dress, and gestures.

Determining the extent to which dolls served as tools for girls' socialization during the Third Reich is beyond the scope of this study. However, it is clear that the government had specific ideas about the social roles it wanted girls and young women to fulfill, that doll manufacturers responded to a market demand for dolls resembling figures of the day, their appearance and attire, and that consumers purchased these dolls for girls to play with. It is also evident that home-made dolls and doll accessories expressed these ideas, whether in imitation of their high-status, shop-bought counterparts, or from ideological motives.

MEMORIES OF DOLLS AND DOLL PLAY 1933–45

In his study of modern autobiography David McCooey (1996) wrote that "[t]he surviving objects of our childhood are magical, even astonishing, because they are the past washed up on our doorstep. Nothing is so distant—nor paradoxically, so immediate—as one's lost childhood" (p. 54). Dolls are icons of memory, vehicles capable of providing links to former times, and forces of recollection. Although inanimate, dolls hold a special power in memory, since to girls they can be real people—lifeless objects invested with life through imagination. Claus Hansmann (1959) began his study of dolls with the observation that girls do not merely *believe* such objects to be alive; they are convinced beyond all doubt that their doll is a real human-being (p. 5).[38] It is this "seeming authenticity," as Fooken (2012) put it, which makes the doll a memory object different from others (p. 63). Fooken argued that dolls can provide a means for adults to access childhood memory and a starting point for autobiographical reminiscences (p. 186). Significantly, this can also be the case even when the doll itself is lost, as the well-loved doll remains a powerful force in the individual's memory (p. 185). As a tangible object from the past, the dolls provide an apparent link to one's personal history—enabling a kind of dialogue between women and the girls they used to be.

In her autobiographical text *Patterns of Childhood* (*Kindheitsmuster*, 1976) the German writer Christa Wolf (1980) described her childhood in the Third Reich.[39] Recalling a picture of her girlhood, Wolf remembered two dolls:

> The stiff-jointed Lieselotte with her golden braids and her eternal red silk ruffle dress. The smell of this particular doll's hair, after all these years, so distinctly, unpleasantly different from the smell of the short, dark-brown, real hair of the much older doll, Charlotte, which had been handed down to the child by her mother, bore the mother's name, and was loved the best. (pp. 5–6)[40]

While Wolf (1980) could recall the doll in great sensory detail, of her own self—the child she was—there is simply "no image" (p. 6).[41]

Since the publication of Wolf's text in 1976, there have been many other autobiographical accounts of the Third Reich that have shed light on children's experiences of Nazism. More recently, the past two decades in particular have seen a steady outpouring, both within Germany and abroad, of memoirs, novels, films, and museum exhibitions about those who grew up in the 1930s and 1940s. From the many autobiographical texts, ego-documents, and anthologies of oral testimony, a range of memories and experiences emerges. These include accounts of different experiences: of the Hitler Youth, of being evacuated to the German countryside (*Kinderlandverschickung*), of the Allied bombing of German cities, of the flight from the Eastern territories in the late 1940s, of Jewish children's life in the ghettos and camps, of the kindertransports, and of Jewish children in hiding.[42] Whether written by Jewish or gentile girls, dolls function as significant memory texts encoded within recollections of their girlhoods.

Dolls figure to varying extents in many such autobiographical accounts. Irmgard A. Hunt (2005) recalled being sent French-made dolls as a present by Emmy Göring, wife of "Reichsmarschall" Hermann Göring. She wrote that she and her sister named the dolls after Frau Göring and her daughter Edda, and that they played with them on Sundays (p. 127). In accounts of girls' wartime experiences, however, dolls take on more central importance. In her autobiographical novel *Jette in Dresden* Helga Schütz (1977) drew attention to the relationship between the protagonist, Jette, and her doll during the time of the Allied bombing.

> Jette does everything it's possible to do with a doll. She carries her, bathes her, combs her hair, goes for walks with her, comforts her, plays at war, and being in the air-raid shelter. She gives her doll a gas mask, sweets, milk and cough medicine. She hangs an identity card around her neck and sings to her. (quoted in Brettschneider, 1982, p. 25)[43]

Dolls appear as objects of comfort to girls but also serve as sources of conflict with parents. The museum curator Mathilde Jamin (2006) showed that memories of the bombing war are often closely linked emotionally with objects. One woman in her study recounted that when she was an 8-year-old girl, she would always try to take her doll along when she raced to the air-raid shelter with her mother. She was deeply affected by the fact that her mother sometimes dragged her to the air-raid shelter before she had a chance to grab her doll. She asserted that this still remains a traumatic experience. In her memories, the doll became a symbol of her "shattered childhood" (pp. 25–26).

In her oral history study *Children of War: The Fate of a Generation* (*Kriegs-kinder: Das Schicksal einer Generation*) Hilke Lorenz (2003) introduced children's understanding of the war through the "experience" of a child's Käthe-Kruse doll, Rosa, whose young owner, Ida-Luise Voigt, always carried it to the air-raid shelter during bombing-raids (pp. 50–51). When the evacuation program (*Kinderland-verschickung*) removed the doll's young owner from Berlin to the relative safety of the provinces, she refused to take the doll with her to prevent it being damaged. This response is, perhaps, surprising. It seems to suggest not, as Lorenz posits, that Voigt might have valued her own safety over the doll's, but rather that she prized the doll's safety more highly than the comfort that its continued presence offered her. It is indicative of the depth of emotion felt by girls towards their dolls. When she returned, she found her family and doll intact. A photograph of the doll is included in the text. Dirty and battered, it appears to bear the bruises of its involvement in war. The doll is personified further in Lorenz's text as she writes that Rosa is a "silent witness" to the fact that hope can come from destruction (p. 65). Here, the object, and by association the child, takes on a dual role, embodying both the silent witness of the event, and hope for the future.

In the face of widespread anti-Semitism, German dolls posed particular challenges for Jewish girls. In *Child of Our Time: A Young Girl's Flight from the Holocaust*, a memoir written by one of the children saved on the Kindertransport, Ruth David (2003) recalled that she owned an "Aryan" doll, which was her favorite. It had blue eyes and blonde hair (p. 15). She recounted that her own and her sister's eyes were not pure blue, which was considered attractive at the time, and was told by her mother that her hair was too coarse to be kept in plaits. Annoyed, she cut off the doll's plaits (p. 16). On the one hand, this violent response suggests jealousy: David was angry with the doll because her own hair and other features were not as "desirable" as the doll's. On the other hand, however, the girl may have been frustrated that the doll did not resemble her. This irreconcilable mix of emotions incited an extreme response, and one which has remained in Ruth David's memory of girlhood. It reveals something of the complex relationship between girls and their dolls, and, in this case, the influence of racial indoctrination on its victims. Winfried Bruckner (1978) recalled a childhood experience during which a group of boys attacked his close friend Sarah for being Jewish. Before the attack, Bruckner had himself turned on Sarah, spouting parrot-fashion Nazi ideology, accusing the Jews of being "evil" and "ugly" (p. 45). Sarah calmly responded by pointing out that she and her dolls are Jewish too, asking whether he thinks they are ugly as well. Bruckner conceded that "there must be exceptions" to the rule (p. 46). A group of boys then appeared and damaged the dolls. Shortly afterwards the Nazis deported Sarah and her family and the reader learns that they perished in a concentration camp.

For the children that the Nazis deported to ghettos and concentration camps, dolls were often the only item they could preserve from their former life. Yad Vashem's exhibition "No Child's Play," curated by Ms. Yehudit Inbar, featured a number of dolls that children carried with them during the war, and which offered an important source of security and friendship.[44] There were home-made dolls, and manufactured dolls that girls brought with them on the transports. Inge Auerbacher (1993), for example, recalled her fear when she and her family were rounded up and searched before deportation. Above all, she remembered, she was afraid that the SS would confiscate her doll (p. 32). Again, in situations of fear, the girl regards her doll's safety alongside, or even before, her own.

In the final stages of the war and in the immediate post-war period, millions of ethnic Germans fled or were expelled from the eastern territories.[45] For those children caught up in the flight, a doll might have been the only object taken with them. Ingrid Flemming (2007) recalled the flight from the Sudetenland with her mother, and that she was only able to take one item with her: she chose her doll (pp. 27–28). Similarly, Giesela Heinrich (2007), aged 12, carried her "Bärbel" doll—produced by the Schildkröt firm—as she fled across Joachimsthal to Nordenstern/Gablonz in what is now the Czech Republic. The doll—an icon of their survival—sits in pride of place in their family home today (p. 10). Another girl recalls taking her Minerva celluloid doll when her family fled from Uivar/Neuburg an der Bega, Romania, to Gornsdorf, Erzgebirge. "During the escape I always had my doll with me, because before we left we were told that everyone should only take the most important things with them."[46] In his study of children who fled from the Eastern territories, Rainer Bendel (2008) found that children recalled small sources of comfort amidst memories of destruction and fear. The discovery of a doll believed lost after the destruction of a family home came to represent "survival and future" (Bendel, p. 182).

Dolls could also be a point of contact to a better time and place (Fooken, 2012, p. 19). In his study of child survivors of the Holocaust, Paul Valent (1994) encountered Eva M., who grew up in Vienna, and whose family sent her to Riga to escape Nazism. When the Germans invaded they sent her to a camp in the area of Novosibirsk in Siberia with her family, where they remained for six years. She recalled her fondness for the doll she had in the camp, which provided a link to the childhood she had lost. In addition to the children, the doll served as a source of comfort to adult prisoners, to whom it symbolized normality (p. 212).

Believing in the importance of dolls for girls, Jewish adults in the worst of circumstances fashioned many out of available materials. In *Children and Play in the Holocaust* George Eisen (1988) wrote that all kinds of toys were produced by adults for children in the camps. The children carried these toys to their death (p. 48). According to Yehudi Lindeman (2007), who chronicled accounts of children smuggled out of the Warsaw ghetto, one girl remembered her mother and cousin making a doll for her from sawdust (p. 138). Similarly, for one family in hiding in the Netherlands, their young daughter's second birthday became an opportunity to "lift the family's morale." A photograph reveals the girl clutching a rag doll made out of old scraps by her nurse (Heberer, 2011, p. 355).

In the official chronicle of the Łódź ghetto, Oskar Rosenfeld reported that unlike "German" children, Jewish children imprisoned in the ghetto had to make their own toys (quoted in Eisen, 1988, p. 70).[47] In his study of Theresienstadt, George E. Berkley (1993) reported that a teacher had a group of girls make their own dolls. The girls' intention was to fashion dolls that resembled princesses, but they were unhappy with the results (p. 114). The teacher's solution was to suggest that the girls make the dolls represent a "cleaning squad," complete with bucket and scrubbing brush. This was successful and the girls were reportedly in good spirits as a result (p. 114). The girls' response indicates that they wanted to create dolls that resembled themselves, or at least those in their situation. It also suggests that they were reluctant to confront a more positive, but ultimately distant, representation of themselves as princesses, free of the drudgery and fear of the ghetto.

In *Witnesses of War*, Stargardt (2006) considered the relationship between girls and their dolls in ghettos and concentration camps. He outlined the experience of Nina Weilová, who was imprisoned in Theresienstadt and Auschwitz, and whose memoir gives an account of her own experience by recounting what happened to her doll (Stargardt, 2006, p. 370). He posited that the doll, which was lost on the ramp from the train on her arrival at Auschwitz, became a psychological crutch necessary to relate her experiences. "It is as if she were withdrawing from the situation and seeing it through the eyes of a third person—except that this third person was a thing, her doll" (p. 370). Stargardt concluded that in different ways a doll might become a substitute, for example, for a mother.

Dolls assumed other meanings to war-weary European children among whom, by 1945, 250,000 Germans had lost both parents and over one million had lost their father (Stargardt, 2006, 342). Margit Hartung (2007) recounted in her memory text "Die Puppe" how, in 1946, she was on the way home from the kindergarten when she discovered a discarded doll in a garbage can (p. 69). Her mother repaired it and it became a symbol of hope in a time of loss and devastation. While later on she was given beautiful dolls purchased from department stores, she would "never forget this first, patched-up doll" (p. 69). The author Peter Weiss, writing for a Swedish newspaper in 1947, observed the traumatic effects of the war as well as girls' therapeutic endeavors. One girl, he reported, did not speak, but simply fashioned a doll and played with it, pretending to hold a funeral for it. He deemed this to be "the beginning of her healing" (quoted in Bode, 2009, pp. 49–50).[48]

Jewish children displaced by the war used a variety of ways to come to terms with their experiences.[49] For some Jewish girls who escaped Nazism, dolls became a symbol of the girlhood they had lost. In 1943 the Nazis deported Bożenna Urbanowicz Gilbride with her parents and siblings from Poland to the Labor Camp in Chemnitz where she spent the war years.[50] After 1945 her family emigrated to the U.S. where she sought to create a version of childhood she had never experienced.

> I never had a doll, I never jumped rope with friends, and I never wore ribbons in my hair....My aunt found me making a rag doll and realized that I had missed that part of growing up. She bought me a paper cutout doll with paper clothes that you can fasten on the doll. (Gilbride, 2009, pp. 42–43)

According to Yad Vashem's "No Child's Play" (1996) exhibition, curated by Ms. Yehudit Inbar, "for some children, ...teddy bears and dolls were the most significant possessions left with them at the end of the war. Even today, as adults, their attachment is so great that they have difficulty separating from them." For example, the Nazis deported one girl, Eva Modval, to the Tolonc and Kistarcsa camps in Hungary, where she kept her doll by her side. On loaning it to Yad Vashem in the late 1980s, Modval wrote a letter to the doll—Gerta—in which she addressed it as "the last witness of a dreadful childhood" (quoted in "Ghettos and Camps," 2013).[51]

CONCLUSIONS

Dolls feature frequently in ego-documents and in autobiographical accounts of life in the Third Reich, and are invested with complex symbolic capital. They can function as an illustration of fascism's disruption of normal life; as symbols of racial superiority and the objects of anger and/or self-loathing; as a representation of loss; as a source of childhood nostalgia; and as an alter-ego constructed to cope with the trauma of a wartime childhood. Dolls are not only objects, but, by their very nature, take on the qualities of friends and family, particularly for those separated from them. Frequently, we find the doll as witness—often the only witness—to the traumas of girlhoods. While dolls are popularly assumed to construct female identity, they can also help children through the trials and changes of childhood

(Bachmann & Hansmann, 1973, p. 151),[52] or, as we have seen here, crises of an altogether more horrific kind. They provide a vehicle of mourning for the past and of hope for the future. These memories demonstrate the continued power of dolls in the imagination, where they hold special significance, not only for girls, but for the women they become.[53] It is the very nature of the doll that makes its memory a particularly potent source and symbol of girlhoods.

NOTES

1. "Ein jüdisch[es], schwarzhaarig[es] Mädchen, die Hölle des Konzentrationslagers Theresien-stadt zu überleben." All translations are my own unless otherwise stated. Auerbacher has written and commented extensively on her childhood, and on the part her doll played in her experience of Nazi persecution. She is also the subject of a documentary by Giora Gerzon (2005), entitled *The Olympic Doll*, which is aimed at children and told through the eyes of a doll.
2. See, for example, Anke and Gauder (1978), *Die Deutsche Puppenindustrie, 1815–1940*; Heimlich (2001), *Einführung in die Spielpädagogik: Eine Orientierungshilfe für sozial-, schul- und heilpädago-gischer Arbeitsfelder*; Fooken (2012), *Puppen—heimliche Menschenflüsterer: Ihre Wiederentdeckung als Spielzeug und Kulturgut* (pp. 18–20); Retter (1979), *Spielzeug: Handbuch zur Geschichte und Pädagogik der Spielmittel* (pp. 194–205); and Merkel and Dittrich (2011), *Spiel mit dem Reich: Nationalsozialistisches Gedankengut in Spielzeug und Kinderbüchern*.
3. This issue is discussed in Mitchell and Reid-Walsh (2002), *Researching Children's Popular Culture* (pp. 55–62). See also Ganaway (2008), "Consuming Masculinity: Toys and Boys in Wilhelmine Germany" (pp. 97–113, 111, n. 31).
4. Kuhn drew on Ginzburg's (1989) essay "Clues: Roots of an Evidential Paradigm."
5. Stargardt used a variety of sources, including children's letters, schoolwork, and artwork; adults' accounts of children's games; autobiographical sources; and memory texts.
6. The background research to this chapter was conducted as part of my doctoral dissertation on post-1990 depictions of childhood in the Third Reich, funded by the UK's Arts and Humanities Research Council.
7. See Fooken (2012, p. 60).
8. Freud stated that the notion that a doll could come to life was far more unsettling for adults than for children. See Freud (2000). For a discussion of the child's doll as uncanny, see Schiffman (2001), "Wax-Work, Clock-Work, and Puppet-Shews: Bleak House and the Uncanny." On the figure of the doll in literature, see von Boehn (1932, pp. 250–51), and Fooken (2012, pp. 58–60).
9. For a discussion of how such "innocence" can be "corrupted," see Thomas (2003, pp. 113–75), *Naked Barbies, Warrior Joes, and Other Forms of Visible Gender*.
10. See Brocklehurst (2006, pp. 72–73), *Who's Afraid of Children?: Children, Conflict and International Relations*. Brocklehurst drew on research by Pine (1996, 91–109): "The Dissemination of Nazi Ideology and Family Values Through School Textbooks."
11. Examples can be viewed online as part of a recent special exhibition at the School Museum in Lohr am Main, "Im Schatten des Hakenkreuzes—Die Kinderwelt im Dritten Reich," retrieved from http://www.bnmsp.de/home/e.huber/schulmuseum/kinderwelt1943/

12. It is unclear whether the doll was one of those wearing a Nazi uniform. For a thorough analysis of the poem, see Ernstmeyer (2007), "On 'The Nazi Doll,'" retrieved from http://www.english. illinois.edu/maps/poets/g_l/komunyakaa/nazidoll.htm

13. The German term is "schwarze Pädagogik."

14. See Stargardt (2006, p. 37); Eisen (1988, pp. 291–302), *Children, Play, and the Holocaust*; and Heberer (2011), *Children During the Holocaust*.

15. I (Lloyd, 2013, pp. 175–183) discussed literary depictions of childhood and the Holocaust in "Writing Childhood in Ruth Klüger's *weiter leben: Eine Jugend*."

16. See von Boehn (1929), *Puppen und Puppenspiele*; Bachmann and Hansmann (1988), *Das große Puppenbuch* ; and, most recently, Fooken (2012). See also the huge body of work by doll historians Jürgen and Marianne Cieslik.

17. Several toy and doll museums in Germany possess artefacts from the 1930s and 1940s in their archives and/or displays. See "Puppenmuseen," retrieved from http://webmuseen.de/puppenm useen.html. I am extremely grateful for the assistance I received from staff and curators during the research for this chapter.

18. See Fisher (2007, pp. 1–2), *Disciplining Germany: Youth, Reeducation, and Reconstruction After the Second World War*.

19. Indeed, the sense of equality between girls and boys it engendered was part of the reason for the popularity of the BDM, see Pine (2010, p. 120).

20. See also Rademacher (2012); and Reese (2006).

21. "Dem Führer ein Kind schenken." See Koop (2007).

22. See Miller-Kipp (2007, pp. 57–167).

23. As the author pointed out, however, this example is not necessarily representative of a widespread phenomenon.

24. See also Retter (1979, pp. 194–205).

25. See Straub (2007, p. 24); and J. Cieslik and M. Cieslik (2002), *Das große Schildkröt-Buch: Celluloidpuppen von 1896 bis 1956*.

26. J. Cieslik and M. Cieslik (2002, p. 158) suggested that the dolls merely reflected the aesthetics favored at the time.

27. As Ganaway (2008, p. 235) noted, Kruse's autobiography offers little comment on the years under Nazism. See *Toys, Consumption, and Middle-class Childhood in Imperial Germany, 1871–1918*. I have come across little research that focuses on Jewish toy and doll manufacturers during the period, and it is difficult to determine the extent to which they were affected by anti-Semitic Nazi policy.

28. See also Sheffer (2011, pp. 22–23).

29. "Die Geschichte der Engel-Puppen," retrieved from http://www.engelpuppen.com/de/firmen geschichte.html

30. Although the doll was marketed as "Das deutsche Kind," suggesting a nationalistic stance, this doll had in fact been available from 1929.

31. Quoted in Heimlich (2001), p. 123.

32. See Merkel and Dittrich (2011, pp. 173–74).

33. Girls would have played with their mother's or even grandmother's dolls, or with other substitutes. Eye-witness accounts held at the Toy Museum in Havelland, for example, suggest that it was common practice for girls during the period to play with dolls—mostly porcelain—that had belonged to their grandmothers (Hahn, personal communication, 2013). For further examples

see also Wolf's (1976) *Kindheitsmuster*, and an anonymous eye-witness statement in Merkel and Dittrich (2011, pp. 208–09).

34. "Puppenstube aus der NS-Zeit," German Historical Museum, inventory no. AK 92/153.

35. I (Lloyd, 2014, pp. 89–105) discussed this artefact as a museum exhibit in "'Institutionalized Stories': Childhood and National Socialism in Contemporary German Museum Displays." See also Paver (2010), "You Shall Know Them by Their Objects: Material Culture and Its Impact in Museum Displays about National Socialism" (p. 172).

36. For further information, see "NS-Kinderspielzeug," retrieved from http://www.dhm.de/lemo/html/nazi/alltagsleben/spielzeug/index.html and "Sammlungen des Deutschen Historischen Museums," retrieved from http://www.dhm.de/sammlungen/alltag3/spielzeug/ak92_153.html

37. According to Section 86a of the German Criminal Code (*Strafgesetzbuch*).

38. This is a view that is widely demonstrated in theoretical literature about doll play.

39. The first influential autobiography of its kind to appear, *Kindheitsmuster* has provided a model for this mode of autobiographical discourse in which the author reflects critically on his/her own part in National Socialism.

40. Die steifgliedrige Puppe Lieselotte mit ihren goldblonden Zöpfen und ihrem ewigen rotseidenen Volantkleid. Der Geruch des Haares dieser Puppe, nach all den Jahren der sich so deutlich und unvorteilhaft von dem Geruch der echten, kurzen, dunkelbraunen Haare der viel älteren Puppe Charlotte unterschied, die von der Mutter auf das Kind gekommen war, den Namen der Mutter trug und am meisten geliebt wurde. (Wolf, 1976, pp. 16–17), original German version, *Kindheitsmuster*.

41. "Kein Bild," in Wolf (1976, p. 17).

42. These include German as well as English-language texts: Y. Winterberg and S. Winterberg (2009), *Kriegskinder: Erinnerungen einer Generation*; Leeb (1998), *"Wir waren Hitlers Eliteschüler": Ehemalige Zöglinge der NS-Ausleseschulen brechen ihr Schweigen*; Schmitz-Köster (2007), *Kind L 364: Eine Lebensborn-Familiengeschichte*; Glassner and Krell (2006), *And Life Is Changed Forever: Holocaust Childhoods Remembered*.

43. Jette stellt alles an, was man mit Puppen anstellen kann. Sie trägt sie, badet, kämmt, fährt spazieren, spricht Trost, spielt Krieg, Keller und Bomben. Gibt ihrer Puppe eine Gasmaske, Bonbons, Milch, Hustensaft. Hängt ihr eine Kennkarte um und singt für sie Lieder.

44. A brochure accompanying the American Society for Yad Vashem's travelling exhibition shows some of the exhibits, retrieved from http://www.yadvashemusa.org/documents/no_child_play.pdf. An educational book, based on the content of the exhibition, explores the experiences of three girls and their dolls: Avramski (2007), *Three Dolls*, based on the "No Child's Play" Exhibition, 1996. Curator: Yehudit Inbar. Designer: Pnina Friedman, Temporary Exhibitions Department, Yad Vashem Museum Division. Retrieved from http://www.yadvashem.org/yv/en/exhibitions/traveling_exhibitions/nochildsplay/index.asp

45. See Rock and Wolff (2002), *Coming Home to Germany? The Integration of Ethnic Germans from Central and Eastern Europe in the Federal Republic*.

46. "Während der Flucht hatte ich immer meine Puppe bei mir, denn vor der Abfahrt hieß es, jeder solle nur das Wichtigste mitnehmen." The account is held at the Coburg Doll Museum Collection (Sammlung Coburger Puppenmuseum).

47. Evidence for this can also be found at the Yad Vashem Artifact Collection, and the Beit Theresienstadt Holocaust Museum in Israel.

48. Funerals are a common aspect of doll play. See Forman-Brunell (2011, pp. 235–36), Thomas (2003, pp. 127–28).

49. See Zahra (2011, pp. 11–13), *The Lost Children: Reconstructing Europe's Families after World War II*.

50. Gilbride's family were Polish Catholics. Her father had repeatedly been caught hiding Jews in their barn. See also Lukas (2004), *Forgotten Survivors: Polish Christians Remember the Nazi Occupation.*
51. The letter inspired a song by Chuck Brodsky addressed to the doll, and includes such lines as: "Some things a small doll shouldn't see / Tell them, Gerta, what you saw with me." Retrieved from http://www.chuckbrodsky.com/gerta.html.
52. See also Fooken (2012, pp. 72–73).
53. There is, perhaps, a kind of universality about the doll, borne out by the fact that dolls have been shown to fulfill these roles not just in Germany during this period, but throughout history. This universality unites memories of those who, because of historical circumstance, experienced the Third Reich as children in wildly contrasting ways.

REFERENCES

Anke, G., & Gauder, U. (1978). *Die deutsche Puppenindustrie, 1815–1940.* Stuttgart, Germany: Verlag Puppen u. Spielzeug.
Auerbacher, I. (2009). Inge's story. In I. Auerbacher & B. U. Gilbride (Eds.), *Children of terror* (pp. 51–102). Bloomington, IN: iUniverse.
Auerbacher, I. (1993). *I am a star: Child of the Holocaust.* New York, NY: Puffin Books.
Avramski, I. (2007). *Three dolls* [Based on the "No child's play" exhibition curated by Y. Inbar]. Yad Vashem, Israel: Retrieved on January 20, 2013, from International School for Holocaust Studies website: http://www.yadvashem.org/yv/en/exhibitions/nochildsplay/intro.asp
Bachmann, M., & Hansmann, C. (1988). *Das große Puppenbuch.* Munich, Germany: Orbis Verlag.
Bachmann, M., & Hansmann, C. (1973). *Dolls the wide world over: An historical account* (R. Michaelis-Jena & P. Murray, Trans.). London, England: Harrap.
Bamler, V., Schönberger, I., & Wustmann, C. (2010). *Lehrbuch Elementarpädagogik: Theorien, Methoden und Arbeitsfelder.* Weinheim and Munich, Germany: Juventa.
Baxter, J. E. (2005). *The archaeology of childhood: Children, gender, and material culture.* Walnut Creek, CA: AltaMira.
Bendel, R. (2008). *Vertriebene finden Heimat in der Kirche: Integrationsprozesse im geteilten Deutschland nach 1945.* Cologne, Germany: Böhlau.
Benzing, R. (1941). *Grundlagen der körperlichen und geistigen Erziehung des Kleinkindes im nationalsozialistischen Kindergarten.* Berlin, Germany: Eher.
Berkley, G. E. (1993). *Hitler's gift: The story of Theresienstadt.* Boston, MA: Branden.
Bode, S. (2009). *Die vergessene Generation.* Stuttgart, Germany: Piper.
Boehn, M. V. (1929). *Puppen und Puppenspiele.* Munich, Germany: Bruckkmann.
Boehn, M. V. (1932). *Dolls* (J. Nicoll, Trans.). London, England: Harrap.
Brettschneider, W. (1982). *"Kindheitsmuster": Kindheit als Thema autobiographischer Dichtung.* Berlin, Germany: Erich Schmidt.
Brocklehurst, H. (2006). *Who's afraid of children? Children, conflict and international relations.* Burlington, VT : Ashgate.
Brookshaw, S. (2009). The material culture of children and childhood: Understanding childhood objects in the museum context. *Journal of Material Culture, 14,* 365–83.
Bruckner, W. (1978). Die Puppe. In W. Bruckner (Ed.), *Damals war ich vierzehn: Berichte und Erinnerungen* (pp. 45–48). Vienna, Austria: Jugend und Volk.

Cieslik, J., & Cieslik, M. (1979). *Dolls: European dolls 1800–1930* (R. Bailey, Trans.). London, England: Cassell.

Cieslik, J., & Cieslik, M. (2002). *Das große Schildkröt-Buch: Celluloidpuppen von 1896 bis 1956*. Jülich, Germany: Verlag Marianne Cieslik.

Curry, R. R. (1998). "I ain't no FRIGGIN' LITTLE WIMP": The girl "I" narrator in contemporary fiction. In R. O. Saxton (Ed.), *The girl: Constructions of the girl in contemporary fiction by women* (pp. 95–107). New York, NY: St. Martin's Press.

David, R. (2003). *Child of our time: A young girl's flight from the Holocaust*. London, England: I. B. Tauris.

Die Geschichte der Engel-Puppen. (2013). Retrieved from http://www.engelpuppen.com/de/firm engeschichte.html

Dröse, R. (1996). Immer zu proper, aber langlebig und heißgeliebt. Retrieved from http://www.hessisches-puppenmuseum.de/alte_seiten/fr050796.htm

Eisen, G. (1988). *Children, play, and the Holocaust*. Amherst, MA: University of Massachusetts Press.

Ernstmeyer, P. (2007). On 'The Nazi Doll.' Retrieved from http://www.english.illinois.edu/maps/poets/g_l/komunyakaa/nazidoll.htm

Fisher, J. (2007). *Disciplining Germany: Youth, reeducation, and reconstruction after the Second World War*. Detroit, MI: Wayne State University Press.

Flemming, I. (2007). "Ich klammerte mich an meine alte Puppe, die einzige, die ich hatte mitnehmen dürfen." In A. Kleinhenz (Ed.), *Mit der Puppe auf der Flucht: Zeitzeugen aus nordhessen und südniedersachsen erinnern sich an die Vertreibung aus der Heimat* (pp. 27–28). Gudensberg-Gleichen, Germany: Wartberg.

Fooken, I. (2012). *Puppen—heimliche Menschenflüsterer: Ihre Wiederentdeckung als Spielzeug und Kulturgut*. Göttingen, Germany: Vandenhoeck & Ruprecht.

Forman-Brunell, M. (2011). The politics of dollhood in nineteenth-century America. In M. Forman-Brunell & L. Paris (Eds.), *The girls' history and culture reader: The nineteenth century* (pp. 222–242). Urbana, IL: University of Illinois Press.

Freud, S. (2000). Das Unheimliche. In A. Mitscherlich, A. Richards, & J. Strachey (Eds.), *Studienausgabe: Psychologische Schriften* (Vol. IV, pp. 241–275). Frankfurt, Germany: Fischer.

Fritz, J. (1992). *Spielzeugwelten: Eine Einführung in die Pädagogik der Spielmittel*. Weinheim and Munich, Germany: Juventa.

Ganaway, B. (2008). Consuming masculinity: Toys and boys in Wilhelmine Germany. In S. Colvin & P. Davies (Eds.), *Edinburgh German yearbook, vol. 2: Masculinity and German culture* (pp. 97–113). Rochester, NY: Camden House.

Ghettos and camps (n.d.). Retrieved from http://www1.yadvashem.org/yv/en/exhibitions/nochilds play/ghettos4.asp

Gilbride, B. U. (2009). Bożenna's story. In I. Auerbacher & B. U. Gilbride (Eds.), *Children of terror* (pp. 3–51). Bloomington, IN: iUniverse.

Ginzburg, C. (1989). Clues: Roots of an evidential paradigm. In C. Ginzburg (Ed.), *Clues, myths and the historical method* (J. Tedeschi & A. C. Tedeschi, Trans.). Baltimore, MD: Johns Hopkins University Press.

Glassner, M. I., & Krell, R. (Eds.). (2006). *And life is changed forever: Holocaust childhoods remembered*. Detroit, MI: Wayne State University Press.

Hamlin, D. (2007). *Work and play: The production and consumption of toys in Germany, 1870–1914*. Ann Arbor, MI: University of Michigan Press.

Hansmann, C. (1959). *Puppen aus aller Welt: Farbaufnahmen*. Munich, Germany: F. Bruckmann.

Hartung, M. (2007). Die Puppe. In I. Höverkamp (Ed.), *Nie wieder Krieg! Die Schicksalsjahre 1933 bis 1949: Eine Anthologie*. Munich, Germany: Allitera Verlag.

Heberer, P. (2011). *Children during the Holocaust*. Lanham, MD: AltaMira in association with the United States Holocaust Memorial Museum.

Heimlich, U. (2001). *Einführung in die Spielpädagogik: Eine orientierungshilfe für sozial, schul- und heilpädagogischer Arbeitsfelder*. Bad Heilbrunn, Germany: Klinkhardt.

Heinrich, G. (2007). Mit der Puppe auf der Flucht. In A. Kleinhenz (Ed.), *Mit der Puppe auf der Flucht: Zeitzeugen aus Nordhessen und Südniedersachsen erinnern sich an die Vertreibung aus der Heimat* (pp. 10–11). Gudensberg-Gleichen, Germany: Wartberg.

Hitler, A. (1997). *Mein Kampf* (R. Manheim, Trans.). London, England: Pimlico.

Hunt, I. A. (2005). *On Hitler's mountain: My Nazi childhood*. London, England: Atlantic Books.

Jamin, M. (2006). Kindheitserinnerungen an den Bombenkrieg. Interviews im Rahmen der Ausstellung Maikäfer flieg... des Ruhrlandmuseums Essen. In H.-H. Ewers et al. (Eds.), *Erinnerungen an Kriegskindheiten: Erfahrungsräume, Erinnerungskultur und Geschichtspolitik* (pp. 19–31). Weinheim and Munich, Germany: Juventa.

Kater, M. H. (2006). *Hitler youth*. Cambridge, MA: Harvard University Press.

Käthe Kruse. (2013). Retrieved from http://kaethe-kruse.de/de/27/historie.html

Komunyakaa, Y. (1979). *Lost in the bonewheel factory*. Amherst, MA: Lynx House Press.

Koop, V. (2007). *"Dem Führer ein Kind schenken": Die SS-Organisation Lebensborn e.v.* Cologne, Germany: Böhlau.

Kuhn, A. (2002). *Family secrets: Acts of memory and imagination*. London, England: Verso.

Kuhn, A. (2007). Photography and cultural memory: A methodological exploration. *Visual Studies, 22*, 283–292.

Leeb, J. (1998). *"Wir waren Hitlers Eliteschüler": Ehemalige Zöglinge der NS-Ausleseschulen brechen ihr Schweigen*. Hamburg: Rasch und Röhring.

Lindeman, Y. (2007). *Shards of memory: Narratives of Holocaust survival*. Westport, CT: Praeger.

Lloyd, A. (2013). Writing childhood in Ruth Klüger's *weiter leben: Eine Jugend*. *Forum for Modern Language Studies, 49*, 175–183.

Lloyd, A. (2014). "Institutionalized Stories": Childhood and National Socialism in contemporary German museum displays, *Oxford German Studies, 43*.

Lorenz, H. (2003). *Kriegskinder: Das Schicksal einer Generation*. Berlin, Germany: List.

Lukas, R. C. (Ed.). (2004). *Forgotten survivors: Polish Christians remember the Nazi occupation*. Lawrence, KS: University of Kansas.

Lukasch, P. (2013). Kinder und propaganda. Retrieved from http://www.zeitlupe.co.at/werbung/propaganda2.html

Malzahn, M. (2001). *Germany, 1945–1949: A sourcebook*. London, England: Routledge.

Mansfeld, H. (1943). *Die Fibel der Mark Brandenburg*. Breslau, Germany: F. Hirt.

McCooey, D. (1996). *Artful histories: Modern Australian autobiography*. Cambridge, England: Cambridge University Press.

Merkel, K., & Dittrich, C. (Eds.). (2011). *Spiel mit dem Reich: Nationalsozialistisches Gedankengut in Spielzeug und Kinderbüchern*. Wiesbaden, Germany: Harrassowitz.

Miller, A. (1980). *Am Anfang war Erziehung*. Frankfurt, Germany: Suhrkamp.

Miller-Kipp, G. (2007). *Der Führer braucht mich. Der Bund deutscher Mädel (BDM): Lebenserinnerungen und Erinnerungsdiskurs*. Weinheim and Munich, Germany: Juventa.

Mitchell, C., & Reid-Walsh, J. (2002). *Researching children's popular culture*. New York, NY: Routledge.

No child's play exhibition. (1996). Curator: Yehudit Inbar. Designer: Pnina Friedman, Temporary Exhibitions Department, Yad Vashem Museum Division. Retrieved from http://www.yadvashem.org/yv/en/exhibitions/traveling_exhibitions/nochildsplay/index.asp

Paver, C. (2010). You shall know them by their objects: Material culture and its impact in museum Displays about National Socialism. In R. Braun & L. Marven (Eds.). *Cultural impact in the German context: Models of transmission, reception and influence* (pp. 169–187). Rochester, NY: Camden House.

Peers, J. (2004). *The fashion doll: From Bébé Jumeau to Barbie.* Oxford, England: Berg.

Peers, J. (2008). Doll culture. In C. A. Mitchell & J. Reid-Walsh (Eds.). *Girl culture* (pp. 25–39). Westport, CT: Greenwood Press.

Pine, L. (1996). The dissemination of Nazi ideology and family values through school textbooks, *History of Education, 25*, 91–109.

Pine, L. (2010). *Education in Nazi Germany.* Oxford, England; New York, NY: Berg.

Pinfold, D. (2001). *The child's view of the Third Reich in German literature: The eye among the blind.* Oxford, England: Clarendon Press.

Rademacher, S. (2012). Die opferbereite Kameradin: Schule, Erziehung und Ausbildung der Mädchen im Dritten Reich. In K. Merkel & C. Dittrich (Eds.), *Spiel mit dem Reich: Nationalsozialistisches Gedankengut in Spielzeug und Kinderbüchern* (pp. 63–71). Wiesbaden, Germany: Harrassowitz.

Reese, D. (2006). *Growing up female in Nazi Germany.* Ann Arbor, MI: University of Michigan Press.

Retter, H. (1979). *Spielzeug: Handbuch zur Geschichte und Pädagogik der Spielmittel.* Weinheim, Germany; Basel, Switzerland: Beltz.

Rock, D., & Wolff, S. (Eds.). (2002). *Coming home to Germany? The integration of ethnic Germans from central and Eastern Europe in the Federal Republic.* New York, NY; Oxford, England: Berghahn Books.

Rösch, M. (2002). *Die Münchner NSDAP 1925–1933: Eine Untersuchung zur inneren Struktur der NSDAP in der Weimarer Republik.* Munich, Germany: Oldenbourg.

Ruder, G-K. (2006). *Holocaust im Gedächtnis einer Puppe: Unterwegs auf Lebensspuren von und mit Inge Auerbacher.* Baden-Baden, Germany: DWV.

Schaumann, C. (2008). *Memory matters: Generational responses to Germany's Nazi past in recent women's literature.* Berlin, Germany: de Gruyter.

Schiffman, R. L. (2001). Wax-work, clock-work, and puppet-shews: *Bleak House* and the uncanny. *Dickens Studies Annual, 30*, 159–171.

Schmitz-Köster, D. (2007). *Kind L364: Eine Lebensborn-Familiengeschichte.* Berlin: Rowohlt.

Schütz, H. (1977). *Jette in Dresden.* Berlin and Weimar, Germany: Aufbau.

Sheffer, E. (2011). *Burned bridge: How East and West Germans made the Iron Curtain.* New York, NY; Oxford, England: Oxford University Press.

Stargardt, N. (2006). *Witnesses of war: Children's lives under the Nazis.* London, England: Pimlico.

Straub, R. (2007). *Eine Reise in die Welt der Puppen und Teddybären: Geschichten vom Puppen- und Bärendoktor.* Norderstedt, Germany: Books on Demand.

This is "Jugend um Hitler." (1937, December 6). *LIFE*, 6–9.

Thomas, J. B. (2003). *Naked Barbies, warrior Joes, and other forms of visible gender.* Urbana, IL: University of Illinois Press.

Valent, P. (1994). *Child survivors of the Holocaust.* London, England: Brunner-Routledge.

Vincenz, K. (1995). Historische Puppen. In P. Schmerenbeck (Ed.), *Puppen, Bären, magische Laternen* (pp. 9–18). Oldenburg, Germany: Isensee Verlag.

Winterberg, Y., & Winterberg, S. (2009). *Kriegskinder: Erinnerungen einer Generation.* Berlin: Rotbuch Verlag.

Wolf, C. (1980). *Patterns of childhood* (U. Molinaro & H. Rappolt, Trans.). New York, NY: Farrar, Straus and Giroux.

Wolf, C. (1976) *Kindheitsmuster*. Berlin: Aufbau.

Wolf, S. (2010). Excursion through a century of children's bedrooms. *Kunststoffe International, 5*, 79–83.

Zahra, T. (2011). *The lost children: Reconstructing Europe's families after World War II*. Cambridge, MA; London, England: Harvard University Press.

Part II: Performance and Identity

CHAPTER FOUR

The "Dollification" OF Riot Grrrls: Self-Fashioning Alternative Identities

MEGHAN CHANDLER AND DIANA ANSELMO-SEQUEIRA

In their 1990 music video for "He's My Thing," American Riot Grrrl pioneers, Babes in Toyland, present a nightmarish world paved with rubble and populated by dolls. Rejecting the typical pacifiers and rattles, these dolls prefer matches and machetes. The lead doll, who bears an uncanny resemblance to lead singer Kat Bjelland, with her messy blond curls, navigates the post-apocalyptic landscape to find a porcelain doll playing with a ballerina figurine. As stand-ins for conventional femininity, this old-fashioned doll and her ballerina plaything embody what girls and dolls should be: dainty, demure, and contained. In stark opposition stands the blade-wielding, Bjelland look-alike doll, who proceeds to amputate the limbs of her porcelain counterpart and set fire to everything around her. By similarly maiming old notions of girlhood, other Riot Grrrls also broke down existent patriarchal notions of what girls should be by carving out an empowered, alternative identity. Through their subversive reworking of doll figures, they challenged the longstanding cultural belief that doll-play cultivated "good" girls.

In *A Study on Dolls*, a pioneering text in the field of childhood psychology published in 1897, G. Stanley Hall and A. Caswell Ellis had argued that dolls fostered girls' feminine identity. After polling over 640 boys and girls attending American and British schools, the two American psychologists concluded that playing with dolls shaped children's understanding of society (p. 22). By making sense of the outside world through small-scale doll-universes, children supposedly formed life-long notions of "goodness" and "badness," which informed their self-perception as well-adjusted individuals. The psychologists claimed that "by trying to teach her doll" manners, morals, and hygiene, a girl tried "to set a good example" that often translated into optimized self-care. In fact, several parents included in the study reported that "car[ing] for [a] doll's body help[ed infants] to know and care for their own" (p. 45). Parents also observed that doll-play stimulated their children's ability to "cultivate taste in dress," ultimately making them "more stylish, more refined [...and with a] love of beauty." Thus, according to Hall and Ellis, the doll functioned as a mirror through which the child learnt formative lessons on beautification, fashion, and self-maintenance. Biased gender-coding, however, undergirded these foundational teachings. Such achievements in fashion, taste, and self-grooming positioned doll-play as a mock-practice for assuming traditional feminine roles, shaping the child's "fit[ness] for domestic life," "the care of children," and "womanliness," while preparing them for heterosexual coupledom (pp. 44–45). In sum, *A Study on Dolls* proposed that, while both genders engaged in childish doll-play, only female subjectivity became radically molded by its formative lessons on ladylike propriety, beauty, and domesticity.

One hundred years after Hall and Ellis, a cadre of teenage girls on both sides of the Atlantic reworked conventional ideas about feminized doll-play. In a variety of ways, these rebellious, riotous girls gleefully embraced the process of "dollification," a term Hall and Ellis (1897) described as "the childish instinct to find or make a doll out of everything—even themselves" (pp. 11, 46). Donning handripped attire and banging on hard-strummed guitars, American and British Riot Grrrls rehearsed a much darker, sexualized play with dolls at the dawn of the 1990s. In an attempt to subvert corseting views on female beauty and girlish passivity surrounding the figure of the doll, these girls—some of them underground singers and working-class performers, many others middle-class high-school students—caked their faces with smeared make-up; gashed their mouths with runny, red lipstick; shaved or teased their "birdnest" hair (http://katiejanegarside. com/press.html, n.d.); and costumed themselves in soiled, flimsy baby-doll dresses that exposed their bruised and tattooed young bodies.

Banded together, these girls birthed an idea-swapping "network and a space for experimentation," which two Portland teenagers first dubbed the "Riot Grrrl" movement. Tellingly, the term originated within their private correspondence, propelled by the 15-year-olds' shared desire to witness young females revolt against America's male-dominated popular culture. In a self-fashioned journey through the proverbial looking-glass, they metamorphosed into outspoken, crude versions of Hall's "elegant French dolls." While in 1897, Hall and Ellis claimed that, "if dolls lose their heads, eyes, or get otherwise deformed, little children are afraid of them," by 1989, those "rude and maimed dolls" no longer scared girls (pp. 11, 42). Rather, Riot Grrrls celebrated such grotesquely reconstructed doll figures by mimicking their scabs, scratches, and sutures. As a result of this perceptual twist, girls ceased to long for dolls that mirrored a beautified notion of self. Instead, dolls became the externalized reflection of girls' hidden fears, personal obsessions, and coming-of-age nightmares. Riot Grrrl artists further played upon these darker aspects by crafting a powerful menagerie of violated prom queens, maimed super models, and strung-out cheerleaders. While their creative reinterpretations dismantled previous models of girlhood, Riot Grrrls nonetheless reused some of the left-over pieces to fashion new feminist images. Sometimes Riot Grrrls posed with dolls for promotional photos, cover-art, and in music videos; sometimes they re-appropriated mass culture depictions of commercial dolls (such as the infamous Barbie) in their confessional writings and self-reflexive art practice. Other times, the performers themselves embodied the wound-up automaton, spasmodically trashing across the stage while fans waited for their batteries to run out. In the end, Riot Grrrls found a voice in the otherwise historically silent figure of the doll, and became "dollified" spokespersons for new feminist ideals.

This chapter aims to extend the parameters of existent histories on Riot Grrrls by investigating the doll imagery appropriated and produced by three ringleaders of dollification: Kat Bjelland from Babes in Toyland; Courtney Love from Hole; and KatieJane Garside from Daisy Chainsaw. While cultural theorists such as Ross Haenfler (2010) and feminist scholars such as Anne Higgonet[1] (1998) and April R. Mandrona (2012) have identified doll images and doll-making within the "do-it-yourself" ethos of the Riot Grrrl movement, we push this perspective further. We ask: in what ways did Riot Grrrls use the doll as a central figure and repeating motif in their artistic works or performances? How did such reappropriation intersect with or diverge from previous meanings ascribed to dolls and their intended cultural work? By exploring these questions, our chapter demonstrates that, in the hands of Riot Grrrls, the doll served as a significant political figure who subverted patriarchal views about young femininity. We utilize material culture, as well as the textual and visual analyses of these three artists' stage personae, their album artwork, music videos, and lyrics to interrogate how and why the doll figured so centrally in Riot Grrrl musical culture.

More than an aesthetic object choice, Riot Grrrls used dolls to become what sociologist Dick Hebdige (1979) dubbed, "subcultural bricoleur[s]."[2] Riot Grrrls gave new meanings to dolls by transforming and re-contextualizing them. They creatively filtered dominant meanings of dolls through their subcultural agenda, consequently re-appropriating them as tokens of feminist resistance. Broken and bruised, lewd and loud, Riot Grrrls rewrote the doll's iconography and cultural meaning of prim beauty, frigid innocence, and passive composure. Their "dollified," animated bodies thus became a vehicle through which Riot Grrrls staged their intervention as subcultural bricoleurs and empowered agents, hell bent on subverting mainstream ideas on proper feminine identity.

While most Riot Grrrl histories tend to focus exclusively on American individuals, our work expands these borders to consider Riot Grrrls and their doll-play on an intercontinental scale.[3] Analyzing Hole and Babes in Toyland in tandem with British band Daisy Chainsaw, our chapter examines the transatlantic as well as transhistorical continuities of doll imagery. In addition to broadening our scope beyond the traditional American-centric perspective, we also move beyond the era typically associated with the heyday of the Riot Grrrl movement. As such, we consider how pro-feminist doll-play continues in the form of contemporary Riot Grrrl acts such as Doll Fight!, a three-woman Riot Grrrl band from Vermont, and the art practice of KatieJane Garside, the iconic lead singer of Daisy Chainsaw. In fact, Riot Grrrls' reappropriation of dolls remains alive in girls' cultural productions, performances, and imaginations.

"REVOLUTION DOLL STYLE NOW:"[4] AMERICAN RIOT GRRRLS

The Riot Grrrl movement first emerged in the early 1990s as an underground feminist punk movement; it continued throughout the 1990s, spreading from its original epicenter in the Pacific Northwest across the United States and the world. Several outspoken, politically oriented feminist artists—including Kathleen Hanna and her Bikini Kill band, Bratmobile, Heaven to Betsy, 7 Year Bitch—led the movement through music as well as other visual art practices, including self-published "zines" and "do-it-yourself" art production. Riot Grrrls attempted to reclaim and self-fashion a counter-hegemonic version of female empowerment through these projects, and utilized hyper-sexualized images of girlhood as a privileged motif.

Even though Courtney Love and Kat Bjelland held complex and at times oppositional positions toward the Riot Grrrls,[5] their early endeavors (musical and otherwise) established the foundational tenets and ethos of the movement. In particular, images of dolls served as a staple in the musical and artistic output of Kat Bjelland's band, Babes in Toyland, as well as Courtney Love's band, Hole.[6] Sugar Babydoll, the musical and artistic collective founded in 1981 by Love and her Portland-based friends, Ursula Wehr and Robin Barbur, is evidence of Love's early exploration of dolls as culturally meaningful artifacts. The collective later relocated to San Francisco during 1982–84, with singer Kat Bjelland and bassist Jennifer Finch replacing Wehr and Barbur. In an interview with VH1, Bjelland admitted that Sugar Babydoll was always "more about taking pictures" than producing real music (Gottlieb, 2010, 1:27:05). Yet these early collaborations introduced two major themes—girlhood imagery and the doll figure—that Love, Bjelland, and other Riot Grrrl artists would explore in their songs, videos, and performances.

Following Sugar Babydoll's lead, Riot Grrrls played upon and toyed with idealized notions of dolls, girlhood, and the "Romantic child." Since the eighteenth century, Romantic girls sporting frilly dresses, coiffed hair, and demurely dimpled smiles served as long-standing emblems of pure, innocent girlhood and idealized femininity (see Higonnet, 1998). Riot Grrrl bands reworked fetishized exemplars of naïveté and innocence—from Victorian fashion dolls to the sickeningly sweet line of Strawberry Shortcake dolls of the 1980s—by ripping their own frilly dresses, disheveling their hair, and turning their smiles into sardonic sneers. Exploding romanticized images of female childhood from the inside out, Riot Grrrls acted as self-aware agents who subversively refashioned themselves into parodied pastiches of childish yet sexual vamps. Their reformulations of girlhood and its associated objects, ranging from baby-doll dresses to actual baby dolls, revealed how girlhood and its iconic images could be used as a powerful cultural critique as well as to empower alter-egos.

Riot Grrrls, however, were not the first to play with dolls or forge public personas that sexualized girlish cuteness. According to Kim Marie Vaz (2013), author of *The "Baby Dolls": Breaking the Race and Gender Barriers of the New Orleans Mardi Gras Tradition*, in 1912 African American women from the New Orleans red light district banded together to form the Million Dollar Baby Dolls. The group masqueraded in baby doll costumes and assumed doll personas in order to carve out new identities in the predominately white male carnival traditions of Mardi Gras. As forerunners to Riot Grrrl Kinderwhore, the Million Dollar Baby Dolls costumed themselves in an ironic mix of short satin dresses, sexy garters, and demure bonnets. Their costuming turned the innocuous cuteness of passive baby dolls into a sexually empowered, alternative pastiche. Paving the way for later Riot Grrrls, these marginalized New Orleans women exploited stereotypes and used images of dolls to make themselves publicly visible.

Similarly, in the hands of Riot Grrrls, the doll ceased to be an embodiment of childish cuteness and passive purity. While Lori Merish (1996) theorized that cuteness de-sexualizes the child's body and facilitates the disavowal or sublimation of eroticism, Love and other Riot Grrrls dollified themselves into living parodies of sexual, girly playthings. Rather than playing the good girl, rebellious Riot Grrrls played with alternative presentations of what girls could be. In doing so, they transformed dollish innocence into a performance of empowered female sexuality. According to feminist scholar Karina Eileraas (1997), the Riot Grrrls' surreal juxtapositions of conventional prettiness with violent, violated images "create[d] a visual economy that emphasize[d] the violence to and alienation from the body that obedient performances of 'pretty' femininity entail" (p. 124). Shattering the glossy veneer of girly prettiness and doll-like cuteness, Riot Grrrls pieced together a tattered quilt of knowing sexuality. Echoing this, Courtney Love even described how she consciously veered away from stereotypical notions of upper-middle-class femininity and prom queens in favor of embodying "subculture, [and becoming] a teenage bag lady" (O'Brien, 2002, p. 171). Thus, by playing with sexualized images of dolls and re-presenting themselves as "child-women, [or] fucked-up Lolitas," as

Eileraas described them (p. 128), Riot Grrrls perverted cute images of girls. Their self-conscious refiguration of the dress and aesthetics of girlhood defined Riot Grrrl style and delineated their politics of oppositional identity-making.

"CRAZY OLD DOLL IN A CRAZY OLD DRESS:"[7] COURTNEY LOVE, KAT BJELLAND, AND KINDERWHORE

Courtney Love and Kat Bjelland defined Riot Grrrl style through their *Kinder-whore* fashion. Their ripped baby-doll dresses, torn stockings, messy doll-like curls, and smudged makeup became the fashion staples of this trademark look. Babes in Toyland's 1990 song, "Lashes," effectively spelled out the crazed, destructive ethos at the core of *Kinderwhore*. As Bjelland's lyrics proclaim,

> She screams sweet hell, in her old white nightie with rips and tears she's too aware / Baby's got ruby jewel lashes that'll whip your spine /....I put on my best Sunday dress and I waltz straight into this mess posing as...a crazy old doll in a crazy old dress. (Bjelland, 1990)

Garbed in tattered nighties and messed-up make-up, Riot Grrrls crafted a twisted style that tore at the decorous dress signifying proper and poised femininity; instead, they replaced these candy-coated stereotypes with "sweets laced with razor blades" (Women on the Verge, 2011).

While some credit Bjelland with pioneering the *Kinderwhore* trend, Love undoubtedly popularized it amongst Riot Grrrl fans. Love "seemed iconic compared to other female musicians on the scene," wrote one Atlanta teen, "all those bands had girls trying to be like the boys or girls too soft and sweet, but Court and Kat [Bjelland] were just right, a marriage between feminine and fierce" (kidsoncrux, 2012). Simultaneously appropriating the styling of naïve schoolgirls as well as tawdry women, Riot Grrrls problematized the fetishistic fantasies constructed around imagined ideals of innocence and passivity in doll objects—the central metonym for girlhood itself. Courtney Love especially turned the innocent cuteness of doll-like girls into an embodied "glistening sex doll" performance by combining ripped baby-doll dresses with smudged makeup and barrette-studded, mussed hair (Attwood, 2007, p. 241).

Love constructed a subversive image of girlhood with her *Kinderwhore* fashions, then beat and battered her dollified image in Hole's songs and music videos. For example, songs such as "Babydoll" graphically explored adult sexuality: "Drill it in my good hole so that I can see / Here she comes Her pants undone / Oh my babydoll what a whore you are" (Love, Erlandson, Emery, & Rue, 1991a). Love also used *Kinderwhore* costuming to produce intentionally twisted visuals and question normative understandings of acceptable feminine behavior.[8] Through her performance of self-abuse and sexual stylization, Love struck back at the very patriarchal constructs that defined idealized femininity as socially and sexually passive.

In music videos for "Violet" (Seligar & Woodward, 1994) and "Miss World" (Muller, 1994), Love's *Kinderwhore* costuming served to further challenge stereotypical notions of how "good girls" should conduct themselves. In particular, "Violet" addressed sexual exploitation and self-exploration by juxtaposing children dressed as ballerinas with women "dressed" as strippers and burlesque dancers. Wearing a gauzy tutu alongside prepubescent ballerinas, Love baited listeners to "Go on, take everything" while she proceeded to stage-dive into a salaciously groping male crowd. Appearing as both the vulnerable child and a sexually active woman, Love effectively blurred the boundaries between these diametrically opposed positions. Hole's "Miss World" video also mixed childish appearances with a more mature type of physical expression, characterized by Love's reckless trashing and aggressive screaming, which flew in the face of prim, good-girl behavior. During the video's chorus, for instance, Love angrily screams and bangs her guitar in front of a twinkling backdrop spelling out the phrase "Cleanliness is next to Godliness." This adage echoes back to cultural demands upon little girls: namely, that they remain pure and grow into decorous women. Love resists this proscription, however, and instead presents a raucous, unruly version of herself. Donning dirty off-white knee-highs, scuffed Mary Jane shoes, and a mussed Peter Pan collar dress, Love defied dominant expectations and investments in hygiene, self-containment, and beautification—the same virtues that, as Hall and Ellis theorized, dolls should instill into little girls.

"I AM DOLL ARMS BIG VEINS DOG BAIT:"[9] SHATTERING DOLLS AND STEREOTYPES

In one of Hole's earliest singles, "Burn Black" (Love & Erlandson, 1990), Love presents dolls as a metaphoric weapon of empowered, violent resistance. The song's lyrics depict a girl pushed over the edge: tired of her unnamed companion's demands and disregard, she lashes out with verbal promises, uttered from her "doll mouth," to "slit your neck" and "[gush] up a violent smear." Becoming her own avenging agent, Love struck back against this marginalizing, stand-in masculine figure. Love pursued this role as an active and empowered doll in a number of her others songs and music videos. In Hole's 1994 "Doll Parts" (Love, 1993), for example, Love again assumed a tattered doll persona. In the video, Love wears a thin, hiked-up nightgown, and sits with her knees spread apart on a dirty, unmade bed. Intercut with images of Love on the bed are images of a child poking the evacuated eye sockets of a corroded, dirt-encrusted porcelain doll. While the child plays, Love itemizes all the pieces of her body that mirror the doll's: "doll eyes, doll legs, doll mouth...doll arms...doll heart." As the song progresses towards its bitterly screamed chorus—"He only loves those things because he loves to see them break....And some day you will ache like I ache"—Love stages her own sinister version of the doll tea party by smashing this quintessential ritual of feminine gentility (Bayer, 1994). Doll bodies lie strewn across a scorched desert landscape and are skewered on naked trees as Love angrily throws the tea party chairs and dolls to the ground. By destroying the dolls and the customary tea party ritual that disciplines girl's bodies and minds, Love retook ownership over her body through this deviant, aggressive resistance.

The physical destruction of dolls also characterizes several of Babes in Toyland's album artwork. Their *Spanking Machine* (1990), *Fontanelle* (1992), and *Painkillers* (1993) albums, for example, respectively feature dismantled, amputated doll parts; a naked female doll with splayed legs and exposed genitals; and a doll whose head has been covered with a frightening female clown mask shellacked with exaggerative, nightmarish makeup. *Spanking Machine* even pictures the band members as destroyed dolls, lying in a pile of amputated plastic limbs. By turning themselves and the bodies of pristine dolls into mutilated fragments, Babes in Toyland reworked hegemonic renditions of femininity and re-scripted a new image of dolls through acts of creative destruction or, as political theorist Ernesto Laclua (cited in Wald, 1998) has termed it, "disarticulation-rearticulation" (p. 591). Riot Grrrls, in other words, used fragmentation and deconstruction as a constructive political tool. They tore down and broke apart previously established images of girls, dolls, and femininity. From this rubble, they constructed new images of themselves as empowered and active agents, with all their cracks and flaws unabashedly worn on their dirtied, ripped sleeves.

While the destructive fragmentation of female figures often results in disempowerment, when wielded by female agents it can be reclaimed as an empowering feminist act. As music historian Robin Roberts (1996) argued, the types of broken, dismantled images adopted by the Riot Grrrls "[call] on the viewer to break down preconceptions about 'proper' roles and narratives; fragmentation disrupts by calling into question each part of a preconception of what is 'natural' and hence unquestioned" (pp. 14–15). Expanding this analysis to the Riot Grrrls themselves, their productive practice of deconstructing the doll into fragmented parts succeeded in breaking down and exposing oppressive expectations of how girls should look and behave. Ultimately, Love and her Grrrl conspirators dismantled previous stereotypes of girls and doll icons, and reconstructed defiant new alternatives to the gendered prescriptions of restrained, neatly contained, and pristine femininity.

"GIRL REVOLUTIONARIES YOU AND ME:"[10] BRITISH GRRRLS JOIN THE RIOT

The formation of Riot Grrrl bands in Great Britain stemmed from a different cultural moment than their American counterparts. Although both shared a commitment to female agency and feminist expression within a male-centric music industry, the British musical landscape in the early 1990s lacked an underground culture driven by young, especially female, voices. "Our situation was different to the one the American Riot Grrrls were responding to," explained Jo Slade from Bristol-based Riot Grrrl band, Huggy Bear. "The underground in London had deteriorated totally, there wasn't really much of an alternative…'indie' just became an abstract term….Punk rock wasn't important. Fanzines were seen as a sad joke….The reasons for being independent were snorted at" (Raphael, 1996, p. 151).[11]

Barbara Hudson's fieldwork conducted in a British high school in 1984 explained why. In "Female Adolescence," the sociologist argued that, culturally, girlhood has always been considered a subordinate of superior masculinity. Hudson further remarked that, "all our images of the adolescent—…the restless, searching youth, the Hamlet figure…—these are masculine images" (p. 35). As a result of this pervasive preconception, in order to perform a socially acceptable version of female adolescence, girls either modeled themselves after "one of the boys," or attempted to impersonate proper ladylikeness, a feminine paradigm defined by an over-investment in fashion, beauty, and romance. At either end of the spectrum, however, growing girls were still being understood as imperfect duplicates of boys or as intrinsically superficial subjects.

British Riot Grrrls grew up within this cultural paradox. Like many of Hudson's 15-year-old interviewees, British teenage girls growing up in the 1990s quickly discovered that, culturally, female adolescence continued to be derisively compared to boyhood. Thus, young women such as Debbie Smith, a self-identified black "dyke" who toured with Curve from 1991 to 1994; Scottish-born Lesley Rankine, who proclaimed the famous lyrics "Hips, Tits, Lips, Power" during her stint in Silverfish (1988–1993); or Niki Elliott, Jo Slade, and Karen Hill, three teenagers from the influential band Huggy Bear (1991–1994), gravitated towards the American Riot Grrrl movement while seeking an alternative outlet for feminist self-expression. "It was so much more of an exciting and alive idea of feminism than we were all coming across in books," Jo Slade reminisced about her first encounter with the Riot Grrrl community; while Debbie admitted that watching "Huggy Bear perform on the TV show *The Word*" was a watershed moment in her musical education. "I thought: 'Fucking hell, yes!' I went and saw a few bands and really got off on the energy. [The Riot Grrrl movement] was spawning a lot of new bands and lots of women were getting on stage: some of them were terrible, some were quite good and some were excellent. But it was encouraging women to play" (Raphael, 1996, pp. 151, 155).

A wasteland for free-thinking teenagers and feminist girls, Great Britain forced a generation of burgeoning artists "to look to the US as if it were a one-sided mirror…as spectators. Girls wanted in, so they began to work towards inclusion" (Raphael, 1996, p. 155). By "dollifying" themselves, British girls (such as 18-year-old KatieJane Garside, the future lead singer of Daisy Chainsaw) donned shredded baby-doll dresses, combat boots, and brightly colored wigs and disseminated a "feminist school of thought" through their writings and performances and gained entry into the American Riot Grrrl community (p. 151). If, in the late nineteenth century, dolls had been the mirror and mediator of girls' aspired feminine identity, at the end of the twentieth century, Riot Grrrls took control over their image by self-fashioning themselves as subversive playthings.

"THIS TIME THE DOLL WAS ME:"[12] KATIEJANE GARSIDE AND THE REAPPROPRIATION OF DOLL-MAKING

Willowy and diminutive Katiejane began her public dollification in 1989, shortly after replying to an ad that musician Crispin Grey placed in the music press. The ad asked for a vocalist to front a punk/Riot band. The resulting four-piece ensemble, Daisy Chainsaw, released their one hit, "Love Your Money," at the end of 1991. The single reached the U.K. Top 30 in February 1992, with critics attributing the unknown band's overnight success to "Garside's kooky delivery… her combination of wide-eyed innocence and ragged rebellion" (Strong, 2003, p. 45) met with "enough breathy growls…to cause genuine concern for her larynx" (Joseph, 1992, p. 22).

Costumed in dirty, little-girls' dresses, moth-eaten wedding gowns, shredded nighties, and elaborate headpieces made of fake flowers, pale-faced Garside resembled a beautiful porcelain doll—a doll that, after being broken and buried by a pack of bored girls, had resurrected to take sinister revenge. Doll-play permeated more than just her appearance; it underpinned every aspect of Garside's public persona. In Daisy Chainsaw's music videos and promotional photos, she rode toy trains, played with miniature tea-sets, or held tiny Kewpie Dolls and mangled teddy bears. On stage, she decorated her microphone and bandmates' instruments with dismembered plastic limbs, cuddled baby dolls, and drank orange juice from a baby bottle. Reviewers responded by comparing Garside's reckless dives into the crowd and her physical elasticity onstage—trashing and slithering in a bare, pink slip—to that of a jointless "mad rag-doll" (Joseph, 1992, p. 22).

Always appearing in public wearing dingy baby-doll dresses, uncombed hair, and bare feet, the waifish Garside performed a nightmarish version of wide-eyed vulnerability and abused innocence that had become associated with Riot Grrrls' perversion of "Romantic" childish femininity. Even the title and cover art of Daisy Chainsaw's first album, *Eleventeen*, reinforced the band's clashing of prepubescent playfulness with adolescent messiness: illustrated in childish crayon colors, the cover sported a monstrous eight-legged animal reminiscent of a bad acid trip through Lewis Carroll's disconcerting Wonderland.

The British press further attempted "to make sense" of Garside's baffling mixture of physical fragility, lyrical rawness, and onstage sexual aggressiveness by dubbing her "one of the originators of the *Kinderwhore* look" (Lobasso, 2009, p. 22). Later, in 1992, the group reinforced their Riot Grrrl affiliations by playing alongside Hole during their first UK tour. Courtney Love's appreciation of KatieJane's live performances allegedly culminated in Love praising her as "one of the first true Riot Grrrls." This seal of approval ultimately helped boost Garside's reputation as Britain's leading kinderwhore. However, reporters often filtered Garside's disquieting image through familiar paradigms of troubled girlhood, comparing the lead singer to "a Dickensian beggar girl" (Strong, 2003, p. 46) or a "battered-Ophelia just escaped from an asylum" (Joseph, 1992, p. 22). Although male authors penned both figures, the duality of mad Ophelia—docile, lovelorn maiden transformed into a deflowered, foul-mouthed ranter due to a claustrophobic, patriarchal society—spoke near and dear to Garside's feminist views. From her garlanded hair to her whispered ditties, dazed stare and spasmodic dancing, Garside projected both sides of Ophelia's personality: the virginal and the sexual, the hopeful and the angry, the frenetically alive and the lethargically suicidal. Moreover, by choosing to identify with Ophelia instead of Hamlet, Garside—alongside Love and other Riot Grrrls—worked to undercut the masculinization of adolescence Hudson had identified in the early 1980s. Having sung her despair and heartbrokenness to her deathbed, Shakespeare's teen heroine gave voice to the type of girlhood many ordinary females experienced: a messy, marginalizing, and sexually charged phase.

By resurrecting Ophelia as their role-model, Riot Grrrls not only reclaimed adolescence as a feminine construct, but also challenged the "boys' club" mentalité that shaped the late-80s music industry. In the song "Belittled and Beaten Down" (1992) Garside sees herself through the eyes of British reporters and musicians who formed a tight-knit oligarchy that believed punk, hardcore, and rock should remain the exclusive province of men:

> You're just a puny annoyingly cutie who couldn't / keep up with us no matter how hard
> you tried / leave the important things up to the big boys / cause you are amusing and
> we wouldn't want you to cry. (Gray, 1994)

In fact, male journalists who reviewed British Riot Grrrls' concerts and albums attempted to defang the bite of their musical testimony. "Despite Huggy Bear's grandiose posturing, this didn't sound like a revolution: it sounded like the same old song," reported *Spin Magazine* ("Huggy Bear/The Frumpies," 1994, p. 85) in a critique of Huggy Bear's 1993 live concert in New Jersey. In 1992, the same magazine remarked of Daisy Chainsaw's first EP, *LoveSickPleasure*: "Dig below the grunge, and you'll find a syrupy core as sweet as sugar" (Joseph, 1992, p. 22). Echoing conventional notions that ascribed superficiality and sentimentality to young femininity, the male-dominated music press continued to suggest that British girls' angry resistance functioned as a paper-thin veneer, ultimately hiding their true "syrupy core, [that was] as sweet as sugar" and lacked any spice. In fact, as soon as Riot Grrrl bands reared their heads on the British horizon, they were almost immediately eclipsed by the so-called "New Wave" or "Brit Pop," a movement spearheaded by "working-class Manchester lads"—such as Oasis and Blur—whose songs dealt with a testosterone-filled worldview of "fighting, beer, and football." Debbie Smith (Raphael, 1996, p. 55) called the emergence of this masculinized genre, "a total female castration of Riot Grrrl." Author Lucy O'Brien (2002) condemned the British media for picking up and skimming off "the top from the [Riot Grrrl] movement before it had a chance to breathe and grow" (p. 168).

By 1993, at the apex of her stardom, Garside abandoned Daisy Chainsaw, claiming that living in the media spotlight had caused her breakdown. Shortly before her premature departure, Garside shaved her mane of blonde hair on stage while painfully cradling a naked baby doll against her soiled chest. Reporters gleefully speculated that Garside's abrupt exit from the band was actually "due to press furor surrounding alleged revelations of childhood abuse" (Strong, 2003, p. 46). Ambivalent about a childlike 22-year-old who thrashed about onstage wearing ripped lingerie and had unshaved armpits, critics scrutinized Garside, using her dollified image as therapists would to treat abused children. Transformed into a life-size doll herself, Garside realized that it hurt everywhere.

Dolls continued to underpin Garside's ambivalent play with possession and dispossession, self-control and abandonment. That tension defined Garside's ongoing engagement with art, music, and self-expression, as well as accounting for interest in "making dolls." Resembling Hall and Ellis's puppets, Garside described herself as a passive channel where "music is at odds with its vehicle" (Toazted, 2005), and as a taken-over medium "that claims to be the reincarnation of Helen of Troy" (ElvisGun, 1992). Possessed by sound and legend, she exists as an evacuated plaything, dominated by external forces. Music reviewers agreed, depicting Garside as a mindless doll that "shows complete disregard for her own safety and has been known to stage-dive headfirst into the audience" (ElvisGun, 1992). When asked about her relinquishing of control both on stage and in her creative life, Garside replied that, "I am just like broken glass. There was never…solid…anything to refer to, there was never any Santa for me.…I have tried to patch the holes in the canvas for a long time" (Toazted, 2005). In fact, she has often described herself as "a vehicle" (Hardy, 2006), "the doll," or "the puppet" (Hare, 2011) animated by musical impulses. In addition to Garside's pliable insubstantiality as a selfless automaton animated by the electric current of music and fandom, she also struggled with the violence perpetrated by some male audiences. After being mauled and undressed while crowd-surfing, Garside confessed that abdicating her agency was,

> complicated because on one hand I have seen it that it's not really me, it's kinda like I am just a vehicle, it's almost like a rite of purification; and then another time I come very much into the foreground, or myself does, or even my mother looking after myself comes into the foreground and I get fucking angry. (Hardy, 2006)

Torn between letting go and fighting back, Garside also presented herself as a firmly defined personality, evinced by the way she painstakingly remade "all of [her] clothes" to reflect aspects of her complex interiority. Clothes may have been "somebody else's design first," the singer conceded, "but I changed it. When it gets on my body, it's been cut and it's mine" (Lobasso, 2009, p. 22). Her repurposed clothes—particularly the bare-boned underwire skirts, the hand-frayed vintage beaded dresses, and the rusty prosthetic limbs—transformed Garside into a life-size doll.

Doll-play and doll-making harken back to Garside's most formative memory: that of spending her teen years sailing the world with her parents and young sister aboard a small boat. She later encapsulated that experience as "seamless days of ocean and two little girls with dolls"—dolls that she remembered making as a childhood pastime. As she grew into girlhood though, Garside discovered that doll-making continued to frame her professional and personal development. Evaluating her career in the late 2000s, Garside admitted that, after coming to shore at age 18 and joining Daisy Chainsaw, "I just carried on making dolls but this time the doll was me" (Hare, 2011). This insight explains Garside's life-long play with dolls: as the dollified lead singer for Daisy Chainsaw in her earlier days, and later in life as an internationally adored underground cult figure who "transcribed [her] dreams onto" the naked "bodies" of repurposed plastic dolls and sold them to loving fans on her personal website (Garside, 2013).

The manual methods employed when "sewing new stitches and patterns into small, ragged dresses" (Garside, 2013) also hearken back to turn-of-the-century feminized practices of hand-stitching, paper-cutting, and scrapbooking (Hall & Ellis, 1897).[13] In the late nineteenth century, arts and crafts became the most popular pastime for middle-class youth growing up in Britain and America. Young mothers and housewives practiced domestic frugality and engaged their offspring in educational pastimes that recycled household scraps—paper, cloth, clay, wood, and wax—while teaching them practical skills. Widely published in both countries, "how-to" books guided girls in sewing, scrapbooking, and doll-making.[14]

One hundred years later, artists such as Garside, who identified with the emergence of the "do-it-yourself" ethos, also engaged in collaging, crafting, and creating artwork that disseminated Riot Grrrls' original message of feminist self-empowerment. Garside reclaimed those domesticated practices of hand-sewing and doll-making, using them as feminist weapons in her late twentieth-century critique of female oppression. Firstly, the labor of repurposing second-hand clothes stitch by stitch, layering new fabrics onto old patterns, created a multi-textured palimpsest of self-expression that not only resembled Riot Grrrls' collaged fanzines, but also conversed with Hole's first album, *Pretty on the Inside*. Juxtaposing facsimiles of handwritten, angry lyrics ("here you are just ugly as me") with cut-out images of the Virgin Mary, sawdust dolls, Victorian children, and pin-up girls, the album sleeve resembled a girl's collaged diary refashioned as a public manifesto (Love, Erlandson, Emery, & Rue, 1991b). Hole's artwork and Garside's repurposed clothes both show how mass-marketed images that promote stereotypical female beauty can be repossessed and reworked, becoming sites of feminist criticism, self-awareness, and cultural deconstruction. Secondly, by utilizing reclaimed garments as tools for subversive dollification, Garside turned them into personalized banners of resistance. Convulsing onstage in her girly frocks or photographed as an autopsied doll cut open amongst a bed of copper flowers, Garside embodied a self-directed plaything—made, cut, sewn, soiled, and dollified by her own hand and not by male objectification. Thus, handmade garments and life-size dolls ceased to be domesticated; they became weapons, flung from the stage, and shoved onto audiences' faces.

Because doll-play and dressmaking are an extension of Garside's self, she "refuse[d] to cover up" long after "[Courtney] Love and many other *Kinderwhore* girls, including Babes In Toyland's Kat Bjelland and The Muff's Kim Shattuck, have put the look to bed" (Lobasso, 2009, p. 22). For Garside, doll-play and doll-making began as a childhood memory, growing with the singer as she travelled through adolescence and adult life, public infamy and underground success. As suggested by Hall and Ellis (1897) in their landmark study, the doll did become Garside's vehicle to understand the outside world and make sense of her budding subjectivity. The same way Garside never retired the *Kinderwhore* look, she also never tired of playing with dolls. In fact, as a middle-aged woman, she fashioned herself as a ventriloquist doll, the receptive loudspeaker through which inner music and creativity flowed. In this movement of dispossession, however, her voice was not lessened, but strengthened. As a doll, an adult Garside gained control over the play. "This time I was the doll. I was the puppet," she explained in the late 2000s, "but I was the one that pulls the strings" (Hare, 2011).

AND THEY LIVED HAPLESSLY EVER AFTER:
RIOT GRRRLS TODAY

Although the Riot Grrrl movement lost momentum as the 1990s wore on, dolls have remained a source of tension and empowerment for twenty-first-century female artists. At the dawn of the new millennium, American and European musicians still privilege dolls as polysemic objects and poseable foils. Nowadays, young artists and performers continue to reinvent the Riot Grrrl movement as well as continuing to play with dolls, further challenging pre-established views on idealized female beauty, girl sexuality, agency, and activism.

For example, in Great Britain, the artificial animation of the doll's body, as well as its plural associations with childhood play and womanly sexuality, continued to fascinate Garside, even as she turned 40. Throughout the 2000s, Garside expanded her feminist reappropriations of doll-making to photography. One of her side-projects, a collection of intimate Polaroids, appeared in the Fall of 2007 at the WOOM Gallery in Birmingham, U.K. Under the title, "Darling, They've Found the Body," the snapshots depict Garside as a gigantic marionette—naked, masked, and smudged, lying amongst fragmented doll limbs and a decapitated mannequin head. Similarly focused on deconstructing ideas of female primness and propriety intrinsic to girly doll-play, Garside chose the plastic doll's bare body as her primary canvas. Sometime in the late 2000s, Garside crafted two pieces ironically dubbed "dream dolls—genica-pussywillow & sleeplikewolves" (2013). Selling them on her personal webpage without a visible price tag (fans had to email for details), Garside described her doll-making process as a nightmarish subversion of the conventional processes of feminine beautification. "I write on them and scratch on them, they don't cry and they don't bite back, they've 'seen some,' the most important thing is that they stay together, one doesn't work without the other." Scratched but impervious to pain, Garside's ravaged dolls stand for a feminist reclaiming of female agency and mindful self-fashioning that once underpinned the Riot Grrrl community.

In true *Kinderwhore* fashion, Garside (2013) also uses these dolls to comment on the double-standard disseminated by media depictions of sexualized young girls: premature self-awareness is encouraged in twenty-first-century females, but only if combined with passive, "full pose-ability" and controllable, "go to sleep eyes" (Garside, 2013). In her subversive doll-making, Garside continues to rework the Riot Grrrl legacy of experimenting with self-ascribed identities: like the doll, Garside tries on many different outfits. However, as a musician, she also refers back to her original childhood memory: she and her sister crystalized as "two girls with dolls." Like KatieJane and Melanie Garside, "genica-pussywillow" has a "smaller sister, 'sleeplikewolves,'" and "their history [is only] completed" when Garside's "dreams are transcribed onto their bodies." The tension established between the impulse to reach back to a protean ancestry while yearning to birth something new has always undergirded Garside's ambivalent relationship with temporality. "You need to destroy the past sometimes to be in the present," she told *Origivation Magazine* in 2009. "But at the same time, I think there might be some value in having some kind of a past" (Lobasso, 2009, p. 22).

This quote aptly encapsulates how current Riot Grrrls relate to their predecessors: although they honor the legacy created by Love, Bjelland, and Garside, contemporary Riot Grrrl artists rework their key themes and motifs—including doll images. This negotiation of Riot Grrrl heritage even extends beyond America and Britain, appearing across the ocean in Russia. Heralding from St. Petersburg, the one-girl act Headless Doll Whores emerged within the online music scene in the Summer of 2012. On one hand, this group attests to Riot Grrrls' transnational impact. On the other, Headless Doll Whores' subversive play with dolls evinces the movement's lasting influence, especially its use of dolls to help young female artists express their creative and cultural agency.[15]

Following in the footsteps of Riot Grrrl artists and fanzine makers, Headless Doll Whores utilizes sampling, collaging, and media reappropriation of doll imagery as a form of self-expression. The cover-art for the group's first album *Incredible Adventures of Dolls Whores* juxtaposes images of dolls from multiple eras: a sepia photograph of a small girl, dressed in communion garb, is surrounded by a multitude of nineteenth-century porcelain dolls with white dresses and "go-to-sleep" eyes. Positioned amidst the army of sitting dolls, an upright human child becomes transformed into an inanimate plaything. Stiff and uncanny in her ill-fitting bridal gown, this image can be read either as an original memento mori or as a clever superimposition of old dolls with a contemporary, living child. Either interpretation equally denounces a residing cultural tendency to "dollify" female children through garb as well as public spectacle.[16]

Furthermore, the anonymous female artist behind the band takes the original *Kinderwhore* look one step further. Costumed in lacy dresses, see-through baby-doll slips, and sporting a pasty-white complexion and bleach-blonde, tressed hair, Headless Doll Whores' tall, skinny leader styles herself on the likes of Courtney Love and KatieJane Garside. Additionally, the few black-and-white photos posted online by this elusive musician show her as a fragmented doll, draped over a vintage record player, with tiny toys and naked Barbie dolls spilling out of the open case. By keeping her anonymity so absolute, the girl behind Headless Doll Whores renders herself even more of a dollified vehicle than any of her famous Riot Grrrl predecessors: she remains a nameless ventriloquist dummy filtering musical creativity.

While Courtney Love attempted a fledging comeback with Hole in the 2000s, a new crop of outspoken American women musicians appointed themselves as the rebuilders of "a Riot Grrrl sound and manifesto for the 21st century" (Dollfight!, 2013). Reusing the doll as their figurehead, these Riot Grrrls craft a "righteous rage with febrile firepower and meticulous musicianship" (Dollfight!, 2013). Armed with enraged dolls, a three-woman punk band from Vermont, named Doll Fight!, recently emerged as contemporary leaders in what *Tom Tom Magazine* (DeRossa, 2011) suggested is the resurgence of the Riot Grrrl movement. Formed in early 2011, Doll Fight! and its members—Christine Mathias, JBA, and Kelly Riel—have since developed a devoted fan base and enthusiastic critical regard. In November 2011, the band released their second full-length album entitled "Revolution Doll Style Now."

With their headlining track, "Plastic Revolution," the group is ushering in a new wave of a doll-fronted revolt. Band leader Christine speaks eloquently about appropriating dolls as a way to pay homage to early Riot Grrrls. However, she also utilizes them to self-fashion a new personal and political revolution. Evoking Hall and Ellis' (1897) foundational study, even if unaware of its historical significance, drummer and percussionist JBA claims that their reappropriations of dolls are conscious reclaimings of the standard social mores that doll-play supposedly instilled. "From doll play," JBA wrote in the band's online manifesto, "girls absorb messages about how their bodies should look, and what domestic role they should play as adults. We're revolting against those (pretty revolting) aspects of 'doll style.'" Significantly, Doll Fight! retakes the master's tools from his own hands and, like the pioneering Riot Grrrls, they use dolls to dismantle the very hegemonic ideals dolls embody. "[W]e're going about this in our own version of 'doll' style," JBA continued, "[w]e like dressing up for shows—[as dolls and] often in clothes we've made ourselves [...we are] getting the Doll Fight! message out in a cheeky, sometimes childish fashion. Revolution through all kinds of playing!" (Dollfight! 2013).

Ultimately, following in the tradition of early Riot Grrrl agents, contemporary girls across the globe continue to play with dolls and toys with their inscribed meanings, by turning them on their heads—or even ripping them off. For bands such as Doll Fight!, artists such as Garside, and other likeminded Riot Grrrls, reclaiming and reappropriating the doll figure is an empowering act of self-made deconstruction that facilitates a refashioning of alternative identities. Rather than play the part of the "ideal" feminine doll, these riotous girls continue to play with the iconic plaything and cobble together something new and completely their own. To this day, Riot Grrrls continue to live by the anthem, sung by Doll Fight!, "[w]e're the dolls, we're human, we're DIY, we're flawed, and we're beautiful exactly how we are" (DollFight!, 2011).

CONCLUSIONS

By the early 1990s, the Riot Grrrl movement had erupted in the American and British music scenes and precipitated a watershed moment in the history of girls' cultural production and political intervention. Armed with disheveled hair, ripped baby-doll dresses, and a fistful of angry lyrics, this cadre of young women and girls in their teens created an international community of empowered artists. Through their angry art and charged music, Riot Grrrls sought to challenge their patriarchal societies, which dismissed young females as passive, unproductive, and frivolous dolls.

At the turn of the twentieth century, pioneering psychologists G. Stanley Hall and Alexander C. Ellis (1897) seminally proposed that ideal ladylikeness was best embodied by the figure of the doll: a beautiful, silent, and inactive object. Playing upon these biased stereotypes, Riot Grrrls reclaimed and reused dolls as a way to dismantle longstanding notions about "proper" femininity. Reacting against Hall and Ellis's theory that doll-play taught girls how to become domesticated ladies, musicians Courtney Love, Kat Bjelland, and KatieJane Garside deliberately turned themselves into nightmarish dolls. By fashioning themselves as broken marionettes, soiled Kewpie dolls, and ravaged Barbie lookalikes, these outspoken singers re-appropriated the doll as a symbol of feminist resistance. Moreover, their reinvention of doll-play, as well as the insistent dollification of their bodies, revolutionized how young female artists presented themselves within a pervasively male-centric music industry. In fact, Love's, Bjelland's, and Garside's dollification became such a powerful tool for feminist reclaiming that it outlived the fleeting Riot Grrrl movement; although the movement faded away by the late-1990s, these Riot Grrrls' doll-play lives on today. Across the world, all-girl bands such as Doll Fight! and Headless Doll Whores continue to rework the iconic figure of the doll, teasing its flexible meanings, expanding its pliable image, and imbuing it with newly crafted feminine identities. Like their predecessors, each contemporary band conducts their dollification with a unique voice. However, their ongoing play with dolls keeps alive the creative spirit of a transnational community of feminist bricoleurs and subversive doll-players who first ignited the Riot Grrrl movement.

NOTES

1. In this work, Higgonet noted that, "groups like Hole, Bikini Kill, and Babes in Toyland have all identified their music with juxtapositions between photographs of abused dolls, photographs of themselves as children, and very tough photographs of themselves as adults."
2. Hebdige noted that in 1976 cultural theorist John Clarke seminally described the bricoleur as a transformative agent that adapts an established tenet to his/hers particular subculture. Thus

[w]hen the bricoleur re-locates a significant object in a different position within that discourse, using the same overall repertoire of signs, or when that object is placed within a different total ensemble, a new discourse is constituted, a different message conveyed. (p. 104)

3. For works that focus on American Riot Grrrls, see: Gottlieb and Wald (1994); Kearney (2010).

4. Title of Doll Fight!'s 2011 MP3, *Revolution Doll Style Now*.

5. Love, for example, was at times at odds with the Riot Grrrl movement. In particular, she criticized other Riot Grrrl bands for sacrificing musical quality for their political agenda and message. Bjelland never officially characterized her band, Babes in Toyland, as a "Riot Grrrl Band," even though they have been identified by other Riot Grrrl bands and fans as influential within the movement, especially at its birth.

6. Love and Bjelland have a colorful personal history together as friends/enemies. They began as bandmates in Sugar Babyboll (1984) and, very briefly, in Babes in Toyland (1987). Their relationship, however, was subsequently marked by volatile collaborations, public fall-outs, lyric stealing, revenge songs against each other, and contested counterclaims over who first started the Kinderwhore trend.

7. Bjelland (1990).

8. For example, in Hole's 1991 song "Good Sister/Bad Sister," Love proclaims to "be the biggest dick that you ever had."

9. Lyrics from Hole's "Doll Parts" (Love, 1993).

10. Lyrics from Huggy Bear's "Her Jazz" (Huggy Bear, 1993).

11. Also see: Downes (2012).

12. KatieJane Garside, as cited in Hare (2011).

13. Hall and Ellis (1897) argued that "many children learn how to sew, knit, and do millinery work, observe and design costumes, [and] acquire taste in color," due to their desire to learn how to construct and costume homemade dolls (p. 53).

14. In fact, from the 1890s until the late 1910s, the Chicago publishing house A. Flanagan Company released a series of guidebooks teaching children how to productively engage in manual work during their leisure time. The "How To" books sported titles such as *How to Teach Paper-Folding, with Scissors and Paste*, and *Busy Hands Construction Work*.

15. On their VK page, the European version of Facebook, the band lists their birthday as August 27, 2012. Further, self-identified as a "sound collage" ensemble that samples and remixes jazz tunes from Soviet composers, the band allegedly recorded their first and only nine-song album, Incredible Adventures of Dolls Whores, in three short days. Each track is intermingled with ghostly snippets of musical instruments and voice-overs: the clinking of busy speakeasies, the static noise of crowded city streets.

16. Further, Headless Doll Whores ascribes a doll-identity for each one of her tracks: Christina, Agatha, Carina, Sasha, Paulina, and Veronica. According to the group's VK profile, each track is also accompanied by doll images: a black-and-white doll hung from a tree; two mannequins dressed in 1940s attire; or a grainy film-still of three dolls limply reunited around a table set for tea.

REFERENCES

Attwood, F. (2007). Sluts and riot Grrrls: Female identity and sexual agency. *Journal of Gender Studies*, *16*(3), 233–247.

Bayer, S. (Director). (1994). Doll parts [Music video]. Santa Monica, CA: DGC Records.

Bjelland, K. (1990). Lashes [Recorded by Babes in Toyland]. On *Spanking machine* [CD]. Minneapolis, MN: Twin/Tone Records.

DeRossa, R. (2011, Spring). Doll fight! [Review of the CD *Morning again* by Doll Fight!] *Tom Tom Magazine, 6*, 52.

Dollfight! (2013). Retrieved from http://dollfight.com/

Doll Fight! (2011). *Revolution doll style now* [MP3 file]. Vermont: Doll Fight! Retrieved from http://dollfight.bandcamp.com/album/revolution-doll-style-now

Downes, J. (2012). The expansion of punk rock: Riot Grrrl challenges to gender power relations in British indie music subcultures. *Women's Studies: An Inter-Disciplinary Journal, 41*(3), 204–237.

Eileraas, K. (1997). Witches, bitches & fluids: Girl bands performing ugliness as resistance. *TDR, 41*(3), 122–139.

ElvisGun. (1992). *Daisy Chainsaw interview on Rapido* [Video file]. Retrieved from http://www.youtube.com/watch?v=ltEmQdaYqzk

Garside, K. (2013). dream dolls, genica-pussywillow & sleeplikewolves. Retrieved from http://katiejanegarside.com/shop.html

Gottlieb, S. (Writer). (2010, June 22). Courtney Love [Television series episode]. In D. Scoccimarro (Production Associate), *Behind the music*. New York, NY: VH1. Retrieved from http://www.vh1.com/video/shows/full-episodes/courtney-love/1642087/playlist.jhtml

Gottlieb, J., & Wald, G. (1994). Smells like teen spirit: Riot Grrrls, revolution and women in independent rock. In A. Ross & T. Rose (Eds.), *Microphone fiends: Youth music & youth culture* (pp. 250–275). New York, NY: Routledge.

Gray, C. S. (1994). Belittled and beaten down [Recorded by Daisy Chainsaw]. On *For they know not what they do* [CD]. London, England: One Little Indian.

Haenfler, R. (2010). *Goths, gamers, and Grrrls: Deviance and youth subcultures*. New York, NY: Oxford University Press.

Hall, G. S., & Ellis, A. C. (1897). *A study of dolls*. New York, NY: E. L. Kellogg & Co.

Hardy, J. [itsjuliahardy]. (2006). *Queen Adreena talk about their obsessive fans* [Video file]. Retrieved from http://www.youtube.com/watch?v=QQzgSVK8S2I

Hare, I. (2011, February 15). The scream of the butterfly: Katie Jane Garside [Blog post]. Retrieved from http://www.frostmagazine.com/2011/02/the-scream-of-the-butterfly-katie-jane-garside/

Hebdige, D. (1979). *Subculture: The meaning of style*. New York, NY: Routledge.

Higonnet, A. (1998). *Pictures of innocence: The history and crisis of ideal childhood*. New York, NY: Thames & Hudson.

Hudson, B. (1984). Femininity and adolescence. In A. McRobbie & M. Nava (Eds.), *Gender and generations* (pp. 31–53). London, England: Macmillan.

Huggy Bear. (1993). Her jazz. On *Her jazz EP* [7-inch vinyl single]. London, England: Wiiija.

Huggy Bear/The Frumpies. (1994, January). *Spin Magazine, 85.*

Joseph. (1992, August). Heavy rotation. *Spin Magazine, 22.*

Kearney, M. C. (2010). Riot Grrrl: It's not just music, it's not just punk. In M. Forman-Burnell & L. Paris (Eds.), *The girls' history and culture reader: The 20th century* (pp. 300–316). Urbana, IL: University of Illinois Press.

Kidsoncrux. (2012, May). What is Kinderwhore? [Blog post]. Retrieved from http://www.kidsoncrux.com/2012/05/what-is-kinderwhore.html

Lobasso, R. (2009, Spring). Ruby Throat. *Origivation Magazine, 22.*

Love, C. (1993). Doll parts [Recorded by Hole]. On *Live through this* [CD]. Santa Monica, CA: DGC Records.

Love, C., & Erlandson, E. (1990). Burn black [Recorded by Hole]. On *Dicknail* [Single]. Seattle, WA: Sub Pop.

Love, C. Erlandson, E., Emery, J., & Rue, C. (1991a). Babydoll [Recorded by Hole]. On *Pretty on the inside* [CD]. London, England; New York, NY: Caroline.

Love, C. Erlandson, E., Emery, J., & Rue, C. (1991b). Good sister/bad sister [Recorded by Hole]. On *Pretty on the inside* [CD]. London, England; New York, NY: Caroline.

Mandrona, A. R. (2012, Summer). Homemade identities: Girls, dolls and DIY. *Girlhood Studies, 5*(1), 98–120.

Merish, L. (1996). Cuteness and commodity aesthetics: Tom Thumb and Shirley Temple. In R. G. Thomson (Ed.), *Freakery: Cultural spectacles of the extraordinary body* (pp. 185–203). New York, NY: New York University Press.

Muller, S. (Director). (1994). Miss World [Music video]. Santa Monica, CA: DGC Records.

O'Brien, L. (2002). *She bop II: The definitive history of women in rock, pop, and soul*. London, England: Continuum.

Raphael, A. (1996). *Grrrls: Viva rock divas*. London, England: St. Martin's Griffin.

Roberts, R. (1996). *Ladies first: Women in music videos*. Jackson, MS: University Press of Mississippi.

Seligar, M., & Woodward, F. (Directors). (1994). Violet [Music video]. Santa Monica, CA: DGC Records.

Strong, M. C. (2003). Daisy Chainsaw. In M. C. Strong (Ed.), *The great indie discography* (p. 45). London, England: Canongate Books.

Toazted. (2005). *Queenadreena Katie interview with Jane Garside by Toazted* [Video file]. Retrieved from http://www.youtube.com/watch?v=qOPDPTagcNM

Vaz, K. M. (2013). *The "baby dolls": Breaking the race and gender barriers of the New Orleans Mardi Gras tradition*. Baton Rouge, LA: Louisiana State University Press.

Wald, G. (1998). Just a girl? Rock music, feminism, and the cultural construction of female youth. *Signs, 23*(3), 585–610.

Women on the verge: An introduction to Punk, *Kinderwhore*, and heroin chic [Blog post]. (2011, February 23). Retrieved from http://fashiontheory.umwblogs.org/2011/02/23/women-on-the-verge-an-introduction-to-punk-kinderwhore-and-heroin-chic/

"It's Barbie, Bitch": Re-reading THE Doll Through Nicki Minaj AND Harajuku Barbie

JENNIFER DAWN WHITNEY

"I had only one desire: to dismember it. To see of what it was made, to discover the dearness, to find the beauty, the desirability that had escaped me, but apparently only me. Adults, older girls, shops, magazines, newspapers, window signs—all the world had agreed that a blue-eyed, yellow-haired, pink-skinned doll was what every girl child treasured."
—TONI MORRISON, *THE BLUEST EYE*

Wide-eyed and voluptuous, hip-hop sensation Nicki Minaj poses on the cover of her 2010 debut studio album, *Pink Friday*.[1] Sporting a super-sleek pink wig, hot pink lipstick, shiny pink lace-up platform boots, and a shimmering corseted dress winged in tulle, the songstress sits propped up, pouting for the camera. Showcased by a bubblegum pink backdrop, Minaj is surrounded by an overabundance of visual cues signaling a girlishly sexy femininity. To accentuate this indulgent spectacle, the photograph has been noticeably altered. Minaj's legs are elongated into caricature, her arms erased in their entirety. The latest princess of hip hop gazes out at her fans as a hyperfeminine and hyperreal representation of a dismembered black Barbie doll.[2]

With promotion from her record label, Young Money Entertainment, Minaj extends this image beyond photoshoots and album covers. Through visual and lyrical allusion, playful appropriation, and ostentatious posturing, the rapper's public persona is constructed in conversation with the Barbie doll. This chapter interrogates the assembly of Minaj's Barbie-doll-like celebrity persona, engaging with the tropes of black femininity in mainstream media and hip-hop cultures, and reads Minaj's celebrity in terms of the themes therein. Further, by investigating Minaj's appropriation of Barbie alongside the doll's racial, economic, and historical underpinnings, this chapter examines whether the emcee troublingly erases the hegemonic narratives that surround the plastic doll, or whether such a performance also leaves room for liberatory, pluralistic, and feminist interpretations. Considering Minaj's album cover, might we be able to read her performance as a dismantling or a dis-arming of the Barbie doll's traditional signification of idealized white femininity?

"WHERE MY BAD BITCHES AT?": CONTEXTUALIZING THE FAME OF NICKI MINAJ

Nicki Minaj's presence in hip hop is exceptional. Women emcees have been involved in the scene since its start, but garnering the same level of commercial success as their male counterparts continues to be elusive. *BitchMedia* blogger Alyx Vesey (2010) elucidated the difficulties women continue to face in the industry. She contended that Minaj's contemporaries, "like Lil Mama, Estelle, Ke$ha, and Kid Sister get some recognition, but not on the level that kingpins Jay-Z, Kanye West, T.I., and Lil Wayne receive" (para. 9). She went on to posit that women who were once hip-hop superstars no longer sell records: "Older female rappers have either become less culturally relevant, like Missy Elliott, or have branched into a variety of creative and merchandising opportunities outside of hip hop, as Queen Latifah has done" (para. 9). When women artists do acquire mainstream recognition, as Latoya Peterson (2010) detailed for the website *Jezebel*, their, "shelf life [in the] limelight is less than two years" (para. 1). In contrast, male performers such as Snoop Dogg continue to tour and release albums on major labels 20 years into their careers.[3] In such a climate of inequality, it is no wonder that when *Pink Friday* went platinum in 2011, it had been preceded by an 8-year drought for women in the business.[4] Considering this history, the rapper's response to her mainstream triumph was understandably exuberant. At the news that *Pink Friday*'s sales had surpassed Kanye West's *My Dark Beautiful Twisted Fantasy*, Minaj exclaimed, "Girl Power! I deserve it this time" (Goddessjaz, 2011, para. 3). Rather than demonstrating the evolution of the industry, however, *Pink Friday*'s critical and commercial success signals that Minaj is a hip-hop aberration. The artist's triumphs call attention to a dearth of highly influential women in the industry, and the misogyny that informs it.

Misogyny in hip hop is a driving force behind many rappers' mainstream success, and is typically emphasized by traditional media outlets. Headlines that sensationalize a small fraction of hip-hop culture, with themes of obscenity, objectification, homophobia, and gendered violence incite controversy and curiosity.[5]

Rappers who court this controversy gain the most fame and commercial success. Conversely, the potential for progressive lyrics and celebrity personas that promote diversity and feminist themes are diminished and dispelled when the genre is co-opted by white mainstream culture. In the documentary film, *Cultural Criticism and Transformation*, bell hooks (1997) contended with this phenomenon. She argued that:

> Rap music is so diverse in its themes, its style, its content, but when it becomes a vehicle to be talked about in mainstream news, the rap that gets in national news is always the rap music that perpetuates misogyny, that is most obscene in its lyrics, and then this comes to stand for what rap is.

The music featured on MTV, popular entertainment websites, and mainstream radio, fits this bill. Crucially, it is this tradition—which is, in itself, the product of institutionalized racism—that begins to explain why there are so few women in major positions of stardom in the world of hip hop. Moreover, misogyny in the hip-hop scene is indicative of how and why commercially successful women rappers market their images and music to consumers in very specific ways.

In order to be successful, black women rappers often must follow a very limited cultural script in the construction of their hip-hop personas. Tricia Rose (2008) contended that the rappers who have met the "commercial demands" of the industry have had to rely "on the product reserved especially for black women: sexual excess" (p. 124). Indeed, exploiting one's (hyper)sexuality through performance is a ubiquitous practice for black women in the medium. Kelis, whose breasts "bring all the boys to the yard" (Williams & Hugo, 2003); Beyoncé (by way of Destiny's Child), whose backside is particularly "bootylicious" (Knowles, Rowland, Fusari, & Moore, 2001); and Lil' Kim, whose "pussy…can break up happy homes" (Jones, 2011), are all chart-toppers who demonstrate the popularity and profitability of sexually explicit lyrics in the world of hip hop. Minaj's performance of celebrity also exhibits the signs of this type of overt sexual expression, and illustrates how it is not confined to the lyrical. Along with these contemporary artists, Minaj asserts her sexuality in song, boasting in "Lollipop" that she has "the fattest pussy in the business" (Carter, Garrett, Harrison, Maraj, Scheffer, & Zamor, 2008). Her frequent "twerking" style of dance, and her uninhibited style of dress both prove that the star brings her sexuality to the fore in her stage and video performances and public appearances.

Sex certainly sells. However, as Rose (2008) suggested, how black women in hip hop are labeled and choose to self-brand is complicated by a broader scope of Western cultural discourses. Not limited to the world of hip hop, black feminine bodies in the West have, for centuries, been equated with sexual spectacle and excess. Of significant influence to the discourse of racial and gendered othering in the West is the narrative construction of Sarah (Saartjie) Bartmann. Though most of Bartmann's biography is uncertain, it is known that she was a woman from the southern region of Africa, who, when brought to Europe in 1810, became "a theatre attraction" known as the Hottentot Venus (Fausto-Sterling, 2002, p. 80). Over the course of five years, her body was the subject of oddity exhibitions, where she was visually and physically examined for both scientific and entertainment purposes. Bartmann's body became emblematic of a racial, gendered, and sexual other, due, in part, to what was constructed to be her "steatopygous backside" (p. 78). The result of such exhibitions, Ann Fausto-Sterling explained, was that African women were "linked [to] the notion of the wild or savage female," which was, in turn, connected with ideas of a "dangerous or uncontrollable sexuality" (p. 78). It is from this model that contemporary black women are still often perceived and represented in mainstream Western culture. Indeed, Zenzile (2010), a writer for the lifestyle blog *LoveJonesLifestyle,* described Minaj's appearance on a morning television program this way: Minaj was "transformed from artist into modern day Hottentot Venus" (para. 1).

Drawing upon longstanding cultural tropes, the rapper has been the focus of incessant media speculation regarding whether or not she has undergone cosmetic surgery for "butt implants" (*Huffington Post,* 2012). Dubious before and after photographs asserting the "proof" of such cosmetic surgery are in circulation online. Further, when Minaj visited the aforementioned American morning television program, *Live with Regis and Kelly,* in 2010, her body and sexuality became the focus of the interview. Zenzile (2010) recalled Minaj's guest appearance in this way:

> While Regis examines the construction of Nicki's dress, a veiled lead into his groping/slapping/grasping of her posterior, Kelly...leads into a discussion of Nicki's waist measurements. In its entirety, Nicki became a museum[-]like display of physical wonder. [In this context], [s]he is no longer an artist, emcee, singer or performer, but a body. (para. 2)

Regis's voyeurism and groping, and Kelly's evaluative inquiries work in conjunction with the general tone of the public interest surrounding Minaj's figure. The emphasis on the rapper's backside is no coincidence, but instead is informed by a confluence of gender and racial stereotypes.

While engaging with the rules of commercial success for black women in hip hop, Minaj has expressed ambivalence. She is frustrated by the way black feminine embodiment is constructed in hip hop and popular cultures in the West. "The female rappers of my day spoke about sex a lot...and I thought that to have the success they got, I would have to represent the same thing." Yet over time, Minaj "made a conscious decision to try to tone down the sexiness" (Vibe Magazine, 2010, para. 3). In a profile piece with *Out*magazine, Caryn Ganz (2010) wrote that the rapper has responded to the racist and sexist demands of the industry "by playing to her female fans" (p. 1). She "started making it [her] business to say things that would empower women, such as, 'Where my bad bitches at?' to let them know, 'I'm here for you'" (p. 1). She extends this approach further on the track "I'm the Best" (Maraj and Johnson, 2010)from *Pink Friday*. Here, she raps, "I'm fighting for the girls that never thought they could win." These examples convey Minaj's alignment with a philosophy of racial and gender solidarity, which seems to have arisen from her personal experiences, and the wider problems black women face, within the hip-hop industry and the mainstream media. As such, Minaj is refusing to be complacent. Her alternative is to present herself as a positive role model for girls and young women. With her traction as a trendsetter, this ambition is a compelling one. Her decision to take on these norms by way of Barbie makes her approach all the more provocative.

SOME ASSEMBLY REQUIRED: THE CONSTRUCTION OF HARAJUKU BARBIE

Minaj's negotiation of her role as a woman in hip hop comes to the fore through the construction of a prominent alter ego. Described as "imaginative" and "fun," she is the *Pink Friday* image come to life in the form of a "coquettish girly girl-fashionista" ("The Harajuku Barbie," 2012). Manifesting in all aspects of the artist's public performance of her celebrity, this Barbie-doll-like character announces her presence accessorized with multi-colored wigs, pink lipstick, a cute and fantastical wardrobe, and whimsically affected voices. Minaj takes her persona beyond allusion, when, in publicity photos, she boldly flashes a sparkly necklace with the word "Barbie" appearing in its familiar cursive script. Explaining the motivation behind co-opting the appearance of this cultural phenomenon of idealized white femininity, she stated simply that, "all girls are Barbies." "We all want to play dress-up" as well as be "icons and moguls" ("Nicki Minaj Explains 'Harajuku Barbie,'" 2009). With this assertion, Minaj identifies Barbie as a figure of accessible aspiration.

The rapper mediates the aspirational language of becoming Barbie into her public persona by combining the doll's signatory characteristics with another set of cultural markers. Harajuku Barbie—the official title for Minaj's alter ego—makes reference to Tokyo street culture. Minaj claims that she named her Barbie character after the subculture of Harajuku because of her appreciation for its "free-spirited, girls just wanna have fun, kick ass" attitude (HipHopStan.com, 2009). Based upon Minaj's description, it seems that the rapper's (cursory) understanding of the tenets of Harajuku already align with many of the signifiers that make Barbie, Barbie. Perhaps what appeals to Minaj, then, is her interpretation of Harajuku as a slightly tougher, more "kick ass" approach to femininity. Or, perhaps incorporating Harajuku into the artist's Barbie performance provides her with a more flexible understanding of what Barbie means. Redefining the doll with the grammatical modifier of Harajuku specifies that Minaj's performance of Barbie is racially specific. Unlike the original and most recognizable Barbie doll, Harajuku is not white or even normatively Western. As such, while claiming many of the conventions of Barbie—the glamour, high fashion, and fun—Minaj takes the narrative that becoming Barbie is an aspirational practice reserved for white women and girls and turns it on its blonde head.[6]

While Harajuku Barbie appears as a vibrant and inventive force on the popular culture stage, taking cues from both mainstream Western iconography and Japanese street culture, her creation also owes much to a tradition of women in hip hop. Despite her wariness in terms of her musical predecessors' expressions of sexuality, Minaj's persona is in direct conversation with the well-established, and potentially subversive, models of black femininity therein. These models, which have contested and negotiated the representational and commercial disenfranchisement of women in the genre, have paved the way for Minaj, both in her stardom and in her performance of her alter ego.

In "Empowering Self, Making Choices, Creating Spaces: Black Female Identity Via Rap Music Performance," ethnomusicologist Cheryl L. Keyes (2004) explained how black women rappers' celebrity can be defined by way of four distinctive identities. She identified these as "Queen Mother," "Fly Girl," "Sista with Attitude," and "Lesbian" (p. 306). Emcees who are inclined toward the "Queen Mother" role "view themselves as African-centered icons" (p. 306). "Fly Girls," she explained, are women who dress "in chic clothing and fashionable hairstyles, jewelry and cosmetics" (p. 309). Keyes qualified the "Sista with Attitude" as rappers who "value attitude as a means of empowerment" (p. 312). The final category of "Lesbian," Keyes explained, is for women rappers who are out both lyrically and publicly. Like many women in the industry, Minaj's hip-hop celebrity construction, and her alter ego of Harajuku Barbie, can be understood to alternate and embody many qualities from all but the "Queen Mother" role.

The importance of these categories as attempts to undermine the traditional trope of the black woman in hip hop, and Minaj's involvement with them as Harajuku Barbie, cannot be overstated. At first glance, the "Fly Girl" may seem superficial, but her performance might also be read as "'flippin da script' (deconstructing dominant ideology)" (Keyes, 2004, p. 310). By wearing "clothes that accent" parts of the anatomy "considered beauty markers of Black women by Black culture," the "Fly Girl" celebrates "aspects of Black women's bodies considered undesirable," unattractive, or excessive by mainstream Western culture (p. 310). Considering the "Fly Girl" alongside Harajuku Barbie's fashionista status suggests that her engagement with elaborate and flamboyant fashion choices is an act of resistance. The "Sista" can be read as empowering black women through confidence and self-expression. The "attitude" of many "Sistas" is punctuated with the word "bitch" as a way to "subvert patriarchal rule" (p. 312). Minaj's lyrics, and overall attitude, indicate a provocative swagger in line with the "Sista." In fact, as Harajuku Barbie, she often ends phone calls with an enthusiastic "It's Barbie, *bitch!*" (Ganz, 2010,p. 2).

Finally, the "Lesbian" subverts narratives that write black women in hip hop as sexual objects—instead reclaiming desire through this identity. Minaj/Harajuku Barbie's relationship to the role of "Lesbian" is contested, at best. Minaj embraces feminine desire, to be sure, but she seems to capriciously shift into and out of a queer or bicurious identity as she shifts alter egos.[7] Reading Harajuku Barbie in terms of these roles situates her performance within a framework that has been contending with the race, gender, and sexual politics of hip hop since its earliest days. Crucially, this conversation equips Minaj with the tools necessary to challenge the racist and misogynistic structure of the industry, while withstanding attacks from critics as well.

Despite Harajuku Barbie's layered construction, popular feminist critics are quick to denounce the spirited enthusiasm of Minaj and her alter ego as a misdirected attempt at feminism-lite. When Minaj performed alongside Mariah Carey in a remixed rendition of the song "Up Out My Face" (Carey, Nash, & Stewart, 2010), both appearing as Barbie dolls in the video, such criticism was acute (Vesey, 2010). However, Minaj is always ready to defend Harajuku Barbie. "It's interesting that people have more negative things to say about me saying 'I'm Barbie' than me saying 'I'm a bad bitch.'" Elaborating further, Minaj explained, "So you can call yourself a female dog because that's cool in our community. But if you call yourself a Barbie, that's fake" (Ganz, 2010). With this articulation, Minaj reveals hypocrisy at work in many of the criticisms about her performance, as well as the contradictions that lie uninterrogated in the industry.

Consolidating and reclaiming both of these terms, as Minaj does in "It's Barbie, *bitch!*" undermines their power as epithets of abuse. This style of appropriation, made popular by the "Sista with Attitude," builds upon Minaj's reputation as Harajuku Barbie, especially with her fans. Indeed, keen followers happily brandish the Barbie moniker, inspired by the star to interpret Barbie style in new and inventive ways. Significantly, these fans have even organized a "Barbie Movement." With it, online communities document both Minaj's doll-like persona as well as that of her fans. Fan-created blogs display discussions about beauty and fashion, and provide helpful tips to achieve the Harajuku Barbie aesthetic, while an endless stream of inspirational images of Minaj circulate.[8] MyPinkFriday.com, the rapper's official website, also hosts forums where fans can communicate. In a thread offering support and friendship, one fan expresses her enthusiasm in being a "diva" (2011). Conversely, another bemoans being called "fake" (2011). Like Minaj, these fans—oftentimes girls and young women of color—seem to be constructing their own interpretations of Barbie. Collectively referring to themselves as the Barbz, their identification offers a sharp and pointed corruption of Barbie.

"BITCH, YOU AIN'T NO BARBIE": RACE, AUTHENTICITY, AND THE COMMODIFICATION OF DIFFERENCE

Vesey (2010) pondered whether "the aspiration [to imitate Barbie by way of Minaj] results from some black girls wanting to find dolls with whom they can identify" (para. 4). This question offers insight into the scarcity of convincingly diverse Barbie doll options. Significantly, analyses of Barbie and race often suggest that while Barbie dolls do come in many different colors, there remains one, iconic Barbie. As Mary Rogers (1999), author of the critical reader *Barbie Culture*, posited through a reading of feminist and queer theorist Erica Rand, media and visual texts that contain representations of Barbie "convey the message *not* that any girl can be like Barbie, but that *any* girl can be like Barbie's friend" (p. 56). Regardless of whether Mattel has created black dolls that bear the name Barbie, in these advertisements and visual narratives, the real and true Barbie is always white—with an assortment of diverse friends. Thus, when Rogers wrote that, "Barbie is an icon whose 'perfect' body is more attainable than ever before" (p. 122), what is implied here is that her body is more attainable for young, affluent, white women. Considering this, what then happens if girls and women of color decide that they, too, will appropriate attributes of the Barbie doll?

In the case of Harajuku Barbie, there is an inevitable cultural backlash. One example, worth exploring further here, involves recent white pop/rap phenomenon and internet it-girl, Kreayshawn. In her self-produced track, "Gucci Gucci" (Negrete, Weiner, & Zolot, 2011), she spits the lyrics "Bitch, you ain't no Barbie," purportedly accusing Minaj and her fans of failing to achieve doll-like perfection. When asked to address this for Complex.com (Ahmed, 2011), Kreayshawn justified her lyrics.

> Honestly man, this is no disrespect to [Minaj] because she's got talent. She's got an image. But when it comes to inspiring young women, her message is to be a Barbie—to be plastic, to be fake, to all have blonde hair. (p. 4)

Kreayshawn condemned Minaj for a lack of authenticity, but she, too, could be accused of an inauthentic persona. A member of the controversially named White Girl Mob, Kreayshawn seems to be appropriating an ethicized stage name in order to connect with a hip-hop audience. Considering this, perhaps such accusations are not simply acrimonious, but reside within a larger context.

Feuding in hip hop has a long and notorious history. Popular culture blogger, Goddessjaz (2011), explained that, "Public 'beef' is a hugely powerful promotional tool and can make or break careers" (para. 5). Indeed, while Kreayshawn may have provoked a rivalry with Minaj, the latter was already embroiled in another feud, with Lil' Kim.[9] Critics have much to say about this tradition, especially when a feud occurs between women. Goddessjaz (2011) pointedly queried: "But what does it mean when the few women on the mainstream scene are bickering?" (para. 5). The races of those feuding invoke further questions. Would Kreayshawn have thought it necessary to criticize Minaj's Barbie-doll-like qualities—or, crucially, what she understands as a lack thereof—if Minaj were not a woman of color? Kreayshawn's comments exist within a tradition of feuding in hip hop, but they should not be read merely as part of the business. Such remarks are situated within a wider cultural narrative that repeatedly insists that black girls cannot be Barbie-doll-like. Further, this discourse troublingly implies that, like the black Barbie dolls to which they are equated, Minaj and her fans are simply counterfeit imitations of a blonde original.

The ubiquity of the original, white, Barbie doll, and the assumed inauthenticity of the black Barbie doll, deserves a closer look. In her book *Girls*, Catherine Driscoll (2002) asserted that, despite her clear and recognizable signification, "Barbie is never complete" (p. 98). While the doll is laden with the meaning imparted by five decades of creators and consumers alike, in her there is a certain blankness that enables interpretive versatility. It is from this ambiguous space that Barbie assumes the flexibility to occupy fantasies, uphold innumerable and conflicting representations of identity, and redefine the meaning she supposedly embodies. Rand (1995), in *Barbie's Queer Accessories*, reasoned that, "Mattel touts Barbie as a catalyst for fantasy and since the 1960s has deliberately refrained from circulating certain Barbie biographical details or narratives—such as age, a geographical location, or a wedding—that might foreclose fantasy options" (p. 8). Thus, while Barbie's signification may never be complete, she is not simply an empty signifier upon which meaning can be written. It is through Mattel's meticulous engineering and advertising ingenuity that Barbie's narrative persists as enigma. As such, this "incompleteness" is incorporated into her branded narrative.

Since Mattel holds specific information about Barbie strategically under wraps, this act of cloistering becomes inseparable from the very story that is cultivated to keep her contemporary—the primary objective of Mattel. Her body, hair, makeup, and fashion ensembles not only reflect the year she was manufactured, but they also work to maintain a superficial narrative that Rand (1995) described. In 1959 "Barbie [began] as a good girl." Now she represents "a paragon of feminism and diversity in their most widely palatable, and co-opted, forms" (p. 193). It is through a combination of attention to detail and subtlety that Barbie remains relevant to shifting ideas of femininity, yet is always narratively secure. The incompleteness that Driscoll described is a calculated feature that functions both to belie and reinforce the elasticity of Barbie's image. It is a well-crafted singular representation to which Barbie always returns, while appearing slightly rejuvenated each year that she re-emerges.

Ann duCille (1994) elaborated on this marketing strategy in her essay "Dyes and Dolls." She argued that Mattel's ventures maintain Barbie's originary white, able-bodied status, which is never in question despite the blankness (read: whiteness) attributed to her. Indeed, duCille stated that Mattel's proliferation of diverse representations of Barbie, including a plethora of racial and ethnic identities, work to perpetuate these "different" dolls precisely as other. Addressing dolls specifically racialized by Mattel as black, she argued that these Barbies are simply "dye-dipped versions of archetypal white American beauty" (p. 49). She explained that, "Regardless of what color the dolls are dipped in or what costumes they are adorned with, the image they present is of the same mythically thin, long-legged, luxuriously haired, buxom beauty" (p. 50). Speaking to the historical process of both manufacturing and naming these dolls, Rand (1995) elucidated this point. She recalled that, "In the 1960s, there were nonethnic Barbie and her sometimes ethnic friends" (p. 83). While today, "some 'ethnic' dolls now get the name *Barbie*, a 'nonethnic' Barbie still occupies center stage, and only she can do anything" (pp. 83–84). Rand specified that if "there can only be one" Barbie "she's white and blond" (p. 84). The variety of skin tones Mattel has created "are merely temporary costumes that Barbie puts on in certain situations, and importantly, that you can buy" (p. 84). Thus, both duCille and Rand contended that while Mattel has been creating and producing an array of visually "different" Barbie dolls, such production works to reinforce the discourse that there is only one "real" Barbie doll, and she is white.

Today, not all ethnic Barbies are dye-dipped versions of the original. Since the 1990s Mattel has been making head and face molds representative of the ethnicity each doll is designed to embody. Yet, the company's attempts to be progressively more diverse remain problematic at best. More recent designs by Mattel, such as the So-In-Style Barbie dolls released in the summer of 2009, again make an effort to encompass black identity. "Courtney, the cheerleader doll, has a fuller nose and fuller lips than regular Barbie. Trichelle, the doll 'into art and journalism,' has curly hair; Kara who loves math and music, has a 'darker' skin tone" (Stewart, 2009, para. 2).[10] Even with these latest versions of Barbie's black friends, however, the white, blonde, and busty Barbie continues to be enforced as the authentic, true and original doll, exemplifying the all-American norm to which all other dolls must measure up.

With the celebration of Barbie's 50th year in 2009, festivities in the world of celebrity—from runway shows, to magazine editorials—commemorated the original white doll's impact on popular culture. Richard Dyer (1997), in his book *White*, described how such occurrences work at normalizing whiteness and perpetuating racial hegemony. He explained that,

> As long as race is something only applied to non-white peoples, as long as white people are not racially seen and named, they/we function as a human norm. Other people

are raced, we are just people. …This assumption, that white people are just people, which is not far off [from] saying that whites are people whereas other colours are something else, is endemic to white culture. (pp. 1–2)

Thus, when, in a fictive interview with *Forbes* (Vander Broek, 2009), the original white Barbie proclaimed that, "I am a big believer in dreaming big and inspiring girls that they can do anything they set their minds to" it seemed like a contradiction; Barbie's ethnic doll counterparts are always a high-heeled step behind. As Mattel persists with Barbie's twenty-first-century image as progressive, feminist, and multicultural, so long as there is one Barbie to which all other Barbies must evoke, such attempts will continue to gloss over issues of whiteness as a non-race, and, in turn, sustain white as the norm to which Dyer (1997) attested.

In terms of manufacturing and marketing, Barbie resides in an awkward position, where Mattel withholds biographical information to encourage fantasy, while simultaneously producing an overflow of diverse fantasy representations. Such representations are dubious, as they may not be understood as representations of identity at all. Rather, race and ethnicity, while reflecting particularities of identities, are being marketed as accessories to the original. Further, as Mattel continues to manufacture ethnic-looking dolls alongside the original, white Barbie, additional questions emerge about racial authenticity. Critically, as duCille (1994) reflected:

The notion that fuller lips, broader noses, wider hips, and higher derrières somehow make the Shani dolls more realistically African American raises many difficult questions about authenticity, truth, and the ever-problematic categories of the real and the symbolic, the typical and the stereotypical. Just what are we saying when we claim that a doll does or does not "look black?" (p. 56)

In "Eating the Other," bell hooks (1992) took up these issues of the commerce of diversity and authenticity. She argued that while contemporary marketing may be promoted with a "postmodern slant" (p. 22) that appears to celebrate diversity and difference, such "commodification of Otherness" (p. 21) reveals a nostalgia for racial authenticity. She insisted that where representations of ethnic identities are introduced into the marketplace, there is a "resurgence of essentialist cultural nationalism [wherein, the] acknowledged Other must assume recognizable forms" (p. 26). According to hooks, these forms often take shape in the primitive. As such, dolls such as the Shani Barbie—which duCille (1994) described as exemplifying what Mattel envisions black dolls to be, complete with African print clothing and "higher derrières"—signal tropes of sexual excess, and limit black bodies in mass culture to the atavistic.[11]

Both duCille (1994) and hooks (1992) troubled the idea that identity is fixed, insisting that representations of race and ethnicity can no longer reside in something so essentialist. Minaj's Barbie-doll-like performance aligns with this analysis, yet attempts by Mattel to present an authentic racial accuracy—even when they created a Nicki Minaj Barbie Doll in 2011—cannot take account of shifting definitions of identities in culture. Instead, they work to uphold a culturally specific single moment in such identities. Mattel's approach prevents the possibility of fluidity of difference, and, as hooks argued, "difference is often fabricated in the interests of social control as well as of commodity innovation" (p. 25). She continued,

> The commodification of difference promotes paradigms of consumption wherein whatever difference the Other inhabits is eradicated *via* exchange by a consumer cannibalism that not only displaces the Other but denies the significance of that Other's history through a process of decontextualization. (p. 31)

Mattel has situated itself within a dilemma where, in its efforts to make the doll more diverse, accessible, and, therefore, more marketable, it has also become more locked into stereotypes and static representations. These, in turn, work to negatively heighten and reinforce difference in one sense, while decontextualizing it in another. Thus, Mattel's efforts to transform the doll into an ethnic body may be doing multiple disservices to the children for whom it is a play and fantasy object. Certainly, duCille's (1994) sentiment that "Barbie's body type constructs the bodies of other women as deviant" (p. 64) is not unorthodox, but this, alongside questions of race and ethnicity, further begs the questions: Can Mattel ever physically represent ethnic and racial identity in its dolls? And, if not, what does it mean that white Barbie is successful at embodying a certain blank signifier that proliferates the notion of whiteness as invisible and thus the norm?

These questions persist within a Western context, and, increasingly, they also take precedence within an ever-growing global consumerist culture. As Barbie's popularity continues to move outside of the West, her subsequent influence has extended to global popular culture. Susie Orbach (2009), on the subject of consumerism, succinctly argued in her popular book *Bodies* that: "Globalism brings uniformity to visual culture" (p. 88). Here, she speaks to the anxiety that idealized white femininity may have a universalizing effect on global identities. However, the issue of Barbie's influence should not be understood as simply universalizing. As Driscoll (2002) attested,

> It may be useful to argue that Barbie imposes undesirable models of femininity on girls, but it is also the dominant public discourse on girls who like to play Barbie. It is not radical to imply that Barbie enthusiasts are co-opted or stupid or to see Barbie as an ideological template, because these criticisms of girl culture are proper to positioning girls as definitively malleable gullible consumers. (p. 98)

While it is worthwhile to critique the production and marketing of Barbie, it would be a mistake to assume that consumers are limited to interactions with Barbie dolls based simply on appearance, or the incomplete fantasies Mattel manufactures. When Kreayshawn insisted that Minaj is perpetuating the message that "all" girls should "have blonde hair" (Ahmed, 2011) like Barbie, she reiterated the universalizing consequences of a singular Barbie doll fantasy.

PLAYTIME'S NOT OVER: THE POSSIBILITIES
OF HARAJUKU BARBIE

Harajuku Barbie and the Barbie Movement's relationship with, and co-optation of, the Barbie brand of femininity complicates traditional feminist readings of the doll and her far-reaching influence. Natasha Walter (2010), a feminist journalist, highlighted this perspective in her nonfiction work from 2010. *Living Dolls* offers a popular analysis of the contemporary culture of girls and young women in the West. In it, Walter worried: "It often seems that now the dolls are escaping from the toy shop and taking over girls' lives" (p. 2). Walter's concern is that many girls and young women have a desire to be doll-like, and that this can have a dangerous effect on their self-esteem and body image. Rather than adhering to this conceptualization of what it means to be doll-like, however, Minaj and her fans toy with it.

Critiques of Nicki Minaj imply that her Barbie-doll-like persona is most abhorrent in terms of being "plastic" and "fake." However, Minaj has decisively embraced these labels. Try as she might, Kreayshawn, for example, is not disrespecting Minaj, but re-articulating what the rapper has already made abundantly clear. Minaj fully indulges in the inauthenticity of her hyperreal Harajuku Barbie alter ego. She plays up its fabrication lyrically, aurally, and visually. Harajuku Barbie manifests in Minaj's songs, videos, and photoshoots, and Minaj seems to take pleasure in how technology is used to reshape and redefine the lengths she is physically willing to go to.

Significantly, Harajuku Barbie, though a prominent persona, is not Minaj's only one. She shifts between several others including Roman, Rosa, and Martha. Each of these personalities materializes in interviews, or while Minaj is rapping, and can be detected as she changes accent and body language to accommodate the character. What is also noteworthy here is that Minaj's biography is inconsistent, at best. While her lyrics sometimes suggest bicuriosity, Minaj insists in interviews that she does not date women, or men (Ganz, 2010, p. 2). There have also been discrepancies involving her age as well as her upbringing. And, most befittingly, Minaj's legal surname is Maraj (recalling mirage).[12] There is so much evidence to support Kreayshawn's claim that Minaj is "fake" (Ahmed, 2011) that instead of it being an accusation, it is simply a statement of the obvious. Considering this, like Vesey (2010), I too am "inclined to read this stylistic choice as an indication of the fragmented nature of female identities" (para. 11).

Rather than attempting to uncover a sort of "true" or "real" feminine identity, Minaj's multiple and fragmented self-interpretation, by way of Harajuku Barbie, offers keen insight into an alternative understanding. Minaj's brand of Barbie-doll-like femininity both imitates and exaggerates the signification of the iconic doll, going beyond straightforward identification. Her gendered personas, pastiched performances, and hyperbolic revelry can be situated within a framework of poststructural and postmodern feminism, touched upon in the quotations by duCille (1994) and hooks (1992) above. In this tradition, the idea of an authentic and cohesive feminine identity is called into question. This logic is echoed throughout French feminisms of the twentieth century, where, most vocally, Simone de Beauvoir (1997) asserted that, "One is not born, but rather, becomes a woman" (p. 295). Such ideas about the fluid nature of gender have resonated with contemporary feminist philosophers, especially Judith Butler. Butler (1999), in her influential research, insisted that all gendered bodies are referential, or an "imitation without an origin"(p. 175). These analyses, while building upon each other, have extended feminist debate by suggesting that there is no essential femininity. It is through this lens that a critical analysis of what is "fake" and what is "real" in terms of a Barbie-doll-like femininity can take shape.

Clearly influenced by Butler, Kath Albury (2002) in *Yes Means Yes* develops her own ideas about femininity in new and exciting directions. In her analysis of what she calls "female female-impersonators" (p. 86), she observed the cliché that "The ideal Western woman is pretty, witty, charming, sexy and blonde" (p. 86). While this assertion should come as no surprise, she suggested that female female-impersonators seek to disrupt this ideal through an exaggerated or distorted presentation of overtly feminine markers. When these women take up these "parodic roles," she explains, "they rub their audiences' noses in the messy fake that lies beneath the accepted myth of 'natural' femininity" (p. 86). Edith Zimmerman (2010) wrote for the feminist blog, *The Hairpin*, that, "somewhere along the line [Minaj] clearly stopped caring whether or not she sounds 'pretty'" (para. 5). Delighting in the vocally strange, while simultaneously exemplifying an overabundance of traditionally feminine markers, Minaj, as Harajuku Barbie, destabilizes the conventions of traditional femininity that align with these female female-impersonators. Moreover, as a pastiched and fragmented alter ego that takes on questions of race, Harajuku Barbie not only reflects a gendered, racialized, and sexualized configuration that deconstructs white femininity as the Western ideal, but also denaturalizes narratives of sexual excess written onto black femininity in Western culture.

Taking the idea of hyperfeminine exaggeration into consideration as a site that is especially productive, Kim Toffoletti (2007), in her critical work, *Cyborgs and Barbie Dolls*, contended that Barbie, and the feminine bodies that inform, and are informed by, the doll, offer a textured interpretation of feminine subjectivity. It is her contention that Barbie is "an in-between phenomenon constantly circulating in the ambivalent space between the image and its referent, between illusion and the real" (p. 58). As such, both plastic and flesh-and-blood Barbies/Barbz call "established categories into question" (p. 58). In this way, there is a transgressive engagement with feminine subjectivity, which enables the subject to be perceived as transformative. Toffoletti contended that, "Figurations such as Barbie, function to encourage alternative understandings of the body and self as transformative, rather than bound to an established system of meaning" (p. 59). Barbie, and those who appropriate her, offer the "potential for identity to be mutable and unfixed" (p. 59). The potential of Barbie's plastic body for "real" women, is that it calls the very notion of "real" into question.

Arguments against Minaj's Barbie-doll-like femininity, especially those that interrogate her authenticity, reinforce an essentialist paradigm. The undercurrent is that femininity is static, and ought to follow specific, well-prescribed rules. Such articulations insist that there is a natural, or more "true" state of femininity. Minaj liberates this convention with her persona of Harajuku Barbie, offering a thoroughly postmodern reading of multiple constructions of femininity in the West. Minaj's performance takes pleasure in the fragmentation and hyperbole of postmodern culture, as is envisioned through her stretched and broken limbs on the cover of *Pink Friday*. She takes on the serious task of deconstructing idealized white femininity, while offering a critical assessment of excess endemic to consumer-based hip-hop and celebrity cultures. Further, with Harajuku Barbie, Minaj puts forth a playful alternative to the static black Barbie doll representations imagined by Mattel. While the traditional Barbie doll assumes a model of aspiration to a specific Western demographic, Minaj mischievously subverts the standard. The Barbie doll is refracted by Minaj's performance into an ever-changing plethora of behaviors and possibilities. In this sense, what is "fake" and "plastic" about Minaj, and what is "fake" and "plastic" about Barbie, become their greatest attributes.

NOTES

1. The album cover art is available on Minaj's official website: www.mypinkfriday.com
2. Minaj is Trinidad-born and of mixed-race ancestry. She has self-identified as black in interviews and song lyrics. In popular media, she is repeatedly labeled "Black Barbie."
3. In 2012 Snoop Dogg changed his stage name to Snoop Lion, but he is still recognized as the former as well.

4. Lil' Kim previously achieved this accolade in 2003, with her album *La Bella Mafia*.
5. See: Guillermo Rebolla-Gil and Amanda Moras (2012), "Black Women and Black Men in Hip Hop Music: Misogyny, Violence and the Negotiation of (White-Owned) Space."
6. Convincing arguments have been established that the rapper is perpetuating Orientalism with her appropriation of Harajuku (Jenn, 2010; Vesey, 2010).
7. In "Go Hard" (Maraj & Carter, 2009), Minaj raps, "I only stop for pedestrians or a real, real bad lesbian." Many other lyrics, full of similar posturing, suggest that her (fictional?) sexual conquests are often women. Troublingly, however, her verses are also peppered with the heterosexist shorthand "no homo" (Ganz, 2010, p. 3).
8. Such fansites include: http://beeleedatbitch.yolasite.com/, http://www.facebook.com/nickiminaj (Minaj's official Facebook page), http://fuckyeahharajukubarbie.tumblr.com/, and http://ifuckinlovenickiminaj.tumblr.com/
9. In 2000, Lil' Kim released the video for her single "How Many Licks?" (Winans, Andrews, Lewis, Combs, & Wallace), wherein she played the role of a factory-assembled living doll. Considering that Harajuku Barbie appears to have formed on the same assembly line as Kim's video persona, comparisons are frequent. As such, a rivalry between the rappers has developed.
10. An image of the So-In-Style dolls is available at: http://www.barbie.com/activities/friends/soin-style/
11. Elizabeth Chin (2001) complicated this issue in "Ethnically Correct Dolls: Toying with the Race Industry." Upon measuring the Shani doll, Chin noted that her "bigger butt is an illusion" propagated in popular discourse (p. 158).
12. In line with how hip hop sexualizes female rappers, Maraj purportedly was changed to Minaj to hint at ménage à trois.

REFERENCES

Ahmed, I. (2011, May 31). In her own words: Who is Kreayshawn? *Complex*. Retrieved from http://www.complex.com/music/2011/05/who-is-kreayshawn/influences#gallery

Albury, K. (2002). *Yes means yes: Getting explicit about heterosex*. Crows Nest, Australia: Allen and Unwin.

Butler, J. (1999). *Gender trouble*. New York, NY; London, England: Routledge. (Original work published 1990)

Carey, M., Nash, T., & Stewart, T. (2010). Up out my face. [Recorded by M. Carey (featuring N. Minaj)]. On *Memoirs of an imperfect angel* [CD]. New York, NY: Island Records.

Carter, D., Garrett, S. E., Harrison, D. J., Maraj O., Scheffer, J. G., & Zamor, R. F. (2008). Lollipop (Remix) [Recorded by N. Minaj (featuring Lil Wayne)]. On *Suckafree* [Mixtape]. Be Records.

Chin, E. (2001). Ethnically correct dolls: Toying with the race industry. In *Purchasing power: Black kids and American consumer culture* (pp. 143–174). Minneapolis, MN: University of Minnesota Press.

De Beauvoir, S. (1997). *The second sex* (H.M. Parshley, Trans.). London, England: Vintage. (Original work published 1949)

Driscoll, C. (2002). *Girls: Feminine adolescence in popular culture and cultural theory*. New York, NY: Columbia University Press.

DuCille, A. (1994). Dyes and dolls: Multicultural Barbie and the merchandising of difference. *Differences, 6* (1), 46–68.

Dyer, R. (1997). *White: Essays on race and culture*. London, England; New York, NY: Routledge.

Fausto-Sterling, A. (2002). Gender, race, and nation: The comparative anatomy of "Hottentot" women in Europe, 1815–17. In K. Wallace-Sanders (Ed.), *Skin deep, spirit strong: The Black female body in American culture* (pp. 66–98). Ann Arbor, MI: University of Michigan.

Ganz, C. (2010). The curious case of Nicki Minaj. *Out*. Retrieved from http://www.out.com/detail. asp?page=2&id=27391

Goddessjaz. (2011). Nicki Minaj: 1st female platinum rapper in 8 years [Blog post]. http://feministing. com/2011/01/06/nicki-minaj-1st-female-platinum-rapper-in-8-years/

The Harajuku Barbie. (2012). Retrieved on January 30, 2013, from http://nickiminaj.wikia.com/wiki/ The_Harajuku_Barbie

HipHopStan.com. (2009). Nicki Minaj explains "Harajuku Barbie" [Video file]. Retrieved from http://vimeo.com/6019791

hooks, b. (1992). Eating the other. In *Black looks: Race and representation* [pp. 21–41]. London, England: Turnaround.

Huffington Post, Nicki Minaj Before Butt Implants (PHOTOS). (18 September 2012). Retrieved from http://www.huffingtonpost.com/2012/09/18/nicki-minaj-before-butt-implants_n_1892922. html

Jenn (guest contributor). (2010). The Orientalism of Nicki Minaj [Blog post]. Retrieved from http:// www.racialicious.com/2010/11/01/the-orientalism-of-nicki-minaj/

Jones, K. (2011). Pussy callin' [Recorded by Lil' Kim]. On *Black Friday* [Mixtape]. New York, NY: IRS.

Keyes, C. L. (2004). Empowering self, making choices, creating spaces: Black female identity via rap music performance. In *That's the joint! The hip-hop studies reader* (pp. 305–319). New York, NY: Routledge.

Knowles, B., Rowland, K., Fusari, R., & Moore, F. (2001). Bootylicious [Recorded by Destiny's Child]. On *Survivor* [CD]. New York, NY: Columbia Records.

Maraj, O., & Carter, D. (2009). Go hard [Recorded by N. Minaj (featuring Lil Wayne)]. On *Beam me up Scotty* [Mixtape]. New Orleans, LA: Young Money Entertainment.

Maraj, O., & Johnson, D. (2010). I'm the best [Recorded by N. Minaj]. On *Pink Friday* [CD]. New Orleans, LA: Young Money Entertainment.

Morrison, T. (1999). *The bluest eye*. London, England: Vintage.

MyPinkFriday.com. The unfortunate part about being a Barbie. (2011, February 15). Retrieved from http://mypinkfriday.com/forum/back/195261

Negrete, A., Weiner, M., & Zolot, N. (2011). Gucci Gucci [Recorded by Kreayshawn]. On *Somethin' 'bout Kreay* [CD]. New York, NY: Columbia Records.

Orbach, S. (2009). *Bodies: Big ideas*. London, England: Profile Books.

Peterson, L. (2010). Nicki Minaj and the issue of female MCs. *Jezebel*. Retrieved from http://jezebel. com/5478800/nicki-minaj-and-the-issue-of-female-mcs

Rand, E. (1995). *Barbie's queer accessories*. Durham, NC: Duke University Press.

Rebolla-Gil, G., & Moras, A. (2012). Black women and black men in hip hop music: Misogyny, violence and the negotiation of (white-owned) space. *The Journal of Popular Culture, 45*(1), 118–132.

Rogers, M. F. (1999). *Barbie culture*. Thousand Oaks, CA; London, England: Sage.

Rose, T. (2008). *The hip hop wars: What we talk about when we talk about hip hop—and why it matters*. New York, NY: Basic Books.

Stewart, D. (2009). Mattel's new black Barbie a step in the right direction. *Jezebel*. Retrieved from http://jezebel.com/5315415/mattels-new-black-barbie-a-step-in-the-right-direction

Toffoletti, K. (2007). *Cyborgs and Barbie dolls: Feminism, popular culture and the posthuman body*. New York, NY; London, England: I.B. Tauris.

Vander Broek, A. (2009). The Forbes fictional interview: Barbie. *Forbes*. Retrieved from http://www.forbes.com/2009/03/05/barbie-doll-interview-business_speaks.html?fd=rss_business

Vesey, A. (2010). Tuning in: Nicki Minaj [Blog post]. Retrieved from http://bitchmagazine.org/post/tuning-in-nicki-minaj

Vibe Magazine, Nicki Minaj & friends cover Vibe Magazine. (2010). Retrieved from http://www.vibe.com/article/nicki-minaj-friends-cover-vibe-magazine

Walter, N. (2010). *Living dolls: The return of sexism*. London, England: Virago Press.

Williams, P., & Hugo, C. (2003). Milkshake [Recorded by Kelis]. On *Tasty* [CD]. Virginia Beach, VA: Star Trak Records.

Winans, M., Andrews, M., Lewis, M. Combs, S., & Wallace, C. (2000). How many licks? [Recorded by Lil' Kim]. On *The notorious K.I.M.* [CD]. New York, NY: Atlantic Records.

Zenzile. (2010). Nicki Minaj: Modern day Hottentot...[Blog post]. Retrieved from http://love-joneslifestyle.blogspot.co.uk/2010/12/nicki-minaj-modern-day-hottentot.html

Zimmerman, E. (2010). Who is Nicki Minaj? [Blog post]. Retrieved from http://thehairpin.com/2010/11/who-is-nicki-minaj

CHAPTER SIX

Technologies OF Gender AND Girlhood: Doll Discourses IN Ireland, 1801–1909

VANESSA RUTHERFORD

INTRODUCTION: IRELAND, GENDER, AND DOLL DISCOURSES

Toys, specifically dolls and doll houses, as semiotic technologies, fashion gender identities, performances, and actions. During the nineteenth century, colonial Ireland witnessed the proliferation of expert discourses regarding objects of knowledge, particularly the sexualisation of children and the female body. Religious, pedagogical, popular culture, medical and scientific discourses, together with institutions of the state, anchored technologies of gender within Irish society (Foucault, 1980). Ideological societal apparatus, which encompassed bourgeois liberalism, colonialism, and imperialism, established a "set of effects produced in bodies, behaviours, and social relations" by the deployment of "complex" technologies (Foucault, 1980).

By 1824 Ireland was "enrolled in what was arguably the first mass movement of organized democracy in Europe" (McCartney, 1987, p. 112). The campaign for the repeal of the Act of Union (1801), the end of the Irish tithe system, universal suffrage, and a secret ballot for parliamentary elections was non-violent, but agitation and the threat of violence was constant. A gulf yawned between colonizer and colony. The passing of the Catholic Emancipation Act (1829) only fuelled the imperial drive to "subdue the Irish," to "make the poor contented with their lot" (McCartney, 1987, p. 119). As the British imperialist administration saw it, early in the nineteenth century, the solution to the Irish problem lay in cultivating the greatest resource the country had, its children, through bodies of knowledge and disciplinary practices. "It is to the child we must address ourselves," wrote Thomas Wyse (1836) in his treatise, *Educational Reform*. He continued, "an infant is capable of belonging to any country," and, given the "flexibility of his nature," he may "with equal facility be moulded ...into an Englishman" (pp. 5, 278). Childhood "moulding" ensured a "second creation," a "useful, obedient, respectful and happy race." The toy industry formed one strand in the overall supreme machine of disciplinary power designed to alter and mould behaviours, to "break down," train, and "rearrange" Irish minds and bodies (Foucault, 1977, p. 138). The micromanagement of the child body and mind through toy discourses combined with the macro surveillance of the body politic and created a disciplinary power that targeted the individual within state power targeting the social body (Stoler, 2010). Designed and marketed to fabricate the child via technologies of power, dolls, and doll houses, impressed in its object an internalization of mental, physical, social, and emotional controls, in order that "the will itself" be "taken captive" (Rousseau, 1979, p. 84). Rousseau defined childhood as a space and time that was not adult. Dolls and doll houses shaped and produced the "natural child" in a specific childhood space during play time.

Childhood, or "a chronological stage and a mental construct, an existential fact and a locus of desire, a mythological country continuously mapped by grownups" (Goodenough, 2000), became recognized as a crucial time within the lifecycle—a stage of development that laid foundations for the future of society. A naturalistic definition of children, with an empirical and scientific basis, emerged during the Enlightenment (Castillo, 2006). The resultant nineteenth-century shift in emphasis on childhood as the *ground floor* of human development and its subsequent growth towards civilization reflects changing scientific, social, cultural, and political attitudes and behaviours that were rooted in the Enlightenment plan to create rational forms of governance over the individual, the nation, and the empire. While some saw the ages between birth and 13 as a mass of native and savage urges that needed to be tamed and civilized (Davin, 1999), others approached it more reverently, and focused on an association between primitive life and paradise (Plotz, 2001; Natov, 2003; Shuttleworth, 2010). Childhood emerged as a site of "pedagogy and socialisation...a domain colonised by a range of social agents and practices—doctors, health visitors, social workers, educational psychologists and so forth" (Rose, 1985). Toy discourses (specifically dolls and doll houses) provided a context from which to explore concepts and beliefs, identities, and behavioural enactments that crucially influenced, enabled, and constrained conceptions, representations, and actualities of childhood in Ireland during the nineteenth century.

The significant growth in the toy industry in Ireland during the nineteenth century is illustrated by *Thom's Directory* (1845, 1855, 1860) and *Slater's National/ Royal National Directory* (1846–1894). In 1855, 10 toy warehouses are listed. By

1856, 34 are noted ("toy warehouses" refers to toy shops and toy factories). Specialist producers of wooden toys included Cushendall, County Antrim, and Killarney, County Kerry (*Thoms*, 1845). Representatives from the Ballycastle toy industry, from County Antrim, appeared at the Irish Industrial Exhibition at the World's Fair in St. Louis in 1904. They displayed reproductions in miniature of McKinley's cottage and peasant furniture (Handbook & Catalogue of Exhibits, 1904). In a similar vein, the Castle Pollard toy and basket industry in County Meath specialized in traditional toy making.

In Dublin city and county alone, the number of toy warehouses increased from 15 in 1840 to 26 by the mid-1880s (*Thom's*, 1855, 1860; *Slater's*, 1856). From mid-century, toy shops competed with each other to provide the best selection of "French, English and German toys." *Thom's Irish Almanac* [Dublin City and County] listed Blum Joseph Brothers, 25 Nassau Street, Dublin, a bazaar of Parisian importers; Johnson, 37 Sackville Street Lower, Dublin, an English toy importer; Hamburgh House Toy Warehouse, located at 17 Nassau Street, Dublin; and Stavenhagen, 67 Grafton Street, Dublin, a German toy warehouse (*Thom's*, 1845, 1855). Mary Plunkett, 3 Earl Street, Dublin, and Maria Russell, 8 Westland Street, Dublin, provided an array of toys to Dublin children. Toyshops Todd, Burns, & Company, and Pim's, South Great George's Street, Dublin, and The World Fair Store, Henry Street, Dublin, targeted parents and children via advertisements that announced assortments of "TOYS, TOYS, TOYS," and "all the most ingenious novelties" (*Thom's*, 1845, 1855; *The Sunday World*, 1895). The expansion of the toy market in Ireland interwove materials, products, life stories, and historically emergent discourses that fashioned childhood ideologies into enacted and lived everyday realities.

There have been active attempts to conceptualise a rigorous understanding of "pedagogy of play" within contemporary Irish society (Murphy, 2006; Kernan, 2007). However, studies that address specific aspects of doll culture and grapple with the theoretical positioning of the child in social-historical culture are unfortunately omitted from the modern Irish discourse. Susan Willis (1991) explored the world of Barbie, He-Man, and MTV to deepen our understanding of the immersion of capitalist society in America. Formanek-Brunell's (1998) study of the United States doll industry provides a rich perspective on the construction of gender in America from 1830–1930. Lynne Vallone (1995) examined girls' culture and the many forms it took in the eighteenth and nineteenth centuries. Claudia Nelson and Lynne Vallone (1994) edited a volume on cultural histories of the Anglo American girl, 1830–1915. Sally Mitchell (1995) looked at girls' culture in England, 1880–1915. Using a variety of intertextual critical approaches, including feminist theory, neo-Freudian Winnicott play analysis, structuralism, and neo-Marxism, Lois Kuznets (1987) focused on how toy characters, like children's play, can be associated with deep human needs, desires, and fears. Ariel

Dorfman (Dorfman & Mattelart, 1975) explored the imperialist ideology amid Disney figures such as Donald Duck. Feminist critics have mapped the images and gender roles of women and girls in children's media, including dolls. Leonore Weitzman (Weitzman, Eifler, Hokad, & Ross, 1972) and others (Gersoni-Stavn, 1974) explored sex-role socialization in picture books for preschool children.

Poststructuralist feminists have rethought the construction of gender, acknowledging the interplay between masculinity and femininity within individuals and culture. For example, Helene Cixous (1975) dealt with the multiplicity of response and desire: gaps, disjunctions, and uncertainty. According to Cixous and her contemporary, Julia Kristeva (1980), not all women and girls enact a single, biologically determined way of playing with dolls. Gender is not essential but is rather constructed in complex ways that are directly tied to how we communicate in society.

In this chapter, the word "discourse" is used in the Foucauldian sense and refers to bodies of knowledge or the social, historical, and political conditions under which statements, come to be regarded as true or false. Statements as components of discursive formations are functional units; they do things and bring about effects. Statements are not fixed but can be understood via the rules that govern their functioning, and are part of historically variable bodies of knowledge and technique(s) for the production of human subjects and institutions (Foucault, 1972). This concept of discourse moves away from a purely linguistic system or social structure. Discourse is the relationships between disciplines or bodies of knowledge and the disciplinary practices or forms of social control, models of power, and social possibility. Toy discourses are a revealing source of children's media and genres and provide crucial insights into childhood tropes from the nineteenth century. This childhood repertoire is intermedial, as the discourses combine and remediate broader mixed media and intermedia, namely magazines and newspapers, periodicals, and educational texts (Rajewsky, 2005).

This chapter employs critical discourse analysis to describe, interpret, and explain the ways in which broader social, scientific, political, ideological, religious, and cultural contexts and struggles for power constructed toy discourses as technologies of gender and girlhood in nineteenth-century Ireland.

CULTURAL WORLDS AND TOYS: FRAMING GENDER

Gender is the product of dominant social and cultural technologies, discourses, and practices rooted in body, self, and society (Foucault, 1980). In the age of colonialism, forceful ideas about domesticity, the home, and the role of the family framed both gender and class. Religious discourse, education discourse, state and social policy, architect and town planning discourse, and toy and popular media discourse generated symbolic, material, and organizational aspects of womanhood and manhood, masculinity and femininity. Female and male are complementary yet mutually exclusive categories and constitute a symbolic gender system that intimately connects social, political, and economic factors, values, and class hierarchies within every society (Ortner & Whitehead, 1981). Gendered meanings mapped bodies.

Motherhood started to be glorified as a woman's chief vocation and central definition during the nineteenth century. Macro political, social, and religious structures sanctioned and prescribed the social and cultural perception and performance of the female body (Butler, 1990). The educator, Maria Edgeworth (R. L. Edgeworth & Edgeworth, 1798) approvingly wrote of "little girls...pleased with the notion that" they are like "mama" (p. 3). Church leaders consistently put forward their vision of motherhood as the "ultimate calling of women" and of its "proper link with marriage" (Kennedy, 2001). Medical professional Dr. Hayden (1836), of Dublin's Anglesey Lying-in Hospital, asked in an 1836 lecture, "What constitutes the chief delight and charm of the domestic circle? Are they not the fond care, the smiling welcome, the tender love of the mother?"

The second annual report of St. Brigid's Orphanage said in 1858 that "it is hard to compensate for the loss of a father's protection, a mother's love and the endearments of a family circle." In 1872 *Dublin University Magazine* warned Irish women of the dire consequences of stepping outside their "natural" homemaking role,

> the moment woman abandons her great work [and] attempts to do the work of man, she is likely to fail; and if she proposes to subvert the laws of her own being, which are the laws of her creator, she will go to the wall. (*Dublin University Magazine*, 1872)

Government agencies such as the Congested District Boards (1881) and Agriculture and Technical Instruction (1898) reinforced the message that home was the proper space for the mother by teaching poor mothers home management skills, hygiene, nutrition, sanitation, and laundry work. An article in *New Ireland Review* in 1904 noted that, "We observe that in the home the chief duties of women are the care and training of the children...the regulation of the household, paying special attention to its cleanliness, sanitation and good order; the prevention of sickness" (Lovibond, 1904, p. 80). According to the Women's National Health Association (WNHAI, 1913), an organization set up by the Marchioness of Aberdeen and Temair (1857–1939) to combat disease, champion child health and well-being, and educate their working-class sisters in the art of motherhood: "no situation is more thoroughly a woman's than that which has as object the care and charge of the infant. Women are born with a natural talent for it" (WNHAI, *Sláinte*, 1909, p. 10). The nineteenth-century woman's world *naturally* betrays the home, mother, and homemaker. Middle-class women reinforced this corporeality to wield power and colonize their working-class sisters (Rutherford, 2013). Boundaries marked and defined woman's space, place, and body. The interwoven maze of nineteenth-century authorships and discourses produced powerful and entrenched expectations of gendered identity.

Toymakers drew on these maternal ideals for inspiration. They designed and marketed artistic objects (dolls and doll houses) that cultivated and regulated worthless bodies into gendered categories. Dolls and doll houses provided the *"corpus vile* on which the first experiments in the art of gendered living are made" (*Irish School Magazine and Junior Teachers' Assistant*, 1878).

> Toys are the alphabet of life through which children learn what poetry, what passion, what property mean…all life is to be found in the toy shop in miniature, however much more polished and sparkling. Everything is harmonious, cheerful, innocent, curious and smooth in a toy world. Children speak to their toys, toys become actors with them in the drama of life and the little owners learn unconsciously what it is to confer ideal qualities on very commonplace objects. Children learn through toys one of our human ways of being well deceived into an interest in life. (*Irish School Magazine and Junior Teachers' Assistant*, 1878, p. 21)

Doll discourses played a powerful role in inscribing the implied player positions within the unfolding toy narrative and beyond.

DOLLS: LITTLE GIRLS' TOYS

Small family craft shops produced a varied selection of wooden dolls in Ireland during the nineteenth century. These handmade plain and sturdy dolls with expressionless faces have fixed individual identities (specific facial features). They represent a legacy of interwoven historical materials, traditions, and imaginaries of the creators. As the century progressed, the family shops fought for survival with the importation of inexpensive foreign doll parts and complete dolls from Germany and the United States. Toy warehouses Kirby's, Grafton Street, Dublin; Lawrence and Company, O'Connell Street and Grafton Street, Dublin; and the Toy Factory at Cushendall, County Antrim produced wooden dolls well into the 1900s.

With the publication of *Practical Education*, Maria Edgeworth and her father (1798), who co-authored the educational treatise, categorized dolls as "little girls" toys (p. 3). The Edgeworths rooted gender in a social reality that had concrete existence in cultural forms. The toy industry duly responded by producing more realistic figures modelled as babies, which offered lessons in the cultural correlates of gender and class. New technological advances and serial mass-production by mid-century facilitated the redesign of doll figures. Irish toy shops competed with each other to provide the "best selection of Swiss, French, English and German" (*Thom's*, 1845). New visions of coming-alive identities abounded. A range of dolls developed "more natural" and "generic" features and represented "every nationality" (*Irish School*

Magazine, 1878). The infiltration of these dolls established a British way of life into the wilderness of colonial Ireland. The physical identity of a doll, her facial features, skin colour, and hair colour interweaved cultural attributes such as hair style and dress (Kress & Leeuwen, 2006). These interactive dolls (designed to have things done *to* them by the child in role play or otherwise) and active dolls (enable the child to make the doll do specific things, such as a movement of the limbs, sleeping dolls) represent technologies of gender and girlhood. The Irish child felt into the doll object and the doll playing activity. Dolls talked to the child's cultural self (Nelson, 2003).

As noted, the female body emerged the true bearer of bourgeois ideology during the nineteenth century. It was a domain colonised by a range of social agents and technologies—doctors, health visitors, social workers, religions, educational psychologists, and toy media. This is reflected in doll sellers who "catered to a clientele of urban middle class woman" (Formanek-Brunell, 1998, p. 16). The fixed physical and cultural requirement for any doll to be "beautiful" persisted (Baker-Sperry & Grauerholz, 2003). Her beauty antipathetically compared to the more primitive and fixed features of Irish wooden dolls. By 1878, toy windows in Ireland displayed dolls with "the most lovely flaxen hair, rosy cheeks and eyes of the most decided blue" (*Irish School Magazine,* 1878). Advertisements focused on the physical characteristics of the modern dolls described as "particularly fine specimen[s]" with pretty faces and curling hair," quite unlike the "good old rag doll," whose "beauty was not its strong point" (Curtis, 1909). These bodily descriptions projected basic, indelible, fixed characteristics of a specific social type. Hyper-idealized feminine features (namely long hair) and frilly clothing reinforced idealized gender "slots" and role models. For example, a *Sunday World* advertisement (1895) described a "lovely dolly (whose limbs are jointed)" bedecked in "a pale green corded silk gown, having a white satin yoke. The large picture hat is trimmed to match, and her golden hair is hanging down her back." Another doll is "dressed in light blue satin, elaborately trimmed with lace." Most important, modern doll makers offered Irish subjects "English dressed dolls" as a "speciality, the entire costume being replaceable, and being in styles and materials thoroughly up to date." These mass-produced doll figures shaped the contours of colonial cultural ideals and fore-grounded femininity through their relationship to their owners. Object, self, other, and experience would be forever interweaved (Rosaldo, 1989). The "unconscious objects that are toys become self consciously alive, [and] they blur the lines between self and other, subject and object" (Kuznets, 1994, p. 5).

A mid-nineteenth-century "sturdy" doll bemoaned the fate of the modern doll. She said "we had entered the world together; her beauty and her fine dress had been the cause of her misfortunes" (Constable, 1846; Kuznets, 1994: p. 103). This mid- nineteenth century lament perhaps aligns with Brown's (1993) assessment of Victorian female powerlessness as well as the "lingering nostalgia" for lost childhoods "in the face of the increasing materialisation of the industrial age."

Nineteenth-century toymakers and toy sellers used magazines, advertisements, visuals, and cartoons to assimilate the female figure to the form of the mother. In an 1882 article for *Irish Monthly* magazine, H. D. Tainter wrote "think for one moment what it means to be a mother. It means to call into existence a new soul to bear the burdens and cares of this world." And,

> Slowly but surely you will see the tiny being develop, and seem to become conscious of its existence. Now…you find that, instead of having a plaything—a live one, in place of your dead dolls—you are confronted by a human being, small, I grant you, but the personality is distinct: there in a miniature, you have all the passions, love, hate and remorse….You can now mould and form the plastic material into what shape you will. Given the right bias, the plant twig will grow into a glorious tree…but cramp and cripple the tender shoot, and you will produce a stunted, dwarfed monstrosity. (p. 47)

The doll "becomes a force that dominates and determines those who come under its spell, acting as a creator in no less a fashion than the individual who form its existence" (Mendelsohn, 1977, p. 83). Dolls style girls with a "mother" performance. An 1895 toy warehouse advertisement described dolls "garbed in velvet" and "light silk," holding "baby dolls suitably attired." The dolls opened and shut their eyes and looked "most intelligent" (*Sunday World* advertisement, 1895). Dolls represented social types in their recognizable identities as "mothers" (Foucault, 1977). These popular doll discourses asserted the social representation of femininity that in turn affected its subjective construction (Wohlend, 2009).

Dolls, as technologies of gender and girlhood, imbue matter with life. They girl the girl. At birth, children are assigned a gender, based on medical interpretation of whether their bodies are "male" or "female." This interpretation sets up how they are treated and what are thought appropriate ways for them to act and play (Butler, 1990, 1993). Female "identity is instituted through a stylized repetition" of play (Butler, 1990). Or, as the Edgeworths (1798) had noted more than a century ago, dolls inspire girls with a European bourgeois girl performance (pp. 3–4). The figure and function of a doll represent an archetype and a prototype. Through play with a literal, physical object, gender identity is understood and reinforced in the earliest stages of development, because, as the Edgeworths observed, "practical education begins very early" (p. 8).

DOLL HOUSES AND ACCESSORIES: IMAGINED WORLDS

Designed materially and semiotically, doll houses offer images of the world constructed in a miniature world. The child is in a sense the miniature of the adult, and the world of childhood, limited in physical scope, offers something fantastic and magical in content. The miniature doll house offers a world that is part of history, a chapter in the life of the child, yet it can also be remote from the presentness of adult life. Within the doll house, "function and representation" become "closely allied." According to Sutton-Smith (2001), the miniaturization of artefacts creates a paradox, which denies its own repression of reality, asserting itself ready instead, for a "reaction of fantasy or phantasmagoria." (p. 132). As a prop for play, doll houses combine space, characters, objects, and subjects that unlock imagination, fantasy, desire, and adventure in tacitly reconstructing time, experience, place, self—a gendered social subject (Brougère, 2006; Foucault, 1980; Kuznets, 1994, p. 6). Dominant ideas of gender penetrate doll discourses.

The National Museum of Ireland has in its keeping three significant doll houses made in nineteenth-century Ireland. Purchased by adults for children, these mnemonic houses reflect homes within homes. These doll houses address the child player as a woman. They frame femininity: space, accessories, character, dress, activity, material, and image interact. At one level, it permits an escape into the child self, and entry into one's own little private world. At another level, the horizon of possible meaning-making extends beyond the walls of the doll house, and reaches out towards the exterior social and cultural life of the female child.

The Strahan doll house dates from around 1820 and is the earliest in the collection of the National Museum of Ireland (Rafferty, 1980). Made by the Strahan family, who were cabinet-makers in Wentworth Place, and later Henry Street, Dublin, the doll house is constructed of pinewood. It is formed in three separate parts, each with a removable front and two storeys. The whole front is painted a brick colour and there are four movable steps that lead up to a double door of panelled mahogany. Each side of the door has a lion's-head knocker and brass door knob. The keyhole has a well-made lock, and this and the brass bolt inside ensure the safety of the contents and persons of the house (Rafferty, 1984–1987). Clara May Strahan and her dolls were accommodated in this large and open doll house, which provided a setting for didactic and orderly lessons of life—the performance of daily domestic female routines.

The Strahan doll house epitomises "neatness and serenity within" (Summerson, 1963). This house is both an object of play for little Clara May Strahan, and also represents an evocative mirror of human nature. Interior design, fabrics, and choice of colours speak female and class. The four-poster bed, constructed of mahogany, rests on four globular feet. The domed canopy has carved pediments in front and two sides. The inside of the head of the bed and the canopy are lined with pink fabric and there is an interior valance of the same material, edged with a matching pink and green braid. Green brocade bed curtains are held back with ornamental cords on metal rings and are matched by top valances with green braid and tassels. The bed is covered with four neatly hemmed cotton sheets. Two white sateen bolsters are filled with lamb's-wool within a white cotton bolster case that has a drawstring through one end. There are also two square pillows, both filled with lamb's-wool and covered with white linen pillow cases trimmed with Valenci-ennes lace and fastened with mother-of-pearl buttons (Rafferty, 1984–1987). The delicate fabrics, accessories, and finishes shape the character of play.

Another Irish doll house, the Wilson doll house, is named after its donor, Mrs. A. H. Wilson of Monkstown, County Dublin. It is dated between 1830 and 1840. There is one chimney at the centre of the pitched roof, which dictates the position of the fireplaces in each of the rooms. The front, provided with a keyhole, opens as a unit and is secured by a metal hook on the top; the hook is hidden by a projecting parapet (Rafferty, 1980).

The doll house has two rooms: a bedroom on the first floor and a parlour on the ground floor, complete with rosewood furniture. Design from the real world is reflected in the composition of the doll house; social structures, class, and income are reflected within. The bedroom features a four-poster bed; the hangings are made of fawn chintz reflecting a coral and seaweed pattern and bordered with faded blue ribbon. A miniature replica mattress and bolster, flannel sheets with red wool blanket stitching, a pillow with lace-trimmed cover, and croquet bedspread with long cotton fringe dress the bed. Gender is reproduced through the cultiva-tion and appearance of bodies into "natural" appearances and dispositions (But-ler, 1990, p. 525). A dressing table is covered with white crochet. An oval swing mirror and large pin cushion, decorated with lace, lie on the dressing table. The discursive feminine scene positions the silent female within a space of sensibility and comfortability, sitting on the scroll-end sofa and matching foot stool that are covered in the coral and seaweed pattern. The bell pull is made of perforated and embroidered card, lined with mauve silk, and trimmed with silk-covered beads and tassels (Rafferty, 1980). These accessories speak woman and class. Through intersection with these objects, bodies are crafted into gender and class through the performance of play, and as Judith Butler (1990) has noted, "the performance renders social laws explicit" (p. 526).

Domestic bourgeois dynamics are captured within. The parlour contains a circular tilt-top table on which lie a croquet mat, plates, and a candlestick. There are six chairs and a scroll-end sofa. The large harp dominates this room and is made from paper and cardboard, decorated with gilt-and-white scraps of thistles and roses and edged with gilt paper. The strings are made of knitting needles. Harp-making was a typical nineteenth-century female pastime (Rafferty, 1980). The gaze of Victorian domesticity placed an emphasis on inherent female pursuits, domains, meanings, positions, and roles—in this case, needlework. Needlework for dolls indexed middle-class maternal homemaking, domestic ideals, values, and expectations (Scollon, 2001; Bowen, 1942).

The doll in the bedroom wears a mauve taffeta dress trimmed with pink ribbon, a golden chain about her neck, and a large white hat with silken embellishments on her head. The doll in the parlor wears a two–tier grey-and-pink taffeta gown. Mauve silk ribbons form large bows on the shoulders and ribbons are also used to make a belt with long streamers in the front. One arm is tucked into a blue velvet muff and the other holds a yellow taffeta reticule. A green bead necklace is worn around the neck. Tacit conventions of dress and appearance structure the way the female body is clothed (Ruble, Lurye, & Zosuls, 2007). Gowns, jewelry, bows, ribbons, silk, velvet, reticule, and pink style the natural configuration of bodies (Butler, 1990).

The doll house is a setting for the playing out of imaginaries; for fulfilling convention petit feminine pastimes and activities directly associated with its image (Davies, 1989). Play unfolds within and between the two rooms of the Wilson doll house; through characters and accessories that suggest *normalized* activities or that imaginatively re-enacted state of traditional perfection associated with sentimentality, domesticity, and childhood. "The playset becomes a self-sufficient [and idealized] universe" that speaks feminine (Brougère, 2006). Further, it reflects "social structures that are mimicked in real domestic arrangements" (Kuznets, 1994, p. 120) yet it remains a privileged place, "exempt from the most serious problems of life and civilization" (p. 149). See Figure 1.

Figure 1. Wilson Doll House.
Source: National Museum of Ireland.

Reflecting the desire to carve out a bourgeois vision of an imagined and real world for the child player is another doll house made in Ireland and shown at the Great Exhibition of London, 1851. The National museum (Rafferty, 1980) acquired the house in 1901 from its owners, the Domville family, of Loughlinstown, County Dublin. Cushendall toy industry, County Antrim, produced the furniture in a variety of styles—Sheraton, Hepplewhite, Chippendale, and Adam. The furniture and interior design shapes the character of the toy. The curtains, carpets, and tiles have painted designs, while the paintings on the doll house walls represent miniature copies of those owned by the Domville family. Behind the doors of the Domville doll house was a perfect, miniature utopian world where the artwork, the decorative, the domestic, and the feminine reigned supreme (*The Sunday World*, 1895; Turner, 1974).

By the late nineteenth century, Dublin toy shops were advertising an array of fashionable and mass-produced doll houses. According to the *Irish School Magazine*, by 1878, Irish toy shops were displaying "glittering furniture of dolls" kitchens and their well-built houses painted in dazzling tints" (*Irish School Magazine*, 1878). The World's Fair Store at 30 Henry Street, Dublin, advertised "Boxes of really nice doll's house furniture, cooking ranges, fitted with complete sets of saucepans for 6-½ d" and "China tea sets in boxes" (*Sunday World*, 1895). These items speak to the idealisation of personal and social values, concepts, experiences, and categories. The mass produced doll house carved out a domain for the domestic that represented an ideal of middle-class culture.

Within the doll house narrative, animal and toy interact freely with girls. Nursery book characters appear on doll house dishes and cups. The flat patterns and images focus on nature and animals (Vanobbergen, 2004). Kate Greenaway's designs (1846–1901); Mabel Lucie Attwell's distinctive characters (1879–1964); and Beatrix Potter's creations (1866–1943), Peter Rabbit and Benjamin Bunny, all feature. These designs created texts that provide messages about a woman's place. The little girl has the potential to change into a human being or subvert social norms by identifying with the *naughty* animals (Potter, 1904). Doll houses represent *magical* technologies that inspire girls with a girl performance.

CONCLUSION

This chapter explores nineteenth-century doll discourses. Interpreting the historic world of dolls and doll houses gives us a glimpse into the construction and reconstruction of childhood in modern Irish society. Dolls and doll houses symbolize powerful objects that gave children shape and form as their lives intersected with them. In the doll world, girls negotiated and recreated, organised and performed identities, agency, meanings, values, knowledge, practices, categories, and discursive positions—all in the name of child's work. As the Edgeworths (1798) noted "children work hard at play; therefore we should let them play at work" (p. 83).

Dolls and doll houses as technologies of gender and girlhood are the product of various social and cultural discourses, epistemologies, and critical practices, as well as structures, practices, and systems of power (Foucault, 1980). Dolls and doll houses materially frame forms of gender, and mediate identities and action. Gender is not a property of bodies, already existent in individuals, but is the "set of effects produced in bodies, behaviours, and social relations" (Foucault, 1980). It moves beyond the "political" to implicate social and cultural technologies. In play contexts real and imagined, identity and performance based on gender is tacitly negotiated, embodied, and embedded in thought, meaning-making, and practice. As Paley (1986) observed,

> Right now the girls are in the block area building a zoo. They have named the four rubber lions Mother, Father, Sister, and Baby and put them in a two-story house. Girls tame lions by putting them into houses. Boys conquer houses by sending them to space. (p. 9)

This reflection symbolises the division society makes between girls and boys at play. It reflects gender separation assigned to natural nurturing instincts, rooted in nineteenth-century developments. Doll discourses represent natural technologies for societal gender modelling.

REFERENCES

Baker-Sperry, L., & Grauerholz, L. (2003). The pervasiveness and persistence of the feminine beauty ideal in children's fairy tales. *Gender & Society, 17*(5), 711–726.

Brougère, G. (2006). Toy houses: A socio-anthropological approach to analyzing objects. *Visual Communication, 5*(1), 5–24.

Bowen, E. (1942). *Bowen's Court.* New York, NY: Alfred A. Knopf.

Brown, P. (1993). *The captured world: The child and childhood in nineteenth century women's writing in England.* Hemel Hempstead, England: Harvester Wheatsheaf.

Butler, J. (1990). *Gender trouble.* London, England: Routledge.

Butler, J. (1993). *Bodies that matter: On the discursive limits of sex.* USA & Canada: Routledge.

Castillo, S. (2006). *Performing America: Colonial encounters in New World writing, 1500–1786.* London, England: Routledge.

Cixous, H. (1975). *Le rire de la méduse.* L'Arc.

Constable, M. (1846). *The two dolls: A story.* Edinburgh: Constable.

Curtis, M. A. (1909). Bricks without straw. *Irish Monthly,* xlvii.

Davin, A. (1999). What is a child? In A. Fletcher & S. Hussey (Eds.), *Childhood in question: Children, parents and the State.* Manchester, England: Manchester University Press.

Davies, B. (1989). *Frogs and snails and feminist tales: Preschool children and gender.* Boston, MA: Allen & Unwin.

Dorfman, A., & Mattelart, A. (1975). *How to read Donald Duck: Imperialist ideology in the Disney comic* New York, NY: International General.

Dublin University Magazine (1872).

Edgeworth, R. L., & Edgeworth, M. (1798). *Practical education.* London, England: J. Johnson.

Formanek-Brunell, M. (1998). *Made to play house: Dolls and the commercialization of American girlhood, 1830–1930.* Baltimore, MD; London, England: The Johns Hopkins University Press.

Foucault, M. (1972). *The archaeology of knowledge.* London, England: Tavistock.

Foucault, M. (1977). *Discipline and punish: The birth of a prison* (London: Allen Lane).

Foucault, M. (1980). *The history of sexuality.* New York, NY: Vintage Books.

Gersoni-Stavn, D. (1974). *Sexism and youth.* London, England: R. R. Bowker.

Goodenough, E. (2000). Introduction to special issue on the secret spaces of childhood. *Michigan Quarterly Review, 2.*

Handbook & Catalogue of Exhibits, 1904.

Hayden, G.T. (1836). *A lecture to a course on midwifery and diseases of women and children delivered in the Aglesea lying-in hospital.* Dublin.

Irish school magazine and junior teachers' assistant. (1878). Dublin, Ireland: Albert E. Chamney.

Kennedy, F. (2001). *From cottage to crèche: Family change in Ireland.* Dublin, Ireland: Institute of Public Administration.

Kernan, M. (2007). *Play as a context for early learning and development.* Retrieved from National Council for Curriculum and Assessment website: http://www.ncca.ie/en/Curriculum_and_Assessment/Early_Childhood_and_Primary_Education/Early_Childhood_Education/How_Aistear_was_developed/Research_Papers/Play_paper.pdf

Kress, T. G., & van Leeuwen, T. (2006). *Reading images—the grammar of visual design.* London, England: Routledge.

Kristeva, J. (1980). *Desire in language* (T. Gora, A. Jardine, & L. S. Roudiez, Trans.). Oxford, England: Blackwell.

Kuhn, D., Nash, S. C., & Brucken, L. (1978). Sex role concepts of two- and three-year-olds. *Child Development, 49,* 445–451.

Kuznets, L. R. (1994). *When toys come alive: Narratives of animation, metamorphosis, and development.* New Haven, CT; London, England: Yale University Press.

Lovibond in *New Ireland Review* (1904).

McCartney, D. (1987). *The dawning of democracy: Ireland 1800–1870.* Dublin, Ireland: The Educational Company of Ireland.

Mendelsohn, L. (1977). Toys in literature. In F. Butler (Ed.), *Sharing literature with children: A thematic anthology* (pp. 81–84). New York, NY: David McKay.

Mitchell, S. (1995). *The new girl: Girls' culture in England, 1880–1915.* New York, NY: Columbia University Press.

Murphy, B. (2006). Child-centred practice in Irish infant classrooms: A case of imaginary play. *International Journal of Early Childhood, 38*(1), 112–124.

Natov, R. (2003). *The poetics of childhood.* London, England: Routledge.

Nelson, K. (2003). Narrative and self, myth and memory: Emergence of the cultural self. In R. Fivush & C. A. Haden (Eds.), *Autobiographical memory and the construction of a narrative self.* Mahwah, NJ: Erlbaum.

Nelson, C., & Vallone, L. (1994). *The girl's own: Cultural histories of the Anglo-American girl, 1830–1915*. Athens, GA: University of Georgia Press.

Ortner, S., & Whitehead, H. (1981). *Sexual meanings: The cultural construction of gender and sexuality*. Cambridge, England: Cambridge University Press.

Paley, V. (1986). *Boys and girls: Superheroes in the doll corner*. Chicago, IL; London, England: The University of Chicago Press.

Plotz, J. (2001). *Romanticism and the vocation of childhood*. New York. NY: Palgrave.

Potter, B. (1904). *The tale of two bad mice*. London, England: Frederick Warne.

Rafferty, C. (1980). Irish doll house: Elegance in miniature. *Doll and Toy Collection, 6*.

Rafferty, C. (1984–1987). The Strahan doll's house. *Irish Arts Review*.

Rajewsky, I. (2005). Intermediality, intertextuality and remediation: A literary perspective on intermediality. *Intermedialites, 6*.

Rosaldo, R. (1989). *Culture and truth: The remaking of social analysis*. Boston, MA: Beacon Press.

Rose, N. (1985). *The psychological complex: Psychology, politics and society in England 1869–1939*. London, England: Routledge & Kegan Paul.

Rousseau, J. J. (1979). *Emile* (A. Bloom, Trans.). New York, NY: Basic Books.

Ruble, D. N., Lurye, L. E., & Zosuls, K. M. (2007). Pink frilly dresses (PFD) and early gender identity. *Princeton Report on Knowledge, 2*.

Rutherford, R. (2013). The panopticon: St. Ultan's infant hospital, Dublin 1918. In C. Delay & C. Brophy (Eds.), *Ordinary and outcast: Poor women, family and sexuality in Ireland, 1840–1950*. New York, NY: Palgrave.

Saint Brigid's Orphanage. (1858). *Second annual report of St. Brigid's Orphanage*, 12–13.

Scollon, R. (2001). *Mediated discourse: The nexus of practice*. London, England: Routledge.

Shuttleworth, S. (2010). *The mind of the child: Child development in literature, science and medicine, 1840–1900*. Oxford, England: Oxford University Press.

Slater's, *National Commercial Directory* of Ireland 1846; Slater's *Royal National Commercial Directory of Ireland*, 1856, 1870, 1881, 1894.

Stoler, A. L. (2010). *Carnal knowledge and imperial power: Race and intimacy in colonial rule*. London, England: University of California Press.

Summerson, J. (1963). *Heavenly mansions and other essays on architecture*. New York, NY: Norton.

Sutton-Smith, B. (2001). *The ambiguity of play*. Cambridge, MA: Harvard University Press.

The Sunday World. (1895, December 22).

Tainter, H. D. (1882). Some practical hints on the education of children. *Irish Monthly, X*.

Thom's Irish Almanac and Official Directory. (1845). Dublin, Ireland: Alexander Thom & Co.

Thom's Irish Almanac and Official Directory. (1855). Dublin, Ireland: Alexander Thom & Co.

Thom's Irish Almanac and Official Directory. (1860). Dublin, Ireland: Alexander Thom & Co.

Turner, V. W. (1974). *Dramas, fields and metaphors: Symbolic action in human society*. Ithaca, NY: Cornell University Press.

Vallone, L. (1995). *Disciplines of virtue: Girls' culture in the eighteenth and nineteenth century*. New Haven, CT: Yale University Press.

Vanobbergen, B. (2004). Wanted real children: About innocence and nostalgia in a commodified childhood. *Studies in Philosophy and Education, 23*.

Weitzman, L., Eifler, D., Hokad, E., & Ross, C. (1972). Sex-role socialization in picture books for preschool children. *American Journal of Sociology, 77*, 1125–50.

Willis, S. (1991). *A primer for daily life*. New York, NY: Routledge.

Wohlwend, K. E. (2009). Damsels in discourse: Girls consuming and producing gendered identity texts through Disney princess play. *Reading Research Quarterly, 44*(1), 57–83.

Women's National Health Association of Ireland (WNHAI). (1909; 1913). *Sláinte.*

Wyse, T. (1836). *Education reform; or, the necessity of a national system of education.* London, England: Longman, Rees, Orme, Brown, Green, & Longman.

Part III: Mediating Contexts of Play

Rescripting, Modifying, AND Mediating Artifacts: Bratz Dolls AND Diasporic Iranian Girls IN Australia

NAGHMEH NOURI ESFAHANI AND VICTORIA CARRINGTON

In this chapter, we analyse the interactions between mass-produced global fashion dolls and diasporic Iranian girls. Heeding Hains's (2012) call that we spend time exploring the detail of how children engage with dolls, toys, and media, the research described here paid close attention to the complexities of interaction between technological artifacts of a global commodity market and the young children who are given them as playthings. In particular, the research made use of concepts drawn from the emerging field of postphenomenology (Verbeek, 2005) to pay very close attention to the ways in which Iranian girls living in a new Western culture both influenced and were influenced by the design features and narratives of Bratz global fashion dolls.

CONTEXT

The influential role of dolls in the relationship between girls and their surroundings identified by Ann DuCille (1994) inspired the choice of Bratz dolls for this examination. According to DuCille,

> More than simple instruments of pleasure and amusement, toys and games play crucial roles in helping children determine what is valuable in and around them. Dolls in particular invite children to replicate them, to imagine themselves in their dolls' images. (p. 46)

Since the 1950s, Barbie has dominated the fashion doll market. Barbie, however, reflects a particular racial and cultural profile that is increasingly out of step with the realities of life for young girls around the world. DuCille's (1994) analysis of Barbie and her critique of Mattel's efforts to represent multiculturalism through dolls references her experience of being "different" as a black girl living in the United States at a time when white dolls predominated (p. 48). Reflecting the shifting racial and cultural profile of the United States, and responding to the limited representation of difference in the Barbie range of dolls (DuCille, 1994), Bratz dolls were launched into the market in 2001.

Unlike Barbie, designed as the all-American white teenager, MGA's Bratz explicitly introduced multi-ethnic dolls to the toy market. The four initial dolls reflect individual interests and a specific contemporary urban character. MGA intended to represent multiculturalism and racial difference, but not necessarily to identify the dolls as specifically African American, Hispanic, or Middle Eastern (Talbot, 2001). As Guerrero (2009) explained, while Chloe had pale skin and blonde hair, Sasha's black hair and skin could have identified her as African American, Jade's jet-black straight hair and pale skin could position her as Asian American, and Yasmin's olive skin colour and brown hair suggested an ambiguous ethnic background that could be read as "Latina, a Filipina, a South Asian girl, or a White girl with a good tan and a talented hair colorist" (p. 191). The combination of names and physical representation alluded to a set of racial and ethic positionings without explicit identification. Guerrero argued that the very existence of the Bratz dolls, with their explicitly non-white styling, represented a move away from the hegemonic white-blonde ideals of Western beauty and cultural norms. However, she remained critical of the ethnic aspects of Bratz dolls, arguing that their ethnicity is being used as a commodity in order to create a more fashionable appearance for the dolls in a global market.

McAllister (2007) acknowledged MGA's effort to create a group of dolls that represent different ethnicities through skin and hair color as well as non-Western names, but pointed out that regardless of these differences, the dolls share a "cartoonish hyper-femininity of an all lips-and-eyes Bratz face and the sassy style of clothing/accessories" (p. 252). McAlister maintained that there can be no in-depth understanding of race and ethnicity apparent when all Bratz dolls have a similar body shape and share basic physical characteristics such as over-sized almond-shaped eyes and generic noses. The similarities, McAlister concluded, flatten any ethnic or racial differences that the dolls may portray (see also Almeida 2009).

While many scholars have critiqued the cleverly designed dolls as contemporary reflections of gender, ethnicity, the sexualization of young girls, and glorification of consumption (DuCille, 1994; Chin, 1999; Rand, 1995; Inness, 1998), this chapter contributes the application of a new theoretical orientation to issues of identity, materiality, and the construction of everyday life. Specifically, the chapter draws from an emerging philosophy of technology based in postphenomenology to view the dolls as mass-produced technological artifacts that influence and co-construct everyday lifeworlds. The chapter demonstrates the efficacy of this approach in bringing our attention, systematically, to the intricacies of dolls-in-use, most particularly in cross-cultural contexts.

VERBEEK'S POSTPHENOMENOLOGY OF ARTIFACTS: A USEFUL THEORY

Peter Paul Verbeek's post-phenomenology has particular relevance to this chapter because of his consideration of how technological artifacts engage us with the world and each other and play a part in setting up the particular conditions of engagement and, consequently, our perceptions and understandings of the world around us, and our actions within it. His framework builds from Ihde's (1990, 2009) repositioning of phenomenology in the context of the twenty-first century, "a deliberate adaptation or change in phenomenology that reflects historical changes in the twenty-first century" (Ihde, 2009, p. 5). A feature of postphenomenology is the focus on the particularities of specific technological artifacts. Verbeek argued that technological artifacts or objects co-shape both human action and human perception, that they effectively "mediate" how we see the world around us and how we act within, and on, it. It is self-evident that an artifact is designed to fulfil a function. Verbeek, however, suggested that while technological artifacts have an obvious functionality, they also have what has been termed "intentionality" (Ihde, 1990). Rather than being inert beyond the scope of a pre-set functionality, technological artifacts play an active role in the relationship between humans and the world they live in. Technological artifacts play a role in both human perception and human action and are "not neutral intermediaries but actively co-shape people's being in the world: their perceptions and actions, experience, and existence" (p. 364). Technological artifacts are mediating technologies: they mediate how the user perceives the world and how s/he acts upon it by suggesting some actions while discouraging others. Thus, for Verbeek, artifacts are not neutral objects. Rather, they are active and complicit in the ways in which social practices are formed and played out. Verbeek contended that artifacts "help to shape a situation which would have been otherwise without the artifact" (Verbeek, 2008; Verbeek & Slob, 2006). Latour (1992) and Akrich (1992) introduced the notion of the "script" in order to emphasize the characteristics of artifacts that might determine human action. However, while Akrich's emphasis was on the technical characteristics of artifacts and the role of the design features in influencing use, Latour focused on the artifacts' physical form and meaning. Verbeek (2005) suggested that Akrich and Latour's notions of script limit the concept to an instruction manual and technical functionality. Verbeek (2008) was keen to differentiate a script from the basic functionality of an artifact, arguing that artifacts, with their material intentionality, "cannot be entirely reduced to their designers' or users' intentions" (p. 95). The influential role of artifacts in the relationship between humans and their world, and the ways in which artifacts influence the organization of human life, has been termed "mediation" (Verbeek 2008, p. 123). As Verbeek (2005) stated, mediation "is not a product's function, but rather a by-product of its functionality" (p. 208). Verbeek's post-phenomenological framing argued strongly that our perspective on our world is formed and transformed through the mediation of artifacts, which are actively involved in the co-construction of our experiences. Interpreting the dolls as technological artifacts opens the way to exploring the script and intentionality of their design, giving explicit consideration to their role in mediating lifeworlds, and consequently identities and engagement with family, peers, and broader social contexts, and the role of agency in these constructions.

IRANIAN GIRLS IN AUSTRALIA

The participants in this study are Iranian girls whose families fled Iran for Australia first during the 1979 revolution, then during the Iran–Iraq War between 1980–1988, and more recently after 9/11. In order to cope with displacement as well as stereotyping, Iranian immigrants sought ways to renegotiate their identities and develop strategies (Aidani, 2007, p. 3). Global anxiety about terrorism in the post-9/11 era generated negative views of Middle Eastern and Iranian cultural and racial identity. Aidani argued that the hostile climate detrimentally impacted Iranians living in Australia, saying that "'Iranian' identity in the diaspora represents popular understandings of current political events and to a large extent is made up of negative modes of meaning" (p. 145). Aidani went on to suggest that, "Iranian identity in Australia is a difficult 'identity' to carry as it is constituted and loaded by so many ideological, cultural and religious meanings" (p. 169).

Consequently, Iranian girls and their families navigate complex cultural contexts in their everyday lives. As this study demonstrates, connections to Iranian family, language, and cultural practices are highly regarded and actively maintained. However, at the same time, Iranians of all ages daily move through an Australian cultural context: children attend local schools, shop at local supermarkets, and encounter Western cultural values and practices modeled on the streets and in the media. Iranian girls' everyday lives, then, involve negotiating pathways between the diasporic complexities of Iranian family culture and the specifically Australian, Western cultural and geographical location in which they are growing up. Dolls have been associated with representation, globalization of production and commodification of identities and are intimately embedded in the everyday lives and play practices of the girls described in the study, therefore a close study of Bratz in this context has potentially much to tell us.

The specific activity that was examined in this study was that of girls playing with Bratz dolls. Migration is a key phenomenon in contemporary global politics and culture. Consequently, the ways in which everyday objects such as dolls take on roles as important facilitators of cultural shifts or as colonising influences is an important issue. This research investigated the role of these global fashion dolls as everyday artifacts in families with diverse cultural backgrounds and beliefs. The research examined a range of issues related to the adaptation of these dolls as they move across cultural boundaries.

This examination, which is part of a larger study of global fashion dolls in the lives of young Iranian immigrants, comprises a set of six case studies of girls between the ages of 5 and 9 living in one Australian capital city. The research utilized an ethnographic, participant observation approach that followed the ways in which young girls interacted with, narrated, and re-designed fashion dolls in home-based play. This chapter focuses on two young girls, Gita and Neli, and their particular engagements with Bratz fashion dolls as they and their families navigate a new cultural landscape.

THE PARTICIPANTS

Neli, 8 years old at the time of this study, is the second child of a middle-class Iranian family living in an Australian state capital city. Both of Neli's parents left Iran as teenagers, because their minority status made it difficult to remain in Iran after the Revolution. Neli's mother left Iran with her family and moved to India when she was 16. After spending 8 years in India, Neli's mother went to the U.S., but later moved to Australia where the rest of her relatives lived. Neli's father left Iran for the U.S., where he studied engineering, when he was 19. While living in Australia with his family, Neli's father, an engineer, travelled frequently to other countries for work, and when back home, he told Neli and her brother stories about his experiences in different cultures.

At the time of the study, Neli and her family lived in a suburban area close to relatives and Iranian friends. Neli's family socializes predominantly with relatives and mostly with friends of the same non-Muslim minority. Neli's parents place importance on maintaining Iranian traditions. Reflecting the family's attachment to their Iranian cultural heritage, photos of their prophet and temple are displayed everywhere as are Iranian handcrafts and carpets. In addition to attending the local Australian primary school during weekdays, Neli also attends weekly religious classes and an Iranian school on Sundays to learn Farsi.

Despite the family's adherence to Iranian cultural traditions, Neli owns a variety of Western dolls. Six Bratz dolls are her most "favourite." Neli keeps all her dolls' hair and dress accessories in separate boxes. In each corner of her room, Neli has built a doll house for her dolls, with her books and other doll furniture. Five of her Bratz dolls are of Yasmin. Her mother bought two of them and she received the rest as gifts. Throughout the study period, Neli kept all of her dolls undressed because, "I like to design the dolls' dresses myself because the [store-bought] dresses are annoying."

Gita, an only child, migrated from Iran to Australia at age 6 with her middle-class parents. Her mother believed that the family would have a better life in Australia and Gita would have a brighter future. While both parents received Australian residency before settling in Australia, Gita's father stayed behind to run his construction business. Gita's mother chose to move to a part of Australia where a close friend from Iran had been living for 5 years. Gita and her mother lived with their friend in a suburban area until Gita's aunt and uncle arrived on study visas. The family then moved to a large house that was still near to the mother's friend. Eight months later, Gita's father joined the family in Australia. Unable to find suitable work after completing English courses and professional classes, he travelled frequently between Iran, where he ran his business, and Australia.

Gita's parents and her aunt and uncle maintain Iranian traditions at the same time as embracing Australian culture. Gita attends the local primary school during week days and an Iranian school on Sundays in order to learn Farsi and become more familiar with her cultural roots. Gita also takes Iranian dance lessons. The house includes Iranian handcrafts as well as old family photos. Gita's family tends to socialize with Iranian friends, family, and neighbours. Gita's grandparents visit regularly and Gita travels to Iran at least once a year to visit her grandparents and other relatives. When not at school, Gita spends most of her free time with her aunt, an Iranian friend and neighbour, and twin African Australian school friends.

Gita, also 8 at the time of the study, owns nine Bratz dolls, six of which were of Yasmin. She received most of her dolls as Christmas gifts or birthday presents because everyone knew "she liked Yasmin Bratz the most." She gave her many

Yasmin dolls different names including Yass, Yasmica, and Yassi. She named her newest Yasmin Bratz doll Gabriella after her favourite character in Disney's *High School Musical.*

SCRIPTING AND MEDIATION: PHYSICAL MODIFICATION AND NARRATIVE ASSIGNMENT

In what follows we apply Verbeek's theory of scripting and mediation in order to make sense of Gita's and Neli's everyday doll play. Our analysis pays particular attention to the resilience of the original scripting of the dolls, in concert with the cultural resources that the girls use to reshape and repurpose the dolls. Studying the interactions of our participants with their Bratz dolls, we recognize two major levels of interaction: (1) the physical modification of the dolls, and (2) the narrative assignment. While these levels overlap in the girls' play, we separate them here in order to build an analysis of the artifacts in use.

Our participants interpreted the physical characteristics of the dolls according to their individual understanding of their world. In many cases they modified the dolls' physical characteristics or embodied scripts to fit them to their setting. While the dolls' original script encouraged the girls to play with the dolls in particular ways, our participants applied changes to the physical characteristics of their dolls to co-construct their relationship with their world. For example, the material characteristics of the dolls enabled Gita to change the gender of one by cutting its hair short and removing its feminine clothing. While the doll often served as an uncle, it also played the part of a boyfriend, husband, and father. By creating male figures for her narratives Gita revealed how she, as a diasporic girl, incorporates men into her fantasy life. Most men in her world are fathers, husbands, or uncles (uncle is a common term for a family's close male friends among Iranians). In one of her play instances, while Gita assigned the role of boyfriend to her doll, she immediately changed her mind and said, "no, he is the uncle." While having a boyfriend is generally not acceptable in most Iranian families, Gita's roleplaying could also reflect her close relationship with her uncle who had migrated with them and lived in the same house at the time of this research. By fundamentally altering the doll's gender, Gita changed the script embodied in the doll's feminine body. For Gita, the doll became a tool enabling her to explore female-male relationships. By transforming the female body (Figure 1) the doll better enabled Gita to mediate her relationship to men.

Figure 1. Gita cut the doll's hair and off her dress and boots to be able to use the doll as boy. Hair, outfits, and boots seem to be the symbols of gender for Gita.

Some of Yasmin's other features enabled Gita to project other Iranian experiences onto their dolls. The dolls' skin colour and ethnic characteristics enabled more fluid readings by the players. Gita identified Yasmin's nationality as Iranian, saying, "Yasmin is an Iranian name and she looks like Iranians." While Yasmin is not marketed as Iranian, Gita does have a friend in Iran named Yasmin. Moreover, the doll's physical characteristics, such as her olive skin colour, dark hair, and dark eyes suggest Middle Eastern racial characteristics. Both participants preferred brown-haired Yasmin Bratz dolls because of their similar physical characteristics to Iranians. Gita drew upon her Iranian background when she confidently assigned an Iranian identity to the doll. The base script of the dolls made it possible for the girls to find a place for their racial characteristics in a Western context. The dolls that more closely reflected the girls' own ethnicity enabled them to rescript and re-narrate the dolls, thereby bridging their home Iranian culture and mainstream Western culture.

Between the two, Neli demonstrated particular interest in assigning different ethnicities to her dolls by creating Indian dolls. In this way, Neli and the doll co-constructed her understanding of Indian culture drawn from her mother's experiences in India. To assign an Indian character to her dolls, Neli drew bindies on her dolls' foreheads with pens and established the physicality of the new ethnicity for the dolls with big earrings. As Neli explained, "they can be Indians not [only] because of their skin colour, [but also] because Indians use this type of jewellery." In these ways, Neli rescripted the materiality of the artifact in line with her own ethnic understandings. Lacking a designated nationality, race, or ethnicity, Bratz dolls enabled Neli to create a variety of multi-ethnic scripts. Taking cues from the dolls' existing physical characteristics, Neli modified them and rescripted her narratives. As Neli explained, "They can be Indian, English or Turkish. In different plays they can be from different places."

The participants used their dolls as mediating artifacts to co-construct their relationship to the ethnic diversity of their everyday lives. As Neli and Gita's interaction with their Bratz dolls showed, diasporic young girls do not have a sophisticated understanding of ethnic characteristics such as bone structure or beauty standards. Their understanding of ethnicity is limited to skin tones, eye and hair color, accessories, and traditional clothing. In fact these are the characteristics that MGA focused on to introduce the multiethnic dolls, and that are probably the reason that kids from diasporic families in Western contexts welcome these dolls. Because each Bratz doll represents different physical characteristics, girls from different ethnic backgrounds and with different racial experiences may more effectively help in the co-construction of girls' relationship with their Western context.

The girls also drew upon their particular diasporic contexts in order to construct play narratives that often centered on food. The kebab, a favorite Iranian dish, featured prominently in many doll play scenarios. In one of Gita's scenarios, a mother and her daughters discussed whether to make kebab or order it at a restaurant. Neli similarly created a story about her dolls who "are going to a restaurant which serves kebab." Almost all Iranian children in diasporic families have the experience of going to Iranian restaurants with their parents or helping their parents make kebab at home. Adding to the strength of this cultural narrative, which elicits memories of family and friends in their home country, is the kebab party. At the same time, Bratz dolls also provided players with other opportunities to create scenarios that integrated family with host-country cultural experiences. Gita, for instance, constructed a KFC (Kentucky Fried Chicken) fast food restaurant backdrop to a social event for her dolls.

Girls made use of the physical capabilities of Bratz dolls in order to create scenarios with a more specifically diasporic context. Neli liked that Bratz dolls' arms moved and that their legs bent, because then they could sit during the religious meetings she created for them. Participating in religious meetings is an important activity in lives in Neli's religion. While appropriate appearance and conservative outfits are required, Neli used her naked dolls and only focused on the dolls' ability to perform specific motions such as sitting, praying, and dancing. While the dolls' absence of clothing can be interpreted in a variety of ways, there is evidence to suggest that in their naked state the dolls better reflected the liminality of diasporic girls' identities. When Gita moved to Australia she attended a school that taught her how to read and write English. Although Gita wore a uniform at school, while at home her naked Bratz dolls helped her co-construct a new relationship to her world.

CONCLUSION

The interaction between our participants and Bratz dolls suggests that rather than serving as carriers of coded scripts, these dolls can serve as flexible mediators. While a range of researchers have criticized Bratz dolls for being unidentifiably ethnic and purposefully shallow, it would seem that for girls these dolls can mediate diasporic experiences and relationships. While it is clear that the dolls' specific physical characteristics shape players' activities, this study reveals that girls agentively modified and rescripted their dolls in order to mediate between their family's localized ethnicity and their new Australian context. Modifications of dolls' physical characteristics and conceptual alterations of play narratives reflected participants' individual experiences of different cultures and their perceptions of the self.

Through the agentive process of interaction, the study participants developed connections between the dolls and the world as they experienced it. This concept foregrounds the mediating role of artifacts in postphenomenology. As Verbeek (2005, 2006) reminded us, we are active participants in the redesign of artifacts, and, as a consequence, influence the mediating role that artifacts play in our relationship with our world. Rather than passive recipients of the embedded scripts of artifacts, we are surrounded by our own re-scripted (Nouri Esfahani & Carrington, 2013) versions that work to mediate interactions. While it may, on the surface, look like these are just little girls playing with dolls in their bedrooms and living rooms, they are, in fact, actively engaged in the serious activity of shaping and interpreting their world through these everyday artifacts. The study showed that Bratz dolls' racial and ethnic characteristics make them suitable platforms to co-construct girls' lived experiences of culture, gender, race, and ethnicity.

The data in this study suggests that the moment we interact with particular artifacts, we actively re-design them in order to mediate our relationships with our worlds. In turn, rather than the originally scripted artifact, it is always the re-scripted version invoked in our relationship with our world. While these diasporic girls see and understand themselves to be different from the cultural and racial context of contemporary Australia, re-scripting their dolls enables them to co-construct their relationship with their new context and family traditions. However, it was also clear that while the girls actively re-scripted these dolls, the dolls displayed what Verbeek (2005, see also Ihde 1990) called intentionality. The dolls, as artifacts actively involved in the process of interaction, also afforded particular physical alterations and engagements. As artifacts, the dolls moderated the tensions that exist between girls in their diasporic home context and their present Western culture. It is evident from the data analyzed here that rather than creating a nostalgic impression of the past, their doll artifacts, alongside the girls, co-constructed a relationship with their present.

We believe that there is a good potential for dolls to play an important role in the everyday lives of young girls. Rather than serving as conveyors of Western values and practices, the dolls can more usefully be seen as mediating artifacts that co-construct the relationship between the girls and their lived experiences. This is an engaged and interactive process. The diasporic young participants use the dolls as a platform to interpret and respond to cultural and racial difference. These young girls agentively re-script their dolls in ways that make them into useful artifacts in their own lives. As the study demonstrated, it is predominantly the re-scripted version of these dolls with which the girls interact. In other words, these diasporic girls use the dolls as the raw material to shape appropriate artifacts to co-construct their relationship with their lived experiences. In opposition to discursive media and scholarly understandings, Bratz dolls in real use context can be transformed into useful mediators. Diasporic girls use these artifacts as tools to build their relationships and act upon their worlds. The customised versions of mass-produced and globally marketed artifacts become important mediators of relationships, and as such, work to co-construct the lived experience and perceptions of young girls.

REFERENCES

Aidani, M. (2007). *Displaced narratives of Iranian migrants and refugees: Constructions of self and the struggle for representation* (PhD dissertation). Faculty of Arts, Education and Human Development School of Psychology, Victoria University, Australia.

Akrich, M. (1992). The de-scription of technological objects. In W. E. Bijker (Ed.), *Shaping technology/building society: Studies in sociotechnical change*. Cambridge, MA: MIT Press.

Almeida, D. (2009). Where have all the children gone? A visual semiotic account of advertisements for fashion dolls. *Visual Communication, 8*(4), 481–501.

Chin, E. (1999). Ethnically correct dolls: Toying with the race industry. *American Anthropologist, 101*(2), 305–321.

DuCille, A. (1994). Dyes and dolls: Multicultural Barbie and the merchandising of difference. *Differences: A Journal of Feminist Cultural Studies, 6*(1), 47–68.

Guerrero, L. (2009). Can the subaltern shop? The commodification of difference in the Bratz Dolls. *Cultural studies ↔ Critical methodologies, 9*(2), 186–196.

Hains, R. (2012). Challenging our assumptions: Is there anything good about Bratz? Retrieved from http://rebeccahains.wordpress.com/2012/01/07/challengingour-assumptions-is-there-any-thing-good-about-bratz/

Ihde, D. (1990). *Technology and the Lifeworld.* The Indiana Series in the Philosophy of Technology. Bloomingdale: Indiana University Press.

Ihde, D. (2009). *Post-phenomenology and technoscience: The Peking University lectures.* Albany, NY: State University of New York Press.

Inness, S. A. (1998). "Anti-Barbies": The American Girls collection and political ideologies. In S. Inness (Ed.), *Delinquents and debutantes: Twentieth-century American girls' cultures* (pp. 164–183). New York, NY: New York University Press.

Latour, B. (1992). Where are the missing masses? The sociology of a few mundane artifacts. In W. E. Bijker (Ed.), *Shaping technology/building society* (pp. 225–258). Cambridge, MA: MIT Press.

MacAllister, M. (2007). Girls with a passion for fashion. *Journal of Children and Media, 1*(3), 244–256.

Nouri Esfahani, N., & Carrington, V. (in press). (Re)Scripting Barbie: Post-phenomenology and everyday artifacts. In S. Poyntz & J. Kennedy (Eds.), *Phenomenology of youth culture and globalization: Lifeworlds and surplus meanings in changing times.* London, England: Routledge.

Rand, E. (1995). *Barbie's queer accessories.* Durham, NC: Duke University Press.

Talbot, M. (2006). Little hotties: Barbie's new arrivals. *The New Yorker.* Retrieved from http://newamerica.net/node/7772

Verbeek, P. (2005). *What things do: Philosophical reflections on technology, agency, and design* (R. Crease, Trans.). Pennsylvania, PA: Pennsylvania State University Press.

Verbeek, P. (2006). Materializing morality: Design ethics and technological mediation. *Science, Technology and Human Values, 31*(3), 361–380.

Verbeek, P. (2008). *Morality in design: Design ethics and the morality of technological artifacts.* In: *Philosophy and Design* (pp. 91–103). Berlin, Germany: Springer.

Verbeek, P. P. & Slob, A. F. L. (2006). *User behavior and technology development: Shaping sustainable relations between consumers and technologies.* In Verbeek & Slob (editors). Eco-efficiency in industry and science. Dordrecht: Springer.

CHAPTER EIGHT

Barbie Sex Videos: Making Sense OF Children's Media-Making

ELIZABETH CHIN

When I tell people that I enjoy watching sex videos that are made by children and starring Barbies, I am generally greeted with a look of horror. I take such looks to mean shock and disbelief that children might actually make something like a "sex video," and shock and disbelief that an adult such as myself might watch such videos. "Perhaps," I can see people thinking, "she's a pedophile." Let me unpack the statement "I enjoy sex videos made by children and starring Barbies." By enjoy, I mean that I find these videos incredibly smart and funny. Sex, in these productions, is rarely, if ever, prurient or pornographic. Let's face it: sex between Barbies, or between Barbie and Ken, or between Barbie and a Cookie Monster or between Barbie and a Teenage Mutant Ninja Turtle is just hard to take seriously. Children's video productions featuring Barbie and having to do with sex certainly engage in a kind of naughtiness, since kids know they're not supposed to be playing with Barbies in "that way" or dealing with "those things." Yet the narratives children pursue in these videos are not reducible either to sex or Barbie per se: they explore a range of complex territories having to do with romance, power, gender, and sexuality in ways that are sophisticated and witty. In this chapter I will focus discussion on one such video made by kids and posted on YouTube: *Barbie Sex Life*: (madiluvzyoo, 2010).

There are hundreds, perhaps thousands of Barbie videos made by children on YouTube. Nearly all of them present narratives that detail aspects of Barbie's life, whether she meets Ken (barbiebabe890, 2007), goes on dates with Ken

(BarbiesStory, 2008), or gets married to Ken (barbiebabe890, 2007). She also has an encounter with an evil dentist (CRAZYCOMMERCIALSR, 2011), takes a driving test (reggie1556, 2011), and goes to McDonald's (SuperJeets, 2011). The range and complexity of these videos is quite broad, both in terms of subject matter and in terms of the level of technical expertise. There are several kid-made multi-episode series, the longest-running of which are *Barbie Happy Family* and *Barbie Dream House*. Leveraging the monetization and branding potential of You-Tube, these series have tight and consistent production values, modeling and incorporating a wide range of media-savvy strategies, such as affiliated web sites, t-shirt sales, and Twitter feeds. At the other end of the spectrum are messily shot clips that are often accompanied by the statement: "I did this one day when I was bored." According to makers' YouTube profiles, all tend to be in what is often identified as middle childhood: between 10 and 12 years of age; most are girls, but boys participate as well; most videos are made by pairs or trios of kids, with a strong sprinkling of videos made by single individuals as well. Looking closely at clues ranging from bedroom décor to faces or hands appearing in the videos, when a maker claims to be a child there are no glaring reasons to doubt this is the case. Being sure of the age or identity of child YouTube participants can often be guesswork, but the same is true when participants claim to be adults. Without strong reasons to doubt the identity profile provided by YouTube media-makers, accepting the ways they identify themselves by age or gender is the default practice in the emergent scholarship in the area (Burgess & Green, 2009; Vonderau, 2010). In the case of *Barbie Sex Life*, the poster, madiluvzyoo, has uploaded 11 videos since joining YouTube in 2007. Of videos loaded several years after *Barbie Sex Life*, two show a cheer squad performing at games; one shows a young, white woman in a cheer outfit getting her tongue pierced; and in another, a different young woman is getting a belly-button piercing (with over 93,000,000 views, this is madiluvzyoo's most-watched video). I did try to make direct contact with madiluvsyoo but my enquiries received no reply. Still, given the internal and external clues, I am reasonably confident that *Barbie Sex Life*, like so many other similar videos, was indeed made by kids, one of whom was likely the young woman appearing in most of the videos.

In terms of production values, technical finesse, and general sophistication, *Barbie Sex Life* falls somewhere in the middle of the spectrum defined by slick series such as *Barbie Happy Family* at one end and the "I did this when I was bored" type of video on the other. However, like Lange (2011), and others who look at children's participation with media platforms, I am less interested in assessing the relative amateur-ness or professionalism of a particular video than I am in excavating individual videos for layers of meaning. While unique, *Barbie Sex Life* is not particularly remarkable in the child-made Barbie video universe: it is neither technically excellent nor especially terrible. In choosing to focus upon a relatively "average" video, I emphasize that the kind of cultural complexity evident in these productions is typical rather than exceptional. Like many other similar videos, *Barbie Sex Life* is scripted, shows purposeful set-making, costuming, and editing, and deals with complex social situations as its subject matter. Narratively complex, this video is like most other Barbie videos in that it is not part of an ongoing series; furthermore, like most, the maker's channel is not marketed or monetized or branded.

One obvious way in which *Barbie Sex Life* is unusual is that it is somewhat sexually graphic as part of the narrative. From the outset, the internet has been perceived to be a territory where children could be exploited by unscrupulous or even dangerous adults. As an indication of the extent of such concerns, an Amazon search using the words "child internet safety" returns 469 results. Among those books are one co-authored by former first lady Laura Bush (Leavitt & Linford, 2006), a safety guide from a "cyber cop" (Klinkhart, 2012), and an American Girl guide to internet safety (Cindrich, 2009). Parents are urged to monitor and even police their children's internet access for a variety of reasons: some biologically rooted arguments focus on the health problems associated with repetitive motion required in keyboarding and in the near-focus typical of looking at a screen; social worries range from children becoming too anti-social from living in fantasy worlds that substitute for face-to-face engagement, to kids becoming too social, in the form of creating relationships on-line that morph into real-world interactions. In many cases, fears regarding the internet and children have risen to the level of a moral panic. These fears are also highly gendered, with cyberspace itself being coded as male (Holloway & Valentine, 2000, p. 139), and girls understood as being especially vulnerable to such characters as "dirty old men" (Buckingham & Bragg, 2004, p. 10). Even as all this energy is spent attempting to protect children from contact with inappropriate material on the internet, they seek it out and, at least in this case, produce the very material from which many seek to protect them. Yet as we all know, children are interested in sex from an early age, and they variously think about, talk about, or imaginatively engage with sex (or what they think is sex). In the interesting and powerful space that is the forbidden, children show themselves to be curious, funny, and remarkably well-adjusted.

Understanding any culture is a complicated task, and children's culture is as complicated as any other. Children and childhood studies have, in recent decades, begun to achieve a legitimate space in the academy, and this has helped to demonstrate, via a growing and dynamic literature, the myriad facets of children's lives, experiences, and cultures. I approach children's culture from an interpretive and constructivist point of view, which is to say I understand children's culture as socially constructed, and in need of careful interpretation. With regard to children, sex, and media, prominent media researchers David Buckingham and Sara Bragg (2004) noted that nearly all the research has been focused on identifying negative effects, and research frameworks nearly universally assume that children are "powerless to resist the 'messages' to which they are 'exposed'" (p. 10). A similar approach dominates thinking about children's engagement with media violence, and the discourse of imitative violence is quite similar to the discourse about children and what might be called imitative sex. Both suffer from similar conceptual and methodological problems, among them what Tobin (2000) described (with regard to media and violence) as "sloppy reasoning and half-baked formulations" (p. 26). When these are the starting assumptions, it is obvious that thinking about the ways in which children might differently interpret what they see or experience is, by definition, outside the bounds of consideration. The work of Tobin, and of Buckingham and Bragg among others, is part of a small but growing cadre of media analysis that demonstrates the fallacy of assuming that kids uncritically reproduce what they witness in media. Like these other scholars, my view is that children engage in highly sophisticated, nuanced, and critical discourses that explore the world around them. This includes having a point of view about Barbie and all that she represents.

The video I analyze here constitutes a very specific form of cultural production by children. Fully engaged with technologies and routines of a variety of media—film, video, and popular music—the videos are actual media productions, often involving the creation of scripts, sets, costumes, and other production elements. As instances of play, this video and others like it are at once private and public, and exist in a play space made possible by social media and the internet, a space in which the play is about media production, while simultaneously the play produces media as its product. The production of play (the video) lives well beyond the spatial confines of the physical play space or immediate social group. In these productions children make use of powerful narratives about gender, class, and race. Using a theoretical framework based in the ideas of Bakhtin, Tobin (2000) rejected the pervasive assumption that children's media engagement is primarily imitative ("monkey see/monkey do") and/or psychological, that is, an expression of an individual's inner thoughts and feelings. Rather, he argued, we can understand this engagement as profoundly social and ideological. Understood in this way, Tobin stated that "we can view children's talk about the media as expressions less of their individual concerns and understandings than of larger social concerns and understandings that get articulated by and through individuals as they speak" (p. 19). Barbie sex videos are explorations and articulations of kids' ideas about such topics as marriage, romance, relationships, and consumerism. As such, they offer a powerful view of the degree to which children are active creators of meaning in their own lives. Like Tobin, I take the position that children actively experiment with social roles; make commentaries whose flavor may take any number of forms from ironic to parodic to serious; use citation to communicate; cobble a range of approaches together in a form of bricolage. Interpretation of what these productions mean, then, is neither easy nor definitive because they engage with multiple discourses and myriad social issues. Therefore, interpretation is and must be at once contingent and emergent.

This approach to interpretation is what Bakhtin (1986) himself called "creative understanding" (p. 7), a concept particularly useful when thinking about how grownups might approach meaning-making with respect to children's media-making. Writing of understanding across culture and time in literary studies, Bakhtin asserted that creative understanding

> does not renounce itself, its own place in time, its own culture; and it forgets nothing.... In the realm of culture, outsideness is a most powerful factor in understanding. It is only in the eyes of *another* culture that foreign culture reveals itself fully and profoundly. (p. 7)

Part of what I find compelling about Bakhtin's position is that it acknowledges the importance of cultural difference in generating complex understanding of cultural materials. In this case, that acknowledgement is one that understands the difference between adults and children without reducing one to the other, or substituting one for the other. Furthermore, he recognizes and embraces the notion that cultural producers may not—indeed cannot—know or understand the totality of meaning contained in the things they make. The "outsideness" of the observer allows for a kind of understanding quite different, and very valuable, from that of the insider, and yet is not a substitute for it. Outsiders can see things that insiders cannot. The subtlety of what Bakhtin is proposing here goes well beyond the old insider/outsider debate. He fully recognizes the degree to which one's own position and identity render the other meaningful in the context of the relationship itself: "we seek answers to our own questions…and the foreign culture responds to us by revealing to us its new aspects and new semantic depths" (p. 7). It is this element of continually unfolding meaning, and a recognition of the otherness and legitimacy of children's culture, that is missing from dominant discourses about kids' engagement with Barbie. Bakhtin concluded by saying that "Without *one's own* questions one cannot creatively understand anything other or foreign" (p. 7).

When attending to children's culture, adults tend to forget quite a bit. They forget how smart and sly children can be, and they forget that children are quite capable of independent thinking. This forgetting is especially evident when it comes to children and Barbie, and even more profound when it comes to children and sex. Feminist critiques of Barbie tend to assume that kids (girls) will directly take on her innate messages about unrealistic beauty standards and vapid social values; Jan Susina's (1999) observation that girls playing with Barbie prepare for lives in the magazine *Cosmopolitan* is one that captures this perspective (p. 124). In this view, Barbie is both an embodiment and cause of problematic and pervasive ideas about gender and beauty in particular (Edut, 1998; Wolf, 2002). Children are cast as uncritical and powerless in their interactions with her (or anything else), and solutions to the problem need to be provided to them. In the 1990s there was the "Happy To Be Me" doll, who addressed Barbie's body issues by having flat, rather than pointed feet and a "more realistic" body shape (although, as a friend of mine remarked: "why are her thighs not touching?")("She's No Barbie, Nor Does She Care to Be," 1991). American Girl Dolls, with their sexless, soft cloth bodies, were created expressly as an alternative to Barbie, emphasizing girls as good at school, and having real-life struggles set in specific periods of American history. In 2011 a college student made a "life-sized" papier-mâché Barbie as a tool for talking about anorexia. This project gained national media attention despite the truly terrible level of craft and finish exhibited in her creation (Slayen, 2011). More recently, a group of feminist scholars developed and implemented a workshop built around the idea of rejecting Barbie so that girls could break away from her limitations (Collins, Lidinsky, Rusnock, & Torstrick, 2012). Each of these solutions shares the assumption that children absorb problematic messages from Barbie about beauty and their bodies, and that these messages need to be counteracted by taking Barbie down.

"Solutions" such as this, confidently addressing the supposed problems children develop because of Barbie, forget the important step of looking to kids themselves to learn what they think about Barbie and/or investigate how they actually play with her (Duhamel, 1994; Messner, 2000; MacDougall, 2003). When British researchers gave Barbie dolls to elementary school children to play with, the results were not what many might assume. Girls shrieked "eeeew," and not "oooooh," going on to chop the doll's hair off and even decapitate her ("Barbie Girls Play Rough," 2009). Over many years of teaching a freshman writing seminar on Barbie, I read personal accounts from dozens of students. To be sure, they played fashion show and let's ride in the Corvette; in addition, however, their accounts gave testimony to a broad and perhaps even startling range of relationships with the doll. One young woman curated huge arrays of handmade couture-style clothing for her Barbies as a way of maintaining a relationship with her often absent mother; others blew their dolls up, melted them, or otherwise destroyed Barbie's perfection in an attempt to fashion their own independence; one young man spent his childhood passing a boxed Barbie back and forth with his best friend as an endless birthday gift joke. Another young man remembered taking a nude Barbie doll into his sleeping bag at a sleepover party. "It felt," he wrote, "like a long, cold, hard teddy bear." Which brings me to the question of sex.

As Erica Rand (1995) documented so beautifully in her book *Barbie's Queer Accessories*, sex play with Barbies has long been part of children's private Barbie activity repertoires. Such play is built around narratives of gender and sexuality, and, I would argue, is less centered upon particular sex acts than it is upon explicating children's own ideas of and observations about sex and its place in peoples' lives. This is not to say that such sex play is not "sexy" or sexual; indeed, it is quite often explicit. However, such sex play is colored by children's lack of information about what, exactly, sex is.

In addition, what looks like sex to an adult may well not read as sex to a kid; as they play, sex may or may not be part of a narrative they construct using butt-naked Barbies in the bathtub. Perhaps those Barbies are hurtling into outer space. Even when doing sex, the details may be fuzzy: for one of Rand's (1995) informants, the culminating elements of "sex" were Barbie serving drinks to Ken on a tray, at which point Ken would hypnotize Barbie, waving his unbendable arms up and down in front of her face. The end. Rand's book was built around grown women's remembered Barbie play and fantasies. We all know that children are interested in what sex is, and how it works both literally and figuratively, in peoples' lives. Most of us, if we are honest, remember making our Barbies have sex, in some form or another. But the way that kids do Barbie sex is—by definition—not adult in its nature. As Rand's work shows, what sex IS and how children articulate it (even in its remembered versions) may or may not include acts recognized by adults as constituting sex. So the real question, as far as I'm concerned, is this: what does sex mean to kids and how is Barbie used to articulate these meanings? Any number of factors make investigating these questions incredibly difficult. My interest is in children's spontaneous sex play with Barbies, something that adults are really unlikely to witness given the charged nature of the very idea of children and sex.

In my analysis of *Barbie Sex Life* I aim to show that the kind of Barbie sex that kids explore is ultimately about ideas and symbols, narratives and stories. Yes, the videos and their makers address sex as a topic; but they also address heterosexuality, relationships, life trajectories, class, race, and gender. Such videos are, in a very basic and classic sense, a form of play: they take place in a space marked off from the real world and they conform to a set of rules and/or boundaries that establish the continuity and legibility of the play itself. The literature on the study of play is extensive, and there is not space to review it in detail here. Drawing from Vygotsky, Huizinga, and Caillois, I emphasize that play is a conceptual space that is set apart from the real world; conceptually "free" from real world constraints, play nonetheless is a highly structured activity, involving rules and boundaries. Furthermore, as Bateson (1972) noted, play necessarily requires cognitive sophistication: far from being simple, play is wonderfully complex (Huizinga, 1950; Caillois, 1961; Vygotsky 1967; Bakhtin, 1982; Bakhtin, 1986).

Ethnographers typically minutely analyze particular cultural moments in spirals of increasing detail, couched in broader knowledge of the larger cultural scene. Such knowledge is acquired by spending long stretches of time embedded in a culture, following the routines of daily life. When dealing with such taboo subjects as children and sex in the United States, it is both ethically complex and methodologically sticky to get much ethnographic access to children's perspectives. Luckily, there's YouTube. From the point of view of an ethnographer who is interested in children's play, YouTube is a combination of goldmine and godsend. The videos discussed here, and many others I have reviewed but do not specifically analyze, have the advantage of dealing with sex and being made by kids in relative privacy. As such, they show a kind of narrative freedom that differs significantly from that which kids might explore in an experimental setting such as a university laboratory or even a formal interview, settings where direct adult engagement frames the encounter. These videos are produced in kids' own homes and rooms, under conditions of their own construction and choosing; while adults might be nearby, they are nearly never "on set," so to speak. They are complex media productions, and they are at the same time an especially interesting form of play: during the making of the video they are at once naughty and secretive, which is much of what makes them fun. Later, when they have been uploaded, the videos are even naughtier for their publicness, being broadcast beyond the confines of the home, and thus no longer secretive at all. The careful scripting, creation of sets and props, editing, and other production values in these videos also showcases the painstaking choice and construction of themes and narratives chosen by kids. Unlike the spontaneous play using toys and sand tables that is used so often by psychologists to gain access to children's unexpressed thoughts and emotions, these Barbie videos are purposeful media utterances that both embody and communicate children's knowledge of and play with powerful cultural themes and ideas. Unmediated by direct interaction with adults, these productions are sites in which a wealth of material about kids' own ideas and perspectives are generated and distributed. These ideas are evident both in the videos and in the comments that others make about them. Quite often, those uploading videos will admonish respondents in advance, telling them not to be "haters," or asking viewers to excuse technical errors. Commenters may engage in discussions among themselves, variously criticizing each other for being mean, or defending the video. The commentary also provides insight into how some people, at least, receive and respond to what they are seeing.

In an essay entitled "Reading the Difficult Text," Brown (2008) wrote that:

> the labor of reading the difficult text should involve an intensive political reflection about our reading protocols, a reflection that asks us to first explore the different ways we read as we read and, second, expose the connections between these reading habits and Eurocentric or imperial ways of knowing.

How is our own ability to interpret and understand bolstered by framing *Barbie Sex Life* as a difficult text rather than a simple one? Returning to Bakhtin, how can we, as outsiders, generate creative understanding of videos such as *Barbie Sex Life* through the disciplined practice of asking questions? What might be the "reading protocols" at work when viewing a YouTube video publicly posted, made by kids, and dealing with "Barbie sex life"? Furthermore, how might these protocols be framed, as Brown (2008) said, by "Eurocentric or imperial ways of knowing?" To this I would also add the question, "How are adult understandings of meaning different from those created by children?" Clearly, if one reads *Barbie Sex Life* from the adult point of view that children's exploration of sexual themes is by definition inappropriate, even dangerous, there is little room left for understanding this production as anything other than perverse or disturbed. Such a point of view is simultaneously imperialist, Eurocentric, and adult-centric, and works to suffocate the rich meanings embedded in the work itself. Alternatively, we can look at *Barbie Sex Life* the way we look at other complex texts, whether works of art, films, or novels. Like any cultural text, *Barbie Sex Life* may well be interpreted and understood in ways unanticipated by the author, maker, or director. Finding meaning in the medium need not reflect upon the personal psychology of the makers. Rather, as Tobin (2000) emphasized, one of the great values of close reading is that it can elicit citations of and commentaries about the larger social and cultural milieu within which both maker and interpreter are embedded. From this point of view, the value of interpretation is not so much to declare a given meaning right and another wrong. Symbols, by their very nature, never have only one meaning. Rather, the value of interpretation done in the spirit of creative understanding is to challenge our own assumptions, to enter other points of view and worlds of meaning, and thereby to expand our own understanding of the world through the act of recognizing—and perhaps even delighting in—the integrity discovered in places where we had previously failed to look.

BARBIE SEX LIFE

The YouTube video *Barbie Sex Life* is a stop-motion narrative lasting just under 2 minutes. Perhaps not surprisingly, Barbie's sex life, in this version, begins with a wedding. The narrative alternates between enactments of stereotypical heterosexual romance and raunchier displays of nakedness and sex. These shifts in tone and content are marked by their accompanying soundtracks: when we are in the syrupy, stereotype mode, we hear Justin Bieber's 2010 song "Baby"; when we are in sex mode, the music shifts to Salt-N-Pepa's 1998 song "Push It (Real Good)." There is no spoken dialogue; the different narrative sections of the story are marked through a series of titles, which appear as white lettering on a Barbie-pink background.

Before moving into detailed interpretation and analysis of *Barbie Sex Life*, let me provide a description of the video itself.

Title: The wedding

[Action is taking place on a well-groomed and very green lawn; in the background is a clean and large parking area with garage spaces, perhaps for an apartment complex.]

Pink Barbie car enters the left side of the frame, pulls to a stop in the center. Barbie in a wedding dress and veil exits the car. There are three to four other Barbies as guests. She walks down the aisle, which is made of toilet paper laid over the grass.

00:12 Cut to: Action taking place on another piece of lawn. In the background there is a wooden fence and tall, trimmed cypress trees, evenly spaced and very tidy. Barbie and Ken holding hands and facing each other. They kiss and she jumps into his arms.

"You know you love me, I know you care."

00:16 Barbie and Ken get into the pink Barbie car.

00:18 Rear shot of car with "Just Married" sign attached to back. Barbie and Ken are seated on top of the back with the car's top down.

"Just shout whenever"

Car drives off into the distance.

"and I'll be—" [sound cuts off]

[instrumental Salt-N-Pepa]

Cut to: Ken reclining naked.

00:23 Cut to:

Title: The honeymoon. [sic]

"P-p-push it real good!"

Ken is naked and seated facing the camera, leaning up against a lavender heart-shaped pillow that has a pink heart-shaped peace sign appliquéd on it. Barbie approaches him, naked also. She kneels down on top of him. They flip over so he is on top of her, her legs are spread open. Beneath the pink heart-shaped peace sign are the letters LOVE (which you can now see). They flip and turn again and Barbie is now straddling Ken, facing the camera as she does so. She rises up on her knees and waves one arm in the air like a cowgirl on a bucking bronco. They flip over and over a few times.

00:37 Cut to:

Title: There first house. [sic]

"You want my love, you want my heart…"

Ken and Barbie drive up to the dream house in the pink car. Barbie is wearing a pink bubble skirt and a black-and-white striped sleeveless top. Ken is still wearing his tuxedo, minus the jacket. Ken is driving.

00:45 "And we will never ever ever be apart…"

Ken walks around the back of the car to Barbie's side and picks her up to carry her over the threshold of the Barbie dream house.

00:47 "Are we an item?"

Now from inside the house we see Ken carry Barbie into the living room of the dream house.

"Girl quit playin'…"

Barbie and Ken get into the elevator and go up to the second floor. Barbie starts to take off her top.

00:49 "P-p-push it real good!"

Barbie removes the rest of her clothes and is naked. Ken is seated on the couch out of the frame (we can see his feet sticking out into the left side of the frame). Barbie sits naked on the floor to take off her black high heels one by one.

00:54 Barbie gets into the shower stall.

00:58 Barbie exits the shower stall.

Cut to:

1:00 Title: Her first pregnancy test.

"We're just friends? What are you sayin'?"

Barbie is standing in the bathroom wearing a long-sleeved top and a pair of pink shorts. She pulls down her shorts and sits on the toilet. She holds a white pregnancy tester in her left hand and looks at it. (It looks like it is made of a small twist of paper.)

"My first love broke my heart for the first time"

Close up:

Barbie's feet. She is now standing.

"and we're like,"

The tester strip falls to the floor by her feet. Barbie turns and walks into the other room.

1:13 "Baby, baby, baby, oh,"

Barbie walks to Ken who is still sitting on the couch; Ken stands up and hugs her.

"Baby, baby, baby no,"

Title: 7 months later.

1:19 Barbie is visibly pregnant, she is standing facing Ken in the bathroom.

"Baby, baby, baby oh!"

Title: Her birth.

1:22 Barbie is lying down on a piece of 8½ x 11 paper that stands in for a hospital bed. She is wrapped in white toilet paper and her legs are bent, knees up. Another Barbie, wrapped in toilet paper, has her hands outstretched between Barbie's open knees.

"Baby baby baby oh,"

Title: They lived happy ever after.

"Like baby baby baby no—"

1:34 Ken and Barbie standing together, Barbie holding a baby (made of toilet paper?) wrapped in pink. Ken is standing behind, Barbie's head is turned toward him over her right shoulder.

1:39 "Thought you'd always be mine."

Credits roll:

Title: Barbie and ken. [sic]

Barbie
Barbie
Ken
Ken
Camera 1
Liz
Camera 2
Ross
Camera 3 and director
Jess

TECHNICALITIES

Let's begin with a technical break down of *Barbie Sex Life* as a way to begin engaging with this text. First it is evident that this video took work and planning. It would have taken much less time to move the Barbies around using hands, but the choice of stop-motion narrative is much more complex to accomplish. Stop-motion has the advantage of creating a more realistic vista in which the Barbies seem to move and come to life. The technique itself is challenging because it requires imagining action in very tiny, incremental bits, and photographing each minute element individually. In the first segment "The Wedding," there are over 50 separate stop-motion images, each of which required the makers to compose and shoot individual moments making up a sequence that lasts only a few seconds. This segment alone could have taken upwards of one or two hours to shoot. The makers needed to know what they wanted to convey, and to carefully position the elements of the scene to create the effect and tone they had in mind.

Throughout the video, costumes and props play an important role. In "The Wedding," Barbie wears a wedding dress and veil, while Ken is in his tuxedo; Barbie changes clothes with each successive scene, although Ken does not—something of an indication of whose story this is. The pink car, the "just married" sign, the pregnancy test, and the baby are all props made specifically for the shots in which they appear.

Framing is also purposeful and varied. The video uses closeups, long, and medium shots in order to communicate point of view and to emphasize aspects of the story. In the section "The honeymoon," an image of Ken nakedly awaiting Barbie briefly appears before the text itself, a powerful way to foreground his (probable) anticipation of the antics to follow. As we proceed into the honeymoon, another shot features Ken in the background, with Barbie's legs in the near foreground; the composition reminds me of something one might find in a James Bond film when the evil temptress is approaching the suave yet savvy spy. Later, in the segment

"Barbie's first pregnancy test," we begin with a medium shot of Barbie in the dream house, standing in the second-floor bathroom. When she is reading the results of the test, we move to a close-up of her feet, and then we see the tester stick drop into the frame from above, as if she has dropped it in surprise. With these and other framed moments, it is evident that the makers of the film are familiar with many of the conventions of framing for visual effect and are able to use them with creative purpose to forward the narrative they are producing.

Comments about elements of the production were common, and show that those viewing *Barbie Sex Life* were interested in and paid attention to technical questions, props, and narrative: of just over 250 individual comments, 54 of them had something to do with the technical elements of the video. User realitymuzic3 wrote: "thumbs up if you noticed barbies hand got stuck in the shower door," while user gleek7478 commented that "the camera is a little shakey." Criticism was offered by four different users regarding attention to detail in the birth scene. Discussion also went back and forth as to the timing of Barbie's birth, with users commenting to each other about why Barbie gives birth 7 months after the pregnancy test. While JulieNCharlie said "LOL It's 9 Months not 7 LMFAO!!!" giana4598 thought "She was 2 months pregnant when she took the test. :|," and SunsetBabli added "or it could have been an early delivery XD maybe she thought she was getting fat." Part of what is interesting in these discussions is the degree to which other YouTube participants are paying careful attention to *Barbie Sex Life*. Noting the exact time (1:23) that a production glitch is visible, as linda123199 did, takes at least two or three viewings, as well as taking the time and making the effort to make the comment. The specificity of the production-related comments indicates that these viewers, at least, were interested in learning, seeing, or evaluating minute technical details.

The use of sound is also centrally important in this production, which features two songs: Justin Bieber's "Baby" and Salt-N-Pepa's "Push It." There were more comments about the music choice (34) than there were about the inclusion of sex (21). Here the comments tended to be about Bieber and/or his music, but not in connection to the way the song was used in the video, in connection to the narrative. The consensus seems to have been, as tellmehaboutit4 succinctly put it "Justin Bieber SUCKS." Interestingly, only two comments showed up about "Push It," one asking what the song was, and the other suggesting that it should have been used as the sound in the birth scene. Only one comment, from alidemoss, noticed the connection between Bieber's song and Barbie's pregnancy, birth, and growing family: "now I get y they played baby," she wrote.

Alternating between Justin Bieber's "Baby" and Salt-N-Pepa's "Push It," these two musical riffs are used to indicate changes in mood and action. "Baby," with its "my-voice-hasn't-changed-yet" vocals singing about first love, is suffused with a kind of soft-focus, dreamy yearning about romance; "Push It," with its aggressive lyrics and pumping instrumental, is in comparison raw and explicit. Interestingly, nearly all of the comments on the music indicated that, given the content of the narrative being created, "Baby" is a great choice, since the culmination of the story is about Barbie actually having a baby; when Justin Bieber keens "Baby, baby, baby, oh—" his words become a double entendre as we see the pregnancy tester fall to the floor, and later, when a toilet-paper-wrapped Barbie is shown in the process of giving birth. The cuts to "Push It" are abrupt. From sweet romance we are thrust (so to speak) into images of nakedness and, in the honeymoon, to some pretty explicit genital-free Barbie sex. Just as "Baby" has words to match the themes of the video, "Push It" also says things that match what is being shown. The two songs were made 12 years apart, with "Baby" being a hit at the time this video was being made, while "Push It" came out before two of the video-makers were even born. While we do not know how many songs were considered for the soundtrack, it is clear that the choice of songs involved selections that were considered and consequential. Furthermore, as the video proceeds, so do the songs themselves, in particular "Baby," which dominates the soundtrack in terms of seconds-on-air. The song is allowed to play out, despite being chopped into as "Push It" intrudes. Such cutting of music took some expertise to accomplish.

All of this work and effort does seem to take its toll. Compare the section "Her birth" to the opening sequence, and the stop-motion has all but disappeared. The framing is sloppy, with an unused Barbie and some other junk lying in the top of the frame, and those who commented on the video pointed out these flaws repeatedly. "1:23 dead chick in the corner," offered linda123199, while likelazo said "wat the hell y is there a dead chich in the corner." The sense is that the film-makers are losing patience or getting tired, and just want to get it all finished. In the segments that follow the birth, the stop-motion virtually disappears and we get sequences of still shots, held for a second or two, rather than the elaborate nearly live action movement we had at the start.

Bringing the whole thing to a close, the credits begin to roll. Actors and their roles come first, followed by the names and jobs of the video makers. Here they distinguish between cameras one, two, and three (although the video itself does not show the kind of variety of shots that a typical three-camera setup would), and Jess is credited with being the director. This is the moment in which we also learn that one of the three video-makers is likely a boy, since camera two is credited to "Ross."

The visual tropes that dominate television are strongly evident in this video. Even the assignment of cameras one, two, and three has been highlighted—a sign that the makers have a working knowledge of the ways in which technical aspects of image-making are represented. The variety of shots, the purposeful framing, the use of props, are all incorporated in ways that bring detail and richness to the narrative and the visual storytelling. These kids are, without a doubt, more than competent media-makers, and those who view the video and have commented on it similarly pay attention to technical details, offering criticism, advice, or asking questions.

NARRATIVES OF SEX AND RACE

Media-making involves a great deal more than technical know-how. It is also about the presentation and use of symbols and images in order to communicate ideas. The titles inserted throughout the *Barbie Sex Life* video follow this trajectory: marriage, honeymoon, first house, pregnancy test, birth, and happily ever after. In this way, the titles neatly replicate—and in proper order—standard milestones in the normative, white, and middle class version of the female life-course. Yet the video makes clear that text does not communicate everything. There is subtext, and there is the physical reality as well, and these need not always match. The meanings communicated in the visuals themselves display a range of moods and content. For instance, although the video is entitled *Barbie Sex Life*, sex is never textually identified; the word sex appears in the title, but never again. In a video one might assume is all about sex, it turns out that sex is shown only in the honeymoon scene; as the video progresses, the sex falls away, and the narrative of heterosexual love and family-making takes over completely.

From the outset, then, the relationship with Barbie and sex, between the child video makers and sex (and Barbie, and Barbie's sex life) is multifaceted and complex. Why is it that the video is titled *Barbie Sex Life* but seems to tell the story of a life in which sex happens only once, to be replaced with a baby and happily ever after? Why is sex visually explicit in the honeymoon, but never textually identified except in the title? There is a way in which the ambiguity on offer here is precisely the ambiguity children experience in contemporary American culture: one in which sex is visually available in all sorts of ways, yet verbally forbidden. Perhaps these children are reproducing the conditions they themselves experience: they see sexualized images in music videos, in magazines, on television, and yet speaking frankly of sex is somehow impossible to do. They leave it to Salt-N-Pepa to do the talking.

At the time the video was made, Justin Bieber had yet to be in a publicly acknowledged romance. Moreover, he was an acknowledged Christian (Ronson, 2010). His public relationship to sex, then, was not only nil, it was one that if it were to be spoken (which it was not) could confidently be summed up as "abstinence." He sings of romance, not sexuality. He embodied virginity, both for the boy and the girl. On the flip side, Salt-N-Pepa actually had a hit song entitled "Let's Talk About Sex." The contrast could hardly be more explicit or complete. As hip hop's first all-female rap crew, Salt-N-Pepa specialized in writing and performing songs in which women were sexually active, sexually aware, and sexually subjectified. In their videos, it was men who were on display for the pleasure of women, and not the other way around. Whether or not the three makers of *Barbie Sex Life* knew the details upon which we might now be able to compare and contrast these two songs and the artists that made them, the contrast itself communicates powerfully at a number of levels. Bieber's angelic innocence vs. Salt-N-Pepa's explicit articulation of sexuality comes through in the song titles. The musical styles—Bieber's sweet teeny-bopper pop vs. Salt-N-Pepa's liberated hip hop—create contrast of their own.

The issue of race, another thing in American culture that is endlessly visible and yet powerfully silenced, is also relevant here. On the one hand we have a yearning and innocent white boy; on the other, a group of self-empowered black women. In the neoliberal twenty-first century, Bieber offers a vision of masculinity in the form of a boy-poised-on-the-verge-of-manhood that is at once deeply sensitive and not sexually coercive in the least: it is he who has had his heart broken, by a girl who exercised her own autonomy and left him. Furthermore, Bieber is an excellent stand-in for the famously sexless Ken. Black women, as happens so often in American culture, take up space as sexually active, and forceful, providing the soundtrack for the racy antics of the honeymoon. Taken as representations of dominance and deviance, we are left not with a radical reimagining of sex and sexuality, but with one that is depressingly consistent with racial formations that associate sex with blackness and animal impulses, while the higher-functioning white (man) can be filled with desire, yet represent the utterly acceptable form of morally upright sex that takes place only in marriage, and mainly for the purpose of baby-making.

Were the three video-makers themselves in the business of intending to make a racial statement? I doubt it. Rather, in Bakhtinian fashion, their narrative takes up powerful cultural concerns—how could it not—and among these concerns is the sexual politics of race. Race is one of the primary ways in which Americans understand the social world around them, and in ways quite similar to sex, race is a realm that is at once eminently visible and yet rarely explicitly articulated. We see it, but we tend not to talk about it. Such racial politics have long been embedded in Barbie herself who is unchangeably white; as my own work has shown, what are commonly called "Black Barbies" by the public are not considered by Mattel to be Barbies at all: they are friends of Barbie, with different names or identities: Christie, Nichelle, Asha, Shani (Chin, 1999).

In *Barbie Sex Life* race is visually absent from the video except in the form of unmarked, normative whiteness. Racial difference nevertheless surfaces in the form of popular music. In the larger world, this is exactly how life and racial dynamics often work: the largest market for hip-hop music is white middle class youth whose closest contact with black life and black people is through consumption of music made by black artists (Bialik, 2005). It is in this doubly silenced space, that of race and sex, where black women do the talking in *Barbie Sex Life*. And what they say is: "P-p-push it!" something no nice girl would ever say (but wish they could?). No wonder a bunch of black women do the talking here.

The Barbie world in the video lacks diversity except in hair color; we know little or nothing about the race of the video-makers, except for one hand glimpsed for an instant in a stop-motion shot when Barbie and Ken are in the dream house: the hand appears to be white. This brings up the question as to who it is exactly that does not speak about race. Although I stated earlier that Americans tend not to speak about race, that generalization was, in fact, untrue and deeply problematic. The Americans who talk openly and critically about race are more often than not people of color. The Americans who do not talk about race are more often than not white Americans. The silencing of race, and of discussions about race and racial inequality, has been widely discussed by people of color, but such talk is often received negatively by whites (Foster, 2005; Lipsitz, 1998; Mullings, 2005; Morrison, 1992; Myers, 2005).

The rapid expansion of the internet, and of social media, has had a marked impact upon the availability of sexual images to children, and of the ways in which children and youth engage in thinking about and participating in activities related to the world of the sexual. These range from the infamous Abercrombie "push up" bikini-bra-top for 7 to 12-year-olds (Wade, 2011) to the advent of "sexting" and the posting of "do you think I'm pretty?" videos. Along with this is what might be called the pornification of sex. Like the "do you think I'm pretty" video, porn is visual material. Both are shaped by filmic practices and norms. With its broad reach, the internet has proven fantastically powerful in reshaping sexual imaginations and intimate practices to mimic and even reproduce porn aesthetics and practices. Both Harvard and Boston University have student-published porn magazines featuring student models (Oleyourryk, 2008). Body norms for women are no longer just about the breasts, face, or wobbly upper arms. Plastic surgery of the vagina—labioplasty, vaginoplasty, and clitoral-hood reduction—are among the fastest growing surgeries for women; this rise in "designer vaginas" is often attributed to the wider reach of porn aesthetics (Goodman, 2011; DiFilippo, 2010).

Can't blame Barbie for that development: she hasn't got a vagina for girls to examine and want for their own!

Given the ubiquitous media availability of sexually themed imagery, the ways in which sexuality is represented in *Barbie Sex Life* is not especially shocking or surprising (Buckingham & Bragg, 2004). What does the sex in this video look like, exactly? First and most obvious, it is heterosexual sex. In the honeymoon sex scene, both Ken and Barbie are completely naked. They are shown in a variety of sexual positions, but that variety is very limited. Barbie straddles Ken, facing him. Ken lies in missionary position on top of Barbie. Barbie straddles Ken again and raises one arm in the air. The sex on offer here is not especially racy. Notably absent are a variety of sexual positions: doggy style, 69, or oral sex are not shown.[1] Yes, sex is being depicted here, but it lacks detail when compared with the realistic attention to minute gestures seen earlier in the wedding scene.

Remembering Bakhtin's (1986) notion of asking our own questions, it strikes me as important to sincerely wonder why does the sex look the way it does in this video. Were the video-makers self-censoring in not showing the racier kinds of sex acts? Or is it that the sex being shown is kind of an encyclopedia of these children's limited sexual knowledge? Were they unaware of the larger variety of postural possibilities or, conversely, did they specifically choose these positions from a much larger universe that they know about? Is the sex on offer a combination of knowledge and imitation, and if so, knowledge of what and imitation of what? Actual sex acts they have seen? Reenactments of scenes from movies? Glimpses of naughty magazines found in a drawer or under someone's bed?

The social context in which these children display what might be called their sexual know-how is one in which the federal government has specified that sex education in public schools must emphasize abstinence rather than other approaches—among those, approaches that frankly describe and discuss sex, without necessarily promoting it. The uncomfortable kid-parent talk where mom talks with daughter and dad talks with son about "the facts of life" is one of our cultural clichés, an emblematic moment that all parties find uncomfortable at best, and where all too often the child lets the parent off the hook by saying, "Oh I know that stuff already!" From the depths of this cultural black hole, somehow children are supposed to emerge as adults who have knowledge of themselves, their bodies, their desires, and to develop notions of sexuality that are at once healthy and fulfilling.

As an affirmation that "I know about that stuff already!" *Barbie Sex Life* is quite effective and perhaps even a little reassuring. There is a light touch when it comes to the sex, and a substantial number of the comments responding to the video specifically mention the honeymoon as especially funny. This sense of parody or silliness is amplified by the abrupt change in soundtrack, which contrasts so starkly with Bieber's sugary moans. (Other comments disparage the music choice.) The bumping, pumping Salt-N-Pepa music brings up the energy, yet the sex itself is neither serious nor pornographic. It is almost as if the video-makers are saying "This is funny because we are not supposed to be doing it!" The clunky positions and the bonking together of the bodies look pretty silly. The lavender fun fur pillow in the background does little to make the scene seem threatening or lifelike, but instead seems to say "It's even funnier because you grownups take it seriously!" This lack of serious intent is cemented when Barbie waves her arm in the air as she sits atop Ken. It's something of an audience-directed moment, a visual "Woo-Hoo!" that includes a gestural quote from popular dance, a genre whose moves often consist of corporeal quotes from elsewhere many-times-over. And while the video-makers may not have done detailed research on the musical performances of the artists on their soundtrack, versions of the arm-raised, fist-pump gesture can be seen in several Salt-N-Pepa music videos that were available on YouTube at the time *Barbie Sex Life* was created (Balton, 2009; SaltNPepaVEVO, 2009). This "Woo-Hoo!" moment may well represent a kind of self-consciousness on the part of the video-makers, almost like a sly wink, as if to say, "Lighten up, mom and dad, it's not really sex. It's Barbies. (Eye roll)."

SINCERE QUESTIONS

Asking questions is one of the basic activities of the social scientist. But as Bakhtin emphasized, not just any question will do. Our questions must be "our own," as he said, but they must also be "sincere" (1986, p. 7). What Bakhtin was getting at is the complexity of engaging across culture or even point of view in a way that avoids being self-serving. Good questions destabilize such preconceptions, and open up spaces in which simplistic, two-dimensional ideas can be exploded into terrains worth exploring. Sincerity, in this case, has involved an attempt to intuit and explore the range of meanings and ideas that the kid media-makers were working with as they created their production.

Barbie Sex Life is, indeed, what Brown (2008) would call a difficult text. My reading of *Barbie Sex Life* is hardly exhaustive: this little-less-than-2-minute video could sustain a great deal more interpretation. With more space than I have here, it would be fascinating to explore more deeply the complexities of gender, both because one of the makers of the videos seems to be a boy, and because Ken (as usual) is such a non-entity in the video's narrative. What might this mean for the children making the video and how might this express their own understandings of boy-girl, Ken-Barbie relationships? Another line of enquiry worth pursuing would be to wonder about the position being taken in terms of the life trajectory outlined here. Do these kids imagine this as the storyline of their own lives? Or are they making fun of the marriage-house-baby storyline? Perhaps their position is some combination of embrace and rejection?

Difficult as this text may be, it is also fun, silly, and surprising.

The point, in the end, is not to answer such questions with a definitive single statement. Rather, the aim is to muddle through and around the territories identified by these questions, as a way of expanding understanding and thinking. It is this process of asking questions, contemplation, and intellectual exploration that is the essence of good enquiry. My interpretive approach is aimed at demonstrating the rich complexity of kids' understanding and deployment of images, narratives, stereotypes, and other forms of circulating social and cultural knowledge. Oriented fundamentally around the notion that culture is meaningful and important, my work here asserts that children and Barbie are part of worlds in which meaning and culture are generated and played with. Raising more questions than I ultimately answer, this kind of interpretive project asserts that engaging with questions, pushing them further, and continuing to explore new territories is, in and of itself, a uniquely valuable mode of engagement.

NOTE

1. These exotic positions typically do appear in adult-made Barbie sex productions. As a point of rough comparison, take the sex scene from the R-rated marionette-acted film *Team America*. Here the romantic protagonists engage in 11 distinctly different sexual positions in less than 30 seconds of screen time. Part of what is funny in this scene is the extremely realistic way in which the sex is enacted by the marionettes; yet because the scene featured marionettes, and not people, the filmmakers could be much more explicit than would have been possible in a live-action film.

REFERENCES

Bakhtin, M. M. (1982). In M. Holquist & V. Liapunov (Eds.), *The dialogic imagination: Four essays* (V. Liapunov & K. Brostrom, Trans.). Austin, TX: University of Texas Press.

Bakhtin, M. M. (1986). In C. Emerson & M. Holquist (Eds.), *Speech genres and other late essays* (2nd ed., V. W. McGee, Trans.). Austin, TX: University of Texas Press.

Balton, C. (2009, August 9). *Salt-N-Pepa "Push It"* [Video file]. Retrieved from http://www.youtube.com/watch?v=cMBh8P1m9Wo&feature=youtube_gdata_player

barbiebabe890. (2007, August 21). *Barbie and Ken's wedding* [Video file]. Retrieved from http://www.youtube.com/watch?v=MYHnfWnScWs&feature=youtube_gdata_player

barbiebabe890. (2007, August 21). *When Barbie met Ken* [Video file]. Retrieved from http://www.youtube.com/watch?v=G2OcsVCBfqU&feature=youtube_gdata_player

Barbie girls play rough. (2009, February 14). *Today*. Retrieved from http://news.bbc.co.uk/today/hi/today/newsid_7889000/7889147.stm

BarbiesStory. (2008, August 25). *Barbie gott a date with Ken*. Retrieved from http://www.youtube.com/watch?v=um4bxYT-fXo&feature=youtube_gdata_player

Bateson, G. (1972). A theory of play and fantasy. In *Steps to an ecology of mind: Collected essays in Anthropology, Psychiatry, Evolution, and Epistemology* (pp. 177–193). San Francisco, CA; Scranton, PA: Chandler.

Bialik, C. (2005, May 5). Is the conventional wisdom correct in measuring hip-hop audience? *Wall Street Journal*. Retrieved from http://online.wsj.com/article/SB111521814339424546

Brown, M. (2008). Reading the difficult text. *Radical Teacher, 82*, 8–12. Retrieved from ProQuest. (Order no. 218833441).

Buckingham, D., & Bragg, S. (2004). *Young people, sex and the media: The facts of life*. New York, NY: Palgrave Macmillan.

Burgess, J., & Green, J. (2009). *YouTube: Online video and participatory culture* (1st ed.). Cambridge, England: Polity.

Caillois, R. (1961). *Man, play and games.* New York, NY: The Free Press.

Chin, E. (1999). Ethnically correct dolls: Toying with the race industry. *American Anthropologist, 101*(2), 305–321.

Cindrich, S. (2009). *A smart girl's guide to the internet (American Girl Library).* Middleton, WI: American Girl.

Collins, L., Lidinsky, A., Rusnock, A., & Torstrick, R. (2012). We're not Barbie girls: Tweens transform a feminine icon. *Feminist Formations, 24*(1), 102–126.

CRAZYCOMMERCIALSR. (2011, April 26). *A Barbie life story–Evil dentist* [Video file]. Retrieved from http://www.youtube.com/watch?v=FBp7bXeH_Uk&feature=youtube_gdata_player

DiFilippo, D. (2010). "Designer vaginas": Here's the lowdown. *The Philadelphia Daily News.* Retrieved from http://articles.philly.com/2010-03-16/news/24957349_1_cosmetic-surgery-plastic-surgeons-vaginoplasty

Duhamel, D. (1994). Differently-abled Barbies. *Chicago Review, 40*(2–3), 14.

Edut, O. (Ed.). (1998). *Adios, Barbie: Young women write about body image and identity.* Berkley, CA: Seal Press.

Foster, K. M. (2005). Diet of disparagement: The racial experiences of black students in a predominantly white university. *International Journal of Qualitative Studies in Education, 18*(4), 489–505.

Goodman, M. P. (2011). Female genital cosmetic and plastic surgery: A Review. *Journal of Sexual Medicine, 8*(6), 1813–1825.

Holloway, S. L., & Valentine, G. (2000). *Children's geographies: Playing, living, learning.* Hove, England: Psychology Press.

Huizinga, J. (1950). *Homo ludens: A study of the play element in culture.* Boston, MA: Beacon Press.

Klinkhart, G. (2012). *A cybercop's guide to internet child safety.* Hersham, England: SecurusMedia.

Lange, P. G. (2011). Video-mediated nostalgia and the aesthetics of technical competencies. *Visual Communication, 10*(1), 25–44.

Leavitt, J., & Linford, S. (2006). *Faux Paw's adventures in the internet: Keeping children safe online.* Indianapplis, IN: Wiley.

Lipsitz, G. (1998). *The possessive investment in whiteness: How white people profit from identity politics.* Philadelphia, PA: Temple University Press.

MacDougall, J. P. (2003). Transnational commodities as local cultural icons: Barbie dolls in Mexico. *Journal of Popular Culture, 37*(2), 257–275.

madiluvzyoo. (2010, March 11). *Barbie sex life.* Retrieved from http://www.youtube.com/watch?v=Y6X6E15cse4&feature=youtube_gdata_player

Messner, M. A. (2000). Barbie girls versus sea monsters: Children constructing gender. *Gender & Society, 14*(6), 765–784. doi:10.2307/190373

Morrison, T. (1992). *Playing in the dark: Whiteness and the literary imagination.* Cambridge, MA: Harvard University Press.

Mullings, L. (2005). Interrogating racism: Toward an antiracist anthropology. *Annual Review of Anthropology, 34*(January 1), 667–693. doi:10.2307/25064903

Myers, K. (2005). *Racetalk: Racism hiding in plain sight.* Lanham, MD: Rowman & Littlefield.

Oleyourryk, A. (Ed.). (2008). *Boink: College sex by the people having it.* Lebanon, IN: Grand Central Publishing.

Rand, E. (1995). *Barbie's queer accessories.* Durham, NC: Duke University Press.

reggie1556. (2011, November 13). *Barbies driving test* [Video file]. Retrieved from http://youtube/OpWQyU7rml8

Ronson, J. (2010). Justin Bieber: One day with the most Googled name on the planet. *The Guardian*. Retrieved from http://www.guardian.co.uk/music/2010/nov/13/justin-bieber-interview

SaltNPepaVEVO. (2009, October 6). *Salt-N-Pepa—push it* [Video file]. Retrieved from http://www.youtube.com/watch?v=vCadcBR95oU&feature=youtube_gdata_player

She's no Barbie, nor does she care to be. (1991, August 15). *The New York Times*. Retrieved from http://www.nytimes.com/1991/08/15/garden/she-s-no-barbie-nor-does-she-care-to-be.html

Slayen, G. (2011). The scary reality of a real-life Barbie doll. *Huffington Post*. Retrieved from http://www.huffingtonpost.com/galia-slayen/the-scary-reality-of-a-re_b_845239.html

SuperJeets. (2011, August 20). *Barbie goes to McDonalds* [Video file]. Retrieved from http://www.youtube.com/watch?v=eisZ3mF-7KU&feature=youtube_gdata_player

Susina, J. (1999). American Girls collection: Barbies with a sense of history. *Children's Literature Association Quarterly, 24*(3), 128–35.

Tobin, J. (2000). *"Good guys don't wear hats": Children's talk about the media*. New York, NY: Teacher's College Press.

Vonderau, P. (2010). In P. Snickars (Ed.), *The YouTube reader*. Stockholm, Sweden: National Library of Sweden. Retrieved from http://www.kb.se/dokument/aktuellt/audiovisuellt/youtubereader/youtube_reader_052009_endversion.pdf

Vygotsky, L. (1967). Play and its role in the mental development of the child. *Soviet Psychology 12*: 62–76.

Wade, L. (2011). Push up bikini tops at Abercrombie Kids. *Sociological Images*. Retrieved from http://thesocietypages.org/socimages/2011/03/19/push-up-bikini-tops-at-abercrombie-kids/

Wolf, N. (2002). *The beauty myth: How images of beauty are used against women* (Reprint). Harper Perennial.

Part IV: Modernism and Modernization

Adelaide Huret AND THE Nineteenth-Century French Fashion Doll: Constructing Dolls/ Constructing THE Modern

JULIETTE PEERS

The rise of the Parisian luxury doll trade in the mid-nineteenth century is a particularly complex period of doll production that, unlike the plastic era of dolls, remains generally outside of scholarly consideration. This chapter places French dollmaking alongside some currently popular and familiar fields of scholarly discussion around the emergence of modern art and modern consumerism, especially in the context of French culture. In recent years the understanding of the role of women in relation to these two phenomena of modern practices of fashion consumption and art making has been revised significantly to emphasise women's agency and relevance to the twinned concepts of modern style and modern city life. Fashion has now been repositioned as central to the lived experience of the modern in the 1860s (Groom, 2012). Via the dolls of nineteenth-century Paris, the culture of girlhood can be linked to this reconsidered definition of modern life. Nineteenth-century French dollmaking resonates with recent discussions of the origins of modernist culture, particularly the importance of modern fashion to current understandings of creativity and the communication of ideas around the modern (Troy, 2003). Adelaide Huret and her contemporaries—gifted female dollmakers, dressmakers, designers, and retailers of Second Empire Paris—and their dolls, place women, girls, and girl cultures within these discourses.

The history of the modern movement in art and culture has been strongly influenced by scholars such as T. J. Clark, who in the early 1970s identified innovation with masculine energy and cultural identity, making the assumption (soon crystalised into accepted fact) that the revolutionary and forward-seeking were driven within the masculine, public sphere. Clark's gendered definition of the avant-garde and revolutionary rendered women invisible (D'Souza & McDonough, 2006, pp. 5–7). Throughout much of the twentieth century, the traditional academic viewpoint claimed that modernity found its concrete and lived expression in the public sphere. Thus it was assumed that respectable women, who largely inhabited the private sphere, were excluded from experiencing, expressing, or creating the modern. However the scholarly questioning of a narrowly politically driven vision of modernity, and the assimilation of "capitalist" art forms such as product design and fashion into the visual culture historical canon in recent years repositions women as modern agents in their own right. Rather than functioning as objects of social and artistic scrutiny, women in the urban retail spaces (Iskin, 2007, pp. 7–14, 184–224) can finally be understood as performers of fashion and urban life.

In 1988 Griselda Pollock (2003), seeking to define women's potential contribution to the emergence of contemporary art in nineteenth-century Paris, wrote of "women's bodies as the territory across which men artists claim their modernity and compete for leadership of the avant-garde" (p. 76). Pollock certainly foregrounded women's exclusion from those spaces that constituted "the 'painting of modern life,'" but also enacted a finely grained scrutiny of space and meaning in nineteenth-century Parisian life that has generated two decades of art historical discussion. Historians and curators Søndergaard, Iskin, D'Souza and McDonough, Groom and others, in recent studies of women, modernity, identity, consumption, fashion, and visibility in nineteenth-century Paris, have repositioned respectable women as more visible agents than Pollock's early—albeit highly insightful—foundational text posited. Finally, after decades of research and debate, the notion of women's absence in the discourses of modernity is being increasingly shifted and diversified (D'Souza & McDonough, 2006, pp. 5–9).[1] An ever-increasing acknowledgement of the power of fashion and appearances as a cultural player in both mainstream French culture and the avant-garde has opened up a greater space for acknowledging the importance of feminine cultural experience in the history of modernism and radical culture.

Placing dolls into this scholarly matrix is not a simplistic and glib combination of two roughly coinciding mid-nineteenth-century historical phenomena. Doll history offers a lesser-known site of female initiative in relation to the developing modern experience in nineteenth-century Paris and therefore the mainstream Western experience, and the history of art and design. Thus this chapter seek: (1) to identify dollmaking as a site where women experienced and proactively shaped the modern experience in both design and lifestyle in Paris, and (2) to indicate, via dolls and doll play, how girls' culture, an emergent discipline over the last 2 decades, can be more firmly integrated into familiar discourses of visual cultural modernity and innovation.

The focus of new interpretations of impressionism and the birth of the avant-garde on the paired phenomena of the city of Paris and the presence of women in the city facilitates my cross reference between art historiography and dolls as cultural artefacts of girlhood. Undeniably, women served as symbols of the city and of the modern life that the nineteenth-century impressionists sought to paint (Clayson, 2003, Iskin, 2007, p. 222). This link between women, fashion, style, modernity, and Paris was familiar to the nineteenth-century French and at times dolls and dollmaking were also included as part of this extended cluster of ideas (Peers, 2004, pp. 41–44). Fashion functioned as a useful visual shorthand of the modern and the connection between fashion and the tangible expression/manifestation into material terms of the avant-garde impetus that has been made since Baudelaire's essay on the painter of modern life, (1863). The role of fashionable dress in the impressionist and dissident art movements of the mid- and late-nineteenth century is well established (Steele, 1988, pp. 123–132). Indeed, in the 1850s and 1860s, French commentators were discussing this nexus between newness and perfection in fashion and the modern woman at the same time that radical artists who advocated the painting and depiction of modern life faced rejection by official institutions in the third quarter of the nineteenth century.

By the mid-nineteenth century a significant cultural investment in the idea of French fashion, particularly as symbolised by the "Parisienne" had crystalised (Rocamora, 2009, 86–125). In 1867 Emmeline Raymond wrote an article entitled "La Mode et la Parisienne" in which the Parisienne was seen as the envoy of fashion, or as Iskin (2007) explained, "the identities of the Parisienne and French fashion constitute each other" (pp. 185, 190). While the association of the entities of "Paris" and "Woman" are commonplace in the twenty-first century at all levels of cultural discourse, from journalism to the academy, the many conscious stratagems over the past century-and-a-half to facilitate the persuasive marketing of French styles and fashion can easily be overlooked (Best, 2008, Rocamora, 2009). These strategically constructed and promoted images centre upon the concept of French fashion and the stylish Parisienne. Modern fashion has been a constituent of French identity for many centuries and is still understood as such at a quasi-official level, despite the increasing threats of globally diffused cultural inspirations and trends (Best, 2008).

The fashionable Parisienne and the superior appeal of women's fashion from Paris testified to French leadership in industry and art during the nineteenth century. "By 1850, France was Europe's biggest textile producer, and by 1860, the foremost industrial power in Europe due to clothing and its ancillary industries" (Best, 2008).

In the nineteenth century, fashion established itself as a key Parisian industry, employing in 1847, "the greatest number of Parisian workers," with activities such as the manufacture of fabrics and shawls and the milling of cotton amongst the most important Parisian industries. The nineteenth century was when the French field of fashion was truly born. Kawamura notes that it signalled the birth of "the modern system" of fashion more generally. (Rocamora, 2009, p. 28)

If we regard the support and accessory industries around the Parisian fashion trade as legitimate players within this fashion-driven impetus of the modern in Paris, then girls' lives and culture, as framed by the luxury Parisian doll design and manufacturing industries, also belong to the "modern." Both the experiential and the theoretical aspects of girlhood have been relatively invisible in the academy until the last two decades, when a rapid expansion of new, revisionist interpretations has both established the importance of girlhood as an academic discipline and consolidated an oeuvre of fresh and informative scholarship (Mitchell & Reid-Walsh, 2008, pp. xxviii–xxxi; Forman-Brunell & Paris, 2011, pp. 3–7). "Girls have mattered across time and place. Until recently, most studies of childhood and youth accepted boys' experience as normative" (Helgren & Vasconcellos, 2010, p. 3). The relative scholarly blindness around dolls until the early 1990s, with consistent and longitudinal scholarly publication attributable to only a small number of academics,[2] parallels the invisibility of girlhood until the recent expansion of the discipline, and, equally, the recent development of both fashion scholarship and the rethinking of the position of female agency within the social history of French painting and its subject matter.

While artists' images of nineteenth-century French women are well known (Clayson, 2003, Simon, 1996, Søndergaard, 2006) and fashionable garments are now widely accepted as museum and gallery pieces (Cumming, 2004, pp. 91–97; Taylor, 2004, pp. 105–199) the beautiful, elaborate French nineteenth-century dolls that equally express and perform this cluster of ideas around women, style, and modernity are less discussed by scholars. If, as Hollis Clayson (1991) and others have argued, the "new" Paris of the Second Empire was a woman, art historians have tended to assume that the woman who symbolised Paris was a prostitute, or the emerging fashionista and consumer of modern fashion, from the empress to the shop girl. Yet equally, Paris-as-woman, that perennial fantasy of fashion marketing (Rocamora, 2009, pp. 86–125), could be the sumptuous, over-dressed, overindulged fashion doll of the Second Empire.

Down the generations the idea that Paris could be a doll rather than a woman has occasionally surfaced. When the Paris correspondent for the *Englishwoman's Domestic Magazine* wished to demonstrate to her readers the abject state into which the city of fashion and pleasure had sunk during the siege and commune of 1871, she could find no clearer metaphor than to report that "the very doll-shops are devoid of new fashions" (Johnston, 1986, p. 66). The importance of expensive dolls to Paris' reputation served as a touchstone to the strange and extreme situation and emphasized the urgent reality of a great crisis in the city. The explicit association between Paris and Jumeau dolls after the Franco-Prussian war again emphasised the link between the Parisienne, her special chic, French artistry, and the city of

Paris. As one contemporary noted at the time, "such a perfect doll, durable and loveable as the Parisienne of which she was a descendent, adorable in her attitude of little woman or charming baby" (Cusset, 1885, p. 76, cited in Davies, 1955).

Even the twenty-first-century guides that highlight quaint, authentic, and "off the beaten track" Paris, mention Robert Capia's antique doll business as a delight awaiting overseas visitors in the arcades of Paris (Belau, 2010, Peers, 2004, p. 42). Capia's merchandise, particularly antique French dolls, still performs the paradigmatic chic that the city has sold for centuries. As recently as 2010, *Girls' Guide to Paris* (Belau, 2010) linked Capia's antique doll shop to its neighbours, an outlet for Christian Louboutin shoes and the signature store for Terry de Gunzburg's cosmetics. These neighbouring businesses, both iconic and popular brands,[3] exemplify how French style is now deployed as a commodity across diverse global cultures. This juxtaposition thus introduces the specialist collector subculture of antique dolls to the more accessible universe of elite brand shopping and accessorising, especially shoes, made broadly popular and rendered synonymous with modern women's understandings of luxury brands in the wake of *Sex and the City*.[4] The use of the term "Girls" in the *Girls' Guide to Paris* is not so much about childhood, but about a friendly sorority between modern professional women (perhaps again referencing *Sex and the City*). The term also highlights popular culture's demand that to maintain their credibility women must stay perpetually young. Many Second Empire doll shops and doll dress shops operated in these same Parisian arcades that are now celebrated in such guides to modern Paris.

THE HURET DOLL

No doll symbolises the nexus of innovation, Paris, and female creative thinking that has recently engaged historians and theorists as much as those made by Adelaide Huret. Her speciality was an 18-inch doll with painted features and a wig. She devised the design and commissioned at least three Parisian manufacturers, Jacob Petit, Letu & Mauger, and Freyon to fabricate a porcelain head made to her specifications from her moulds. Despite the fragile head, the innovative polymer body of both elegant and naturalistic appearance represented a new era of flexibility and durability in dollmaking. Huret's custom-designed doll body was the first of the ubiquitous plastic dolls of the twentieth and twenty-first centuries. Having devised the form of her doll, Huret did not develop the model further and had only one size (18 inches) of mould tooled.

Huret was the daughter of the most prominent locksmith in Paris,[5] Leopold Huret, renowned for serving the Bourbon family in the Restoration period 1814–1815, 1815–1830. He was responsible for producing locks that secured government documents and top-secret despatches carried in haversacks and attaché cases by couriers across the country and into foreign territories. The Huret family also pioneered the manufacture of light, robust, but elegant metal furniture in brass and other substances deemed suitable for chic urban interiors as much as for specialist use such as colonial expeditions or military campaigns. As metal furniture became madly popular in the second quarter of the twentieth century, the family were already forward-looking as designers. Leopold Huret's children, Leopold junior, Olympe, Adelaide, and Marie Therese, conducted business at the same premises (Theimer & Theimer, 2008, pp. 82–83) and extended the family's pre-existing experience in serving an exclusive luxury market. The family's highly admired full-scale furniture—chairs, tables, and jardinières—was augmented by doll-sized iterations for Adelaide's dolls. Such product integration from doll to doll furniture and accoutrements is often assumed to be typical of the "Barbie extended world" and thus associated only with the late twentieth century.

The Huret doll symbolised the new ways of thinking about material objects that arose in Second Empire Paris that have proven so influential to the histories of both fine art and product marketing. While representing a child,[6] the doll simultaneously emphasized the style and exclusivity of classic high fashion in its bespoke clothing that was made to measure and limited in its production runs. Although Huret's family had commercial links back to the French monarchy and the early nineteenth century monarchical period—a time of relative modesty and social cohesiveness—the visible luxury and aggregated meaning and status of her doll clearly articulated the stress upon materiality and display within the values of the Second Empire, characterised by what D'Souza and McDonough (2006) termed "realms of leisure, consumption, the spectacle and money" (p. 5). In particular, one notes the strict limitation of retail distribution—the doll only being sold at the Huret family's own premises—and the exclusivity of innovative design that demanded a specific commitment from the consumer to pay a premium price.

Huret's use of reputation and her product's formal and consistent visual identity to value add and extract a surcharge from the buyer is truly innovative in terms of the history of retailing and branding. Half a decade before Charles Frederick Worth made his breakthrough in placing and marketing high fashion and bringing a new sense of mystique and power to the designer/supplier (Troy, 2003, pp. 19–22; Okonkwo, 2007, pp. 47–58; Tungate, 2009, p. 13) that overwrote the volition and commands of the purchaser as the leader in driving the design and production of goods, Adelaide Huret had already transformed the ad hoc and anonymous production of dolls in Europe by creating a product with individual style and identity exclusively associated with her name.[7] From the start her product, superior to her commercial rivals' and unique in the eyes of the buying public, served as its own advertisement. These innovations changed the identity of the doll in the Second Empire and shifted it from a domestic product to a product of display, moving it from the home circle to being a locus of the public gaze and envy. Adelaide Huret effected changes in her rivals' dolls as they sought to match the appeal of her products to consumers.

Beyond dollmaking, Huret's career raises important academic questions about women's agency and the range of female personae usually discussed by historians of nineteenth-century France (Clayson, 2003; D'Souza & McDonough, 2006; Iskin, 2007; Pollock, 2003; Søndergaard, 2006). She was neither aristocrat nor prostitute. As an active business woman and entrepreneur, moreover, Huret commissioned other Parisian women to dress the dolls she patented and thus her business supported a further circle of skilled women. As an unmarried woman and aging spinster, she would be regarded as a failure in petty bourgeois and bourgeois households and—in the normal course of events—be considered irrelevant and invisible by the society around her. Yet by designing and developing a more beautiful doll than had hitherto existed, Huret brought foreign capital to France and made a tangible contribution to quantifying the elusive idea of "French style" in an international marketplace with her significant artform. The transformations Huret made in the marketing of luxury consumer goods in Paris via her dolls survive into the present day. Likewise her innovations—the provisioning of dolls with ready-made wardrobes and accessories—survive in a cheapened format in every pink aisle of discount stores such as K-Mart and toyshop chains such as Toys R' Us.

The complexity of Adelaide Huret's innovative approach can be traced due to François Theimer translating and publishing details of her patent application. By her own admission, Huret was spurred onto doll designing by the poor appearance of previous French dolls. "The deformed shapes of dolls found in shops today must have made many people think that an improvement is possible," said Huret, adding, "what's more its roughly designed shape in no way suits it for dressing up, almost completely discouraging the decorator" (Theimer, 1997, p. 85). Yet it was not only visual appeal and visual commodity that Huret sought to address, she was also motivated by a concern to anticipate the needs of the child, referencing traditional expectations of women's roles as bound up in nurturing and child rearing. Huret's positioning of her intentions as being about making more appropriate dolls for children strongly resonates with Formanek-Brunell's (1993) identification of professional commercial dollmaking in the late nineteenth and early twentieth centuries as a site where domestic feminist values could be asserted in the marketplace and put into tangible practice (p. 3). In Huret's concern for the "justness" of the doll to the perceived needs of the well-adjusted child in a well-regulated home, we can plausibly see forward to the more clearly stated and intentional political and social dimension of domestic feminist aspirations of the nineteenth and early twentieth century. Her patent application gives an indication of her aims when developing the doll and documents how she had thought about fitness of the doll to the purpose of serving the needs of the child.

> An articulated body, capable of imitating basic human movements and whose shape, without being over perfect for a child's toy, nevertheless is close enough to reality to please the eye—such an idea must have gone through the heads of all those in contact with the sorry examples available at present.... Even [the jointed lay figure] belonging to the painter, though cleverly made is equally unsuitable as a child's plaything. (Theimer, 1997, p. 85)

Huret showed concern that the child should play with that which is relevant to her. The lay figure was "cleverly made" but unsuitable as a toy. No reason is given, but certainly the lay figure was associated with artmaking and thus belonged in the loucheness of the artists' studio. From this discussion it would appear Huret sought to identify what is appropriate to the child and demarcate the child's things from those that are appropriate to the adult, implying that childhood was a vulnerable state, easily corrupted or distorted by contact with the adult world.

Many of the anxieties generated by Barbie (Collins, 2011; Linn, 2004, pp. 125–144) are those of contagion and confusion: she introduces adult concepts into a child's world and educates girls to be materialistic and vapid, the least socially useful of women. Yet this anxiety about the permeable borders between the adult and the child arose a century before Barbie. If Huret saw a seriously pedagogical function in her dolls as training girls in womanly duties of sewing and diligent thrift in homemaking, the industry that rapidly developed in the wake of her innovative dollmaking encouraged conspicuous consumption and brought the celebration of rituals and dress of high society women into the milieu of girlhood. Huret herself condoned this change of direction when her original intention of educating young girls proved unworkable. In the late 1860s a French journalist, Henri Nicolle, summarised Huret's achievements:

> The lady-inventor's original idea was that the dolls ...should be clothed by the child owner. However, little girls' fingers are sometimes clumsy and the busy mothers called to help with the sewing had other things to do. The call went out for ready-made clothing...and so it is now seamstresses, furriers, shoemakers, fine woodworkers and a whole range of other occupations are engaged in work related to this new industry which the Huret doll created and which in its turn gives rise to new specialists.... Around the Rue de Choiseul a number of dolls' clothes makers have set up their workshops, and made their fortune several times over. (Theimer, 1997, p. 88)

Huret apparently condoned the luxury production standards of dolls, clothes, and accessories marketed under her name, as well as the high prices. Documentation does not speak of her introducing a budget or accessible model, so the appeal of the gaze won over the instructional value of improving needlework and the prudent guardianship of the unprotected child's interests. Huret became renowned as the founder of the luxury Parisian doll industry, not as a reformer of childhood playthings. At the time of the 1867 Paris exhibition, in a long discussion of Huret's dolls, the aforementioned French journalist, Henri Nicolle, stated "the Huret dolls have created a whole new industry in the field of luxury dolls and have rightly earned a place in toy history" (Theimer, 1997, p. 87).

Within a decade of the launch of Huret's doll, the doll industry generated vast income and was a significant player in the national economy. During the early 1860s the doll industry in France greatly outpaced the production of male-oriented toys in revenue. According to the *Adelaide Advertiser* (1864),

> M. Ladomie has been going into statistics which may amuse our Statistical Society. He says there are £60,000 worth of dolls manufactured yearly in France; and military toys, "guns, drums, and swords, Heaven save the mark" figure only for £32,000. But then boys expend £2,000 a year in tops and balls and ninepins....But the passion for dolls has always prevailed in France; they vary in price from £60 to one penny; but whether they come in the form of papier-mâché from Germany, or in wood from the Tyrol, or in porcelain from Baccarat, they are not presentable in Paris until they have been dressed by a French modiste. (p. 3)

In considering the relative social importance of boys' to girls' toys, the manufacturing and retailing of military themed boys' toys throughout this period had a significant presence in public culture as a preparation for the values of adult life. The 1860s were an extremely bellicose decade with substantial international and intra-national armed conflicts on several continents, from Savoy to Paraguay. This virtually constant warfare culminated in the Franco-Prussian War of 1870–1871 that brought down the Second Empire and ushered in the New Imperialism of the later nineteenth century. Photographs and engravings of the period from many different nations document boys with miniature drums, rifles, uniforms, and other such toys. Thus the success and scale of the Parisian doll trade are even more striking. Given the stronger hold that "boys' toys," including construction sets, toy robots, military- and space-themed playsets, and the majority of digital games still have even today over both academic and curatorial imaginations, dollmaking's dominance over other toy industries in mid-nineteenth-century France as documented at the time contrasts with the subsequent weighting of public culture and material histories against the cultural objects of girlhood.

Huret's success led other women to establish ancillary businesses as doll seamstresses/dressmakers. Madame Farge's garments bore, in some cases, a stamp identifying these dresses to be products of "Huret à Paris" (F. Theimer & Theimer, 2008, p. 98). This absolutely unprecedented innovation dates from the mid-1850s. Labels in adult clothes appear only a few years later, with the Maison Worth circa 1860, begetting *fake* Worth labels as early as the 1880s (Troy, 2003, pp. 24–25).[8] Huret also developed a clearly identifiable packaging format using a signature shade of green (F. Theimer & Theimer, 2008, pp. 106–107), anticipating the modern practice of visual branding and unity of a commercial undertaking. The Parisian doll shops not only sold dolls, their dresses and accessories, but also promoted them through specialty magazines and promotional events aimed at the dolls' owners. Adelaide Huret and her sisters kept a register of girl owners of their dolls. They invited these girls to parties and sewing classes held at their shop (F. Theimer & Theimer, 2008, pp. 78, 83, 131). These sponsored social events were an extended crossover activity intended to encourage further sales. Such activities are closely parallel to the recently devised emotive and immersive sales techniques of the American Girl Dolls.

MARKETING THE MODÈLE: TRANSGRESSION AND CONDEMNATION

In 1863 doll shop owner Madame Lavalée Peronne founded a doll-themed magazine for girls, *La Poupée Modèle*, and soon two rival publications, *La Poupée* and *Gazette de la Poupée*, vied with *La Poupée Modèle* for readers' attention in Second Empire Paris.[9] This proliferation of journals directed at girls was a remarkable moment of both doll and girlhood history that has hardly registered in the academy. *La Poupée Modèle* and its competitors offered a fantasy world where elegantly dressed dolls enjoyed a life of mysterious independence. Girls and ladies lived without chaperons or visible male authority figures, clearly surrounded by luxury in palatial interiors with gilt mirrors and elaborate finely carved and richly upholstered furniture of the Second Empire. They ate in cafes, visited the races, and walked the streets, a sign of modernist agency and liberal autonomy that constituted the "modern" world. These dolls were themselves the legendary *flâneur*, the stroller in the streets of Paris who has been a focus of scholarly attention, particularly over the last three decades. The *flâneur* symbolises the privilege or freedom to move about the public areas of the city, "observing" (D'Souza & McDonough, 2006, p. 6). The colourful plates reveal girls and their dolls laying claim to the urban and modern.

In other plates dolls hold glamorous balls and receptions, where there are male guests, but women and girls are not under the visible protection of father figures or a chaperon. Moreover there is a strong age dysphasia, as in one plate in which toddlers and young girls are present at an elegant social event that they would have been excluded from in real life until after their formal debut in Second Empire Paris society. In the engraving of "Lily's costume party," *La Vielle Poupée*, the old doll, in 1840s-style dress, spectacles, and a demure white cap, attends perhaps as a chaperon, but her regime is most lax. A doll dressed as a Watteau shepherdess is being asked to dance by a multicultural collection of male jumping jacks, a tableau of male importuning and address that is even discussed in the text of the magazine without qualm or censure. Another female doll in a hussar or lancer outfit plays the piano for a matador doll about to sing. The matador, of course, also recalls Manet's fascination with Spanish costume in the early 1860s. Nothing like this world is documented in sources around real Second Empire society, as these charming ladies of no visible means of support and unrestricted socialising with the opposite gender have no logical life outside the visual fiction of the illustrations in the doll magazines.

The *Poupée Modèle* plates are also early examples of a persistent genre in illustrating children's fiction about dolls. Here, in a doll-centric world, the doll is no longer an inanimate object, passively and patiently waiting upon a child or an adult to pose or move her/him, and thus to love or abuse her/him. In the plates, the doll has full life and agency, moves, speaks, and thinks, within a parallel but well-appointed universe that has no interaction with the real human world, except insofar as we can follow the intelligences gathered by authors and artists reporting upon this other world. Occasionally in these magazines dolls break the fourth wall, and address the wider human world by offering moral and metaphorical guidance. The texts are supposed to be written by a doll herself who offers her young human readers advice on etiquette, fashion, and behaviour. Thus the dolls are assumed to be au fait with correct social usages and formats.

Fashion press and journalism kept ideas of newness and modernity in public circulation and were essential in communicating information about fashion, both within the French nation and globally (Tetart Vittu, 2012 a, 2012 c, Groom, 2012). Parisian fashion journals equally informed the visual style of modern French nineteenth-century painting (Steele, 1988, 123–132). These doll-based fashion journals again place dolls within the cultures of display and communication that underpinned the immediacy of fashion in Paris. The design and presentation of the *Poupée Modèle* plates and those in other doll journals of the 1860s, steel engravings of vignettes of fashionable life, strikingly and vividly tinted with watercolours, is the same as fashion plates from the myriads of adult titles published in nineteenth-century Paris. The fashionableness of dolls is further emphasised by the frequent inclusion of engravings, paper patterns, and comments about doll fashions alongside adult fashion in the major journal, *La Mode Illustrée*, during the 1860s and 1870s. Today, doll fashions would never be regularly discussed or illustrated in high-end journals such as *Vogue* or *Harpers' Bazaar* as worthy of attention alongside major labels and adult haute couture. The girls' journals not only closely mimicked mainstream adult titles in format and appearance, they were also associated in production and management. By the turn of the twentieth century, *Poupée Modèle* shared its offices with a well-known Parisian fashion magazine, the *Journal des Demoiselles*, and recommended that publication to mothers and elder sisters.[10]

This world of pleasure in dress via the doll illuminates the girl-centric fiction of *Les Petites Filles Modèles* by the Comtesse Sophie de Ségur (1906). This book, and other titles by the Countess, are classics of French girls' literature, as are, for example, *Little Women* and *What Katy Did*, in English. Chapter 10 details the myriads of items in a doll's trousseau, so numerous that they are stored in a full-sized armoire. Marguerite wishes to take her large doll out for a walk, despite her sister Madeleine's warning that the doll would get bedraggled, especially if Marguerite let her trail on the ground. When the girls hurriedly run home to escape a thunderstorm, Marguerite, frightened by a noise, accidentally leaves her doll behind.[11] After the doll is stolen by a peasant girl, its retrieval provides a morality tale about taking care of expensive items. Marguerite learns the value of material goods and experiences grief at the loss of her doll, but equally is informed of the social geographic parameters of her social class and appropriate demeanour (De Ségur, 1906).

Yet the comparisons with the appearances and gestures of modern life, and also sexual negotiation, celebrated by Baudelaire and the impressionists are tangible in the *Poupée Modèle* plates and similar doll magazine plates from the 1860s. The dolls visit the country in their finery like Courbet's *Girls by the Seine*. Other dolls attend the races (as painted for adult society by Degas) and the doll Lily receives visitors while her hair is being styled by another doll in a maid's uniform in a plate dated 1863. This scene recalls Manet's *Olympia* or *Nana* or Cezanne's *Modern Olympia* images, and some of Degas' and Jean-Louis Forain's dancers in their dressing rooms, in the image of a woman receiving guests while either being dressed or in a state of undress, although Lily is fully and elegantly dressed. Scholars over the past three decades have discussed the nature and implication of these images of women at their toilette,[12] suggesting that the granting of such an audience was a sign of one of the duties of public women and prostitutes and marks a clear difference from the behaviour of the respectable woman.[13] We can also ask questions about the morals and lifestyle of Lily's female visitor out on her own on the streets of 1860s Paris dressed to the nines.

However, the commentary in the magazine disavows the scenes, reminding the reader that Mamma would assure them that all good little girls dress themselves without a maid. (Perhaps this also indicates that *La Poupée Modèle* had an aspirational function in that, unlike Lily, the magazine's readers may come from families that may not have been well supplied with personal servants). The caption declared that the engraving was merely a picturesque scene to show some charming ideas in doll costuming. Likewise, the vain and foolish doll Chiffonette also conveyed a morally mixed message. Chiffonette's misadventures as a less-than-*Modèle* doll formed an ongoing literary theme in the *Poupée Modèle* magazine. Her adventures were even anthologised as standalone publications as late as the 1880s, 20 years after her first appearance in print, suggesting that this anti-heroine had a community of fans and admirers that belied the fact she had been intended to function as a warning against transgressions.[14]

An image of Chiffonette in the country carried a warning to the reader that walking about in the country in elegant town clothes invited their imminent despoliation. Her wiser companion wears stout[er?] boots, a serviceable and plain pinafore and a rustic hat trimmed with meadow flowers, poppies, cornflowers, and daisies.[15] Poor Chiffonette, as the story advises, having soaked her chosen dress, had to face the shame of attending a social event in a dress that everyone had seen before, as there was no time to refurbish her dress or to have a new one made.[16] The textual caveats indicate that the visual material is potentially ambiguous, if not transgressive, and seeks to normalise the moral universe that the engravings present.

The moral ambiguity of these engravings of elegant doll tableaux brings to life the misogynistic essay by English journalist George Augustus Sala from 1868, inspired by viewing the displays of French dollmakers at the Paris Exhibition of 1867. Sala's main theme is ostensibly a contrast between dolls of different nationalities. The miniature British doll lives a respectable domestic life with her husband and children in a British-made doll house (p. 152). The larger British wax doll is a little girl of chunky, non-threatening body shape, who can withstand the rough play of childhood.

> A doll undressed was a sight which would not have raised a blush to the cheek of the most prurient prude. Dolly was a mere bifurcated bag of bran. Sometimes she had pink kid legs, but they were entirely innocent of calves. She had a waist, but no purist would accuse her of wearing a bustle. She was a doll, in fact, made to be nursed, and tossed, and tumbled about by little children (p. 146).

However the French doll is beautiful, highly fashionable, single, and heartless. Unlike plainer, less elaborate dolls she is not a playmate, nor does she offer comfort, but merely demands that the hapless owner buy her more overpriced dresses, accessories, jewels, and furniture.

For grace and symmetry of form the old bifurcated bran-bags cannot, of course, compare with them, but it is their toilettes that cost the money. It is their mahogany and rosewood furniture, their mirrors and consoles, their chandeliers and their Aubusson carpets that ruin the young prodigals of 'Sixty-seven. If you buy a doll in Paris now-a-days you must not only put her *dans ses meubles*, but furnish for her a luxurious boudoir in the Pompadour or the Empire style. She must have a carriage. She must have a saddle-horse. She must have a "ghroom" and a "jockei." She must have a grand piano from Erard or Pleyel. Her gloves must come from Madame Causse, her bonnet from Jenny Navarre, her watch from Leroy, her diamonds from Mellerio. She must have seventy-two petticoats, like the Russian countess who lives at the Hotel Bristol. She must bathe in milk of almonds, or *sang de menthe*. And I am very much afraid that, if you are suddenly called away, and return, in about a fortnight, unexpected, you will find your doll drinking champagne with your "ghroom." Don't think I am talking about real men and women. I am discoursing simply about the dolls, who, in the French Bimbeloterie Court at the Exhibition, are flirting, lounging, waltzing, jingling on the pianoforte, surveying themselves in mirrors, and ogling each other through consoles. The old child-doll type seems entirely lost. The French toy-men have taken to the manufacture of adult dolls. They look like dolls that have vices—dolls that don't care much about the Seventh Commandment—dolls who, to feed their own insatiable appetite, would eat you out of house and home, mortgage your lands, beggar your children, and then present you with a toy revolver to blow out your brains withal. They are so terribly symmetrical, so awfully lifelike; they carry their long trains, and nurse their poodles, and read their *billets doux*, and try on their gloves, and gamble at lansquenet with such dreadful perfection…. And this is the chief count in my indictment against the modern French dolls in the Exhibition. They have nothing to do with the happy, innocent, ignorant time of childhood. They look like dolls who know the time of day, and whom no young man from the country—or any other man—can get over. (pp. 146–147)

As the essay unfurls, Sala's (1868) intended target is actually not the difference between British and French dolls, but a sophisticated complaint about elite prostitution in Second Empire Paris. At the heart of the essay he contemplates the venal nature of women per se, who are false, artificial dolls and worse, living corpses, corrupt and over-painted with cosmetics and fitted with hair from the dead who abounded—their death agonies, blood, and wounds often visible in horrendous detail in parlour stereoscopic photographs—in this extremely militarised decade. This harvest of death would culminate at the end of the decade in the Franco Prussian war, the collapse of the Second Empire and the mass executions ending the Paris Commune, again documented by widely circulated images by the fashionable former imperial photographer Disdéri. Sala continued:

What would you have? It is a merry age, a dancing age, a jovial, lighthearted, devil-may-care age. *Vive la joie! Vive la bagatelle*! Long live the Cafe Riche and the Jardin Mabille, and the Closerie des Lilas, and the Thirteenth Arrondissement! Let us paint our faces, and put black under our eyes, and pad our haunches, and wash our hair in a solution of soda till it turns red, or, if we have not enough hair of our own, let us unthatch the heads of the dead for our chignons and our false curls. When we grow tired of sham red hair let us smear our pates with dark unguents, and stain our skins with walnut juice, and become sham brunettes. (pp. 144–145)

Beneath the beauty of the dolls of Paris lies putrefaction, again iterating the fear of women and contagion within the Second Empire. Modern life luxuriated upon falsehood and literal corruption. The fashionable French doll is a sign of the Empress Eugenie at whose feet, as Olympia, the spirit of dominant capitalism and heartless depersonalised social relations, much of this death was cast.[17]

Sala (1868) drew a moral alignment between the excess of the French doll and the superficiality and corruption of the Second Empire.

> A review of the remarkable development which within the last ten years has taken place in the French doll trade, not only as regards the manufacture of the puppets themselves, but in the artistic taste and ingenuity lavished on the decoration of objects essentially puerile and intrinsically worthless, might strengthen the position of those who argue that the most palpable fruits of the actual era of French civilisation have been dissipation and frivolity, senseless luxury and frenzied prodigality. (p. 140)

Prior to the collection of Sala's writings about the 1867 exhibition in a book, his comments on dolls had been distributed via the press, and had a high profile internationally.[18] Sala's scornful fascination with the doll display provided a template that was widely followed by fellow journalists. Other writers described the dolls at the Paris exhibition in similar terms, even down to the same focus on criticising the unjustifiable, female-driven expense of high fashion as a sign of the unsustainability and corruption of French society, as well as the French doll's capacity to drain masculine wallets as much as a demanding mistress. According to *The Argus* (1867),

> The triumphs of art appear to be reserved for the dolls, which are perfectly gorgeous in their apparel; and well may they be so when a single lady attired in court dress is ticketed at 1,000 francs. Heaven have mercy on the men who are now little boys, for if the same taste for expensive dress that is now implanted in the breast of young Paris goes on increasing in the same ratio, no purse will be long enough to stand it. (p. 7)

These mid-nineteenth-century discussions of "inappropriate" overtly sexualised dolls, the tawdry meaningless of their (overpriced) high-fashion wardrobes, and their potential to corrupt and distort (innocent, pure) girlhood vividly encapsulate mid-nineteenth-century gendered stereotypes. Concurrently, Sala's (1868) essay, by its vehemence and the emphasis at its core upon the sexualised personae of both women and dolls, raises the possibility that the sustained oeuvre of recent critiques of Barbie and Bratz dolls could have a paradigmatic, conventionalised element as well as being a direct response to an image of womanhood that is judged by some as offensive. Just as the imbrication of adult sexuality and glamour with child size and proportion in the later French bébé dolls—made following the Franco-Prussian war of 1870–1871—gives a historical precedent to the child beauty pageant, so too do mid-nineteenth-century critiques of "bad" dolls give a history and context to more recent narratives around inappropriate dolls. These historical precedents do not necessarily justify, or remove or excuse the later phenomena, but they serve as a reminder that the images of women presented by modern adult and fashion dolls, and the dolls themselves, are not simply alien signs of late capitalism. Nor should modern fashion dolls be read only in a direct cause-and-effect manner, as a reflection of a society in which images of empty but physically perfect young women are in constant circulation via the media. The images and constructs of women and girls as communicated by nineteenth-century French dolls, to a certain degree, predate current debates about body image and feminism. They have a particular value in contextualising what may be assumed to be recent cultural trends.[19]

Sala's (1868) essay indicates the importance of the symbolic discussion of "doll as woman" or "doll as girl" in cultural readings of the feminine. His writings also indicate the importance of the images of femininity represented by dolls, and the interplay of dolls and girls, and how these images can be linked to scholarly analysis of modernity. Via Sala, the doll is again brought into recurrent themes of recent art history scholarship as discussed above, particularly around the meanings of nineteenth-century images of women in Paris. Ruth Iskin (2006), in her essay for the *Invisible Flâneur* anthology, problematises the moral disdain for the insatiable and material woman flourishing within conventional ideas of the avant-garde. She asks the reader to circumvent the modernist denigration of consumption, if we are to write histories of "mass cultures" that allow for positions other than the "autonomous, rational individual of the liberal and Marxist tradition," tied up with images of "progress, reason and masculinity" in transforming the world (p. 114).

Sala's (1868) essay about British and French dolls and expensive prostitutes ascribes agency to the doll as symbol of women and of modern life. No longer just a toy, the Second Empire doll metaphorically represented the fundamentally corrupt nature of the society in which she was made. Moreover, Sala has shifted the doll into the public sphere, giving the doll a spectacular cultural presence generally denied her throughout the twentieth century. Adelaide Huret is implicitly present in Sala's essay. He stated that one person was responsible for the corruption of morals represented by these expensive dolls, and beyond them the flagrant commercialism and flashy surfaces of the Second Empire. For Sala, this culprit is an unnamed proprietor of a doll shop in the Passage de Choiseuil opened before the Crimean War broke out in 1853. Many imitators have been launched and made fortunes for many proprietors of doll shops. He does not name the shop, but there were several doll shops around the Passage Choiseuil, including Huret's (Coleman, 1975, p. 104). As Sala indicated that one shop was the forerunner of them all and as Huret's shop predated Crimea by a couple of years, it is not implausible to suggest that he was thinking of Huret's shop. Sala mentioned her business (by this date managed by her younger brother) as one of the foremost dollmakers of Paris (p. 145). Beyond Sala, other commentators raised moral qualms about the cost of the Huret doll. Such expensive dolls made their girl owners hard, venal, and demanding. It was even claimed that little girls refused to play with children whose family could not afford to buy them an expensive doll.[20]

Adelaide's "rival," Mademoiselle Leontine Rohmer, specifically sought to produce a cheaper doll as a corrective to Huret's high pricepoint (Murray, 2011, pp. 18–19). Rohmer's lifestory again indicates an enterprising and free-thinking woman. Daughter of an Alsatian engineer and, like Huret (cf. Theimer, 2011, p. 18) educated more broadly than many girls of her era, Rohmer spent long periods of her early life in Russia, but later returned to France, having refused to marry a Russian and stay in that country. Back in France, she started a dollmaking business in Paris. Huret and Rohmer battled each other in the courts over the design and invention of doll models. Rohmer's intentions were assumed to be malign, and although she appealed twice, she finally had to surrender those of her dolls and moulds that had been judged to be too close in design to Huret's. A modern commentator suggested that the grounds for Huret winning the case would not stand today, at least in the United States legal system, as the similarities between the dolls were generic and can be equally seen in dolls made by companies not sued by Adelaide Huret (Murray, 2011, p. 21).

Madame Lavallé Peronne commissioned Rohmer to produce Lily, the flagship doll of the journal *La Poupée Modèle*. Lily was sold exclusively at Lavallé-Peronne's shop *A La Poupée de Nuremburg*. Rohmer's dolls also made a broad cultural impact upon French design as Lavallée Peronne's dolls' clothes, worn by Rohmer's dolls, were so popular that she began selling her designs in full-scale versions. This upscaling from doll to human couture is documented in the tiny doll-sized fashion journal that was enclosed with certain issues of *La Poupée Modèle* (*Journal des Poupées*, 15 Mai 1865, 3 Odin, 2010a). A whole industry was catalysed by women, such as Adelaide Huret, Jenny Bereux, Madame Lavallé, the Parisian dolls' elaborate dresses (F. Theimer and Theimer, 2008, p. 136). "Many children's couturiers specialised in dolls' clothes and an entire neighbourhood between Boulevard Montmartre, the Bourse and the Opera became the neighbourhood of dolls' couturiers. As well as serving a demand for children's fashions based upon her designs for dolls, Lavallé Peronne opened an atelier to produce clothes for adult women, again in response to the widespread admiration of her doll fashions (*Journal des Poupées* 15 Mai 1865, pp. 4–5). Thus she too also contributed to the nascent haute couture in industry of the Second Empire. Journalists of the 1860s claimed that French dolls "serve another purpose than that of amusing the young folks, for they are in constant use amongst the dressmakers and milliners as models for their trousseaus and fine raiments." (*The Argus*, 1867, p. 7).

Artefacts suggest the interchangeability of style between little girls and their dolls. A photograph from Paris in a private collection, inscribed Amelie Beaufort aged 9 years 10 August 1866, shows Amelie wearing a layered skirt with a lighter overskirt and sharply cut vandycked edge outlined in a contrasting colour; Jenny Bereux designed a virtually identical skirt in doll size (F. Theimer & Theimer, 2008, p. 133). Amelie holds a doll dressed more plainly than she is. Due to the image being slightly over-exposed the doll lacks detail in the photograph, but from her size and proportions she is similar to the dolls of either Huret or Rohmer. Madame Lavallé-Peronne's doll-sized fashion magazine, given away with a girls' magazine about doll fashion, already itself a juvenile version of adult fashion literature, densely imbricates fantasy, real life, play, and apprenticeship into the role of the Parisienne, the apex of style and of fashion. As Ruth Iskin (2007, pp. 184–222) argued, the Parisienne was lively and chic. She symbolised the commercially prosperous city with its boulevards and department stores, rather than being a sign of moral degeneracy or a threatening sexualised lower class. To be a visibly fashionable woman as in the paintings, the advertising posters, and the fashion plates, as well as the three-dimensional format of the French doll, was a valuable responsibility in terms of constructing a sense of the modern and the inherently French.

The talented and inventive women in the French doll industry can be likened to the major trio of nineteenth-century Parisian artists, the Collin sisters: Anaïs, Heloise, and Laure. In an era when working women were regularly assumed to be prostitutes, and art critics openly belittled women artists, these three sisters, and some of their daughters in turn, established substantial careers for themselves between the 1840s and 1880s as leading fashion illustrators (Steele, 1988, pp. 11–13, 102–111). Like the dollmakers, they served a world that was strongly feminine in its dominant traits and produced items that were substantially consumed and patronised by women. Similarly to Huret and Rohmer et al., the Collin sisters opened up professional lives that have hardly registered in later academic accounts.

LA PRINCESSE EN PLASTIQUE: THE DOLL AS A SIGN OF MATERIAL PROGRESS

Huret's dolls innovate beyond high fashion as well. They are very early examples of plastic toys. Rather than sewing her doll's body from cloth or leather, Huret chose a pliable material, gutta percha, which is derived (like rubber and latex) from the sap of a Malaysian tree (Meikle, 1995, p. 4), and was used for insulation of undersea telegraph cables and small consumer goods in the mid-nineteenth century. Though now superseded, gutta percha was among the earliest commercially viable plastic compounds, albeit, like shellac and rubber, a "natural" plastic rather than a chemically synthesised plastic such as celluloid. Huret's choice of body material further demonstrates the complex positioning of her dolls. The novelty and relative unfamiliarity of this substance to the feminine domestic world must not be underestimated. Adelaide Huret's dolls were, in effect, a smash-and-grab raid upon science and technology from the worlds of creative arts, high fashion, and women's social sphere.

Even today, in Western society, science and technology still guard not only the esteem that their masculine identity guarantees, but also their privileged status in the eyes of government, educational, and economic bodies, against the relatively undervalued creative vocations. Elsa Schiaparelli is routinely commended by fashion historians for her intellectual perspicacity that permitted collaboration in the 1930s, not only with surrealist artists, but with manufacturers of synthetic fabrics and substances, to expand the range of possibilities for fashion (Martin, 1997, p. 98; Parkins, 2013, pp. 82–83, 97–98). In marketing an early, successful plastic-polymer-bodied doll, and developing a luxury industry and mystique around her name, Adelaide Huret consistently paralleled the mindset of acknowledged fashion innovators, including Schiaparelli, as well as Worth. The widespread use of plastic for children's toys today obscures Huret's achievements, but there could be no Toys R' Us, no injection moulding plants on upper stories of Hong Kong high rises or in polluted industrial estates in China, no legions of Pedigree, Regal, Ideal, or Mattel dolls in their collective billions, without such early successful examples of plastic technology as the Huret doll. That gutta percha would, in the long run, prove to be fragile, and many Huret-designed porcelain heads ended up being fitted to replacement bodies, did not prevent this plastic-bodied doll being produced and sold for at least 3 decades. Only in the 1880s did carved wooden-bodied dolls increasingly become the norm for the Huret firm (F. Theimer & Theimer, 2008, pp. 202–204, p. 259). Changes of ownership in the company took the Huret doll off the market, not customer dissatisfaction.

If Haussmann and Worth became household names in the Second Empire, the no-less-spectacular and transformative rise of Adelaide Huret and her dolls equally expressed the zeitgeist. Huret's dolls were as modern and finely wrought as the creations of Worth and Haussmann. As with Worth in dress and Haussmann in city planning, Huret visibly consolidated a position from where the experience of modernity could never retreat or degenerate. Huret's dolls share this grand modernising vision of Worth and Haussmann—the faith in the mutability of matter, and triumph of style and construction, the unification provided by the eye and mind of the designer. If Haussmann constructed a city of sweeping, united direction and a visually cohesive style, from the foetid alleys and crumbling buildings of *le veille Paris*, then the beautiful Huret poupée, with her superbly constructed garments and her pretty, but naturalistic, face likewise swept aside and improved upon the often ramshackle doll norms of yesteryear.

Certainly, for the Jumeau company, the development of the City of Paris, with its transformed public life and amenity, seemed to mirror in analogy the development of a new, sophisticated, improved format of doll. In an 1885 booklet outlining the achievements of the Jumeau firm, author Jules Cusset (cited in Davies, 1955) defined the development of the doll trade as a positivist expression of public benefit that fulfilled the Third Republic's belief in science, system, and order.

Time marches on and new inventions were everywhere surprising the world, which could hardly believe its eyes. After the railroads there were telegrams, then sewing machines and a host of innovations which will make this period renowned.

The old shops full of dust were demolished wholesale, and on their ruins arose elegant and spacious new ones full of light and luxuriously appointed. In place of smoky oil lamps gas flared in opalescent globes, windows sparkled to attract the passers-by and the old people, astonished, wondered by what wave of the fairy wand all these miracles have taken place. The whole world was turned upside down and in no time all the antiquities disappeared and their place taken by novelty and progress.

Today, scarcely 30 years after this industrial revolution, it is only very seldom, in some small hidden corner of the capital that one finds a "boutique" of our parents' time to serve as a reminder of what we all were like. It is at this period that the two Jumeau sons wanted to follow the new ideas. (pp. 63–64)

For Cusset and Jumeau, retailing, and the public appearance of retail premises, are the chief calibration of urban growth and development, thus prefiguring the current scholarly interest derived from Walter Benjamin's (2002) *Arcades Project* in the Parisian shop as a catalyst for modernism. Likewise Cusset's imagery precedes later academic analysis of the modernity of Paris, especially the sense of transformation and the virtu ascribed to the cleansing/salvation/rebirthing of the city under Haussmann's civic redevelopment. This passage prefigures other elements of Benjamin's *Arcades Project* where the new architecture of cast iron and new modes of commerce, display, and human movement and interaction within the arcades both symbolised and facilitated an expanding sense of the modern. The arcades are literally the world of the dolls, not only in modern Paris, but in the Second Empire: many of the doll shops and dolls dressmakers selected retail premises in and around the Parisian arcades, such as the Passage Choiseuil. Again we see how the culture that produced the French doll links into recent scholarly focus upon Paris as a highly informative case study around emergent modernism.

CONCLUSION

This chapter only touches the surface of the extraordinary and relatively under-researched "golden age" of French dollmaking from 1850 to 1900 and its multiple relationships to recent scholarly recapitulation of the lived experience of the modern. Dolls—apart from Barbie—have attracted little research until recently.[21] Moreover, some examples of this small oeuvre of scholarship, such as A. F. Robertson's (2004) analysis of middle-aged collectors of present-day overpriced collectors' dolls, seem to be written with a clearly articulated prophylactic irony—lest the scholar and his/her subjects become intermingled.[22] Yet from a number of perspectives, we can legitimately claim the doll of mid-nineteenth-century Paris as an agent of modernism, from her evocation of the fashionable Parisienne—herself a symbol of the nation, no less, "embodying the glory of France and its civilisation through the superiority of its fashionable women" (Iskin, 2007, p. 222) to the fantasy visual culture to be found in the early pages of *La Poupée Modèle*.

The images from *La Poupée Modèle* in the 1860s evoke the racy social life of the Second Empire. Yet placing dolls as the main actors remarkably and ingeniously erases the foregrounding of patriarchal heterosexual needs and fantasies that has been such a central and persistent feature of Western modernism and its scholarship, by suggesting that the modern could also spin out in a fictitious doll-utopia of lively fashionable girls and women of independent means and virtually invisible masculine presences. These illustrations also suggest that the young girl's world of fantasy enacted by doll tableaux and narratives could express the modern as eloquently as bohemian sexual freedom. The women who designed, made, and promoted these dolls can be legitimately recognised as modernist innovators. Adelaide Huret consolidated and deployed recognisably modern retail and promotion techniques that still shape present-day commercial activities, some years before they appeared in full-sized human-scale fashion.

There was also something modern in the *personae* of the dolls themselves, likened by a number of commentators to high-class prostitutes. Classifying dolls as prostitutes precurses the highly sexual identities freely assigned to Barbie and the Bratz dolls in popular commentary a century and a half later. Likewise, the girls who owned the new Parisian dolls represented something different and strange, seen in their hardness and their consciousness of status conferred by accessories, which did not conform to traditional notions of polite, mild, and non-assertive girlhood. In De Ségur's (1857) *Les Petites Filles Modèles*, the first clue to finding Marguerite's vanished luxurious doll emerged when working-class Suzanne boasted to Camille, Madeleine, and Marguerite that she had seen a more beautiful doll than the one the girls were currently playing with (Chapter 11).[23] Even working-class girls were taught to appreciate the superior power and presence of beautifully designed objects.

The neglect of the Parisian doll by historians of art and design, fashion and women's social life, not only erases an extraordinary moment of girls' material culture, as well as the creative products of some highly successful women, including Adelaide Huret, Leontine Rohmer, Jenny Bereux, and Madame Lavallée Peronne, but also removes an informative site for documenting the emergence of formats and practices of design, retailing, and consumption that are ubiquitous in the present day. Via dolls and the play with and consumption of dolls, women and girls can be placed as active and experientially embedded within the emergence of modernism rather than being marginalised observers and subjects of the masculine gaze of the avant-garde artist.

NOTES

1. Judith Walkowitz's (1992) and Elisabeth Wilson's (1991) writings are insightful here. Both charted female presence, both real and metaphorical/narrative, in the growing public cultures of modernity and the city—although Walkowitz focused on women in 1880s London, two decades after the Second Empire.

2. Outside of texts centred upon Barbie, full-length texts published in the last 2 decades solely devoted to dolls include those by Formanek-Brunell (1993), Peers, (2004), and Robertson (2004).

3. Christian Louboutin is listed on the Luxury Fashion Brands List compiled by Uché Okonkwo (2007) in *Luxury Fashion Branding: Trends, Tactics, Techniques* (p. 47). His shoes are globally recognised due to their red soles (Venkatesh, Joy, Sherry, Deschenes, 2010, p. 465). Terry de Gunzburg is a newer luxury brand and a younger entrepreneur: for *The Wall Street Journal* she is "the Steve Jobs of makeup" (Lennon, 2013).

4. On June 16th, 2012, *The Age* newspaper in Melbourne reported that

> Sadly, the shutter has descended on Catherine Deneuve's favourite antique doll shop at No. 26. Its former owner Robert Capia now devotes his time to running the *Association Passages et Galeries*, which campaigns for the preservation of Paris's historic arcades and organises regular walking tours (Street, 2012).

In defining Capia's shop as "Catherine Deneuve's favourite antique doll shop"—antique French dolls are linked into discourses of celebrity.

5. Details of his career may be found in F. Theimer and Theimer (2008, pp. 11–58).

6. F. Theimer and Theimer (2008, pp. 67–68, 77) emphasised that during Adelaide Huret's era the doll was intended to be a 12-year-old girl, and the original clothes and fashions produced for the doll during her management reflected that persona. He noted that the doll has a flat chest on her shoulderplate, and when fitted to replacement bodies, modifications must be made to bridge the gap between the Huret shoulderplate and the more mature proportions of the body it is fitted to (pp. 260–261). Huret dolls survive frequently redressed as grown women, including wearing clothes dating from the Second Empire, as well as those made by collectors and dealers at a later date. Samy Odin (2010b, p. 46) suggested that Huret's and Rohmer's dolls could play the part of both girl and grown woman.

7. There is a direct parallel between Huret's methods and the retail and promotional strategies of Charles Frederick Worth. Whilst Nancy Troy (2003) associated the rise of the "magic" brand name with the late nineteenth-century "Gilded Age" of exceptionally wealthy American capitalists (p. 26), Worth exemplifies the Second Empire. He had established his business practice of value adding and celebrating the mystique of his name in relation to clothing the court of the Second Empire. The importance of expensive garments, such as Worth's, in court life contributed to a general suspicion that the circle of Napoleon III was an eternal "masquerade" (Steele, 1988, p. 140).

8. Coleman (2010, p. 738, however, noted that "Although often credited with the innovation, Worth was not the first dressmaker to use a label."

9. There was at least one other, not specifically doll-focused, magazine for girls in Paris at the same date, *Cendrillion*.

10. A nineteenth-century advertising flyer in my own collection offers subscriptions to both titles.

11. Valerie Lastinger (1993) suggested that the large doll is more intentionally left behind by being laid down so that Marguerite could gather strawberries with her sister and friend (pp. 34–35), indicating a refusal of the domestic and mothering duties implied by the doll. The text already anticipates the loss of the doll potentially highlighting Marguerite's inability to care for her properly on the walk, and thus Marguerite being clumsy, immature, and unable to reason, as much as refusing maternity. Certainly, she panics with the thunderstorm and does not think clearly. Research into nineteenth-century French dolls is important precisely because the dolls are about display and self-expression via fashion and consumption as much as home making or mothering.

12. Eunice Lipton (1988, pp. 162–177) discussed bathing and the presence of male viewers/visitors in Degas' pastels and monotypes.

13. In eighteenth-century French art women of various classes including the elites are seen publicly receiving guests whilst at their dressing tables.

14. The stories of Chiffonette seem to follow the pattern established by the Comtesse de Ségur in *Les Malheures de Sophie* (1858), of a wilful, wayward girl lurching through a chain of disastrous misadventures and learning experiences.

15. These flowers of course reference the French tricolour and appear on one of the dresses in the couturier design trousseau for the 1938 Bébé Jumeaux presented to the British princesses—where it was noted that these flowers are a symbol of the French countryside and country hospitality and were presented to honoured guests in the country.

16. The expectation that a woman be seen at every social event in a new outfit was known to be a hallmark of the circles around the emperor Napoleon III. It also underpinned the viability of couture and dressmaking businesses.

17. In Chapter Twelve of *The Bostonians* (1921), Henry James lets his character Basil Ransome state of the Franco-Prussian war "It is well known that the Empress of France was at the bottom of the last war in that country" (C.f., McQueen, 2011, p. 287; Dolan, 1994; Dolan, 1997).

18. E.g., *South Australian Register* (1867, November 11, p. 3).

19. A related discussion, which deserves an extended examination in its own right and cannot be engaged with in the space of this chapter, is the 1860s "girl-of-the-period" debate in the English-speaking press, which was perhaps the first moral panic about teenagers and their inappropriate behaviours and dresscodes. Like the discussion about expensive French dolls, the girl-of-the-period debates were riven with anxieties about the sexualised fashions of the day that were based upon falsehood, padding, corsetry, cosmetics, fake hairpieces, and wigs and promoted by expensive Parisian prostitutes.

20. A primary source reproduced in F. Theimer and Theimer (2008, p. 150) appears to be an illustration of a story by the Comtesse de Ségur's daughter Viscomtesse Olga de Pitray, *La Ronde des Tuilleries*. Two richly dressed girls holding elaborate dolls refuse to play with a girl and a doll who are more plainly dressed. F. Theimer and Theimer also quoted Edmond About, writing around 1865–1866, where one little girl sees her doll as superior to another because it has jointed arms, "*mais surtout parce ce qu'elle coute dix francs plus cher*"—but above all because she costs 10 francs more (p. 227).

21. The first academic journal specially themed around dolls was only published in 2012: *Girlhood Studies*, 5(1).

22. Jerry Oppenheimer's *Toy Monster* (2009), the recent sensationalist history of Mattel, is nominally a critique of Barbie, but also foregrounds anxieties bordering on the pathological about women in senior management positions, leaving an impression of a vicious and gendered attack. Sala's 1868 essay is of value here as a cross-referencing context to indicate the traditional and nineteenth-century values at the heart of *Toy Monster* and the denial of women as agents of innovation and entrepreneurship. The doll is yet again a medium for attacking live women.

REFERENCES

Adelaide Advertiser. (1864, June 18). 3.

The Argus (1867, September 7), p. 7.

Belau, D. (2010). Perusing the passages. Retrieved from http://girlsguidetoparis.com/archives/perusing-the-passages/

Benjamin, W. (2002). *The arcades project*. Cambridge, MA: Harvard University Press.

Best, K. N. (2008). Fashioning the figure of French creativity: A historical perspective on the political function of French fashion discourse. *The Web Journal of French Media Studies*, 7.

Boime, A. (1997). *Art and the French commune: Imagining Paris after war and revolution*. Princeton, NJ: Princeton University Press.

Clayson, H. (2003). *Painted love: Prostitution and French art of the Impressionist era*. Los Angeles, CA: Getty Institute. Retrieved from http://www.getty.edu/publications/virtuallibrary/0892367296. html

Coleman, D. S., Coleman, E. A., & Coleman, E. J. (1975). *The collector's book of dolls' clothes: Costumes in miniature, 1700–1929*. New York, NY: Crown.

Coleman, E. A. (2010). Charles Frederick Worth. In V. Steele (Ed.), *Berg Companion to Fashion* (pp. 737–740). Oxford: Berg.

Collins, L. (2011). Fashion dolls and feminism: How do you solve a problem like Barbie? In J. Wolfendale & J. Kennett (Eds.), *Fashion—Philosophy for everyone: Thinking with style* (pp. 151–165). Oxford, England: Blackwell.

Cumming, V. (2004). *Understanding fashion history* (pp. 38–39). Hollywood, CA: Costume and Fashion Press.

Davies, N. (1955). *The Jumeau Doll story* (N. Davies, Trans.). Author. (Reprinted from *Notice sur la fabrication des Bebes Jumeau*, by J. Cusset, 1885, Paris, France: Grand Imprimerie).

De Ségur, S. (1906). *Les petites filles modèles*. Vignettes par Bertall, Paris: Hachette. (First published 1857) Retrieved from http://www.gutenberg.org/files/35404/35404-h/35404-h.htm

D'Souza, A., & McDonough, T. (Eds). (2006). *The invisible flâneuse? Gender, public space, and visual culture in nineteenth-century Paris* (pp. 1–18). Manchester, England; New York, NY: Manchester University Press.

Dolan, T. (1994). The Empress' new clothes: Fashion and politics in second Empire France. *Women's Art Journal, 15*(1), 22–27.

Dolan, T. (1997). Skirting the issue: Manet's portrait of *Baudelaire's Mistress, Reclining. Art Bulletin, 89*(4), 611–629.

Forman-Brunell, M., & Paris, L. (Eds.). (2011). *The girls' history and culture reader: The nineteenth century*. Urbana, IL: University of Illinois Press.

Formanek-Brunell, M. (1993). *Made to play house: Dolls and the commercialization of American Girlhood*. New Haven, CT: Yale University Press.

Groom, G. (Ed.). (2012). *Impressionism, fashion, and modernity*. Chicago, IL: Art Institute of Chicago in association with Yale University Press.

Helgren, J., & Vasconcellos, C. A. (Eds.). (2010). *Girlhood : A global history*. New Brunswick, NJ: Rutgers University Press.

Iskin, R. (2006). The flâneuse in French fin de siècle posters: Advertising images of the modern in Paris. In A. D'Souza & T. McDonough (Eds.), *The invisible flâneuse? Gender, public space, and visual culture in nineteenth-century Paris* (pp. 113–128). Manchester, England: Manchester University Press.

Iskin, R. (2007). *Modern women and Parisian consumer culture in Impressionist painting*. Cambridge, England: Cambridge University Press.

James, H. (1921). *The Bostonians*. London, England: Macmillan London. Retrieved from http://www.gutenberg.org/cache/epub/19717/pg19717.txt

Johnston, E. L. (1986). For the love of the ladies. *Doll Reader, 24*(2), 61–67.

Journal des Poupées 15 Mai 1865 (reproduction published by Musée des Poupées, Paris, and also as bonus enclosure in Odin 2010 a).

Lastinger, V. C. (1993). Of dolls and girls in nineteenth-century France. *Children's Literature, 21*(1), 20–42.

Lennon, C. (2013, March 8). Terry de Gunzburg. *The Wall Street Journal*. Retrieved from http://online.wsj.com/article/SB10001424127887324678604578340813718638862.html#articleTabs%3Darticle

Linn, S. E. (2004). *Consuming kids: The hostile takeover of childhood*. New York, NY: New Press.

Lipton, E., (1988). *Looking into Degas: Uneasy images of women and modern life*. Berkeley, CA: University of California Press.

Martin, R. (1997). A note: A charismatic art: The balance of ingratiation and outrage in contemporary fashion. *Fashion Theory: The Journal of Dress, Body & Culture*, *1*(1), 91–104(14).

McQueen, A. (2011). *Empress Eugénie and the Arts: Politics and visual culture in the nineteenth century*. Aldershot, England: Ashgate.

Meikle, J. L. (1995). *American plastic: A cultural history*. New Brunswick, NJ: Rutgers University Press.

Mitchell, C. A., & Reid-Walsh, J. (Eds.). (2008). *Girl culture: An encyclopedia*. Westport, CT: Greenwood Press.

Murray, L. (2011). The resourceful mind of Leontine Rohmer. *Antique Doll Collector*, *14*(11), 17–22.

Odin, S. (2010a). Lilas: The exemplary life of a Rohmer Lady Doll. *Antique Doll Collector*, *13*(2), 18–23, 43–49.

Odin, S. (2010b). *Lilas: la vie exemplaire d'une poupée de mode sous le Second Empire Paris*. Paris, France: Cahiers de la Musée de la Poupée.

Okonkwo, U. (2007). *Luxury fashion branding: Trends, tactics, techniques*. New York, NY: Palgrave Macmillan.

Oppenheimer, J. (2009). *Toy monster: The big, bad world of Mattel*. New York, NY: Wiley.

Parkins, I. (2013). *Poiret, Dior and Schiaparelli: Fashion, femininity and modernity*. London, England: Bloomsbury.

Peers, J. (2004). *The fashion doll—From Bebe Jumeau to Barbie*. London, England: Berg.

Pollock, G. (2003). Modernity and the spaces of femininity. In G. Pollock (Ed.), *Vision & difference: Femininity, Feminism, and Histories of Art*. London, England; New York, NY: Routledge.

La Poupée Modèle. (1863–1867). Paris, France: Bureau de la Journal des Demoiselles.

Robertson, A. F. (2004). *Life like dolls: The collector doll phenomenon and the lives of the women who love them*. London, England: Routledge.

Rocamora, A. (2009). *Fashioning the city: Paris, fashion and the media*. London, England: IB Tauris.

Sala, G. A. (1868). *Notes and sketches of the Paris exhibition*. London, England: Tinsley Brothers.

Simon, M. (1996). *Fashion in art: The Second Empire and Impressionism* (E. Jephcott, Trans.). London, England: Zwemmer.

Søndergaard, S. M. (2006). *Women in Impressionism: From mythical feminine to modern woman* [Exhibition]. Copenhagen, Denmark: Ny Carlsberg Glyptotek.

Steele, V. (1988). *Paris fashion: A cultural history*. Oxford, England: Berg.

Street, J. (2012, June 16). Passages of time. *The Age*. Retrieved from http://www.theage.com.au/travel/activity/shopping/passages-of-time-20120614-20cee.html#ixzz2Ks9aZAjf

Taylor, L. (2004). *Establishing dress history*. Manchester, England: Manchester University Press.

Tétart-Vittu, F. (2012a). Eduard Manet "the Parisienne." In G. Groom (Ed.), *Impressionism, fashion, and modernity* (pp. 78–81). Chicago, IL: Art Institute of Chicago in association with Yale University Press.

Tétart-Vittu, F. (2012c). Who creates fashion? In G. Groom (Ed.), *Impressionism, fashion, and modernity* (pp. 63–77). Chicago, IL: Art Institute of Chicago in association with Yale University Press.

Theimer, T. (1997). Huret: A side product of a lock company. *Doll Reader*, *25*(2), 84–88.

Theimer, T. (2011). The birth of the Poupée Huret. *Antique Doll Collector*, *14*(4), 18–24.

Theimer, F., & Theimer, D. (2008). *Maison Huret.* Paris, France: Author.

Theimer, T., & Theriault, F. (1994). *The Jumeau Doll.* Annapolis, MD: Gold Horse.

Troy, N. J. (2003). *Couture culture: A study in modern art and fashion.* Cambridge MA: MIT Press.

Tungate, M. (2009). *Luxury world: The past, present and future of luxury brands.* London, England: Kogan Page.

Venkatesh, A., Joy, A., Sherry, J. F., & Deschenes, J. (2010). The aesthetics of luxury fashion, body and identify formation. *Journal of Consumer Psychology, 20*(4), 459–470.

Walkowitz, J. (1992). *City of dreadful delight: Narratives of sexual danger in Victorian London.* London, England: Virago.

Wilson, E. (1991). *The sphinx in the city: Urban life, the control of disorder, and women.* London, England: Virago.

CHAPTER TEN

The Doll-Machine: Dolls, Modernism, Experience

CATHERINE DRISCOLL

My preliminary proposition in this chapter can be stated quite boldly. The modern doll is something quite different than the dolls that preceded it. Let's say "a doll" has always meant a crafted humanoid figurine, and what is done *with* and *as* a doll could always be called "cultural"—encompassing various kinds of ritual, play, and aesthetics. Under the aegis of modernity, however, the doll has also come to signify an encounter with culture itself, extending ritual to nostalgia, play to experiment, and aesthetics to style. All of these new concepts—of and for culture—are integral to modernity, but not often considered together. I want to suggest that understanding the relationship between them could begin by taking the doll as a central figure. In exploring the significance of the modern transformation of the doll I will consider how it unites a set of iconic Modernist doll-figures and their relation to more banal doll-forms and doll-practices on which they draw.[1] My central examples include three very different Modernist artworks—Fritz Lang's film *Metropolis* (and its robot-girl, Maria), Igor Stravinsky's ballet *Petrushka* (and its dancing puppets/dolls), and Hans Bellmer's photographs collectively known as "The Doll" (centred on distorted "dolls" and doll-pieces he had made)—and finally, Mattel's Barbie dolls, which I want to place in the same history of modernising dolls as those artworks. Across these examples the modern doll is both animate and inanimate, both subject and object, but emphatically also gendered. What I will call the girl-ing of the modern doll relies on these entanglements and makes of the doll-machine an icon of modern experience.

"ALL IT NEEDS IS A SOUL!"

My first Modernist doll-figure is the least avant-garde and thus perhaps the most important to a broad cultural transformation of what dolls mean and how they work: Robot-Maria (played by Brigitte Helm) in Lang's famous expressionist science fiction film, *Metropolis* (1927). Unlike the other artworks I discuss, Robot-Maria is truly iconic. That is, she exceeds her own origins and context—working even when she can't be named and entirely outside the film that created her. What Robot-Maria *means* in the famous images from the film and its promotion is culturally apparent, and relies on an intersection between doll and machine that is crucial to the transformation this chapter explores.

While the plot of *Metropolis* may not need paraphrasing, it's important to my argument. *Metropolis* is a city divided: the workers man the city's necessary machines and live regimented lives; the leaders live enlightened lives of leisure as well as managerial authority; and a sub-stratum of catacombs and mysteries manifests the margins of this society, where the resentment of both oppressed workers and leaders whose authority is not recognised can be found. This is where Robot-Maria appears, created at an interface of science and magic by Rotwang in order to ferment worker unrest against his rival. She appears, as one possible intertitle puts it, on "the threshold of an alien world," raising urgent questions about where modern life is going. She represents not only the force of science, able to blur boundaries between man and machine, but also a will at odds with the moral resolution of the plot. In one of the many moral-political homilies in the script, Joh Fredersen tells his son Freder that in the present and future world, "There are millions of hands, my son. Millions of men. Cogs on a wheel that cannot turn without a driving power." It's who or what will be this power that drives the plot, and the important difference between "who" or "what"—man or machine—centres on this doll-figure. Even before she has been "turned on," the question of the robot's soul matters.

The famous scene in which Rotwang's robot is animated with the face, but not the spirit, of the girl Maria invokes Mary Shelley's *Frankenstein* (1818), indeed setting influential cinematic parameters for filming the Frankenstein story by integrating with the animating electricity images of soulless mechanisation. But the intertextual network now invoked by this scene is far more extensive, not only looking back to Ovid's (1953) Pygmalion story and *Frankenstein* but also forward through their many adaptations and towards Philip K. Dick's (1968) or Ridley Scott's (1982) androids/replicants. Robot-Maria is also a primary visual reference for the even more popular figures of Iron Man (Marvel) and C3PO (the Star Wars franchise). But it might not be immediately obvious what dolls have to do with this intertextual field beyond noting that these are all crafted humanoid figures, with dolls only lacking the animation characterising robots, androids, or Frankenstein's monster. This demands more consideration. When Pygmalion's statue of Galatea comes to life, that's his reward for piety, and the question of whether living Galatea has an independent will and chooses to love him is never at issue; her artificiality is simply erased. The robot is quite different, always remaining an animated machine. Rotwang's plan to create mechanical humans is thus part of the cultural history of the robot as a branch of automata bound to both mechanical toys and automated tools (see Wood, 2003).

The robot is always speculatively linked to the problem of labour, beginning with Karel Capek's (1921) 1920 play, *R.U.R. (Rossum's Universal Robots)*. The robot is always more a tool than a toy. Even the various "pleasure model" androids appearing in science fiction (e.g., Scott, 1982) locate sex as work before it is a leisure activity. The doll is quite the reverse. The work a doll does is largely invisible, extending the robot's questioning of the human beyond the man/machine opposition. It is gender, I will suggest, that the modern doll primarily *does*. As the fascinating images of Helm being sustained inside the difficult robot costume for *Metropolis* suggest, there was a girl inside this animated doll.

Capek's (1921) robots—or androids, we might call them now, because they're built of artificially produced biological materials like those in Dick (1968) or Scott (1982)—are crucially male *and* female, telling a story about sexual as well as mechanical reproduction and closing on an attenuated Adam-and-Eve story. In the intertextual field that situates both Capek's robots and Robot-Maria we must also locate the once famous Elektro, best known for his appearance at the 1939–1940 World's Fair in New York. Unlike Capek's dimorphic robots in their drama of reproduction, Elektro was very specifically a man. Appearing in the Westinghouse exhibition, Elektro as promotional spectacle invoked both science and authority for the labour-saving work of electrical domestic appliances (including, implicitly, him). He is the man in a drama centred on women's work, which is why he spectacularly smoked cigars amidst the first displays of dishwashers, and so on, in model domestic spaces.[2] But Robot-Maria is a woman because she is also a doll, splicing the robot story to earlier doll romances. She invites connection to an influence on *Metropolis* as important as Capek's robots, and rather better known, if not often labelled "modernist"—Olimpia from E. T. A. Hoffmann's (1816) story "The Sandman" and its many adaptations.[3]

Olimpia is not Pygmalion's Galatea, because she is a trap and a fraud rather than a reward. Like Galatea, however, and Frankenstein's monster, she is an experiment in producing perfect humanity without the involvement of women. Like Robot-Maria, she is a tool designed to harm a romantic rival. A lover (rather than worker) standing in place of authentic relations, Olimpia herself does nothing, wants nothing, and is no-one. But she does perform: she's a singer and a dancer and these emphatically feminised performances are more perfect than any woman would be capable of. This is itself frightening—everyone but the hero, Nathaniel, finds her exact perfection uncannily off-putting. And Nathaniel's desire for her, and his madness at the exposure of her mechanisation, combine with her uncanny performance of ideal femininity to make Olimpia an automated doll.

In his famous essay on "The Uncanny" (1953), Freud focused on Hoffmann's story only to say that it is not really about "the doll Olympia, who is to all appearances a living being," but about the narrator's association of her creator with a childhood bogeyman "who tears out children's eyes" (p. 227). It cannot be about Olimpia, Freud claimed, because living dolls are more pleasurable than frightening, more wish fulfilment than threat:

> We remember that in their early games children do not distinguish at all sharply between living and inanimate objects, and that they are especially fond of treating their dolls like live people. In fact, I have occasionally heard a woman patient declare that even at the age of eight she had still been convinced that her dolls would be certain to come to life if she were to look at them in a particular, extremely concentrated, way. So that here, too, it is not difficult to discover a factor from childhood. But, curiously enough, while the Sand-Man story deals with the arousing of an early childhood fear, the idea of a "living doll" excites no fear at all; children have no fear of their dolls coming to life, they may even desire it. (p. 233)

The remembered uncertainty here—remembered by both analyst and analysand—nevertheless reveals just how uncannily dolls work. Indeed, Freud (1953) took Ernst Jentsch's account of how frightening and compromising dolls can be as impetus for claiming the uncanny relies on a nexus of three psychic forces: the ongoing power of childhood anxieties, the dramas of repetition by which all neuroses are played out, and the necessity of coming to accord with the real world, which makes any blurring of the boundary between reality and fantasy frightening. Freud wrote:

> We proceed to review things, persons, impressions, events and situations which are able to arouse in us a feeling of the uncanny in a particularly forcible and definite form. … Jentsch has taken as a very good instance "doubts whether an apparently animate being is really alive; or conversely, whether a lifeless object might not be in fact animate"; and he refers in this connection to the impression made by waxwork figures, ingeniously constructed dolls and automata. (p. 226)

In the popular afterlife of Hoffmann's story, it is Olimpia who iconographically represents it, as is the case with Robot-Maria in the afterlife of *Metropolis*. Both represent the bound-together desire for and fear of the doll-come-to-life. Both stories represent giving in to this desire—trying to make the doll live—as an immoral act. The fascination of dolls-come-to-life in these classic Modernist texts, and also in later horror movies, lies partly in the mystery of their animating will. Rotwang is not misnamed when he's called a "wizard" in many of *Metropolis*'s possible intertitles, for all his laboratory equipment. Rotwang proceeds by invocation of substance rather than falsification, to take a Heideggerean line on what distinguishes modern science (see Heidegger, 1977). Robot-Maria requires a soul, a "driving power," her own, but not, of course, quite her own. To be what Rotwang desires, she need not *experience*, only *do*, but what she does is not entirely explicable by motives outside her.

Desire for and fear of the doll's soul is also central to Charles Baudelaire's (1853) short but excellent essay, "The Philosophy of Toys." It opens with what Freud would surely find a telling turn to the past, but Baudelaire saw in children's animating games more diversity than is allowed by Freud's theory of the uncanny. When it comes to that question of the soul, something irrationally destructive is nevertheless involved:

> The overriding desire of most little brats… is to get at and *see the soul* of their toys, either at the end of a certain period of use, or on occasion *straightaway*. On the more or less swift invasion of this desire depends the lifetime of the toy. I cannot find it in me to blame this infantile mania: it is the first metaphysical stirring. When this desire has planted itself in the child's cerebral marrow, it fills his fingers and nails with an extraordinary agility and strength. He twists and turns the toy, scratches it, shakes it, bangs it against the wall, hurls it on the ground. From time to time he forces it to continue its mechanical motions, sometimes in the opposite direction. Its marvellous life comes to a stop. The child, like the populace besieging the Tuileries, makes a last supreme effort; finally he prises it open, for he is the stronger party. But *where is its soul?* This moment marks the beginnings of stupor and melancholy. (p. 5)

It matters that Baudelaire (1853) wrote of toys rather than dolls, and that his child is generically male, distinctions to which I'll return. But another Modernist artwork will help foreground the importance of connecting the doll's soul to melancholy as well as uncanniness.

"VOCIFERATION OF PETRUSHKA'S GHOST"

Every iteration of a ballet is inevitably different, like games played with the same doll. The heightened problems of repetition and originality in ballet, even over theatre given the added difficulties of synchronisation, make it particularly useful for "modernist studies" and, I think, also for considering "play." *Petrushka: Burlesque scenes in four tableaux* is a ballet to music by Stravinsky (1911), originally choreographed by Mikhail Fokine and performed by the Ballets Russes starring Vaslav Nijinsky as Petrushka. As a ballet it can never quite be Stravinksy's alone rather than also Fokine's and Alexandre Benois' (the set designer) and perhaps even Nijinsky's as well. While it has been reinterpreted many times in the ensuing century, the Ballets Russes production—especially Fokine's choreography, despite limited notation of it, but also the sets and the libretto by Stravinsky, Fokine, and Benois—dominate all later performances.[4]

The serious matter on which *Petrushka* (Stravinsky, 1911), is a burlesque is the human condition. Petrushka is one of three dolls, alongside The Ballerina and The Moor, owned by a Magician who sets them to dancing at a Shrovetide Fair. The two middle tableaux are set afterwards, inside the dolls' rooms: in the second, Petrushka expresses his personal angst and his pained love for The Ballerina, who briefly enters to reject him; in the third, The Moor more happily contemplates his own circumstances and then romances The Ballerina only to be confronted by Petrushka. In the final tableau, The Moor chases Petrushka out into the Fair and kills him. The outraged crowd are reassured that Petrushka is only a doll by being shown his inanimate form, but as they disperse Petrushka's ghost taunts the horrified Magician from above the theatre. The ballet's direct plays on will, freedom, and limits support there being an existential narrative here. As Jann Pasler (1986) recorded,

> The real challenge of the [second] tableau, according to Benois, was to express Petrushka's "pitiful oppression and his hopeless efforts to achieve personal dignity without ceasing to be a puppet." To do this, he notes, "both music and libretto are spasmodically interrupted by outbursts of illusive joy and frenzied despair." (p. 61)

Petrushka becomes his own pitiable object, an interpretation for which we might draw on Jean-Paul Sartre to account for modern man's unfreedom and the ties by which he binds himself. But Petrushka is also a doll, even if he is his own properly named character, while The Moor and The Ballerina appear only as types. Indeed, a "petrushka" is a generic "folk" doll; a type of Russian rag-and-straw doll or puppet. Why use a doll to tell this story for the Modernist revolutions in dance and ballet that Fokine, Stravinsky, and the Ballets Russes represent? After all, imprisonment and thwarted love are staple stories for ballet. And modern ballet also does not lack its existential dramas, even if *Petrushka* (Stravinsky, 1911) is one of the most famous.

The setting of *Petrushka* (Stravinsky, 1911) matters here. Despite attempts to pin it down by styling or even dating, this St. Petersburg Shrovetide Fair belongs narratively to the border between industrial and pre-industrial worlds. The long opening to the fourth tableau, seemingly extraneous to the main dramatic narrative, is populated by dancing wet nurses, gypsies, coachmen, jugglers, masqueraders, and so on. This scene is not reducible to either a folkloric exhibition of Russian music or a series of *divertissements*. It appears to locate a disturbing encounter between the wonders of the old and modern worlds. The compiled rustic dances, games, and rituals that open the first and last tableaux constitute each time a public that awaits spectacle. Their wonder at animated dancing dolls in the first tableaux cannot be sustained as such through the intervening display of Petrushka's pain, and is transformed in the final scene by their belief that he lives. When they confront the puppet-master, in most productions by calling the police, and thus the modern state, to rule if this is magic or science (and thus murder), they briefly demand explanation rather than mystery. When the Magician demonstrates that Petrushka's corpse is only a doll they are satisfied and leave, applauding with wonderment once more. His closing lone encounter with Petrushka's ghost disturbs this certainty, but not for "the public" of the ballet.

While ballet characters are not expected to speak, Petrushka's staging and choreography shows a yearning for expression, and his impossible individuation *as a doll* emphasises his muteness. As a doll he cannot speak any more than he can love or live. It is thus as a doll that Petrushka represents the always constrained subject of modern life. We could approach this through Martin Heidegger's (1977) account of the modern subject as the one that is represented in the act of representing.[5] Petrushka's drama plays out that of the simultaneously objectified subject and subjectified object. There is always a puppeteer pulling Petrushka's strings and leaving the authenticity of his emotions in question until this very last scene where he appears as the ghost of a doll and thus as one who has lived. If this doubt about his ontological status still allows that the Magician's theatre might move on to another fair and play the drama out again, Petrushka's vociferation happens outside any domain in which he remains a doll: theatrical exhibition, magical interior, or play. Thus, *Petrushka* (Stravinsky, 1911) works because, as Baudelaire (1853) suggested, dolls always entangle the experience of subject and object in an expressively mute form that inspires questions about whether it lives or not. *Petrushka* further questions Freud's (1953) claim that toys that come to life are wish fulfilment rather than horrifying. Living dolls can turn on their maker, even when the maker is pulling the strings.

Petrushka is definitively unfree: he rails against the harm done to him and limits placed on him by others while he aspires to a freedom neither The Moor nor The Ballerina seem able to comprehend. But the kind of existentialism we need to understand *Petrushka* (Stravinsky, 1911) might be less Sartre's than Simone de Beauvoir's (1949). Like all modern dolls, *Petrushka* is a ballet about constraint and repetition in the drama of identity but it offers no transcendence even as a project. This is inseparable from the modern doll's entanglement with gender. Like all modern ballet, *Petrushka* is also a drama of embodiment. In ballet rather than theatre the human form seems especially doll-like because it has no words: all expression comes from movement, or its absence; from stylised embodiment. Beauvoir insisted, and certainly via Freud as much as Hegel, on an embodied self. This "body is not a *thing*, it is a situation," phenomenologically speaking; "it is the instrument of our grasp upon the world, a limiting factor for our projects" (p. 66). Moreover, this embodiment is categorically sexed, the meanings of which can only be understood with "due regard" for the subject's "total situation" (p. 83). Beauvoir's account of any subject's situation is framed by limits such as political economy, genre, race, science, and law that even the most effective strategies for self-realisation cannot simply exceed. And to understand Petrushka's situation we must look beyond his expression of existence and have due regard not only for the Magician and his audience but also for the other dolls.

Engaging with the doll through de Beauvoir (1949) foregrounds sexual difference and what we now call its gendered meanings. As is the case with all dolls, the gender of Robot-Maria, Olimpia, or The Ballerina comes from their styling, which means in each case that the recognisability of gender precedes them but that specific context is crucial. The narrative centre of *Petrushka* (Stravinsky, 1911) is the rivalry between Petrushka and The Moor for The Ballerina. The Moor can be a controversial figure in performance because of the racial stereotypes his form expresses. But what of The Ballerina? Fokine's choreography plays at all times with the idea of strings pulling at Petrushka. It's an elaborate choreographed pun on heartstrings and puppet-strings. But Petrushka at least has a heart, as The Moor also has apparent desires (for food, religion, sex, and property). The Ballerina, however, is just a doll—her only purpose is dance, and we should recall here that Robot-Maria and Olimpia are both also dancing dolls. If The Moor is constrained by racial stereotypes, The Ballerina represents jointly the proper gender of the loved-object—a doll to admire and employ, as de Beauvoir would suggest—and the constraints of "classical ballet." The Ballerina is as stilted and free of feeling and action as Fokine and Stravinsky believed the assembled genre of ballet to be. In comparison to the fluid expressiveness of Petrushka and the caricature personality of The Moor, The Ballerina is expressionless and stiffly en pointe. The only feeling she is characteristically given, and fleetingly, if so, is alarm. Even whether she chooses The Moor or not remains open to interpretation in performance, compared to Petrushka and The Moor's narrative clarity. The Ballerina is The Magician's puppet, The Moor's toy, and Petrushka's object, but nothing in herself except a dancing doll. If alienation is objectification of the self in one's own experience, this is inescapable for the modern subject from the existentialist point of view—we're all Petrushka. Unless, of course, we're one of the other dolls. For de Beauvoir, the doll specifically signifies a gender regime in which her in-animation and object status are political devices. Dolls belong, for her, to the lessons of gender conformity. And that's an excellent place to turn to Hans Bellmer.

"VARIATIONS ON THE MONTAGE OF AN ARTICULATED MINOR"

Even the strongest expressions of Modernist style—as individual, to paraphrase Fredric Jameson (1983), as fingerprints (p. 114)—have to be assembled with others in ballet. But this dispersal of authority still allowed for many forms of avant-gardism, including neo-classicism, primitivism, and minimalism. But ballet was a less-promising medium for surrealism, relying too literally on the body that does or does not do things. Lynn Garafola (1998) commented on Jean Cocteau's libretto for one of the few key surrealist ballets, *Le Train Bleu* (1924), that "Again and again Cocteau stylized the action, casting it in the form of a mechanically reproduced image" (p. 109), but it made "few allusions to dance. In fact, it contains very few dances" (p. 110). By contrast the breakable, disassemblable, and re-assemblable subjectified object-body of the doll was not only a promising figure for surrealism but practically a totem. Peter Webb (quoted in Gordon, 2005) has suggested that the doll was the "ideal Surrealist object," a significance the surrealist Jean Brun explained through its "conjunction of the everyday and the imaginary, the animate and the inanimate, the natural and the artificial" (p. 103). I want to suggest, instead, and in the light of the previous two sections, that if film was in many ways the perfect surrealist medium, the doll was the perfect surrealist *subject*.

Conceptually caught somewhere between the 1929 films *Un Chien Andalou* and *Man with a Movie Camera*, both of which feature their own dolls, is *Ballet Mécanique*, a film by Fernand Léger and Dudley Murphy (1924) to a score by George Antheil, which offers some context for how something as culturally ancient as a doll could offer that sense of the "new" sought by Modernists. *Metropolis* (Lang, 1927) blends the doll and the robot in figuring inhuman labour and *Petrushka* (Stravinsky, 1911) insists on the horror of the doll-subject, but neither foregrounds one of the most important influences on the transformation that brought dolls in the contemporary world to be overwhelmingly associated with girls rather than boys: the fashion mannequin. Machine-human connections comprise the key narrative thread holding *Ballet Mécanique* together: a girl on a swing dissolves into a set of mechanically reproduced objects, and back again (upside down); a working woman repeatedly climbs the same set of stairs, intercut with a machinic part repeatedly turning the same arc. But in the closing minutes the occasional shots of a heavily made-up girl's mouth and eyes coalesce into a model's doll-like face (Kiki de Montparnasse). She's like a statue, then she's cut up into a turning kaleidoscope of expressive parts. She's rhythmically intercut with looming figurines, abstract shapes, and domestic tools. But most of all she's the disembodied living face of a mannequin, whose stockinged artificial legs are editorially arranged into a clockwork dance with men's accessories and wine bottles as the film builds to its climax, fading into an animated Chaplin-esque dancer who disassembles back into the girl in a garden.

The derivation of fashion mannequins from the mannequin as articulated artist's model suggested in the surrealist films provides an important point of access to the overlaps between modernist avant-gardism and fashion. These overlaps have been extensively discussed (e.g., Troy, 2003; Lusty, 2007) and the conjunction girl-model-doll-surrealism has also been considered (e.g., Caws, 1986; Suleiman, 1998; Gordon, 2005). As Nancy Troy's *Couture Culture* argues, modern fashion intersected with modern visual art in their shared approach to product differentiation and to the manipulation of taste as style in engaging with such "recalcitrant and (compelling)" (p. 292) issues as mass production's transformation of both art and social life. Modernist fashion and visual art, moreover, took the doll and the girl's body as together forming an articulated tool for representing modern subjectivity. For neither Baudelaire nor Freud is the doll especially associated with girls rather than children in general. But the problem of the lifelike doll that represents modern subjectivity precisely in having neither will nor soul is brought to the foreground in Modernist art as a gendered machine. It isn't that the Modernists themselves girl-ed the doll, but the girl-ed doll emerging contemporarily with Modernism told a compatible story.

"The Doll: Variations on the Montage of an Articulated Minor" is the title applied to a collection of 18 images by Bellmer (1934) published in the surrealist journal *Minotaure*.[6] Each image differently assembles "articulated" pieces into a partial and distorted doll figure. Bellmer's "Doll" is worn, unfinished, broken, mutated, prosthetically enhanced, and/or amputated—but specifically a *girl* doll, and the mute expressive body of a *doll* girl. As Sue Taylor (2000, 2001) and Terri J. Gordon (2005) both recounted, Bellmer's success with his doll figures was immediate, notably within the French surrealist art community of which he was otherwise not a part. They also belong to the intertextual field connecting *Metropolis* (Lang, 1927) and *Petrushka* (Stravinsky, 1911) as another Modernist play on the uncannily animated doll (even inspired by Offenbach's Olympia, see Gordon, p. 103). I want to take Bellmer's dolls as also exemplifying the modern transformation of the doll from ritual token to a categorically gendered component system operating simultaneously as image and tool.

Bellmer's (1934) dolls generate a fairly consistent critical response, although it has two sides. On one side, Bellmer exemplifies the surrealist exploitation of the female body as a particularly violent reinvigoration of the way a patriarchal system of artistic production had always used the female body. On the other, Bellmer is represented as using images of girlhood to rebel against violent patriarchal authority at both personal and political levels. Taylor's (2001) account of the *Minotaure* publication makes the technical case for both:

The images show Bellmer's assemblage, made of wood, flax fiber, plaster, and glue, under construction in his studio or arrayed on a bare mattress or lacy cloth. Seductive props sometimes accompany the doll—a black veil, eyelet undergarments, an artificial rose. Naked or, in one case, wearing only a cotton undershirt, the armless doll is variously presented as a skeletal automaton, a coy adolescent, or an abject pile of discombobulated parts. In one unusual image, the artist himself poses next to his standing sculpture, his human presence rendered ghostly through double exposure. Here Bellmer's own body seems to dematerialize as his mechanical girl, wigged, with glass eyes, wool beret, sagging hose, and a single shoe, takes on a disturbing reality.

It is indisputable that Bellmer (1934) violently sexualised his dolls, and that their apparent knowingness opposes the declared innocence of some dolls and the unconsciousness of others. But the modern doll always does much of this work. Bellmer's dolls are fashion mannequins before anything else and speak, in their material fabrication and symbolic effects, to technical and cultural developments in doll production beyond avant-garde art.

Drawing on Seigfried Kracauer's (1927) discussion of popular girl dance revues as a "Mass Ornament," Gordon (2005) connected these revues' "*femme-machine*" to girl-model-doll-surrealism by arguing that both symbolise the mechanised dissassemblage and reassemblage of the body after the trauma of war. If the works of Man Ray and Bellmer collapse "female sexuality and technology" into "the figure of a mechanical woman" they also, Gordon argued, "provide instances of a figuration of trauma in a displaced form" (p. 101). I am suggesting a broader context for the uncanny presence of the gendered doll in Modernist art. The sexualised drama of dissecting girl-dolls and constructing girl-doll-machines in art and dance are continuous with both new forms of fabricating dolls and the girl-ing of dolls.

To accompany a later set of images, Bellmer (1938) wrote an essay, "Notes on the Subject of the Ball Joint," which claimed philosophical consequence for the new manipulability of dolls:

> For such a doll, full of affective contents but suspected of only being a representation and a fictitious reality, to seek out in the external world, in the shock of encounters the unquestionable proofs of its existence, it is necessary, besides, that this external world… suspected of being only perception, demonstrate what the me has gathered there of the you. In a word, it is necessary that an amalgam be formed of the objective reality that is the chair and the subjective reality that is the doll, an amalgam endowed with a superior reality since it is objective and subjective at once. (p. 212)

Taylor (2000) argued that, "like Freud in his essay on the uncanny," Bellmer's essay "is little concerned with the intellectual uncertainty that derives from the dolls being lifelike and lifeless at once" (p. 100). For her, Bellmer's assertion that the doll as paradigmatic "provocative object" primarily depends on "the mechanical factor of its mobility, of the JOINT" (Bellmer, 1938, p. 212) is a sleight of hand (Taylor, 2000, p. 100) obscuring a symmetrical sadomasochistic anxiety (pp. 98–152). But for Bellmer (1938) the doll's place in "the confusion between the animate and the inanimate" depends on its material manipulability aided by the ball-joint that enables it to simultaneously hold and distort bodily form. It can be a "personified thing," he suggested, precisely because it is "mobile, passive, adaptable, and incomplete" (p. 212).

The "disturbing reality" of Bellmer's dolls is, I suggest, continuous with de Beauvoir's (1949) phenomenological account of how one becomes a woman through play, and at what price. When a boy is 3 or 4, de Beauvoir claimed, he may be told to be "a little man" (p. 298), but at this stage, instead, "a girl is given a doll as an alter ego and compensation" (p. 306), and as a way of learning the benefits of obedience to sexual norms. Drawing on psychoanalysis, de Beauvoir paralleled the doll and the penis as tools for developing identification of the self in the world (pp. 306–309, 642). Both doll and penis, she stressed, are "puppets" (p. 299) that enable games with identity and power. The "main difference" between them is

> that, on the one hand, the doll represents the whole body, and, on the other, it is a passive object. On this account the little girl will be led to identify [her body with] her whole person and to regard this as an inert given object. (p. 306)

The girl's identification of body and person leads, de Beauvoir (1949) argued, not only to games of comforting and tending to the doll that involve identification with the doll as vulnerable object, but also to the feminine fascination with dressing up and being on display, whether through the doll or through the body—one of her examples is a little girl who dresses up to have everyone watch her dance (pp. 306–307). While the opposition between penis and doll cannot, for de Beauvoir, be read directly onto sexual difference (p. 307), it is the means by which the girl learns to make herself an object; to be a living doll (p. 308). As critics such as Whitney Chadwick (1998) and Natalya Lusty (2007) stressed, self-representation, and indeed mirrors and mirroring, were particularly important to the surrealist *women* artists I am not discussing here, and this might be brought back to the progression from doll to mirror proposed by de Beauvoir as the process of internalising femininity. But such a proposition should also remind us that, even for de Beauvoir, with the doll, such internalisation remains incomplete.

While the above Modernist doll-figures all come with their authorial masters—inventor, magician, wizard, artist—they also speak to a context in which new technologies were rapidly disseminating and reconfiguring ideas about girlhood as much as about leisure, art, and work. Amidst changes to ideas about the meaning and management of girlhood, across the late nineteenth and early twentieth centuries girls came to constitute not only a new marketplace or workforce, but also a new image of modern identity produced through entertainment and leisure. The diversification of mass-produced toys across this period specialised a relation between childhood play, women's fashion, and the dress-maker's mannequin, and the dressing-up doll became a standard girls' toy speaking to new shop windows in new shopping spaces and new images of feminine beauty and its affordances in a proliferating array of media forms. Artists responded to the modern efflorescence of style as play in many ways, but the doll/mannequin offered a particularly promising connection between such pleasures and the alienation associated with mass production. Lotte Pritzel's waif-life dolls were climbing down off their display pedestals in the early 1910s (see Rilke, 1994), and mannequins became entangled with the new images of movie stars as living dolls (see Eckert, 1991).

Bellmer's success at exposing a fit between new ideas about girlhood and the newly manipulable mannequin/doll explains the ongoing resonance of his work, not only through avant-garde art but as a speaking image continuous with a popular field.[7] It is because Bellmer articulated sex through the doll in a language we still recognise that his work continues to generate strong responses. Bellmer reminds us that it's the reality of the doll that makes her uncanny—that insists on confronting our experience of the self as starkly as a mirror. It is the (girl-ed) doll's strangeness in play as much as art that offers her up as a representation of modern experience. Freud (1953) cautioned that we should not confine the uncanny to fictions, however engaging they make it, and although "What is *experienced* as uncanny is much more simply conditioned but comprises far fewer instances" (p. 247). Uncanniness is a key source of the doll's possible pleasures, horrors, and utility.

"SOMETIMES YOU HAVE TO BREAK A FEW DOLLS TO BUILD A BETTER BARBIE"

The Modernist works discussed thus far insist that the doll is a complex object from which gendered formations of subjectivity—gendered experiences of being in the modern world—are inseparable. Moreover, they insist that we cannot think about dolls as what Teresa de Lauretis (1987) called "technologies of gender" without considering the material techniques of producing them. I want to conclude, therefore, by turning to Barbie dolls. I both want to situate "Barbie" as a Modernist work (by most periodising accounts 1959 is still Late Modernism) and, far more significantly, I think, to use her as a way of thinking about how the rise of the mass-produced articulated doll relates to its becoming girl-ed.

Barbie's physical form and available components change constantly as part of Mattel's endeavour to keep the brand's appeal fresh. After more than 50 years of Barbie doll production, collectors generally group the core (unspecialised) "Barbie" dolls into 10 major body formats, primarily distinguished by materials and degrees and types of articulation. Variations in shape and colouring for these core Barbies are more minor. Her neck, shoulders, upper torso, waist, hips, elbows, and knees offer different combinations of articulation across these designs. There are also variations not named by this taxonomy for specially marketed releases, including additional articulated or exchangeable parts and even hidden mechanisms for sound-boxes, extra movement, or reversible growth. Barbie appears stiff compared to some dolls, and notably so, compared to boy-directed "action figure" toys, but ball-joints, or equally flexible double-pin joints, articulate different parts of Barbie's body for different campaigns. There are three consistencies to Barbie viewed in this way: firstly, her invitation to assemblage, so that no Barbie is complete (Driscoll, 2005, pp. 220–222); secondly, the prioritisation of articulation over style in "playline" as distinct from "collectible" Barbies, which need only ideal and not malleable poses; and, thirdly, plastic itself.

Roland Barthes' (1957) reflection on plastics and toys in his collection *Mythologies*, which appeared around the same time as Barbie, offers a useful way to place her in relation to the living/dead (self/other) doll that fascinated Modernists from Hoffmann to de Beauvoir. From the beginning, Barbie had "life" narratives constructed around her despite being both controversial and successful because of her dissimilarity to any living girl. But neither marketing nor ideology are sufficient to explain Barbie's special conjunction of aliveness and death. For this, the flexibility and redundancy of plastic is as important as the joint articulation that enables her to play at life and marks where she is likely to break. Barthes opened his piece "Plastic" with an invocation of its magic. Plastics, he wrote, have the "names of Greek shepherds (Polystyrene, Polyvinyl, Polyethylene)" but are "in essence the stuff of alchemy," involving "the magical operation par excellence: the transmutation of matter" (p. 97). The magic in this case comes not from any wizard-artist, but from a machine: "at one end, raw, telluric matter, at the other, the finished, human object and between these two, nothing; nothing but a transit, hardly watched over by an attendant in a cloth cap, half-god, half-robot" (p. 97). The older magic that proceeds by invocation of substance, to return to Heidegger's (1954) terms for the emergence of modern science, is displaced in plastics by modern technology that shapes or manages nature rather than responding to it.[8]

For Barthes (1957),

> more than a substance, plastic is the very idea of its infinite transformation; as its everyday name indicates, it is ubiquity made visible. And it is this, in fact, which makes it a miraculous substance: a miracle is always a sudden transformation of nature. Plastic remains impregnated throughout with this wonder: it is less a thing than the trace of a movement. (p. 97)

Barbie, too, can be anything; can "Do Anything" to quote a longstanding Barbie slogan.

Yet this changeability is not entirely a virtue. Here, and discussing "Toys" in another piece, Barthes (1957) suggested that something is lost in the plastic toy, which lacks the aura of wooden toys: "made of a graceless material" with "an appearance at once gross and hygienic, [plastic] destroys all the pleasure, the sweetness, the humanity of touch" (p. 54). Bellmer's dolls were principally made of painted wood and papier-mâché, distinguished from other wooden objects (chair, stairs) by their animation as dolls. The mass-produced fashion doll remains something else, although it is a necessary context for that intervention. The "spectacle" constituted by plastic, Barthes insisted, appears in its multiplying "end-products"—"it can become buckets as well as jewels" (p. 97). But it cannot imitate or relay nature, not even in its displays of colour, and its only specific attribute is that of "resistance," of not yielding (p. 98), as opposed to the warm pliancy of wood or skin. These brittle things "die very quickly, and once dead, they have no posthumous life for the child" (p. 55). But if "Plastic is wholly swallowed up in the fact of being used" (p. 99), meaning it is tailor-made for redundancy and the invention of "objects... for the sole pleasure of using them" (p. 99), at the same time Barthes saw in plastic the promise of plasticising life itself. The portent of the replicant appears in Barthes' essay in the promise of plastic aortas (p. 99) as much as the threat of disposability.

Barbie is rightly located at this juncture that brings Barthes (1957) to a plastics exhibition, but she arrives at this scene to mark a difference. She marked the emergence of a new softer plastic, one Barthes named but did not realise the ramifications of following his experience of the harder plastic toys of earlier years. Barbie is crafted of polyvinyl chloride (aka vinyl or PVC), including a plasticizer to make her softer and more pliable. By the 1960s all major doll manufacturers were making vinyl dolls and the modern doll's fabrication shifted from wood, rag, paper, and porcelain largely to plastics for the combination of resilience and resistance conjured in the word "plasticity," just as articulation became standardised for fashion more than baby dolls, with their more limited need to live and die. Trying to make Barbie's complexion and feel more lifelike has been a preoccupation of much Barbie design. In a design review, Joseph Ogando (2000) recorded Mattell's end-of-the-century search for an elastomer with a "fleshy feel" that could withstand child play—forced poses, biting, abandonment in one position, and exposure to sun, heat, and bodily fluids. This new plastic was designed to "flex" over an acetal ball-and-socket joint. Overall, plastic aided the smoother stylisation of dolls' gendered images along with their openness to varied use. The animating something behind Barbie is thus plastic (half-god, half-robot) in its reproducible malleability—its many-at-once-ness—producing pliant but solid meanings which break only at a limit. Barbie may stop being Barbie in enough dispersed pieces but she can also survive even in a shoe or a disembodied arm.

This flexibility remains tightly coherent. Barbie's array remains unified under her name and under the sign of a gender ideal. As she accumulates monumental status, becoming one of the Great Names of doll history, her coherence exceeds all doll play and she is, like Petrushka, choreographed by her past for audiences in the know. In the ball-and-flex renovation period discussed above, the collector Barbie lines were also renovated, recast in a weightier and more densely resilient plastic (called "Silkstone"; see Ogando, 2000) moulded to fit vintage rather than recent fashion outfits. This combination of nostalgia and imperviousness is designed to preserve "Barbie" and yet produces something new. Barbie, like gender itself, is strikingly coherent (wherever recognised) but remains fragmented (requiring assemblage every time) and eminently changeable (if never in a linear way).

For Barthes (1957), most modern toys "*mean something*, and this something is always entirely socialized." They are, he said, and de Beauvoir would likely agree, "constituted by the myths or the techniques of modern adult life" (p. 53). For both, doubtless, Barbie would appear designed "to produce children who are users, not creators" (p. 54). But it is here that the question of dolls who exceed or question the will of their makers comes back into play. Like all machines, the modern doll is a tool that automates a kind of work, and the work they automatically do is girl-gender, however we choose to play with them. Indeed, if a humanoid figurine emphasizes any other kind of work now, we call it a toy and not a doll.[9]

Certainly, the doll as girl-machine is not a single kind of tool, but mirror, pedestal, modelling clay/pencil/stylus/program, lever, and more. I think we might best understand the field in which dolls become visible and meaningful in this way as a social technology producing gender (de Lauretis, 1987, p. 2). For de Lauretis, the "representation of gender *is* its construction… which goes on as busily today" as it did in the past and as much in its critique as in its affirmation (p. 3). It cannot be resolved into unity or diversity as both identities and social relations are, as some post-Althusserian scholars put it, "articulated" with ideology. The necessary activation (articulation) of the doll-object in subjective relations—whether collection or play—combined with the plastic power of her gender statements, provides a useful example of the way gender, for de Lauretis, involves continual "slippage" between representation and "subjects of 'real relations'" (p. 10).

This brings me back to Heidegger's (1934) account of modern technology, which stresses less technical progress than the changes wrought by new relations between being and tool. His insight into the way tools become visible when redundant or malfunctioning—or else when strikingly *new*—might offer a conclusion here. The Heideggerean tool is collective, situated, and ordered when it works. Then, it is invisible/habitual and "ready to hand." But it can "interrupt" or become visible when it estranges, either as new or as broken or redundant. All of the doll-machines discussed in this chapter operate on a line between broken and new integral to Modernism. The tool, poised between wonder and redundancy, is a form of banality always on the edge of being displaced. Heidegger saw technology as making the world strange, both when it is habitual—"At bottom, the ordinary is not ordinary; it is extra-ordinary, uncanny" (p. 32)—and when it is unfamiliar. The doll's representation of objectified subjectivity, and the other way around, enables it as a tool for estrangement; for sex as estrangement, de Beauvoir might suggest. The visibility with which Barbie does gender also involves continual breakage; an endless renovation trying to remain in sight while inviting habit. When she is cliché, Barbie's gender is as smooth as her various plastic surfaces and concealed articulations. But in her vulnerability to uncanny exposures and to redundancy she is always on the edge of being broken.

Dolls are in a constant state of technological renovation and the modern doll, subject to the fashions it represents and always poised on the edge of redundancy, maps that change. Moreover, modernity marks the emergence of technology as the way of operating in a world populated by tools it organises into ways of knowing that world. Tools and machines can be deployed within different technologies, but the history of the modern doll is one of coming to be a specialised gender-machine. This is neither a developmental nor strictly an ideological proposition. By juxtaposing Modernist artworks with the more banal figures on which they draw, such as fashion mannequins and doll toys, I'm arguing for the importance of "the doll" to understanding modernism as an experience of technology. The Modernist doll-figure is poised at the point where a doll begins to ordinarily express gender, a point mediating future, past, and present. We may routinely take technologies of gender to the doll, as she invites us to, but we just as routinely turn to dolls to see them revealed.

NOTES

1. Throughout this chapter I'm distinguishing between Modernism—as a canonised historical field of aesthetic objects—and modernism—as an ongoing reflexive experience of modernity. I discuss this distinction at length in *Modernist Cultural Studies* (2010), where many key concepts and objects discussed in this chapter appear, but not gathered together around dolls. The final section of this chapter also draws on my previous discussion of Barbie dolls, where I focused on the complex girl's body imagined by Barbie through the philosophy of Gilles Deleuze (Driscoll, 2005).

2. The Exhibition context is important to Elektro's possible meanings and one useful record of this is available in an amateur film from the Prelinger collection (Medicus, 1939).

3. Including, looking towards the next section, many audiovisual adaptations, of which the most influential are Jacques Offenbach's opera *The Tales of Hoffmann* (1881), from which the now more common spelling Olympia derives, the 1870 ballet *Coppélia* (choreography, Arthur Saint-Léon, music, Léo Delibes), and Michael Powell and Emeric Pressburger's film based on Offenbach, *The Tales of Hoffman* (1951).

4. Andrew Wachtel (1998) reconstructed a *Petrushka* libretto from varied sources (p. 118ff), while stressing that "There will always be blank spots of indeterminacy in our reconstruction of a ballet 'text'" (p. 115). The subtitle I use is Wachtel's, which restores to it the concept "burlesque"—a comedy of exaggerating the serious. I discuss *Petrushka* more generically, however, drawing also on multiple performances. An example of the third scene, featuring Petrushka, The Moor, and The Ballerina, is at http://www.youtube.com/watch?v=bmf5T57sFHw

5. The modern subject, Heidegger (1977) suggested, becomes object of his own knowledge through the process of knowing the world subjectively: "Man makes depend upon himself the way in which he must take his stand in relation to whatever is as the objective"; this is "the event of man's becoming *subiectum* in the midst of that which is" (p. 132).

6. For a selection of Bellmer's dolls see http://theredlist.fr/wiki-2-16-601-787-view-conceptual-profile-bellmer-hans.html

7. Cindy Sherman's 1992 series "Sex Pictures" that reply directly to Bellmer's dolls should be inseparable from her images of dolls and girls for covers and other artwork for punk (or Riot Grrrl) band Babes in Toyland in the early 1990s. On Bellmer and Sherman see Susan Rubin Suleiman (1998) and Lusty (2007, pp. 120–145). For Sherman's work with Babes in Toyland see her covers for *Fontanelle* (1992) and *Painkillers* (1993).

8. For Heidegger (1954), differently approaching the terms Barthes used to express concern about plastic, the definitions of technology as "a means to an end" (as instrumental) and as "a human activity" (as anthropological) necessarily "belong together": "For to posit ends and procure and utilize the means to them is a human activity" (p. 4). This is a suggestive frame for thinking about de Lauretis's argument as well.

9. The toys of the *Toy Story* franchise exemplify this, and among them Barbie, fashion dolls as a collective, and Barbie's gender accessory, Ken, work with gender and sex norms. Thanks to Julian Murphet for suggesting *Toy Story* to me in response to an earlier version of this chapter.

REFERENCES

Barthes, R. (1957). *Mythologies*. London, England: Granada.

Baudelaire, C. (1853). The philosophy of toys. In I. Parry (Ed.), *Essays on dolls* (pp. 1–6). London, England: Syrens.

Bellmer, H. (1934). The doll: Variations on the montage of an articulated minor. *Minotaure*, 6, 30–31.

Bellmer, H. (1938). Notes on the subject of the ball joint. In S. Taylor (Ed.), *Hans Bellmer: The anatomy of anxiety* (pp. 212–218). Cambridge, MA: MIT Press.

Capek, K. (1921). *R.U.R. (Rossum's Universal Robots)*. Rockville, MD: Wildside Press.

Caws, M. A. (1986). Ladies shot and painted: Female embodiment in surrealist art. In S. R. Suleiman (Ed.), *The female body in Western culture* (pp. 262–287). Cambridge, MA: Harvard University Press.

Chadwick, W. (Ed.). (1998). *Mirror images: Women, surrealism and self-representation*. Boston, MA: MIT Press.

De Beauvoir, S. (1949). *The second sex*. London, England: Picador.

De Lauretis, T. (1987). *Technologies of gender: Essays on theory, film, and fiction*. Bloomington, IN: Indiana University Press.

Dick, P. K. (1968). *Do androids dream of electric sheep*. London, England: Random House.

Driscoll, C. (2005). Girl-doll: Barbie as puberty manual. In C. Mitchell & J. Reid-Walsh (Eds.), *Seven going on seventeen* (pp. 217–233). New York, NY: Peter Lang.

Driscoll, C. (2010). *Modernist cultural studies*. Miami, FL: University Press of Florida.

Eckert, C. (1991). The Carole Lombard in Macy's window. In C. Gledhill (Ed.), *Stardom: Industry of desire* (pp. 30–39). London, England: Routledge.

Freud, S. (1953). The uncanny. In J. Strachey (Ed.), *The standard edition of the complete psychological works of Sigmund Freud* (Vol. 17, pp. 219–252). London, England: The Hogarth Press.

Garafola, L. (1998). *Diaghilev's Ballets Russes*. New York, NY: Da Capo.

Gordon, T. (2005). Girls, girls, girls: Re-membering the body. In A. Brueggemann & P. Schulman (Eds.), *Rhine crossings: France and Germany in love and war* (pp. 87–118). Albany, NY: SUNY Press.

Heidegger, M. (1934). *Poetry, language, thought*. New York, NY: Harper & Row.

Heidegger, M. (1954). The question concerning technology. In *The question concerning technology, and other essays* (pp. 3–35). New York, NY: Harper & Row.

Heidegger, M. (1977). The age of the world picture. In *The question concerning technology, and other essays* (pp. 115–154). New York, NY: Harper & Row.

Hoffmann, E. T. A. (1816). The Sandman. In *Tales of Hoffmann* (pp. 85–126). Harmondsworth, England: Penguin.

Jameson, F. (1983). Postmodernism and consumer society. In H. Foster (Ed.), *The anti-aesthetic: Essays on postmodern culture* (pp. 111–125). Seattle, WA: Bay Press.

Kracauer, S. (1927). The mass ornament. In T. Levin (Ed.), *The mass ornament* (pp. 75–88). Cambridge, MA: Harvard University Press.

Lang, F. (Director). (1927). *Metropolis* [Motion picture]. Germany: UFA.

Léger, F., & Murphy, D. (Directors). (1924). *Ballet Mécanique*. France: André Charlot.

Lusty, N. (2007). *Surrealism, feminism, psychoanalysis*. Aldershot, England: Ashgate.

Medicus, P. (Producer). (1939). Amateur film: Medicus collection: New York World's Fair, 1939–40 (Reel 3) (Part I) [Amateur film]. Retrieved from http://archive.org/details/Medicusc1939_3

Ogando, J. (2000, December 18). Engineering Barbie. *Design News*. Retrieved from http://www.designnews.com/document.asp?doc_id=222831

Ovid. (1953). *The Metamorphoses*. Harmondsworth, England: Penguin.

Pasler, J. (1986). Music and spectacle in *Petrushka* and *The Rites of Spring*. In J. Pasler (Ed.), *Confronting Stravinsky: Man, musician, and modernist* (pp. 53–81). Berkeley, CA: University of California Press.

Rilke, R. M. (1994). Dolls: On the wax dolls of Lotte Pritzel. In I. Parry (Ed.), *Essays on dolls* (pp. 26–39). London, England: Penguin.

Scott, R. (Director). (1982). *Blade runner*. United States: Blade Runner Partnership.

Shelley, M. W. (1818). Frankenstein; or the modern Prometheus. In B. Bennett & C. Robinson (Eds.), *The Mary Shelley reader* (pp. 11–166). Oxford, England: Oxford University Press.

Stravinsky, I. (Composer) & Fokine, M. (Choreographer), & Benois, A. (Set designer). (1911). Petrushka: Burlesque scenes in four tableaux [Ballet]. France: Ballets Russes.

Suleiman, S. R. (1998). Dialogue and double allegiance: Some contemporary women artists and the historical avant-garde. In W. Chadwick (Ed.), *Mirror images: Women, surrealism and self-representation* (pp. 128–155). Cambridge, MA: MIT Press.

Taylor, S. (2000). *Hans Bellmer: The anatomy of anxiety*. Boston, MA: MIT Press.

Taylor, S. (2001). Hans Bellmer in The Art Institute of Chicago: The wandering libido and the hysterical body. Retrieved from http://www.artic.edu/reynolds/essays/taylor.php

Troy, N. (2003). *Couture culture: A study in modern art and fashion.* Cambridge, MA: MIT Press.

Wachtel, A. (Ed.). (1998). *Petrushka: Sources and Contexts.* Evanston, IL: Northwestern University Press.

Wood, G. (2003). *Living dolls: A magical history of the quest for mechanical life.* London, England: Faber and Faber.

Part V: Commodifying Multiculturalism, Nationalism, Racism, and Girlhoods

CHAPTER ELEVEN

Girls' Day FOR Umé: Western Perceptions OF THE Hina Matsuri, 1874–1937

JUDY SHOAF

[T]here are two days set apart in April for what is called a "Doll's Festival," and all the girls, and even big women, make a great time of it....[T]he poor Japanese women have a very aimless life, and I think playing with dolls is about as harmless a way for them to get pleasure as they could find.

—MARY PRUYN, 1876

Nothing better illustrates inherent Japanese ideas of life and enjoyment, and gentleness of manners, than this bringing out of all the dolls for one long fête week in the year, and the handing them down from generation to generation.

—ELIZA SCIDMORE, 1891

The Dolls' Festival is one of the gala-days. Almost every family has its store of dolls, wonderful, ancient dolls....But the children doubtless love best of all the torn, dirty little dolls they fondle and strap on their backs while they themselves are strapped on their mother's back.

—KATHERINE STANLEY HALL, 1912

Little girls in America have their dolls for their constant companions and carry their favorites about with them. Little girls in Japan, on the contrary, never play with dolls.

—MARION LUCEY, 1928

These voices tell us that the Japanese Doll Festival demonstrates how silly, and how wise, the Japanese are: just like us and not like us at all. Adult women in

Japan play with dolls… and little girls in Japan never play with dolls. The tension between the concept of the doll as an everyday toy and the Japanese holiday to honor "wonderful, ancient dolls" is resolved by each of these American women in a different way.

Japanese play dolls were known in America, throughout the period when these women were writing, not only from depictions in books, illustrations, and advertising, but also "in the flesh" in the form of imported baby dolls representing Japanese children (Shoaf, 2010). But the dolls of the Japanese Doll Festival, or *Hina Matsuri*, were not depicted and adopted in the same way; they did not belong on the Western toyshelf. They came to be understood as "The Dolls that are never played with" (Strack, 1937, chapter title). Hina Matsuri involves the respectful display of figures (*hina*), which are considered by the Japanese to be a subset of the larger category of dolls (*ningyo*), which also includes various types of play dolls.[1] For Americans, and Westerners in general, in the late nineteenth and early twentieth century, dolls were a subset of children's toys, and meant to be treated with some *disrespect* by their owners. That the Japanese have a Doll Festival at all fed into the desire to see Japan as a somewhat childlike (or very child-loving) nation, but its solemn nature introduces other questions: Are these really dolls? What is a doll festival?

In this chapter, I examine the tension between doll play and the Doll Festival display, as perceived (or explained away) by American writers in the last quarter of the nineteenth century and the beginning of the twentieth. The first American writer to propose that the Doll Festival involves *play* was William Elliot Griffis, whose writings were an important channel for information about Japan in America and the British Commonwealth; he wrote two descriptions of the Hina Matsuri, one in 1874 for a learned audience and one in 1875 for children. In Griffis's opinion, based on observation, little girls in Japan do play on this holiday, though he has one answer to the question "are these really dolls?" for adults and a different one for children. Some later writers, especially those who had opportunities to observe and discuss Doll Festival displays, had more trouble reconciling the rituals involved with the assumption that dolls are (by definition) toys for girls to play with. The overwhelming impulse, however, especially for children's writers, was to present the holiday as a "girls' day" or "girls' festival," and to see whatever went on that day as the common province of little girls everywhere.

Since few scholars have approached this particular subject, I will devote my efforts here primarily to setting out the situation: what the Doll Festival was in Griffis's time, the Western options for trying to understand it, and the strategies of various writers for making the festival into some kind of mirror for the doll culture of American readers. My purpose is to introduce this rich topic and examine one aspect of it, the festival as an occasion for play.

JAPANESE DOLLS AND THE DOLL FESTIVAL

Many types of dolls figure in Japan's rich doll culture; dolls are associated with children's play but can at the same time be vectors to divert adverse spiritual forces and reinforce benign ones, and they can be objects for display, gift-giving, and connoisseurship as well (Rupp, 2003, pp. 131–35; Pate, 2008, pp. 25–29). The hina dolls partake of many of these functions, depending on who is looking at them. The *Tale of Genji* (written before about 1014 CE by a woman known as Murasaki Shikibu or Lady Murasaki, 1976) provides a kind of prehistory of the festival. *Hina asobi*, "playing with hina dolls," is featured in many chapters: daughters of the elite families delight in elaborate doll houses and spend many hours imagining their dolls' adventures, often with participation from men or boys.[2] The word "hina" means something like "pretty little thing" and is also used for a baby bird (Pate, 2005, p. 83); these dolls were evidently not "baby dolls" but little models representing the child's family and other court members. Relevant to the Doll Festival itself is a purification ritual described in the *Suma* chapter of the *Tale of Genji*, where the problems of an imperial family member are loaded onto a doll, which is then disposed of in the ocean. Lady Murasaki mentioned that *the third day of the third month* is particularly auspicious for this ceremony. This is the day of the year that later became Hina Matsuri.

The Doll Festival, properly speaking, developed more recently, with the first recorded festival display of hina traced back to 1625, under the auspices of the women of the emperor's family (Lillehoj, 2011, p. 147). During the Edo (Tokugawa) Period, from 1616, when the shogun imposed isolation, until 1854, when Commodore Perry forced Japan to begin to allow Westerners in, Japan maintained its cultural and economic independence insofar as possible. Doll-making was one of a number of art forms that developed to a high level in this society, leading to sumptuary laws limiting the size and type that could be owned by various castes (Pate, 2005, pp. 98–99). The modest figures used in the *nagashi-bina* ("floating dolls") purification ritual by Prince Genji, presumably made of paper or straw, gave way to elaborate mixed-media dolls, which were stored away most of the year but brought out to be arranged by the women and girls of the family for display on the third day of the third month. The association with the festival conferred a sacred quality on the hina. In 1749, the scholar Watarai Naokata (quoted by Pate, 2005), wrote that "*Hina asobi* originated as a divine ceremony which we inherited from mythical times, so it is not something which should be treated lightly. If we simply consider it girls' play, then shouldn't we fear some divine retribution?" (p. 100).[3] But *hina asobi* was, 750 years earlier, a term for "girls' play" in the *Tale of Genji*. The scholar's complaint reflects a period when handling the hina was perceived as a solemn religious ritual; but it also tells us that mid-eighteenth-century girls were in fact playing with hina on that day.

The Doll Festival was one of five national seasonal holidays during the Edo period, each of which had a number of names (relating to numbers, zodiac animals, seasonal flowers, and so on; Casal, 1967). They took place on the first day of the first month[4] of the lunar calendar, the third of the third, the fifth of the fifth, the seventh of the seventh, and the ninth of the ninth. The lunar calendar ran about a month later than the Western, with the new year beginning in February. The earliest Western discussions of the Doll Festival presented it as one of these five religious festivals, and as part of Japanese religion.[5] The cycle became confused after 1873, when the new imperial government of Japan changed from a lunisolar calendar to the Gregorian year. The same proclamation eliminated the five festivals in favor of holidays focused on the new Meiji Emperor and his ancestors. The five festivals continued to be celebrated in Japan, but there was confusion about which calendar to use to calculate "the third of the third" and the other days (Bacon, 1902, p. 29; Casal, 1967, p. 59).

These changes also posed problems for Westerners. The more knowledgeable writers about Japanese culture were aware that these festivals changed and evolved over time (and might in fact disappear),[6] but as ethnographers they felt the need to present the festivals as very old, very Japanese, and unsusceptible to change.

Figure 1. Hina-dan with 15 dolls and furniture (dougu). Inset: The principal female doll, crowned. Author's collection and photo.

What does the doll display look like? The most basic display is two dolls, a male-female pair (*dairi-bina*), set out on a platform or piece of red cloth. The dolls may have one of two forms: standing or seated. The *tachi-bina* (standing hina) are the older format, and can be home-made, e.g., of paper. The seated hina are more complex in construction but equally iconic. The faces and hands are shining with white lacquer (*gofun*), and the roughly pyramidal bodies are of specially woven brocade, seamed to suggest the traditional costumes worn at the imperial court. The male doll carries a sword and a ceremonial baton; the female doll has a fan and a tiara or crown. Special food and drink are set before these dolls in miniature dishes, and during the festival participants—particularly little girls—enjoy such foods in human-size portions.

Many variations and additions are accepted and encouraged. The doll pair may be made of almost any material so long as the iconic shape and format is evoked. In the course of the eighteenth and nineteenth centuries, other doll groups were developed (musicians, servants, etc.), so that eventually a full display required 15 hina dolls with screens, flowers, and lanterns, as well as lacquered miniature furniture appropriate for a dowry, including tables for food service, an ox-cart, and a *kago* (sedan chair). Set out on a *hina-dan*—a tiered structure with five or seven steps covered in a red cloth—this display today suggests the glories of an aristocratic household in Edo-era Japan, with references to earlier periods as well. A typical display in the nineteenth century, to judge from descriptions by Westerners and artistic representations, would have lacked this hieratic format, because it would feature a number of the male-female pairs belonging to women of the family, as well as the family's collection of lesser hina and furniture, which might be somewhat haphazard (Bacon, 1902, pp. 28–31; Griffis, 1874, pp. 149–50). Everyday play or amulet dolls could be placed in the display to join in the honor of the day.

What does the display mean? As I have noted, the use of dolls on 3/3 in the *Tale of Genji* appears to involve ritual purification of an emperor's son, a religious rite performed by a male prelate or shaman. The display of expensive, treasured dolls by women in the home clearly has other implications—most obviously, domestic and gendered. The few Western descriptions of the festival surviving from the Edo period, though they contextualize it as a religious holiday, emphasize this side of the festival. Engelbert Kaempfer (1727) said that the festival is devoted to "pleasure and diversion for young girls, for whose sake a great Entertainment is commonly prepared by their Parents" (vol. I, pp. 218–19). Isaac Titsingh (1822), probably working from Japanese texts,[7] records an alternate name, "Women's Festival," and notes that girls of various classes, in manipulating the miniature furnishings, "are taught, by their very amusements, from their earliest infancy, to become in time good and skilful housewives" (pp. 133–134). Aimé Humbert (1874), visiting Japan at the very end of the Edo period, says "the festival is consecrated to feminine youth" and emphasizes the roles of the mother and older daughters in preparing the display and meal (p. 327).

Lexically, the hina have a political meaning. The dolls are associated with the emperor's court, since the male-female pair is called the *dairi-bina*, meaning "dolls of the Imperial Palace in Kyoto." In the Edo period, the Shogun, whose capital was Edo (modern Tokyo) wielded political and economic power; the hereditary emperor stayed in Kyoto, in his palace, the *Dairi*, with his wives and aristocratic court. There was a considerable tension between the two powers; the Shogun's financial and moral support was needed by the emperor, but the emperor would be asked to appoint, promote, and eventually deify the Shogun. "Dairi" or "dairi-sama" ("master of the dairi") was also a metonymic term often used to refer to the reigning emperor (Lillehoj, 2011, 16).

The earliest records of doll displays on 3/3 come from the Kyoto court in the 1620s, when the most prominent woman in the Dairi was Tokugawa Masako, granddaughter, daughter, and sister of three successive Shoguns and the most important wife (*chugu*) of the Emperor Go-Mizuno. In 1624 she gave birth to a daughter, and the following year there is a record of hina asobi on the festival day (Lillehoj, 2011, p. 147); in 1629, this daughter became the Emperor[8] Meisho. There is evidence that dolls were displayed on 3/3 during Meisho's reign, not only in her Dairi in Kyoto, but also in the Shogun's palace in Edo (Pate, 2005, p. 96). "Dairi-bina" would then have meant something like "dolls *of the type that are displayed in* the Imperial Palace." When the doll-makers began to produce hina costumed in the style of the Kyoto nobles (Pate, 2005, pp. 108–109), "dairi-bina" would refer transparently to "dolls *representing* the imperial court."

The typical Western interpretation of "dairi-bina" is "dolls representing the emperor and his consort." This is strongly opposed by some post-war scholars ("such an idea is contrary to the Japanese spirit," Casal, 1967, p. 52). Westerners in the Edo period identified the dolls as representations of the emperor and his court.[9] In the Meiji era, when the emperor was the sole head of state, ruling in both Kyoto and Edo, and receiving Western embassies, this identification took on a new meaning. Moreover, the Meiji emperor was the first Japanese ruler to have a wife who was presented in public as his empress, a situation designed to earn the approval of the West (Pate, 2011). In this period the doll display seemed to imply both a moral and a national agenda, to Western eyes: "The origin of the celebration lay in the devotion of the people to an always invisible sovereign" (Fraser, 1899, vol. I, p. 301). Since the Meiji emperor was perceived as favorable to progress and Westernization, the Doll Festival was seen as admirably patriotic by most Americans.[10] The same implications were however seen as dangerous "national self-worship" in 1917 by the American John Bovingdon. However, the Doll Festival as an expression of complete devotion to the emperor could still be praised by Lillian Strack as late as 1937.

Postwar Japan rarely links the hina with imperial power. The dolls' religious function continues to be defined in various ways, often looking back to its roots in purification or fertility rituals. A twenty-first-century commentator, Katherine Rupp (2003) said "The 3/3 dolls involve female reproductive potential"; she saw "the food given to dolls on 3/3" as comparable to New Year's "offerings to gods" that "reinforc[e] human relations of hierarchy" (pp. 143, 152). A search of You-Tube on "Hina Matsuri" brings up home videos of tiny girls singing a song for the day or enjoying treats, but also explanations from NHK documentaries that the day is now used "to pray for the happiness and healthy development of girls in each household," since if one touches the dolls "all illness and bad luck will be transferred to them" (Stuart Varnam-Atkin, interviewed in 2010 on the program. *Japanese Trad*, NHK Educational TV; see cae12810, 2011). The dolls are, if anything, farther from being toys or playthings than they were 150 years ago.

IS A JAPANESE FESTIVAL DOLL A DOLL?

Given the fact that the festival dolls clearly do have some kind of spiritual meaning, Western students of Oriental culture—and their adult readers—struggled to reconcile this aspect with the concept of the doll as plaything. Is the doll "really" a doll or "really" the focus of an irrational, or un-Christian, belief? An English missionary wrote in 1903, "some of these dolls at the Hina Matsuri are in reality treated as idols, and have offerings of rice…placed before them" (Ritson, 1903). The hina, she added, are "not sufficiently interesting for a child to wish to play with," and she noted that Japanese girls do own proper play dolls, "miniatures of themselves." Walter Hough (Anonymous 1, 1927) of the National Museum, quoted in an article entitled "From Heathen Idols to Playthings," expressed the possibility that, as a culture evolves, idols can become toys: "[a]mong civilized people, dolls… awake no thought of their former import." The problem with the Hina Matsuri was that the dolls seemed to be displayed precisely to awaken thoughts about the past and about their "import."

The entry "Doll" in the 11th edition of the *Encyclopedia Britannica* (1910–1911), excludes the hina display from the definition:

> Dolls proper should be distinguished from (a) idols, (b) magical figurines, (c) votive offerings, (d) costume figures. The festival figures of Japan, like the bambino of Italy, given to the child only on certain saints' days, hardly come within the category of dolls.

While the author does not state that the Japanese figures are idols, the comparison with a *bambino* ("Baby Jesus," presumably, but shorthand for any local image that might be fêted on a particular day of the year in Catholic Europe) and the reference to "saints' days" suggest Popish image-worship. The Sinologist Gustave

Schlegel, in 1896, asserted that the Dutch must have introduced into Japan "the doll, as an article to play with for little girls" (p. 101). The play-doll is, for Schlegel and the *Britannica* author, characteristic of an advanced society in which human images are relegated to the nursery and have no place in religious life.

Sympathetic Westerners who understood the wide range of doll culture in Japan also struggled to define the spiritual element in the festival dolls. Oddly enough, Frederick Starr (1921), in exalting the spiritual qualities of the dolls, ends up being as condescending as Ritson or Schlegel in evaluating them: "*Hina* are ceremonial dolls; they…are symbolical—so deeply so that few Japanese realize their significance; so deeply so, that no Japanese can think of them as merely toys" (p. 17). Only an outsider, he implied, can analyze this Japanese mystery.

An author who wishes to emphasize that the hina are not toys may use terms such as "figures," "images," or "effigies." Kaempfer's 1727 translator chose the word "puppet," which, while cognate with German *Puppen*, imports overtones of idolatry that would not attach to the word "doll" (pp. 218–219).[11] While the term "idols" is a clear label of the Doll Festival as a pagan ritual, these other terms allow some ambiguity. Adult readers will notice the term and perhaps be alerted to the possibility that this is not a "real" doll, while children may pass over the implications.

WILLIAM E. GRIFFIS

In 1874, William Elliot Griffis delivered a paper on "Games and Sports of Japanese Children" to the Asiatic Society in Yokohama, a paper that nudges the Doll Festival out of the realm of religion and into the realm of child culture. He recontextualized the Hina Matsuri as a celebration of and for children, rather than a national religious holiday. Although he allowed for the religious (i.e., pagan) aspect of Hina Matsuri, he emphasized elements that he, an American Christian, approved of: children's educational play and admiration for the (Westernizing) emperor. The following year, he went further in his story for children, "The Feast of Dolls," where he depicted the day entirely devoted to girls' doll play, comparable to American family festivals such as Christmas and Thanksgiving.

Griffis must have felt in 1874 that he was born to interpret Japan to Americans (Beauchamp, 1976). He had been preparing for the Dutch Reformed ministry, and teaching Japanese men studying at Rutgers, when the lord of the Echizen domain offered him a contract to set up a science program there. He arrived in Japan in 1871, and lived through the upheaval of the abolition of the feudal system and the new Meiji laws and practices. He learned spoken Japanese and made friends in Tokyo; he returned home in July 1874. In 1876 he published *The Mikado's Empire*, which immediately became an indispensable reference for Japanophiles; Griffis saw this tome through many editions and updated it at least until 1913. "Games and Sports" formed a chapter of *The Mikado's Empire*, and endured only the tiniest changes during the decades of editions.

In 1874, a paper for the Asiatic Society on the five religious festivals, recently eliminated from the national calendar, would have been backward-looking. Griffis (1874), however, found room for the first three holidays in his "Games and Sports": New Year's, with many associated indoor and outdoor games; the 3/3 Hina Matsuri; and the 5/5 "Feast of Flags," with its pride in sons and martial play. Griffis's contention was that these celebrations were worthy of attention (both Western and Japanese) because they enriched the lives of children with healthful and educational activities. Moreover, he said, "in the toy-shops of Japan one may see the microcosm of Japanese life" (p. 125), so play offers insight into serious adult concerns and culture.

The description of Hina Matsuri consists of a single paragraph, which became a standard reference for writers on Japan, perhaps because Griffis in this 1874 paper achieved such a precise and authoritative tone. He provided apparently exact (though actually inaccurate) details about the dolls' height ("from four inches to a foot") and the materials used ("wood or enameled clay"). He avoided the problematic questions of the festival's origin and history, which might have led into religious myths or purification rituals. Everything was described in the present tense, with great emphasis on the fact that the dolls were heirlooms owned by the women and girls of the family.

Griffis (1874) avoided the word "doll" for the hina, however; they were "images" or "effigies," and he implied that "some foreign works" are wrong to translate Hina Matsuri as "Feast of Dolls." The little girls "make offerings" of food and drink to the "effigies." To a Christian, these terms clearly indicate idolatry. However, Griffis mitigated this implication by calling the miniature furniture *toys* and speaking of *play*: "A great many other toys…are also exhibited and played with on this day." Girls "spend the day with toys, mimicking the whole round of Japanese female life, as that of child, maiden, wife, mother and grandmother." Dolls are finally mentioned in his very last sentence, as sharing space in the display with the "images"—that is, the exhibition includes both "images" (the hina) and the everyday playthings a precise Westerner would call "dolls."

Like Titsingh (1822), Griffis (1874) followed Japanese moralists who see in the festival an educational display of the apparatus of domesticity. However, whereas Titsingh emphasized that girls learn, according to their class, "decoration of a house, and…whatever is necessary for housekeeping" (p. 134), Griffis pointed to the biological destiny of a woman as a potential wife and mother (and grandmother). Normal play with baby dolls seems more likely to develop such skills than the "amusement" of a miniature court. But for Griffis, the display demanded an understanding of history and even politics that ought to be part of a mother's education.[12]

Griffis's next publication on the Doll Festival presented it as doll-play pure and simple. After returning to the United States, Griffis was publishing as much as he could on Japan, and the new *St. Nicholas* magazine for children enabled him to recast some of the ideas in "Games and Sports" in a pair of 1875 articles on "The Feast of Dolls" and "The Feast of Flags" (the "great day" for boys as the Doll Festival is for girls; this article appeared in May). In "The Feast of Dolls," Griffis told a story about the eve of the holiday and the day itself, moving among the points of view of two little girls anticipating the festival, of the mother preparing the display, and of himself as a foreign visitor paying a call on the father and staying to watch. Here, in contrast to "Games and Sports," he referred to the hina as "dolls" throughout, and reminded his readers that "Japan is, above all others, the land for dolls." Thus, for the first time, the role of the festival dolls *as dolls*, admired and loved by little girls for their own sake, is emphasized in a Western account.

The evocation of American holidays was key to Griffis's 1875 presentation. He balanced comparisons with contrasts between Japanese and American customs with respect to writing, food, clothing, bedtime rituals, and so on. Christmas provided a strong thread of similarity: the children go to bed early because the mother's preparations need "as much time as Santa Claus requires to fill stockings or to trim Christmas-trees."[13] Griffis brought in other Western customs, though; the mother prepares "the dolls' dinner and tea-service." He thus replaces the "Games and Sports" notion of "making offerings to effigies" with the secular picture of a little English or American girl having a tea-party with her dolls. Also, because the dolls had belonged to the little girl's "great-grandmother's great-grandmother," "it was like a Thanksgiving party at home, when grandpa and papa and mamma and all the children meet together. Only they were dolls."

Griffis (1875) presents the girls' games as having a dramatic relevance to the political situation of the 1870s. The girls placed the emperor doll in a vehicle "and played taking the Mikado to Kioto" in a procession. This trip would have been inconceivable before the Meiji Emperor moved from Kyoto, where previous emperors had lived for centuries, to Tokyo, in 1868. Arrived in Kyoto, the dolls "were very hungry, and all sat down to dinner"; the children were treating the imperial figures not as divine rulers but as babies to be fed. After the feast, the emperor doll was placed on his throne and a girl brought a doll representing the Shogun (Tycoon, in Griffis's term) to bow to him. Now, this is the only record I have seen of a hina doll representing a Shogun. It seems possible that the ceremony Griffis describes was an innovation particular to the family he visited (assuming he did not invent it himself); it could be a commemoration of the replacement of the last Shogun by the Meiji Emperor in 1867–1868, or just possibly a fantasy that the emperor would leave the power center in Tokyo, return to his palace in Kyoto, and restore a secular executive power in Japan (subject in principle to the imperial throne, as the Shoguns had been). For adult readers aware of Japan's recent history, this scene presented the Doll Festival as an opportunity for children to learn something about current affairs as well as household management.

The play described by Griffis (1875) ended with the girls treating the dolls to a traditional bit of mothering. They put the dolls to bed: "their curious sleeping-coats were put on, and each head was laid on its pillow." As I have noted above, hina dolls are fixed in a seated or standing position, and cannot be dressed even with a loose "sleeping coat" (the *yogi*, a cross between a quilt and a kimono). On the other hand, ordinary Japanese play dolls were made to be moved, posed, dressed and undressed, so one could infer that Griffis had abandoned, in the interests of storytelling, the hina dolls and switched to talking about the girls' *ichimatsu* or jointed "babies." Griffis here sacrificed clarity for the sake of reaching out to his audience of children to remind them that, at the passage from waking to sleep, children are to dolls as mothers are to children.

Thanks to Griffis, Americans could look at the Doll Festival as a celebration of childhood, different from American Christmas but comparable, and even admirable in its exaltation of the domestic feminine. However, in the end, Griffis's authority backed up the 1874 "offerings to images" interpretation of Hina Matsuri rather than the 1875 "day for playing with dolls" vision. When he published *The Mikado's Empire*, "Games and Sports of Japanese Children" appeared intact as a chapter in edition after edition. Thus this description of the Hina Matsuri was readily available to other writers who recycled it freely.[14] The 1875 *St. Nicholas* article, since it was intended for children, was less widely available or used, though traces of it (particularly the vignette of a girl making a doll bow to the emperor) show up in some children's books. Still, through the two works, he succeeded in detaching this festival from the context of religious festivals and presenting it to the West as a day honoring little girls, paired with the Feast of Flags as a day for boys.

MAKING HINA MATSURI INTO GIRLS' DAY

An author who wished to present the Doll Festival to American readers needed some kind of strategy. Works interpreting Japanese culture for American readers fell into a number of overlapping genres: fictional "ripping yarns" or romantic novels, ethnography and geography (often disguised as a story about a Japanese family through the year, especially when directed at children), missionary propaganda (also, if written for children, profiling a typical child), guidelines for teachers, and personal memoirs. The memoirists aside, few of the authors had actually visited Japan; fewer still had been invited into a Japanese home on "the third of the third" to see the doll display. This is why so many of them simply extract, or paraphrase,

Griffis's account or that of Alice Bacon in her widely-read *Japanese Girls and Women*. This is particularly true of writers for adults.

The preponderance of these texts are however written for children, and most of these tell about little girls whose doll festival involves the same kind of emotion and imagination American girls show in their doll play. However, there were narrative tensions which had to be balanced. One note almost always struck was the potential discontent of boys, excluded from the girls' festival or made to serve their sisters; this was resolved by looking forward to the Boys' Festival on 5/5. On the other hand, the exotic festival required little girls to handle valuable antiques and to know how to place and honor them, to prepare the correct refreshments, and so on. To make American child readers more comfortable with this ritual aspect, some authors redefined the festival in order to focus on play-dolls instead of the festival dolls. Another strategy was to define girls' play as the kind of decorous hostess activities the festival required.

The most honest and scholarly approach was to admit that hina dolls are not play dolls, while emphasizing that Japanese girls did in fact play with other types of dolls. Edward S. Morse, an American scientist who taught in Japan, focused on Hina Matsuri in an 1886 article for children. He told his readers that "The dolls are not played with"; the hina were "really diminutive models" or "little effigies" (compare Griffis's 1874 "images" and "effigies") not dolls as American children understood them. At the same time, he commented that the holiday "finally became an inheritance for the girls alone," so that Japanese girls felt free to include in the festival "dolls of less official dignity"—their everyday play dolls. Stewart Culin, in a 1922 article for adults, "The Story of the Japanese Doll," took care to preface his discussion of the Doll Festival by noting that the ichimatsu play doll, familiar on American toyshelves, "has nothing to do with the hina, although the little girl carries it on this occasion and may place it, as a visitor, with the hina." He saw, however, a form of play in the honor done to the hina: "The ceremonies of the festival may be regarded as playful and not connected with serious homage to the emperor."

Many narratives went farther than Morse and Culin to emphasize the inclusion of a play doll in the Doll Festival, by giving "her" a more active role. In Haines's *Japanese Boys and Girls* (1905), O Haru San imitates the girls in Griffis's *St. Nicholas* article by making a doll bow to the "emperor doll," but in this case it is her everyday play doll, O Matsu, not a "tycoon," who does homage (pp. 2–4). Perkins depicted the same ritual in *The Japanese Twins* (1912), where the "everyday doll" Morning Glory is made to bow (pp. 163ff.). In other works, the relationship between the favorite doll and the hina dolls is blurred. In the novel *The Heart of O Sono San*, the heroine receives a large doll named "O Hinna Sama" (i.e., O-Hina-sama, "Honored Hina"); this doll displaces the "little paper dolls" Sono had formerly displayed for the Feast of the Dolls, but is also a year-round play "baby" to mother, make new clothes for, and so on (Cooper 1917, pp. 72–74, 89). In *Little Americans from Many Lands* (Ridge 1929), Matsue is resigned to leaving most of her hina dolls with her grandmother when she emigrates to the U.S. with her parents, but she tries to smuggle her favorite, Tama San, "the very first doll Matsue ever received," who is evidently a display doll stored with the festival hina. Matsue's parents prevent Tama San from coming along, but before leaving Japan her father gives Matsue "[a] real American doll with golden curls" which she prefers to the less "gorgeous" Tama.

At the other end of the range of strategies, the author could simply present the Doll Festival as an occasion for doll play, ignoring the hina display and its rituals. Mary Pruyn's much-reprinted 1876 *Grandmamma's Letters from Japan* depicted the festival as an occasion for taking dolls for walks and dressing them (pp. 151–152). It's possible that Mrs. Pruyn was honestly describing what she saw in the streets on that day, and that she was unaware of the hina displays inside the houses. But this was not the case for Mae St. John Bramhall, who drew on and acknowledged Griffis's "Games and Sports" in two sections of her 1894 *Wee Ones of Japan*.[16] She ignored his description of Hina Matsuri entirely, instead depicting the Doll Festival as a day when little girls vied to purchase dolls from vendors ("an excited, chattering, pushing, and elbowing mob of whimsical mites") and visited each other with baby dolls strapped on their backs (pp. 111–112). Bramhall hid the hina ceremony itself behind a jesting phrase, "perches of doll breakfasts, rods of doll tiffins or dinners, and acres of doll tableaux." Clearly Bramhall was aware of the hina-dan, but did not want to present it to her readers. A scholarly essay by Charlotte Salwey from 1894, like Bramhall, ignored the hina entirely; in her view, the doll festival was the occasion for Japan's future mothers to receive doll gifts: "these gifts are calculated to instil a mother's love into their young hearts, and at least to teach them how to dress and attend to their little ones when the appointed time arrives" (p. 151). A number of other authors simply stated that the Doll Festival was a day for showing off all a little girl's dolls and doll houses, perhaps assuming that's what a doll festival ought to be, or unable to understand the available descriptions of the hina-dan.

This notion that the purchase of a new doll is central to the Doll Festival carried over to many works for children. O Haru gets a "creeping baby" (an authentic Japanese doll type) from her aunt in Tokyo (Haines, 1905, pp. 2–4); the sister of the eponymous Kenjiro (Mayne, 1908), Metzu (Campbell, 1905, pp. 50–51), or Taro (Entwistle, 1920, pp. 22–24) gets a new dolly, as do Umé San (McDonald & Dalrymple, 1916, pp. 26ff), Haru (Yule, 1927, pp. 20–25), and every Japanese girl, rich or poor (Carpenter, 1917, p. 57; Canning-Wright, 1922, pp. 10–12); sometimes the sister even gets a new doll house (Peltier, 1903, pp. 88ff; Perkins, 1912, 163ff). The festival can be reformed by the presence of the Christian West: Miss Open Sea asks her parents for a new doll representing her friend the missionary lady (Applegarth, 1923, p. 99), and little Tomo shows the visiting English missionary lady her English doll on the hina-dan (Anonymous 4, 1930, pp.44ff). In all these works, the new doll was presented as an addition to the girl's doll collection, not a replacement for the hina themselves. This emphasis on dolls as toys to purchase, dress, mother, or manipulate in a doll house distracted gently from the less familiar hina dolls, and enabled the American reader to identify with the Japanese girl.

A fruitful mistake was the notion that all Japanese girls celebrated their birthdays together on March 3, and boys on May 5 (the date of the "Feast of Flags" or "Boys' Day"). The idea probably originated in Mary Fraser's (1899) *Letters:*

His birthday feast it [the Boys' Festival] is, at whatever time of year he may have been born. Except for the purpose of casting a horoscope, the real day of his birth will be seldom remembered; and just as every girl's festival is March third, so every boy's festival proper is May fifth. (vol. II, 240)

Fraser's point was that this is the day when the child is made much of, receiving gifts and hosting parties; it was an analogy, and unlike the Christmas analogy it "explained" why boys don't get presents on the girls' festival and vice-versa. Although Dr. Sidney Gulick (1903), a few years later, declared "these festivals have nothing to do with birthday celebrations" (p. 96), the idea had a powerful appeal in the West and turned up in many explanations of the two festivals. Sometimes it was modified by claiming the little girl had actually been born on March 3 (Peltier, 1903, p. 90), or by specifying that the girl knew perfectly well she had not been born on the "big birthday of all little girls" on March 3 (Little, 1909, p. 8). But other works present this gendered birthday idea without qualification (e.g., Perkins, 1912; Lucey, 1928, p. 3). The birthday analogy unhooked the celebrations completely from the seasonal calendar, as well as from all religious overtones, Japanese or Western. For authors and educators working towards a gender-specific presentation, this specious explanation reinforced the pairing of the Girls' Festival and the Boys' Festival with their contrast between the domestic and the military, dolls and swords. Authors could in fact define play appropriate for girls by Americanizing somewhat Griffis's 1874 statement that the Hina Matsuri involves "mimicking the whole round of Japanese female life," that is, by emphasizing gendered preoccupations with dressing up, decorum, and decorating the home. Many descriptions simply assumed that admiring one's dolls, preparing and offering food on tiny dishes, and hosting a party for other little girls was a form of doll play. While Griffis and others depicted the parents preparing the display, many narratives showed a little girl becoming involved in the process of unwrapping and setting out the dolls, under her mother's supervision. In one story, young Ishi-Ko sets up the display herself, with considerable anxiety (Sowers, 1934, pp. 37ff). In another, a Japanese princess from next door drops in to help an American girl who is worried about placing the dolls (Hoyer, 1926). The very common emphasis on all-girl parties with the dolls, with each girl in her best kimono and special foods served by the hostess, was accurate enough and it had an analogy built in to American girls' birthday or tea parties. The analogy could elide the specifically Japanese elements: "all the ceremonies sacred to young housekeepers, serving the meals on fairy table-services suited to the size of the hostesses" (Harris, 1878, p. 349) would fit an American girls' doll-party, too. The traditional drink of *shiro-sake* (unfermented sake) offered to dolls and also drunk by the little girls is often replaced in children's stories with tea (e.g., Yule, 1937, pp. 20–25; Hedrick & Van Noy, 1938, pp. 54ff), emphasizing the community of little girls and their dolls (in an era when American children were not even supposed to pretend to drink alcoholic beverages).

We have seen how Western, especially American, authors presented Hina Matsuri as a friendly, girl-centered day of play in the decades before the World War. This could be done by redefining the dolls involved to include everyday play dolls, or by redefining girls' play to include the decorum (and even anxiety) with which the hina dolls were treated. By emphasizing the purchase of new dolls or doll houses, and the expense of both hina dolls and the celebration in general, authors brought into touch the different consumer patterns of American and Japanese societies; spending money on a daughter was presented as a good practice.

CODA

I have not touched on the most spectacular effort to co-opt the Japanese Doll Festival for American play dolls: the 1926–1927 Friendship Doll Exchange (originally called the Doll Messenger program by its founder, Dr. Sidney Gulick). It is a subject worthy of a book, not a paragraph (Gulick, 1929, is incomplete even in its revised edition). Gulick, co-ordinating with friends in the Japanese government, initiated the preparation of over 12,000 American play dolls (mostly blonde, blue-eyed babies), which American children, working mostly through church groups, dressed, equipped, and named. The goal was to arrive in time for the 1927 Hina Matsuri celebration, and enough dolls had arrived in Tokyo by March 3 to permit a formal reception, in the presence of seven imperial princesses and many political dignitaries. The program of course included educating American children about the doll festival; a verse composed by Mary C. Moffat to advertise the project began, "Come, dolls of America, you're asked to go / To a festival quaint, and you'd like it, I know" (quoted in Gulick, 1929, p. 13). The American dolls were distributed to schools and kindergartens throughout Japan, where possible repeating locally a ceremony in which an American child handed the doll to a Japanese girl (Erickson, 1929, pp. 75–78). The program became an exchange of gifts when the Japanese commissioned 58 large dolls—32-inch versions of the ichimatsu play doll, jointed and dressed with the expectation that the new owners would want to undress them—to be sent to America in return, aiming for Christmas (Pate, 2013). The "blue-eyed" dolls inspired affection and became part of Hina Matsuri displays in schools for more than a decade, but most of them were destroyed by the Japanese government after Pearl Harbor. They had been sent as play dolls to dilute the solemnity of the hina-dan, but in the end they became as symbolic and politically charged as the emperor and shogun dolls with which Griffis's friend's daughters played.

NOTES

1. The broadest generic term for dolls in Japanese is *ningyo*, and hina are sometimes referred to as *hina-ningyo*. *Ningyo* embraces the whole array of dolls, whereas *hina* are the festival display dolls (i.e., dolls appropriate for the display, either by form or construction).

2. As a child, Murasaki (the heroine of the *Tale of Genji*) plays with dolls in Chapter Five (*Waka Murasaki*), and Chapter Seven (*Momiji no Ga*). In Chapter 34 (*Wakana: Jo*), she comforts Genji's very young new wife with talk of doll play. Like his father, Genji's son Yugiri takes an interest in girls' doll play in Chapter 21 (*Otome*), 25 (*Hotaru*), and 28 (*Nowaki*). I rely on Seidensticker's 1976 translation for details.

3. Pate cited "Waterai Naotaka" but the correct transcription for the author of *Hina-asobi no ki* is Watarai Naokata.

4. The 1/1 festival was displaced to 1/7 (the feast of the seven herbs).

5. The Doll Festival is described by the following authors who visited Japan in the Edo era: Kaempfer (1727), in Book III, "Of the State of Religion in Japan"; Titsingh (1822), under the heading "Great Festivals" in a chapter called "Feasts and Ceremonies"; Humbert (1874), in Chapter 10, "Religious Festivals."

6. "The children's festivals and sports are rapidly losing their importance, and some are now rarely seen" (Griffis, 1874, p. 125); "with the abandonment [of the holiday from work and school] by the government this festival, like so many charming observances of the Japanese, was sadly neglected" (Morse, 1886).

7. As Westerners in Edo Japan, Kaempfer's and Titsingh's movements were monitored and restricted, so they had no opportunities to see a hina display. According to the prefaces to their respective works, Kaempfer had a Japanese assistant who knew Dutch and could answer his questions, relying on Japanese books as well as personal knowledge; Titsingh could read Japanese and collected various Japanese essays to translate for his book.

8. That is, the girl Meisho held the same title as would a male emperor.

9. The dolls are identified as representing "The court of the *Dairi*, or Ecclesiastical Hereditary Emperor, with the Person of *Finakuge*" (Kaempfer, 1727, p. 219; *fina*=hina, *kuge*=nobleman); "The Dairi himself, his wives, called *Dairi Bina*" (Titsingh, 1822, p. 133); "the Mikado, the Kisaki, and other personages of the imperial court" (Humbert, 1874, p. 327). "Mikado" is another metonymy for the emperor, while "kisaki" is a title bestowed on one of the emperor's wives.

10. The assumption that the dairi-bina are "the emperor and empress dolls" is found also in some works written in English by Japanese authors of the period (e.g., Takashima, 1897, Anonymous 2, 1898, Harada, 1911, p. 191). It is still fairly common.

11. See OED s.v. "puppet, n." The use of "puppet" to mean "idol" predates its use to refer to a child's doll; the (unambiguous) word "doll" came into use later. In 1727, either word would have been available, with the different connotations, to Scheuchzer, Kaempfer's translator.

12. Bovingdon in 1917 attacked the doll display as inappropriate for the education of women; to his mind the "love of little things" distracted women from their "real and normal" interests.

13. The Christmas analogy is an important one, evoked by other knowledgeable Westerners trying to understand the festival, including Greey (1882), pp. 360–61, Morse (1886), and Elmer (1888). Casal (1967) drew out the analogy to suggest the evolution from heathen symbolism (tree/purification doll) to a display of things children can enjoy sensually (edible tree decorations/dolls to play with) to, finally, a display of expensive ornaments (p. 60).

14. Among the authors who quote or paraphrase Griffis (1874) on Hina Matsuri: Knox (1879), pp. 121–22; Dixon (1881), pp. 448–49; Anonymous 3 (1884); Angus (1885), p. 85; Hall and Ellis (1896), pp. 57–59; Forbes (1898); Cook (1891), pp. 85–87; Ainslie (1900), pp. 60–61; Sladen (1892), pp. 295–96, and (1903), pp. 87-95; Huish (1902); Jackson (1908), pp. 37–39; D'Autremer (1910), pp. 85–86. Some of these writers acknowledged Griffis, but not all.

15. Griffis (1874) is cited on p. 51 and p. 117 of Bramhall (1904); Bramhall's description of the Doll Festival is on pp. 111–112. Bramhall's hina-less description was in turn borrowed, without acknowledgement, by Barrett (1895), pp. 135–136, and Newton (1900), p. 202.

16. Morse's careful presentation of the festival, discussed above, is illustrated by a lovely frontispiece to the entire issue, "Preparing for the Festival of Dolls—'The Favorite'": a girl in kimono chooses among four ichimatsu play dolls, with no sign of a hina or hina-dan. The artist knew how to portray a "Japanese doll" of this type from various angles, but had no models for the festival dolls.

REFERENCES

Note: Japanese authors are listed with no comma between last and first names. A more extensive bibliography of source material for this topic is posted at http://www.clas.ufl.edu/users/jshoaf/ Jdolls/jdollwestern/hinamatsuri/

Ainslie, P. (1900). *Bertie Linton, or lost in Japan.* Edinburgh, Scotland: W. P. Nimmo, Hay & Mitchell.

Angus, D. C. (1885). *Japan: The eastern wonderland.* London, England: Cassell.

Anonymous 1. (1927). From heathen idols to playthings. *Popular Mechanics, 47*(5), 738–741.

Anonymous 2. (1898). Hina Matsuri. *The Far East, 3*(25), 149–150.

Anonymous 3. (1884). Children of all nations: Their homes, their schools, their playgrounds: IX.— Japan. *Frank Leslie's Sunday magazine, 16*(4), 267–269. (Reprinted in various collections, one of which lists "Lindley Smyth" as the author.)

Anonymous 4. (1930). *Other boys and girls by those who know them.* London: Highway Press, n.d. (ca. 1930). 44ff.

Applegarth, M. T. (1923). *The Honorable Japanese fan.* West Medford, MA: The Central Committee on the United Study of Foreign Missions.

Bacon, A. M. (1902). *Japanese girls and women* (Rev. ed.). Boston, MA: Houghton Mifflin.

Barrett, R. N. (1895). *In the land of the sunrise: A story of a Japanese family and the wonderful land they live in.* Louisville, KY: Baptist Book Concern.

Beauchamp, E. R. (1976). *An American teacher in early Meiji Japan.* Honolulu, HI: UP of Hawaii.

Bovingdon, J. (1917). The Girls' Doll Festival: An educational study of a Japanese custom. *School and Society, 6,* 549–556.

Bramhall, M. S. (1904). *Wee ones of Japan.* New York, NY: Harper.

cae12810. (2011). Hina matsuri—Japanese Doll Festival [Video file]. Retrieved from https://www.youtube.com/watch?v=PCiB2f2EvWM.

Campbell, H. C. (1905). *Story of little Metzu, the Japanese boy.* Boston, MA: Educational Publishing Company.

Canning-Wright, H. (1922). *Peeps at the world's dolls.* London, England: A. & C. Black.

Carpenter, F. G. (1917). *Around the world with the children: An introduction to geography.* New York, NY: American Book Company.

Casal, U. A. (1967). *The five sacred festivals of ancient Japan.* Tokyo, Japan: Sophia University/Tuttle.

Cook, M. B. (1891). *Japan: A sailor's visit to the island empire.* New York, NY: J. B. Alden.

Cooper, E. (1917). *The heart of O Sono San.* New York, NY: Frederick A. Stokes.

Culin, S. (1922). The story of the Japanese doll. *Asia: The American Magazine on the Orient, 22,* 782–785.

D'Autremer, J. (1910). *The Japanese Empire and its economic conditions.* New York, NY: Scribner.

Dixon, W. G. (1881). *The land of the morning: An account of Japan and its people, based on a four years' residence in that country.* Edinburgh, Scotland: James Gemmell.

Elmer, G. W. (1888). Hina No Matsuri, or "Doll's Day." *Heathen Woman's Friend, 19*(10), 280–282.

Entwistle, M. (1920). *Taro, a little boy of Japan.* London, England: United Council for Missionary Education.

Erickson, L. J. (1929). *Highways and byways in Japan.* New York, NY: Fleming H. Revell.

Forbes, A. (1898). Japanese games. *Pearson's Magazine, 6,* 195–198.

Fraser, M. (1899). *Letters from Japan* (2 vol.). New York, NY: Macmillan.

Greey, E. (1882). *Young Americans in Japan.* Boston, MA: Lee and Shepard.

Griffis, W. E. (1873–74): Games and sports of Japanese children. *Transactions of the Asiatic Society of Japan, 2,* 140–158.

Griffis, W. E. (1875). The Feast of Dolls. *St. Nicholas, 2*(5), 317–318.

Griffis, W. E. (1876). *The Mikado's empire* (12th ed.). New York, NY: Harper & Brothers.

Gulick, S. L. (1903). *Evolution of the Japanese.* New York, NY: Fleming H. Revell.

Gulick, S. L. (1929). *Dolls of friendship* (2nd ed.). Pittsburgh, PA: Friendship Ambassadors Press.

Haines, A. C. (1905). *Japanese boys and girls* (also issued as *Little Japs at home*). New York, NY: A. Stokes.

Hall, G. S., & Ellis, A. C. (1896). A study of dolls. *The Pedagogical Seminary, 4*(2).

Harada Jiro. (1911). The five festivals of the seasons in Japan. *Transactions of the Japan Society of London, 9,* 182–202.

Harris, F. B. (1878). The daughters of Dai-Nippon. *Potter's American* Monthly, 10.

Hedrick, E., & Van Noy, K. (1938). *Kites and kimonos.* London, England: Macmillan.

Hoyer, R. C. (1926). Ancestral dolls: A story of the Dolls' Festival in Japan. *Everyland, 16*(8), 3–6, 11.

Huish, M. (1902). A collection of toys. *Transactions of the Japan Society of London,* 90–92.

Humbert, A. (1874). *Japan and the Japanese illustrated* (F. C. Hoey, Trans.). New York, NY: D. Appleton & Co.

Jackson, E. (1908). *Toys of other days.* London, England: Offices of "Country Life," Ltd.

Kaempfer, E. (1727). *History of Japan* (J. G. Scheuchzer, Trans.). London, England: MacLehose.

Knox, T. W. (1879). *Boy travelers in Japan and China.* New York, NY: Harper & Brothers.

Lillehoj, E. (2011). *Art and palace politics in early modern Japan, 1580s–1680s*. Boston, MA: Brill.

Little, F. (1909). *Little sister Snow*. New York, NY: Century Company.

Lucey, M. (1928). Hina Matsuri or the Dolls' Festival. *John Martin's big book #12*. New York, NY: John Martin's Book House.

Mayne, E. (1908). *Kenjiro, the Japanese boy. Children of many lands: Part III*. Dayton, OH: Paine.

McDonald, E. B., & Dalrymple, J. (1916). *Umé-San in Japan*. Boston, MA: Little Brown.

Morse, E. (1886). Japanese boys and girls. *Wide Awake, 23*(1), 55–57.

Murasaki Shikibu. (1976). *Tale of Genji* (E. Seidenstecker, Trans.). New York, NY: Knopf.

Newton, J. C. C. (1900). *Japan: Country, court, and people*. Nashville, TN: Publishing House of the M. E. Church, South, Barbee & Smith.

Pate, A. S. (2005). *Ningyo: The art of the Japanese doll*. Tokyo, Japan: Tuttle.

Pate, A. S. (2008). *Japanese dolls: The fascinating world of Ningyo*. Tokyo, Japan: Tuttle.

Pate, A. S. (2011). Japanese dolls and the Imperial image. *Doll News*, 80–99.

Pate, A. S. (2013). The Japanese Friendship Dolls of 1927 and the birth of the Japanese art doll. *Doll News*, 30–53.

Peltier, F. (1903). *A Japanese garland*. Boston, MA: Lothrop.

Perkins, L. F. (1912). *The Japanese twins*. Boston, MA: Houghton Mifflin.

Pruyn, M. (1876). *Grandmamma's letters from Japan*. Boston, MA: James H. Earle.

Ridge, M. L. (1929). *Little Americans from many lands*. New York, NY: Gabriel.

Ritson, E. (1903). Hina Matsuri: The Doll-Festival in Japan. *The Round World, 3*, 156–158.

Rupp, K. (2003). *Gift-giving in Japan: Cash, connections, cosmologies*. Stanford, CA: Stanford University Press.

Salwey, C. M. (1894). On symbolism, and symbolic ceremonies of the Japanese. *The Imperial and Asiatic Quarterly Review, 8*(16), 439–453.

Schlegel, G. (1896). Review of Stewart Culin. *Korean Games. T'oung Pao Series 1, 7*, 94–102.

Scidmore, E. R. (1891). *Jinrikisha Days in Japan*. New York, NY: Harper & Brothers.

Shoaf, J. (2010). Queer dress and biased eyes: The Japanese doll on the Western toyshelf. *Journal of Popular Culture, 43*(1), 176–194.

Sladen, D. (1892). *The Japs at home*. London, England: Hutchinson.

Sladen, D. (1903). *Queer things about Japan*. London, England: A. Treherne.

Sowers, P. A. (1934). *Yasu-Bo and Ishi-Ko: A boy and girl of Japan*. Boston, MA: Thomas Y. Crowell Company.

Stanley Hall, K. (1912). *Children at play in many lands: A book of games*. New York, NY: Missionary Education Movement of the United States and Canada.

Starr, F. (1921). *Japanese collectors and what they collect*. Chicago, IL: The Bookfellows.

Strack, L. H. (1937). *Swords and Iris: Stories of the Japanese Doll Festivals*. New York, NY: Harper & Brothers.

Takashima Suteta. (1897). Fêtes and flowers. *The Far East, 2*(1), 163–164.

Titsingh, I. (1822). *Illustrations of Japan* (F. Shoberl, Trans.). London, England: Ackermann.

Yule, E. S. (1927). *In kimono land*. New York, NY: Rand, McNally & Company.

CHAPTER TWELVE

The Secret Sex Lives OF Native American Barbies, FROM THE Mysteries OF Motherhood, TO THE Magic OF Colonialism

ERICH FOX TREE

Barbie could never play it safe. At least since that doll Ken entered her life in 1961, the idealized fashion doll has been deflowered and corrupted millions of times over in the doll houses, backyards, and imaginations of precocious children who never accepted the supposedly innocent storyline repeated by her over-protective maker, Mattel Incorporated.

Despite this dirty reality of children's play, Mattel has spent decades promoting the official image of the world's most popular doll as both chaste and nubile. Sure, over the years, she has worn lots of wedding outfits, and she even once had a wedding ring, but the official storyline says that Barbie is unmarried and childless. Indeed, Barbie has no children *because* she is unmarried, according to what unofficial Barbie historian Evelyn Burkhalter once told fellow ethnographer Genevieve Bell and myself in 1995, when we did a few hours of lighthearted fieldwork on pop-cultural race/class/gender ideology at the Barbie Hall of Fame, the private museum Burkhalter had founded and curated in in Palo Alto, California from 1984 to 1999.

Spurious rumors that Barbie is either pregnant or had her own baby circulate periodically, but they have typically been pranks, misreadings, or conflations of the official Barbie character with other dolls. Over the decades, scores of true Barbies have been packaged with doll children actively marketed as her siblings, cousins, or clients of her numerous business careers, such as baby-sitter, dentist, or ice-cream fountaineer. Since 2001, Mattel has even supplied one hotel near the primary U.S. consulate processing adoptions in Guangzhou, China, with special doll sets to be given complimentarily to hotel clients adopting Chinese children (DiDanielli, 2004): GOING HOME BARBIE consists of a Barbie with European or Asian features, packed with a doll representing an androgynous Asian infant. Yet the context and imagery of these dolls makes clear that this Barbie is an *adoptive*, rather than a *biological* mother. Mattel has never marketed its fair-complected "classic" Barbies as having "biological" children of their own, since nothing would mark their fall from youthful grace more indelibly. Instead, it allowed other characters in the product line—Barbie's supposed "friends" or "relatives"—to be marketed as "biological" mothers. For example, in 2002, as short-lived additions to the "Happy Family" line, Mattel produced "pregnant" versions of Barbie's married friend Midge, each with a removable, racially matching baby concealed beneath a detachable magnetic belly (c.f. dolls #56663 and #56664).

Nonetheless, plastic infants packaged with several less-classic dolls suggest that some Barbies' biological clocks actually went off decades ago. The manufacturer allowed the perpetual single, the idol of American glamour, and the icon of feminine professional success to become a mother, but it did so without tarnishing the chaste-yet-sexualized image of all Barbies, by restricting the duties of "natural" motherhood to a small selection of ethnically marked dolls. In the 1990s, without fanfare or public alarm, Mattel mass-produced three Barbies that represent Native American women as mothers with babies, while carefully protecting (non-Native) Barbie's trademarked, multi-million-dollar character.

By depicting Native women as uniquely inclined toward motherhood, the toy maker articulates and commodifies durable racial stereotypes through the varied plastic identities projected by its "multicultural" toys. Commodification of maternal images of Native America through Native toys—that is, toys purporting to iconically represent Native peoples, rather than toys produced *by* or *for* them—only succeeds because it tacitly invokes an enduring American colonial myth that reframes imperialism as colonization by carnal consent: the archetypal myth of Pocahontas. While contrasting the idealized Barbie image, maternal Native Barbies are iconically congruent to the ubiquitous image of the "Indian Princess," a visual and vernacular motif that American arts, letters, and merchandising have exploited since at least as far back as the sixteenth century, as Cherokee folklorist Rayna Diane Green (1975) long ago noted in her study of the "Pocahontas Perplex" (p. 701).

In addition to commodifying racialized representations of motherhood, Native Barbies articulate complex race, gender, and class subjectivities that North Americans tend to repeat and accept as natural. Native Barbies with babies testify to the mutual constitution of ethnicity and gender by occupying the definitive maternal role of women while simultaneously representing a folklorized vision of Native Americans as people bound by both obligatory tradition and irresistible nature. All the while, they serve to naturalize class ideologies by depicting Native women not merely with the domestic occupation of maternity, but also outside the modern world of leisure, jobs tabulated and valued as "economically productive," and the individual free will and agency they represent. Maternal Barbies thereby contribute to the representation of Native peoples not merely as an underclass, but as a non-class in an imaginary realm outside of capitalism itself.

In short, the dolls represent and embody what Inderpal Grewal (1999, p. 806) has referred to as "heteronormative, gendered racism as a marketing strategy," but they also commodify particular racialized and gendered ideologies of class as well. By calling attention to the particularities of these degrading fantasies that maternalized Native identities structure, my goal is not to rank the severity of the negative depictions of non-White minority groups. The important issue is not whether the icon of Natives as mothers is any more or less offensive than Black "Mammies" or screaming, tomahawk-bearing "Injuns." Rather, I ask readers to question why racist icons of Native mothers continue and seem so natural in popular culture.

This study of the commodification of gendered racism consists of four parts. Part One explains the peculiar "ethnic marketing" of Native toys and describes the Barbie products that are the center of this study, contrasting them with the archetypically single and childless persona that Barbie has idealized for 5 decades. Part Two discusses the role of material culture in the commodification of subjectivities, arguing that toys structure consumers' fantasies about Native Americans at the same time they articulate particular ideologies regarding the class position of Native Americans and the intersection of gender and ethnicity. Part Three reviews how Mattel exploits the popular and historically inaccurate Pocahontas myth in order to sell maternalized Barbies. Finally, Part Four discusses the more general racialized imagery in Native toys, spotlighting non-Mattel merchandise that also represents Native women as mothers, often while simultaneously representing Natives as animals or aspects of a feminized Nature. I conclude with a few remarks about what maternal Native Barbies teach about the nature of identity.

PART ONE: PRODUCTS AND MARKETING

Marketing Ethnicity: [Re-]Producing for the Rez, or for the Rest?

Native toys draw crucial attention to how ethnic marketing strategies can differ dramatically for different ethnic groups. Popular theory dictates that for at least a generation, companies in the USA have manufactured dolls in the images of minorities principally as a means of "Reaching out to Minority Consumers," to borrow the words of journalist Mitchell Zuckoff (1992, p. 73). Scholar Ann DuCille has described Mattel's attempts to produce multicultural Barbies as part of a larger industry trend to "capitalize on ethnic spending power" (1994, p. 49).

Similarly, in a nuanced analysis of Black children's reactions to the "Ethnically Correct Dolls" that Mattel has been producing since the 1980s, Elizabeth Chin (1999) acknowledged that Black girls constitute the target market for Black dolls:

> The primary appeal toy makers offer with their ethnically correct playthings is the idea that such toys can help minority kids to feel more at home in the world through allowing them to play with toys—and especially dolls—that look like them. (p. 309)

Yet general marketing of Native products does not follow the same strategy. While Mattel manufactures Hispanic Barbies for Latina girls, or Black Barbies of several shades for a niche market made up of young African American girls, the toy corporation does not cater its Native dolls to a niche market of Native American girls, let alone to traditional girls from tribal reservations. The potential market of young Native girls is far too small—and statistically too scattered and poor—to be of significance to toy companies. They manufacture quantities of toys representing Native peoples that are far out of proportion with the relative population of Native peoples. From 1993 to 2000, Mattel produced six editions of its (childless) NATIVE AMERICAN BARBIE for its multicultural *Dolls of the World* series, each consisting of a production run of at least 100,000 dolls. The collection also included two editions of ESKIMO BARBIE and one Inuit ARCTIC BARBIE. No other ethnicities and nationalities of the 40 or so represented in the series went through more than two editions during that period. The ethnicities of eight dolls produced between 1995 and 1997 for the *American Stories Collection* further confirm the disproportionate use of Native imagery: six White Barbies and two editions of NATIVE AMERICAN BARBIE. From 2001 to 2003, Mattel produced an entire doll series dedicated entirely to Native American dolls, the *Native Spirit Collection*, made up of three limited-edition dolls: a feat not done for other non-White races.

Unlike what seems to be the case for Black and Latina dolls, the scheme behind the production and sale of Native dolls is not a matter of flexible, post-Fordist niche marketing. Rather, to borrow a phrase from anthropologist Bill Maurer (1997), it is a case of "marketing the niche."[1] Scholars sometimes need to look beyond abstract notions of ethnicity and acknowledge the divergent treatments and trajectories of certain ethnicities. Native toys differ from toys representing other groups because the industry commodifies and markets Native ethnicity with almost no concern for Native consumers. Furthermore, while scholars may point to the novelty of corporate marketing to certain ethnic minorities, the active marketing of the Native niche to the general public has been a consistently successful strategy for many decades.

Natives sell, and they possess trans-ethnic appeal. The multiple editions of the various Native Barbie dolls are a symptom of this awkward economic reality: Non-Natives purchase most toys representing "American Indians" or "Native Americans," whether or not these products are Barbies. Sales further indicate that White Americans are not the only ones infatuated with Nativeness. According to dealers, the major market for Barbie's girlfriend NIA (1990)—a dark-haired, but blue-eyed doll wearing nothing distinctively "Native," but advertised on the package as being American Indian—was made up of young Latinas.

Yet Barbies are inevitably designed with children's tastes and parents' pocketbooks in mind. Whether buying for children or as collectors, adults are the real primary markets, especially if dolls appear rare or unusual (by accident or by design). Mattel advertised most of the dolls discussed in this chapter not only in "children's collection," but also as part of "collectors' editions." Online advertising for about 10% of dolls, typically retailing for $50–$150, includes the phrase, "[f]or the adult collector" (Barbie Collector). Yet dolls' appeal to collectors is enhanced by the outward illusion that it is a toy for little girls. Packaging regularly refers to *girls*, *play*, and *fun*, without acknowledging adult collectors, except obliquely. For example, the back of the box of the second edition AMERICAN INDIAN BARBIE doll (# 17313) says, "Whether you play with them, or display them."

Whether adults or children, non-Native consumers seem infatuated with all things Native. The small market of Native American children is of little significance to manufacturers who can count on the size of this diverse consumer market. There is little financial incentive for the toy industry to consult with Native American parents or child development experts, as DuCille reported Mattel did two decades ago while developing a new line of African American dolls (1994, p. 53; 1996, p. 50). Native toys have been little affected by toy makers' strategy of making ethnic dolls to profit from the overcoming of racial bigotry, such as the Black dolls made by Olmec described by Chin (1999, p. 310). The marketing of Barbie fashion dolls continues to convert Indian-ness into a mere fashion. Tribal outfits can be tossed off and replaced by whatever fad follows. Native Barbies' cross-ethnic appeal might better be seen as a prelude to the various racially ambiguous dolls, such as some in MGA Entertainment's Bratz line, which have chipped deeply into Mattel's dominance of the fashion doll market since their first release in 2001.

In contrast to the new ethnic mystique of racially ambiguous dolls, the general popularity of all things Native is a fad with surprising durability. Manufacturers have long capitalized on the fact that children and adults apparently love both *buying* Indian and *playing* Indian. The public has long dressed up and acted out stereotypes that have grown up over generations, perpetuating the symbolic violence and the racist and colonialist conceptions that such games structure. Economics and politics have also long favored such play. Native authors such as Cherokee folklorist Rayna Green (1988) and Dakota historian Philip Deloria (1998) have long noted that non-Natives have played Indian since the colonial era in large part because North American nationalist ideology has continually appropriated Native Americans as symbols.

Romanticized Hollywood images of Native Americans have added to the sale of "Native" identities. Walt Disney and its toy industry allies began an international toy and game marketing blitz months before the release of its summer of 2013 box-office flub *The Lone Ranger,* as it had previously done before the release of its re-visionist cartoon-blockbuster, *Pocahontas,* in the spring of 1995. And even earlier, the box-office success of the 1990 film *Dances with Wolves* corresponded to an explosion of toys representing Native peoples, and a simultaneous commodification of their identities. That film may even have contributed to an unprecedented explosion of American Indian self-identification on censuses. Clearly, "playing Indian" and "*being* Indian" are popular in ways unlike playing or being a member of any other minority.

Distinctive Imagery for the Native Niche: Brown Barbie Babies

In 1999, Mattel released a new doll as part of its large and successful *Dolls of the World* series, the second edition (1999) PERUVIAN BARBIE (#21506). Brown-eyed and taw-ny-complected, the doll wears earthen sandals and a colorful patterned outfit reminis-cent of *traje* from the highlands of that South American country (Figure 1). Her box depicts pre-Columbian gold jewelry and an image of the Incas' mountain refuge of Machu Picchu. Yet the doll's most telling mark of indigeneity may be how she carries a tawny infant, hooded in a typical Andean woven cap and wrapped in a multi-colored woven shawl.[2] Nothing on or inside the packaging pretends to explain the identity of this indigenous Andean Barbie's brown baby, as if no explanation were necessary.

No other doll in the "collector edition" was equipped with an infant, and the debut of the second edition PERUVIAN BARBIE's baby was masterfully muted, as if tacitly recognizing that consumers typically do not consider babies to be glam-orous fashion accessories. Rather, for Native Barbies, infants are appealing *cultur-al* accessories that mark their racial or ethnic affiliation like garments or crafts. The partial product-line depicted on the package of the second edition PERUVIAN BARBIE even shows the doll without her baby. Instead, she has a hat, reminiscent of those still used by Native Peruvians today. Boxes of later dolls in the same series depict the second-generation PERUVIAN BARBIE with a disconcerting note that confirms the undervaluing of Native infants as cultural trifles: "Comes with baby doll! Hat not included with Peruvian Barbie® Doll." CHILEAN BARBIE (1998), a White doll of the same series, wears a similar hat to go along with her European fashion. Yet nothing announces that the White doll comes with an Andean hat and lacks a baby doll.

Mattel has produced some 30 different Native Barbies, with combined pro-duction runs totaling many millions of dolls. The exact number depends on which models one chooses to count as Native. Among the childless Native Barbies, I include six editions of NATIVE AMERICAN BARBIE, Arctic Barbie, two editions of ESKIMO BARBIE, and the first edition of PERUVIAN BARBIE, which was released in 1986 wearing an outfit that was almost identical to that of the doll described above, except that it possessed neither the multi-colored imitation-indigenous shawl, nor the miniature plastic infant, that accompanied the second-generation doll. More of the nearly naked body of AMAZONIA BARBIE (2009) is covered by "her tribal tattoos" and feathers than clothes. The first edition MEXICAN BARBIE (1989) wears a colonial-style outfit like that still used by some indigenous women of the Yucatan, while the front of the doll's box features a large image of an ancient pyramid. All of the preceding Native dolls belong to special multicultural series, such as *Dolls of the World*, rather than being included among the normative White, Black, Hispanic, and Asian Barbies.[3]

Table 1: A Sample of "Native" Barbies.

COLLECTION NAME (# of different dolls in the collection)	DOLL NAME (original price)	YEAR	SPECIAL NATIVE ICONGRAPHY
Barbie National Convention dolls	ESKIMO BARBIE (250 given free for registrants of the Barbie Convention in Troy, MI)	1982	Fringed buckskins
	AMERICAN INDIAN BARBIE (200 given to registrants of the Barbie Convention in Phoenix, AZ, along with a doll called BARBIE'S POWWOW, which featured a White blonde doll in a rodeo outfit). 25 Kens in buckskins were also distributed	1983	Fringed white or brown buckskins and **baby**
Dolls of the World Collection (203)	ESKIMO BARBIE, 1st ed.	1982	Parka and Mukluks
	ESKIMO BARBIE, 2nd ed.	1991	Parka, Mukluks, and pants
	ARCTIC BARBIE ($21.99)	1997	
	NATIVE AMERICAN, 1st ed.	1993	White buckskins
	NATIVE AMERICAN, 2nd ed.	1994	Tassels, beads, feathers, and buckskins
	NATIVE AMERICAN, 3rd ed.	1995	Tassels and beads
	NATIVE AMERICAN, 4th ed.	1998	Brown buckskins
	NATIVE AMERICAN, Toys "R" Us exclusive ($24.99)	1996	Blue buckskins
	Northwest Coast Native American	2000	Painted buckskin cloak

COLLECTION NAME (# of different dolls in the collection)	DOLL NAME (original price)	YEAR	SPECIAL NATIVE ICONGRAPHY
	PERUVIAN BARBIE 1st ed.	1986	Textiles
	PERUVIAN BARBIE 2nd ed. ($24.99)	1999	Textiles and **baby**
	AMAZONIA BARBIE ($12.99)	2009	Feathers, tattoo, loincloth
	MEXICAN BARBIE, 1st ed.	1989	Pyramid on package; colonial outfit
	Polynesian Barbie ($19.95)	1995	Grass skirt
	Hawaii, USA ($29.95)	2012	Grass skirt
American Stories Collection (8)	AMERICAN INDIAN, 1st ed. ($24.99)	1996	Blue buckskins, feather, and **baby**
	AMERICAN INDIAN, 2nd ed. ($24.99)	1997	Brown buckskins, feather, and **baby**
Native Spirit Collection (3)	SPIRIT OF THE EARTH	2001	Fur and buckskins
	SPIRIT OF THE SKY	2002	Blue buckskins
	SPIRIT OF WATER	2003	Painted buckskins
Princess Collection (21)	PRINCESS OF THE INCAS ($19.95)	2001	Textiles and gold
	PRINCESS OF ANCIENT MEXICO ($19.95)	2004	Textiles and feathers
	PRINCESS OF THE NAVAJO ($19.95)		Textiles
	PRINCESS OF THE PACIFIC ISLANDS ($19.95)	2005	Lai of Blossoms
More World Culture (15)	WIND RIDER BARBIE ($149.95)	2006	Buckskins
	INUIT LEGEND	2005	Painted designs
Celebrity Dolls	70's Cher *Bob Mackie* Doll $34.95	2007	Feather bonnet

Table 1: Mattel produces quantities of "Native" dolls far out of proportion with the number of indigenous girls in the USA, although the company has not always marketed them explicitly with words. The non-exhaustive selection of Barbies with Native Pacific and Amerindian-themed iconography listed in the table shows that Native dolls made up a significant proportion of several Barbie Doll series marketed between 1982 and 2012.

In 2001 Mattel released its third Native Andean doll, PRINCESS OF THE INCAS BARBIE, as part of its 21-doll *Princess Collection*, which also included at least three other Native Barbies: PRINCESS OF ANCIENT MEXICO (2004), PRINCESS OF THE

NAVAJO (2004), and PRINCESS OF THE PACIFIC ISLANDS (2005). The small *Native Spirit Collection* is made up of three limited-edition dolls, each garbed in faux leather or fur, and each sporting stereotypical symbols of Native identity and spirituality: SPIRIT OF THE EARTH BARBIE (2001), SPIRIT OF THE WATER BARBIE (2002), and SPIRIT OF THE SKY BARBIE (2003). The limited edition WIND RIDER BARBIE (2006) had a total production run of fewer than 5,400 units (barbiecollector.com). Over the years, Mattel has also produced several (Native) Hawaiian and Polynesian Barbies. In all cases, whether they wear archaic buckskins, fur parkas, or modern pow wow garb, these Barbies glamorize Native cultures (or more generic "Native American culture") through their ethnic fashions or the exotic backdrops on their boxes. The one exception to the ethnic ghettoization is Barbie's Native American companion, NIA, who uses popular non-Native clothes. Yet NIA is not a true Barbie doll by name, but rather, one of Barbie's "friends." Regardless of the exact number of childless Native Barbies, one point is clear; they are disproportionately numerous.

Figure 1. To mark her as a Native woman, second edition PERUVIAN BARBIE (#21506) sports a tawny baby wrapped in a multicolored shawl reminiscent of those made and used by indigenous women in the Andes.

On the other hand, out of more than 3,500 Barbie models that Mattel has produced since 1959, there are only five maternal Barbies, all of them Native American: two versions of an experimental doll distributed at a convention in 1983, two editions of AMERICAN INDIAN BARBIE produced in 1996 (#14715) and 1997 (#17313), and the second-edition PERUVIAN BARBIE produced in 1999 (#21506). Though the dolls are few, thematic reiteration shows Mattel's commitment to a particular vision of Native womanhood.

Marketing the Mythology of Motherhood

The first Native Barbie dolls equipped with babies were never mass-produced for the retail market. Rather, they were made for a small number of Barbie's most loyal fans: dealers and customers who attended a national Barbie doll convention in Phoenix, Arizona, in 1983. Distributed as part of a package called BARBIE'S POWWOW, which featured a White blonde doll in a rodeo outfit, the "Indian Princess with feather" (as its medallion read) came in two versions sporting dark braids, a headband, a feather over its forehead, a fringed buckskin made of either white or brown suede, and a small bag containing an infant doll with a "Mohawk" hairdo painted onto its scalp. Its complexion—the color of the infant-doll's plastic—was far darker than that of the mother, as if the baby were co-opted from another product line with Black dolls. The baby doll possessed no accompanying literature to explain its identity; the reference to the ubiquitous and insulting image of the "Indian Princess," one of Native America's most despised epithets, was apparently enough.[4] Because the doll's distribution was limited to only about 200 units, few people had the opportunity to question how this doll's baby contradicted Barbie's official image, let alone how the doll's association with motherhood projected fertility and implicit promiscuity onto Native women. Yet they nonetheless set a precedent, being the first explicitly "American Indian" Barbies, and having been preceded by only two earlier Native Barbies, both released the year before as "ESKIMO BARBIE": one a convention doll and the other, one of the first in Mattel's *Dolls of the World* series.

The first Native doll with a baby released for general retail was the 1996 first edition AMERICAN INDIAN BARBIE (#14715). This Barbie formed part of Mattel's *American Stories Collection*, a collectors' series that would eventually consist of eight dolls, including two editions of the Native doll and six fair-complected dolls in colonial or nineteenth-century apparel. The White dolls possessed objects appropriate to their historic occupations: a basket of corn for PILGRIM BARBIE, a bag marked with a physician's caduceus for a Civil War nurse, and a milk canister for a pioneer shopkeeper. Yet Mattel supplied a baby mounted on a cradleboard as the appropriate occupational accessory for AMERICAN INDIAN BARBIE.

By doing so, the manufacturer presented a racialized domestic occupation of *Indian mother* that combines two persistent stereotypes: that being an American Indian is itself a career (cf., Hirschfelder, 1982)[5] and that Natives make good mothers. Rayna Green (1992, p. 15) has written, "Historically, Indian women have been portrayed as caretakers, but rarely have they been represented in their roles as traders, farmers, artisans, and healers." How the *American Stories Collection* depicts American Indian women perfectly fits Green's characterization of the aforementioned caretaker stereotype, given that the White historical figures are presented in exactly those roles from which Indian women are excluded. To top off the package, Mattel placed its dark-skinned Barbie in a stereotyped pose. Her left hand is raised to eye level, palm outwards, as if to connote the generic and linguistically deficient film Indians who converse with limited hand gestures and grunts of "ugh" and "haw!"

In an article previewing and promoting Barbie products, the co-founder and editor of the collectors' magazine *Barbie Bazaar*, Karen Caviale (1996), labeled these dolls "Early American Barbie With Papoose" (p. 70). The phrase categorizes Native Americans as anachronisms. It is consistent with popular nostalgia that makes cultural stasis into a criterion of Native identity and folklorizes Native Americans as "lost" or "vanishing" people. None of the companion dolls of the series was likewise identified as "early," even though they also supposedly represented eighteenth- and nineteenth-century women. PILGRIM BARBIE, for example, was *not* identified as an "Early American Barbie with a basket of maize."

The two editions of the maternal AMERICAN INDIAN BARBIE were the only non-White Barbies in the collection. One can only speculate what occupations might have been selected for the Black, Asian, or Mexican women whom Mattel Eurocentrically omitted from American history via the *American Stories Collection*. Yet while Mattel ignored these groups, Native people were depicted as icons of the past and of outmoded tradition. The confinement of Native Americans to the realm of the historical enables racially perverse imagery to persist. The images that decorate the packaging of Native dolls regularly include wildlife and landscapes alongside historic cultural paraphernalia; snowy igloos and polar bears for ESKIMO BARBIE and ARCTIC BARBIE, and llamas and Inca gold for (Native) PERUVIAN BARBIE.

Indeed, Mattel uses Native Barbies as icons of a sanitized nationalist narrative that erases violence and power from colonial history. It is a peaceful narrative that conforms to the peaceful character that Mattel has sought to promote for the entire Barbie product line. Other than temporary setbacks such as broken legs or broken tennis rackets, Barbies typically do not depict suffering, especially that inflicted by other people. Indeed, while toys for boys, such as "cowboys and Indians" figurine sets, regularly feature ethnic conflict, most consumers do not expect children's toys directed at girls to depict similar social realities. Yet, just as wars and campaigns of racial extermination find no place in Barbie's world, the dolls' imagery situates Native Barbies outside (or historically antecedent to) the oppressive mechanisms of colonialism, racial persecution, and industrial capitalism.

To avoid controversy, the packaging is also predictably silent regarding the imaginary paternity of Native Barbie's "papoose." Nonetheless, working within the boundaries of the historicized Barbie society Mattel has established, one can presume that the father was not Native, given that Mattel has never produced a Native American Ken. Paternity would have been a question of power, since the colonial administration would have denied this child the possibility of rising within the colonial ranks, as Ann Stoler (1991) has argued was the case in colonial Indonesia.

Mattel markets "Early American Barbie with Papoose" as an educational toy, symbolizing a sanitized history that confines Native women to a tacitly unnoted niche of colonial conquest and sexual submission, not to mention racial otherness. Caviale's (1996) product preview reported, "The special edition Barbie doll as an early American Indian teaches *girls* about *another* [emphasis added] culture and lets them nurture a little papoose. This doll comes with an inspirational storybook that tells about Barbie doll and her tribal role" (p. 70). The passage reveals how non-Native girls who know little about (generic) "American Indian" culture are the target audience for AMERICAN INDIAN BARBIE.

Mattel reinforces the maternal imagery of the dolls through the ambiguous denials of maternity that accompany the doll. Statements that the swarthy babe does not represent Barbie's biological child are not only weak, but hidden. The storybook mentioned above reveals that the baby's name is "Baby Blue Feather," and that she is Barbie's infant *cousin* (Smithen, 1995), yet to discover this one must open the package: a no-no for serious adult collectors. Furthermore, the doll's box refers to Barbie's cousin, Baby Blue Feather, without ever stating that this is the name of the baby packaged with the Barbie doll; rather, it implies that Blue Feather is some mythical character:

> Listen along with the children as American Indian Barbie tells the story of the legend of the blue feather. Share in her wonder as a simple act of kindness ends in a magical surprise that comes full circle the day her cousin, Baby Blue Feather, needs her most.

The doll combination exploits an implicit maternal relation, with Barbie as surrogate mother. Even the book inside reveals that "Barbie loved to help care for the baby, and have him close to her as she carried him on her back," suggesting that AMERICAN INDIAN BARBIE loves playing mother as no previous Barbie ever has. It is her proper social role; but it is not an economic one. Whether Barbie's nurturing urges are due to her familial ties, Native ethnicity, or individual desires, she is not labeled "baby-sitter." She can thus be excluded from the economic system in which temporary surrogate mothers would normally be paid.

The identification of the baby as Barbie's cousin is especially unsatisfying, given that Baby Blue Feather, an ethnically marked figure, is not an established character in Mattel's product line. Mattel has not incorporated this infant figure into Barbie's "family tree" made up of family, friends, and pets.[6] The revisions made for the 1997 second-edition AMERICAN INDIAN BARBIE only make the situation more suspicious. Mattel identified the baby more explicitly as Barbie's *sister*. Mattel also revised the text on the back of the box and gave the baby a new "ethnic" name:

> Listen along with the children as American Indian Barbie and her baby sister go on a picnic together. On the way, Barbie tells her sister, Little Cloud, about the animals they live with and how each has given their tribe a special gift that lets them live in harmony with each other.

Yet, while the revised edition avoids the ambiguous portrayal of Blue Feather as a mythical character and explicitly identifies the infant doll as *not* being Barbie's baby *on the outside* of the packaging, the product still endorses other stereotypes. It denies financially profitable occupations to Native women by associating them with motherly nurturing, instead. The association is made more natural by references to animals and traditional tribal "harmony" with them. The equivocal and inconsistent identification of the plastic baby even makes the denial of Barbie's biological motherhood unconvincing. One recalls the timeworn practice of unwed teenage mothers deflecting suspicious inquiries by calling their babies their "cousins" or "sisters," and perhaps forgetting the explanation they last used.

Admittedly, there are few products that depict Barbie as an ethnic mother, and each has its own quirks. Still, one cannot overlook the awkward status of these maternal dolls. And even though Mattel has revised the NATIVE AMERICAN BARBIE, the company has not publicly explained the other Barbie babies. Nothing printed on the outside or inside of the packaging of the second edition (Native) PERUVIAN BARBIE explains her baby, for example, although shoppers I talked to were more than willing to offer justifications for the doll, which they did not find at all peculiar. "It make sense; just look at her clothing," one White woman told me, "She's Mexican, right?" When I pointed out that the doll was actually meant to be a Native Peruvian, the woman answered, "Well, they have lots of kids, too."

Even years after their manufacture, some stores still sell these dolls. PERUVIAN BARBIE'S nameless baby still testifies not only to Mattel's attitudes towards Natives of the Americas, but to the public's desire to consume and perpetuate stereotypes. All these maternal dolls, like so much of popular American material culture, articulate hegemonic visions of Native people.

PART TWO: COMMODIFIED IDENTITIES

Narcissist, Not Nurturer: The Symbolism of Single Status

Native Barbies are made more stereotypically Native through their association with supposedly natural maternal instincts that few consumers question. Mattel has constructed a fantasy society inhabited almost exclusively by childless professionals. Baby-burdened Native women are the only exception. Their maternal femininity fundamentally contradicts one of the most basic principles of the standard Barbie's affluent and nubile femininity. Mattel exoticizes motherhood by overvaluing the independence from children (and spouses) that "successful" modern women like (non-Native) Barbie enjoy. Such role models implicitly exercise individual freedom and choice, centerpieces of capitalist and consumerist economic philosophy. Such choice is denied to Native women. And regardless of however consumers manipulate the merchandise to resist Barbie hegemony, her hardened plastic society symbolically marginalizes Barbies with babies.

Since Barbie first debuted on store shelves in March of 1959, Mattel has marketed her as a model of female success, whether she was modeled as a middle-class girl looking for class respectability, or a flexible and ambitious achiever who could "be anything" (Lord, 1994, pp. 9, 286). In the words of her designer, the late Ruth Handler (1994), "Barbie helped—and continues to help—little girls achieve their dreams" (p. 98). As neither a wife nor a mother, Barbie was a bold icon in the early 1960s. Mattel responded to the women's movement of that decade by associating Barbie with professional achievement and by trying to convert the doll into a symbol, icon, and token of economic liberation. Barbie's extra-domestic activities were meant to represent the supposed possibilities open to the "modern woman." Of course, as Urla and Swedlund (1995) have pointed out, such liberation was held in check by the fact that Barbie's careers have disproportionately favored exhibitionist professions such as fashion model and ballerina, not to mention the career consumer who changes her professional identity by changing her clothes (p. 283). In her 1996 book *Skin Trade*, Ann DuCille (1996) notes that the erotic styling of many doll outfits suggests that Barbie engages in the oldest of professions, though Mattel pleads innocent and accuses consumers of having dirty imaginations (pp. 18–21). Yet, whatever her profession, Barbie consistently expresses her "feminine" side through conspicuous leisure and glamorous public self-maintenance, symbolized by hairbrushes and a seemingly endless wardrobe.

All of this success has only been possible while archetypal Barbie remained single, as if to say that married women cannot succeed professionally. Of course, Barbie has come perilously close to marriage and the loss of independence it symbolizes, as attested by dolls sporting rings or wedding dresses and by dozens of different bridal outfits and accessories "sold separately." Yet she has always managed to stand up her "boyfriend" Ken at the altar.

The manufacturer has always insisted that Barbie is unwed. As mentioned earlier, Evelyn Burkhalter, former curator and founder of the now defunct Barbie Hall of Fame, once commented to me that Barbie has no children *because* she is unmarried. Barbie's numerous wedding dresses suggest a near pathological desire to find a husband and start a family. The marketing strategy idealizes Mattel's model of feminine beauty as desperately nubile. But until recently, that was the limit of what the manufacturer would suggest. Mattel's aversion to Barbie's potential association with fertility, sexual activity, and their swaddled consequences set the stage for a rumor that circulated in 1993 that Mattel had unwittingly produced its first edition AMERICAN INDIAN BARBIE (#1753) dressed in a tasseled outfit that supposedly resembled a dress Apaches use for menarche rituals. It is unlikely that the toy maker was under pressure to recall the doll, as some people supposed. Nonetheless, hearing that Barbie was dressed to celebrate her first menstruation, collectors reportedly rushed to buy the doll.

While menstruation can mark passage into female adolescence, perhaps nothing genders the feminine body more publicly than the generating of a baby. Barbie's nativizing of maternity shows how motherhood can mark race or ethnicity as much as it marks gender. But the process of symbolic linkage is two-way; motherhood defines indigeneity, as indigeneity comes to define motherhood, giving rise to both a racialized gender and a gendered race. The ideologies that frame these subjectivities likewise constitute a sort of gendered racism or racialized sexism.

Yet motherhood can mark not only race and gender, but also class, as clearly shown by recent political debates about the social and economic fitness of "welfare mothers" (even years after Welfare officially ended). Recent proposals to reform safety net legislation, discourage single parenthood, and retrain inner-city mothers should remind us of the links between motherhood and class that U.S. society has constructed.

The occupation of mother prevents AMERICAN INDIAN BARBIE from having a professional occupation like the other Barbie dolls in Mattel's *American Stories Collection*. As erroneously career-less mothers, Natives are supposed to be professionally unproductive, while they are biologically productive. In sum, the imagery of maternal Native Barbies "offers a fantastic conflation of gender, race, and class," to borrow a phrase from Anne McClintock (1995, p. 4).

Classic Barbie managed to step around what most people consider a natural stage in the life cycle of a woman. According to DuCille (1994), "Barbie's curvaceous, big-busted, almost fully female body... summons not the maternal but the sexual, not the nurturant mother but the sensuous woman" (p. 62). Mattel has carefully controlled Barbie's contact with children, effectively prohibiting her from one domestic profession: motherhood. Urla and Swedlund's (1995) anthropometric analysis of Barbie dolls supports this conclusion:

> One could argue that, like the anorectic body she resembles, Barbie's body displays conformity to dominant cultural imperatives for a disciplined body and contained feminine desires. As a woman, however, her excessive slenderness also signifies a rebellious manifestation of willpower, a visual denial of the maternal ideal symbolized by pendulous breasts, rounded stomach and hips. Hers is a body of hard edges, distinct borders, self-control. It is literally impenetrable. Unlike the anorectic, whose self-denial renders her gradually androgynous in appearance, in the realm of plastic fantasy Barbie is able to remain powerfully sexualized, with her large, gravity-defying breasts, even while she is distinctly unreproductive. (p. 301)

The White women whom the archetypal Barbie represents are converted into high-status role models through Barbie's apparent postponement of motherhood and by her professional success, symbolized as much by her leisure and shopping habits as by her careers. Her class position, her implicit pre-marital chastity, and her hyper-sexualized glamour make her even more marriageable; she is an idealized modern woman for today's consumer society.

Native models can only be understood in contrast to their alter egos. White, Black, Asian, and Hispanic women can hold professional careers ranging from fashion model to astronaut to Army grunt, or conspicuous consumer and "lady of leisure" with no career at all. On the other hand, Native Barbies with babies communicate that sexual reproduction is the only proper occupation for Native women. The latter become icons of three supposed plagues of contemporary society: presumed sexual promiscuity, the economic non-productivity of reproduction, and single parenthood. As individuals who are presumed to be incapable of restraining natural or animalistic reproductive urges, whose economic contributions are erased because they do not have extra-domestic careers, Native women are little better than a contemporary Republican portrait of non-White "welfare mothers." Native Barbies' motherhood is a mutely accepted burden from which non-Native Barbies are "liberated" by their freedom to choose other jobs. Mattel's symbolic undervaluing of motherhood is ironic for a business that tries so hard to be a "family company." Perhaps more noteworthy are the profits that drive Mattel and other toys makers to commodify not only exotic Native identity, but exotic ethnic motherhood, and the popular fascination with all things Native that fuels these profits.

As mentioned previously, Mattel has actually included numerous baby dolls in the Barbie product line. Yet formerly, whenever Mattel sold Barbie dolls packaged with babies, the infant companions were explicitly identified as friends, clients, or younger siblings, or understood to be such in the context of other Barbie products. Over the years, Barbie products firmly established that Skipper (1964), Tutti (1966–71), Todd (1966–68), Stacie (1992), and infant Kelly (1995) were all just siblings. In other contemporary cases, such as that of a baby packaged together with Mattel's DENTIST BARBIE (#17255), the fashion doll's outfit and accouterments suggest that her relationship with the baby is purely professional and not familial. The same applies to "Doctor Barbie," despite DuCille's (1996) note that the baby she carries is a potent gender marker:

> The most recent manifestation of Dr. Barbie comes with a pink plastic stethoscope, a White lab coat, and blue spike heels to match her short blue dress. What's new with this edition, though, is the baby Dr. Barbie holds tucked under one arm—perhaps the most appropriate accessory for a real woman. (p. 24)

However, the designers have no need to deny maternity in this case, because the implied non-maternal doctor-patient relationship between the dolls is so clear. Even DuCille begins her description by noting the doctor's medical gear.

Although the maternal pair of mother and baby might be naturalized as "appropriate" in the real world, it does not conform to the standard Barbie image. The simple fact is that the Mattel Corporation aggressively protects Barbie's image. It has carefully and intentionally crafted the authorized vision of its valuable Barbie character. Given all its resistance to matrimony and its implicitly inevitable companion, motherhood, it is surprising that Mattel has now chosen to represent some Barbies as mothers. It is the ethnic marginalization of motherhood and its racialized commodification that protects Barbie's multi-billion-dollar trademarked persona.

Jobless Native Barbie Mothers in a Class by Themselves

The contrast between Mattel's portrayal of Native and non-Native women facilitates the commodification of both ethnic motherhood and a strange Native subjectivity situated at the margins of capitalism. Outside of academic or activist circles, most people tend not to envision mothers, Native peoples, the jobless, and animals as agents of capitalism, or at least not as primary agents. By representing all these marginalized identities at once, Native Barbies with babies are consigned to a position not only outside the professional and leisure class represented by Barbie, but also outside of the economic system that her lifestyle symbolizes. I have already mentioned how Native Barbies in the *American Stories Collection* lack the accouterments of professions or domestic avocations that accompany the archetypal White Barbie dolls of that series. This jobless status only heightens Native Barbies' awkward position.

Of course, merely being without a job is not the same as being without a social class or marginal to capitalism. That imaginary status is created by the other features of the Native subjectivity that Barbies articulate, such as the notion of "tradition," cultural and historical stasis, and lack of agency, not to mention occasional descriptions of antimodern socialism. For example, the packaging of the second edition ESKIMO BARBIE (#3898) released in 1991 reads, "Eskimos live in small groups and believe in sharing. Only the most personal property is considered private." The archetypal White Barbie commodifies the presumed free will celebrated in capitalist ideology. Not only can children *choose* from among thousands of Barbie dolls and accessories, but also the animated imaginary persona of Barbie can *choose* to be a doctor, fashion model, or secretary. Yet while the corporate designers have endowed the Barbie persona with infinite occupational plasticity, they have also energetically disassociated the archetypal Barbie from motherhood, except as a temporary and surrogate task. In other words, White Barbie can choose to baby-sit.

However, according to the imagery of Mattel's maternal Native Barbies, Native women naturally have babies, and they can do so without acknowledgement or further explanation, as in the case of PERUVIAN BARBIE. The occupations chosen for White Barbies contrast with the timeless and unquestioned cultural obligations projected onto Native women. The packaging of Native dolls is littered with visual and textual references to "nature," "culture," "heritage," and "tradition." The personas constructed for Native Barbies lack the economic choice that capitalist ideology presumes, except as limited by tribal tradition. The back of the box for the (childless) 1996 edition of NATIVE AMERICAN BARBIE (#15304) attests,

> All Native Americans believe in *tradition* as a way of life. During our ceremonial events, we have certain rituals to follow and special foods to eat. Each tribe has its own special choices to make about each celebration. Some of us eat only fruits and vegetables, while other tribes eat only what they can catch off the land.

In other words, NATIVE AMERICAN BARBIE consumes nothing from the dominant economy, since her people are self-sufficient hunters or gatherers who are close to nature. By not depicting Native people as equal members of contemporary society—by not using toys to depict Native Americans as stereotypical consumers, as is now the case with White, Black, Asian, or Hispanic ethnicities—Mattel subtly justifies a marketing strategy that basically ignores Native American consumers. But in doing so, it also perpetuates a colonialist ideology. Denial of choice to Native peoples and their obligation to follow cultural norms, rather than acting as free-thinking individual agents, further situates them within a pre-capitalist world, without the agency presumed by the capitalist economy.

Of course, the symbolic exclusion of Native women from capitalism is doubly ironic. It denies the important role Native Americans have played in the world economy for centuries, and it denies the contemporary consumption of almost anything associated with Native America, including Barbie dolls. Native people have been not only the objects of colonial violence and oppression driven by capitalism, but also active agents in world capitalism in their own right for centuries. Like much of popular culture, toy manufacturers endorse images of Natives who are trapped in a folklorized lost world of tradition, historically antecedent and external to capitalism. They deny the capitalist economic realities in which these toys are imbedded: Barbie is the centerpiece of a multi-billion-dollar worldwide toy industry in which Native things sell. Barbie merchandise contributes to society's broader commodification of Native identity. The production, marketing, and consumption of toys such as Barbie helps convert the image of feminized, maternalized, animalized, and economically marginalized Native women into objects of economic value to be bought, sold, and invested.

PART THREE: THE POCAHONTAS MYTH

Where Do Native American Barbie Babies Come From?

The maternal persona of the Native Barbies articulates potent stereotypes about Native subjectivity. In large part, that subjectivity depends on a tacit recollection of a national mythology that envisions Native women as prototypical mothers. Pocahontas serves as the principal figure symbolizing this mythology. The legend of the "Indian Princess" who married an English colonist is still well known today, though people may have forgotten its original purpose: the legitimation of European occupation of Native lands during the colonial period. While modern political economy has rejected miscegenation as a basis for territorial occupation, the belief that miscegenation articulates power nonetheless endures in the image of Natives as mothers. As Mattel relies upon an iconic association of its baby-burdened Barbies with Pocahontas for marketing success, it structures children's fantasies to promote the propagandistic nationalist mythology supported by her legend.

The lingering question of the implicit paternity of Barbie's baby links baby-burdened Native Barbie dolls to Pocahontas symbolism. As mentioned earlier, there is no Native American Ken. In fact, only three types of Kens have ever existed; ethnically unmarked White Kens that have been produced with hundreds of variations since 1961, Black Kens (which were never actually labeled as "Black" or "African American"), and Chicano Kens (the only Kens to have their ethnicity labeled explicitly). Thus, within the Native Barbie's plastic society, her children probably result from miscegenation. This is an important leap given Mattel's general reluctance to show inter-racial personal relations. Television commercials do not show a dark-complected Ken visiting White Barbie in her pink plastic condo or going for a drive with her in the Corvette convertible. Nonetheless, since White Kens handily dominate the never-very-brisk sales of Ken dolls worldwide, toy-owning children who seek a father for Barbie's baby amongst the Barbie characters they own should be more likely to imagine that the father is a White Ken doll.

Yet one cannot forget other compatible dolls that Mattel has sold in recent years, such as foot-high dolls of Captain John Smith, the man whom Disney portrayed as the lover of Pocahontas, despite all of the historical evidence to the contrary. Indeed, the timing of the release of the "Barbie With Papoose," the first of the maternal Barbies to be mass-marketed and retailed, provides a potent rationale for supposing that John Smith was meant to be the father, and not some generic White Ken. The doll went on the market during the merchandising craze sparked by Disney's 1995 animated feature *Pocahontas*. Mattel also manufactured a posable and disproportionately busty Pocahontas doll using Barbie's patented body molds.[7] Thus, Pocahontas' sexualized and anthropometrically unlikely proportions were exactly those of Barbie, though Pocahontas' head mold, her plastic skin tone, and her tattoos were distinctive, as were her imitation Indian accessories. Perhaps to symbolize her symbolic pregnancy as a prelude to baby-nurturing Native Barbies, the Pocahontas doll was even barefoot; her bright, pastel-colored plastic moccasins and matching felt handbags were all sold separately.

Although Disney's portrayal of Smith and Pocahontas as wistful lovers is not true history, Mattel exploited myths put forward by the film to promote the sale of Native dolls. Framing Barbie and baby as a continuation of the Pocahontas myth was a good commercial strategy. Children using AMERICAN INDIAN BARBIE to continue the Pocahontas storyline where Disney left off meant millions of dollars of extra profits for Mattel, without royalties to Disney for the use of trademarks. Barbie's baby is symbolically the child of the mythical Pocahontas figure and John Smith, the man who replaces Pocahontas' historic spouse John Rolfe in popular legend. But the toy child symbolically plays the role that was expected of Pocahontas' true son, Thomas Rolfe. His mother, "Princess" Pocahontas, was the daughter of "King" Powhattan, the werowance who, to Western eyes, lorded over the Chesapeake Confederacy like a European feudal monarch. As a result, Thomas Rolfe could stand for the union of the "royal family" of Virginia with English blood. This blood made him and the lands he supposedly inherited automatically subject to the English crown.

This story only succeeds because of a curious sleight-of-hand on the part of Anglo colonizers, who misread, mistranslated, and purposefully misconstrued the social order of Native Virginians. Powhattan was not a king, and Pocahontas was not his royal heir, either by European or by Chesapeake standards. Though predominantly patriarchal, the Natives of Virginia were matrilineal, as Smith (1969) himself was aware: "their heyres inherite not, but the first heyres of the Sisters, and so successiuely the woemens heires" [*sic*] (p. 189). Furthermore, the story of the transfer of the land by miscegenation requires projection of European-style notions of sovereignty and royal property onto groups outside of those European discourses. Chesapeake Natives probably did not consider land to be a commodity that could be individually owned, sold, and inherited, but rather, an inalienable setting that was communally administered and used. Individuals held only usufruct. This (mis-)translation of "place the terms of which the West has never granted legitimacy" into "place as property" is central to what literary critic Eric Cheyfitz (1991) termed the "Poetics of Imperialism" (p. 58). The vernacular Pocahontas myth disguises the colonial assault by obscuring the ideologies dividing Europeans and Natives.

In the context of the Pocahontas merchandise, Native dolls with babies represent the "Indian Princess" turned "squaw": honored autochthonous royalty turned submissive Native concubine. They are concrete examples of what Green (1975) called the "Pocahontas Perplex," the use of images of Native women to represent the European colonial experience. The mythological Pocahontas is one of the most memorable personas in popular stories of early colonial America. Native Barbie is just one more monument to her. Within the polyvinyl-chloride society Mattel has manufactured, children are meant to imagine that the father of Barbie's baby is no anonymous White Ken, but the mythologized figure of English sea captain and lusting pedophile, John Smith.

The popular story of Pocahontas' love for John Smith that Disney and Mattel remythologized is wholly apocryphal. In his original 1608 "Trve Relation of Virginia," Smith (1969) declared that the real Pocahontas, the daughter of "King" Powhattan, was only "tenne yeares old" when Smith arrived in Virginia a year earlier (p. 206). According to the 1612 testimony colonist William Strachey offers in his *The Historie of Travaile into Virginia Britannia* (cited in Tilton, 1994), she was also married to a Native man named Kocoum by the time the Jamestown colonists abducted her and made her live among the English. Pocahontas married and had a son with English seaman and tobacco promoter John Rolfe, not John Smith. Yet, perhaps most importantly, Smith did not write down the famous event during which Pocahontas reportedly saved him from execution until 16 years after the events supposedly occurred, after "Princess" Pocahontas had already become famous in England and hobnobbed with English royalty, and even after death made her incapable of contesting Smith's yarns. Smith's earliest account, his "Trve Relation," makes no reference to his rescue by Pocahontas. At least one historian has noted that Smith claimed to be rescued by noble maidens at least two other times in his life (Josephy, 1994, p. 199).

The marketing success of maternal Barbies depends on the myth of Pocahontas' love for John Smith, a story that creatively re-imagines colonialism as a process by which Native people willfully submit to colonizers because of irresistible amorous feelings and familial obligations. Rather than expecting parents and children to invent Barbie's life, the industry expects them to recollect the life of Pocahontas, or rather, how American legend and Disney falsely recount her life. Even if the historical details that I have sought to expose might seem obscure for most adults, the dolls' iconic allusions are perfectly clear to children.

Mattel's implicit and asymmetrical advocacy of inter-ethnic unions is not accidental. It is in accord with dominant European attitudes and policies regulating sexual contact with subjugated peoples in colonial contexts around the world. Especially at the start of colonial enterprises, invaders often advocated interracial unions between White males and colonized women as an aid to long-term European settlement. Historian Robert S. Tilton (1994) reported that Captain John Smith of the Virginia Colony had advocated in a letter to Queen Anne that miscegenation would be an effective strategy whereby England could acquire uncontested title to the lands of America (pp. 1–33).

Importantly, the model of consensual submission and miscegenation opened an alternative to the theretofore dominant logic of colonization, the Law of Discovery, an originally papal doctrine which dictated that lands unoccupied by Christians should belong to the first European nation to "discover" and claim those lands. Natives of the area had traded with Europeans for decades prior to Smith's adventurers in Virginia, and even prior to England's failed Roanoke colony. Spain had not only claimed the lands around the Chesapeake, but had made an attempt to found a colony of Jesuit missionaries there in 1571. The missionaries had reportedly been killed by one of their company, known to historians as Don Luis de Velasco, a Native of the Chesapeake who had been captured and enslaved in the Caribbean before traveling to Spain and scheming his return to America under the pretext of converting his brethren. Smith would have known of Spain's prior claims to the Chesapeake, not to mention the story of Don Luis; indeed, having had little time to learn Algonquin, Smith more than likely communicated with the Natives of Virginia in Spanish. Yet he could mention none of this in his accounts of his adventures, for risk of weakening England's claims to the lands and his own economic investments. To solidify English claims, he thus supported an alternative to the religious and legal authority of the Law of Discovery: a model of consensual submission, symbolized and structured by the myth of Pocahontas.

Europeans typically denounced and prohibited such unions once they established colonial control, even though they often continued the practices simultaneously. However, there was little ambiguity when it came to enforcing asymmetrical laws applied to White European women. Colonial policies often forbade unions between White women and Native or colonized men, not so much to restrain the proliferation of mixed-race children and the supposed racial degeneracy, as to defend the racial, sexual, and socioeconomic hierarchies that justified colonialism. Describing colonial Asia, Stoler (1991) has noted that, "hierarchies of privilege and power were written into the condoning of interracial unions, as well as into their condemnation" (p. 86). The point is also valid for the Americas. The contrast between miscegenating Native Barbie and her White alteregos perfectly materializes colonialist ideologies that simultaneously interpolate and constitute race, class, and gender.

While the model for the peaceable merging of peoples and their cultures that Pocahontas' miscegenation with a European colonizer symbolized was officially rejected by colonists at the start of the eighteenth century, its latent ideology survives, preserved in plays and legends about the "Indian Princess" that have been repeated and recomposed since the seventeenth century. The fantasies structured by Disney's Pocahontas and baby-burdened Native American Barbies are only recent iterations of an enduring colonial logic.

PART FOUR: PERVASIVE AND ENDURING IMAGERY

Persistent Papooses and Other Animalizing Traditions

Barbie's baby and her submission to "natural" reproductive urges and sexualized familial occupations make NATIVE AMERICAN BARBIE seem closer to nature than her ethnically unmarked and non-Native namesakes. Of course, Westerners have long seen indigenous groups as part of nature. What is more natural than reproduction? As Yanagisako and Delaney (1995) put it, "sex and reproduction [are] held to be quintessentially natural activities; indeed they are considered our 'animal' behavior" (p. 6). Babies mark the natural feminine gender of their mothers. Now, the social inequalities of Barbie's manufactured society enable us to see how babies also mark ethnicity. Mattel projects the natural career of motherhood only upon the Native women, symbolically linking maternal femininity to racial or ethnic identity, and contrasting extra-domestic professional productivity with traditional domestic reproduction.

Out of nearly 4,000 models produced by Mattel, these five dolls are few; they are important precisely because of their distinctive contradiction of Barbie's standard marketing. With sales totaling more than a billion dollars annually, Barbie is the world's most popular manufactured toy. Yet Mattel's racist depictions exploit a popular colonialist mythology that the wider industry also references. I have focused on Barbie because she is such a well-known doll icon, but countless other toys use similarly racist imagery.

Take for example a line of fashion dolls made by Kid Kore. In 1996, the company produced two series of posable fashion dolls. The first series of dolls for the *Shenandoah Riding Club* consisted of White-complected human dolls, horses, and certain equine accouterments. The dolls came in two sizes: 11.5-inch dolls compatible in size with Barbie doll, and 7.5-inch dolls meant to represent younger siblings. Though no text stated their ethnicity explicitly, the dolls were meant to represent young White women or girls of leisure. The second series, titled *Native American Heartland*, consisted of similarly sized, but dark-complected figures representing Native women and girls. Like their unmarked White counterparts, they were sold with horses. However, the packaging depicted the Native American women in racially folklorized association with those animals, or performing stereotypical activities such as canoeing, and more importantly, child-rearing. The package of a doll sold under the name "Princess Running Deer" contained the figure of a woman wearing colorful "Indian" garb, accompanied by two babies, mounted in backpacks. The text on the back of the box read:

> Princess Running Deer has her hands full with her babies. Riding, clothing, bathing, and entertaining these two takes most of her time. Papooses have a special place in the heart of the Native American tribe. She has lots of extra outfits to wear but may not find the time. She has her hands full with these two cuties.

The statement about papooses' "special place" suggests that babies are something less-than-special for non-Indians—as if children were not important to White people. Still, papooses seem to have an even *more special* place in the toy industry. Numerous dealers, including the nation's largest toy retailer, Toys "R" Us, sold the AMERICAN INDIAN BARBIE of the *American Stories Collection* with a sticker saying "Indian Barbie With Papoose." This was the same doll Caviale (1996) had called "Early American Barbie With Papoose." Responsibility for the offensive ethnic slur should rest with Mattel; as of July 2013, the company continues to describe the baby as a *papoose* even on its "Barbie Collector" website:

> It's Barbie as an American Indian caring for her cousin, Baby Blue Feather. This Collector Edition Barbie wears a tan buckskin-like dress with matching boots. The tiny papoose she carries has a "buckskin" headband and diaper and comes with a matching backpack. Children will love the magical story Barbie tells. From the American Stories Series, this very special Barbie doll comes with her own historical storybook, so she's educational as well as fun.

Dorling Kindersley (Greenwood, 2000) recognized the offensiveness of Mattel's use of the term *papoose* to denote Native children when it printed a photo of AMERICAN INDIAN BARBIE in the picture-guide *Barbie: A Visual Guide to the Ultimate Fashion Doll*. The book used the term *papoose* to denote a Native apparatus for carrying a baby, rather than a Native baby itself, when it labeled Barbie's baby as "baby in papoose (sling)" (p. 94).

American English employs no other term for children of a particular ethnicity so readily. Such terms tend to exoticize and animalize Native Americans. Non-Native women and men have babies, but Native American women ("squaws") and men ("braves" or "bucks") have papooses, just as cows and bulls have calves or mares and stallions have colts. Applied to children of inter-ethnic unions, terms such as "half-breed" only intensify the implicit animalizing.

Such racist innuendoes are old and pervasive. Almost from the moment they first arrived, Europeans argued that Native Americans were natural people, an exotic fauna of the Americas. Today, people persist in tolerating the animalization of Native peoples so much that mass-marketed toys can freely use old racist terms. They are part of a colonialist othering: a dehumanizing ideology that today is incorporated into hegemonic discourses and craftily exploited by Mattel in its presentation of Native Americans. Since Barbie babies are implicitly half-blood or half-breed offspring, their miscegenating mothers thereby qualify them as unique Barbie breeders.

This naturalized association of Native women with motherhood is tied to pervasive metaphoric portrayals of Natives as animals or as beings with a culturally dictated closeness to animals: creatures that synecdochically represent nature itself. Toy stores offer numerous representations of Native peoples with supposedly irresistible social ties to animals. Over and again, toys asymmetrically represent Whites' and Natives' relation with horses.

Naturalizing and Nativizing of Motherhood

What people see as natural is inevitably socially constructed. Moreover, as examinations of power by feminists of color have long revealed, the purportedly separate and natural domains of identity such as race, ethnicity, class, and gender are overlapping and mutually constituting (e.g., Anzaldua, 1987; Moraga & Anzaldua, 1981). The ironies of Native Barbies highlight these generalities about how identity and power operate. Motherhood has come to be a defining marker of gender for women in Western culture, and by disproportionately loading motherhood on Native women, whether as a privilege or burden, Western culture naturalizes motherhood as a defining marker of indigeneity as well. The process diverts attention from the socially constructed power asymmetries between those representing and those represented, between colonizer and colonized, and between producers of popular cultural images and Native peoples reproduced as reproducers.

Playing on ambient cultural beliefs, the toy industry commodifies these stereotypes through products that structure children's fantasies. Yet it can only do so because of the popular persistence of contemporary racial (and racist) ideas about Native women. Even the U.S. government exploited and reinforced a certain racialized exoticism of maternity: since 2000, dollar coins have offered a portrait of Shoshone guide Sacagawea carrying her infant child. Such images depend on the materialization of historical fantasies that sanitize colonialism, such as Mattel's and Disney's versions of the Pocahontas myth. Such distorted visions of Native peoples are reminiscent of what Churchill (1992) described in *Fantasies of the*

Master Race: "Only a completely false creation could be used to explain in 'positive terms' what has actually happened here in centuries past. Only a literal blocking of modern realities can be used to rationalize present circumstances" (p. 241).

Native people are feminized, partially animalized, and used as personifications of an anthropomorphized and feminized Nature. In the European colonial fantasy that Native Barbies symbolize, Native women, wildlife, and personified Nature must be sexually conquered, domesticated, and transformed into things that are productive. Told from the perspective of a prototypically masculine immigrant colonizer, this colonial myth equates the sowing of mixed-race children to the legal occupation of land, "Mother Earth." Using the bodies of Native women to represent the natural landscape of the Americas is a potent colonialist trope. The ideology of "Manifest Destiny" depended on the idea of taming, cultivating, and civilizing an empty but fertile virgin *terra incognita*. Frederick Jackson Turner's famous "Frontier Thesis" even proposed that the West that had shaped American character was a woman, a mother. Annette Kolodny (1975) creatively captured this ideology with the metaphoric title of her study of the American landscape and letters: *The Lay of the Land*. McClintock (1995, pp. 21–74) later used the same phrase to highlight the gendered intersection of power and colonial subjectivity.

Native women remain emblems of a feminized American landscape that is stereotypically wild, archaic, uncivilized, and *awaiting* colonial penetration. The story of Pocahontas retold through baby-burdened Barbies objectifies the ultimate colonization of this "virgin" landscape, with mixed-blood offspring eventually used as a justification for colonial authority.[8] Kolodny (1975) wrote that Pocahontas' 1614 marriage to Englishman John Rolfe "served, in some symbolic sense, as a kind of objective correlative for the possibility of Europeans' actually possessing the charms inherent in the virgin continent" (p. 5). The union only attains such significance when Native women are seen as sexually available, if not promiscuous, in conformity with an androcentric vision of the colonial enterprise. But with the autobiographical tales of men such as Columbus, Cortés, and John Smith dominating histories of early colonial America, the metaphoric feminization of America and its personification as a Native woman are unsurprising.

Conclusions about "Plastic" Identity

All too often, we discover that which we consider to be natural is really man-made. How better to illustrate the point than by doing an ethnographic sketch of a natural woman who is entirely artificial and synthetic; that is, by exploring durable ascribed identities through an ethnography of the most plastic of societies, the world of plastic toys?

Mattel could make greater efforts to specify more explicitly that the children packaged with future Barbie dolls—Native or otherwise—are not Barbie's progeny.

The corporation also could strive for a more even-handed ethnic distribution of infant sidekicks, too. Nonetheless, any action Mattel takes will principally serve to protect the financial value of the Barbie character, rather than reducing discrimination against the (implicitly mixed-race) babies whom it presents as natural cultural accessories of Native women.

Mattel cannot single-handedly undo the images of Native mothers that pervade popular culture, let alone other naturalized stereotypes of Native peoples. Ultimately, *identity* does not mean just *self-identity*, but also what society ascribes to others, including the fantasies commodities structure. Such identities are never as malleable, never as situational, and never as plastic as the identities we ascribe to ourselves. The enduring stereotypes in Native Barbie's plastic society should remind us that imposed identities are not just ad hoc presentist concoctions based on contemporary perceptions; they are also mass-produced formulations that articulate hegemonic histories. Stores do not just sell dolls, but pre-packaged fantasies of Native identity and a racist legend of European colonization. The magic of colonialism is that the toys can impart race/class/gender ideologies almost without words, and almost without notice, within a culture in which colonialist stereotypes persist so pervasively.

ACKNOWLEDGMENTS

I am grateful to anthropologist Dr. Genevieve Bell for offering important insights into (and wisecracks about) the Barbie phenomenon. I also thank friends formerly in Stanford's Department of Anthropology for useful commentary years ago. Yet I owe my biggest debt of thanks to dozens of anonymous security guards in toy stores that prohibit the use of cameras by shoppers, without whose negligence, I would never have been able to peruse, study, and photograph so many toys.

NOTES

1. Maurer's essay "Creolization Redux" (1997) describes the marketing of Caribbean islands as sites for offshore investments, by creating themselves as an important niche with the social pedigree that can insure international economic arrangements.

2. While no longer in production, a photo of this doll, sans packaging, can be viewed by accessing Mattel's official Barbie Collector website.

3. Ironically, this collection was originally called the *International Collection* when it began in 1980, but was renamed *Dolls of the World* in 1984. The original name would have had strange implications for the various Native groups of the United States represented in the series. The earliest of these, ESKIMO BARBIE, came out in 1982.

4. The phrase "Indian Princess" erroneously projects European feudal arrangements upon peoples who lacked them. It serves to convert the Native consort to a European colonizer into a mythical ancestor for the nation: what Philip Young called "The Mother of Us All" (quoted in Green, 1975, p. 699). By being posed as a Native monarch, Barbie becomes an incarnation of the royal "Indian-Grandmother," the typically nameless female ancestor invoked by countless Americans. Dakota author Vine Deloria (1969) has described this as an awkward attempt to use kinship with the colonized to erase their hereditary "guilt for the treatment of the Indian" (pp. 2–4)— what Rayna Green (1975) identified as their personal "Indian Problem" (p. 713). Such weakened claims of Native ancestry or identity rely on a flawed assumption that simple miscegenation inevitably leads to more peaceful co-existence, allegiance, and prosperity: a colonial myth that ignores the context of any such union. Regardless, Barbie-with-baby personifies both the Native consort and the Native ancestor upon which such myths depend.

5. The costumed members of the 1970s disco band the Village People have memorably symbolized this stereotype, with Lakota founding member Felipe Rose dressing in plains Native American garb while other band members played fantasy personas with professions such as construction worker, soldier, cowboy, and cop.

6. Barbie's intriguing "family tree" deserves fuller analysis as an example of a non-traditional family. Over the years, Mattel has exhibited various family trees on its Barbie websites. A family tree that formerly appeared on the 2001 "Barbie Showcase" and the 2005 "Barbie Collector" websites was supposedly based on one that appeared in DK Publishing's *Barbie: A Visual Guide to the Ultimate Fashion Doll* (Greenwood, 2000, pp. 114–119). The book skips all of Barbie's Native kin.

7. Those interested in the unrealistic proportions of the standard Barbie should consult Urla and Swedlund's (1995) "The Anthropometry of Barbie." Though I do not question their conclusions, I believe anthropometric analysis should not be carried out only with naked dolls. Barbie should be clothed because the difficulties of scaling the miniature clothing might partially justify the fashion doll's distorted body proportions. This very issue has actually become a source of contention between the Barbie's makers and artist Nickolay Lamm, the designer of a new line of Lammily fashion dolls, which, when unclothed, reportedly have the same proportions as an average teenage girl (Stampler 2014).

8. Although Pocahontas' homeland was renamed Virginia after the "Virgin Queen," Elizabeth I of England, the name was apropos for a colony imagined to occupy "virgin" territory. The sexualized and feminine personification of the landscape once again conforms to Kolodny's (1975) metaphor.

REFERENCES

Anzaldúa, G. (1987). *Borderlands/ La Frontera: The new mestiza.* San Francisco, CA: Spinsters/Aunt Lute Book Company.

Caviale, K. (1996, January–February). Hot line: Sneak a peak today! Toy Fair preview. *Barbie Bazaar: The Doll Collector's Magazine,* 67–71.

Cheyfitz, E. (1991). *The poetics of Imperialism: Translation and colonization from The Tempest to Tarzan.* New York, NY; Oxford, England: Oxford University Press.

Chin, E. (1999). Ethnically correct dolls: Toying with the race industry. *American Anthropologist, 101*(2), 305–321.

Churchill, W. (1992). *Fantasies of the master race: Literature, cinema, and the colonization of American Indians.* Monroe, ME: Common Courage Press.

Deloria, P. J. (1998). *Playing Indian.* New Haven, CT: Yale University Press.

Deloria, V. (1969). *Custer died for your sins: An Indian manifesto.* New York, NY: Macmillan.

DiDanieli, M. (2004). Should "Going home Barbie" go to more homes? *International Adoption News.* Retrieved from http://internationaladoptionnews.com/archives/article_white_swan_barbie.html

DuCille, A. (1994). Dyes and dolls: Multicultural Barbie and the merchandising of difference. *Differences: A Journal of Feminist Cultural Studies, 6*(1), 46–68.

DuCille, A. (1996). *Skin trade.* Cambridge, MA: Harvard University Press.

Green, R. D. (1975). The Pocahontas perplex: The image of Indian women in American culture. *Massachusetts Review: A Quarterly of Literature the Arts and Public Affairs, 16*(4), 698–714.

Green, R. D. (1988). Playing Indian in America and Europe. *Folklore, 99*(1), 30–55.

Green, R. D. (1992). *Women in American Indian society.* New York, NY and Philadelphia, PA: Chelsea House.

Greenwood, M. (Ed.). (2000). *Barbie: A visual guide to the ultimate fashion doll.* New York, NY: Dorling Kindersley.

Grewal, I. (1999). Traveling Barbie: Indian transnationality and new consumer subjects. *Positions: East Asia Cultures Critique, 7*(3), 799–826.

Handler, R. (with Shannon, J.). (1994). *Dream doll: The Ruth Handler story.* Stamford, CT: Longmeadow.

Hirschfelder, A. B. (Ed.). (1982). *American Indian stereotypes in the world of children: A reader and bibliography.* Metuchen, NJ: Scarecrow.

Josephy, A. M. (1994). *500 nations: An illustrated history of North American Indians.* New York, NY: Knopf.

Kolodny, A. (1975). *The lay of the land: Metaphor as experience and history in American life and letters.* Chapel Hill, NC: University of North Carolina Press.

Lord, M. G. (1994). *Forever Barbie: The unauthorized biography of a real doll.* New York, NY: Morrow.

Maurer, B. (1997). Creolization redux: The plural society thesis and offshore financial services in the British Caribbean. *New West Indian Guide/Nieuwe West-Indische Gids, 3–4*(71), 249–264.

McClintock, A. (1995). *Imperial leather: Race, gender and sexuality in the Colonial contest.* New York, NY: Routledge.

Moraga, C., & Anzaldua, G. (Eds.). (1981). *This bridge called my back: Writings by radical women of color.* Watertown, MA: Persephone Press.

Rand, E. (1995). *Barbie's queer accessories.* Durham, NC: Duke University Press.

Smith, J. (1969). A Trve Relation of such occurrences and accidents of noate as hath hapned in Virginia since the first planting of that Colony, which is now resident in the South part there of, till the last returne from thence. In P. L. Barbour (Ed.), *The Jamestown voyages under the First Charter, 1606–1609.* Cambridge, England: Cambridge University Press, 165–208.

Smithen, K. (1995). *Baby Blue Feather.* Sumatera Utara, Indonesia: Mattel and El Segundo.

Stampler, Laura (2014, March 5). The New Barbie: Meet the Doll with an Average Woman's Proportions. *Time.com* retrieved from http://time.com/12786/the-new-barbie-meet-the-doll-with-an-average-womans-proportions/

Stoler, A. L. (1991). Carnal knowledge and Imperial power: Gender, race, and morality in colonial Asia. In M. di Leonardo (Ed.), *Gender at the crossroads of knowledge* (pp. 51–101). Berkeley, CA: University of California Press.

Tilton, R. S. (1994). *Pocahontas: The evolution of an American narrative*. New York, NY: Cambridge University Press.

Urla, J., & Swedlund, A. C. (1995). The anthropometry of Barbie: Unsettling ideals of the feminine body in popular culture. In J. Terry & J. Urla (Eds.), *Deviant bodies: Critical perspectives on difference in science and popular culture* (pp. 277–313). Bloomington & Indianapolis, IN: Indiana University Press.

Yanagisako, S., & Delaney, C. (1995). Naturalizing power. In S Yanagisako & C. Delaney (Eds.), *Naturalizing power: Essays in feminist cultural analysis* (pp. 1–22). New York, NY: Routledge.

Zuckoff, M. (1992, June 28). Reaching out to minority consumers. *The Boston Sunday Globe*, pp. 73, 77.

CHAPTER THIRTEEN

Canadian "Maplelea" Girl Dolls: The Commodification OF Difference

AMANDA MURPHYAO AND ANNE TRÉPANIER

One summer Taryn, Brianne, Alexi, and Jenna happened to meet…[and] pledged to remain friends forever. They even chose a name for themselves—the Maplelea Girls! Then, Léonie from Quebec City joined the group, and now Saila from Iqaluit is the newest Maplelea Girl!…Taryn, Brianne, Alexi, Léonie, Jenna and Saila are all very different—they like different hobbies, sports, school subjects, foods, colours and even have a different personal fashion style! However, there are some things that they have in common—they are all bright, caring, energetic Canadian Girls who think Canada is one terrific country. ("Meet the Maplelea Girls," n.d.)

In 2003, Avonlea Traditions, Inc. launched the Maplelea Girls, a collection of four "Canadian Dolls for Canadian Girls!". The dolls represent a range of geographically based cultural communities in Canada: Taryn Brady from Alberta, Brianne Kovac from Manitoba, Jenna McAllister from Nova Scotia, and Alexi Neele from Ontario.[1] Like the more widely known American Girl dolls, Maplelea Girls are 18-inch (46-centimeter) dolls that come with storybook journals, expensive accessories, detailed doll outfits, matching outfits for their real-girl-sized owners, and a pedagogical purpose marketed through direct-order catalogues to girls between the ages of 6 and 12, as well as to their relatives. The original four dolls have since been joined by two other Maplelea Girls with backstories, Léonie Bélanger-Leblanc from the province of Québec and Saila Qilavvaq from the territory of Nunavut, as well as 12 unnamed Maplelea Friends that are similar to the choose-your-own-backstory American Girls of Today.

A CANADIAN BY ANY OTHER NAME

We suggest that American Girl dolls and Maplelea Girls are pedagogical tools for addressing the uncertainties of national identity and belonging in the settler-invader colonies of the United States and Canada.[2] Both doll collections were developed by businesswomen interested in educating young girls about their history and heritage through cross-marketed dolls, books, and products. The pro-social intentions behind Maplelea Girls are comparable to American Girl creator Pleasant Rowland's intentions to teach girls about American (U.S.) history with dolls that offer a modestly dressed alternative to Barbie (Inness, 1998). Likewise, Maplelea Girls creator and Avonlea company president Kathryn Gallagher Morton (n.d.) created the dolls in response to "'diva' type dolls… that emphasize body image, dating, glamour and sophistication." Despite similar impetus behind their creation, the Maplelea Girls offer an implied retort to American Girl dolls, emphasizing pride in Canada as "a distinctively *Canadian* [emphasis added] play experience featuring a collection of premium play dolls that celebrate *our* [emphasis added] country's spirit and identity" ("The Maplelea System," n.d.). Furthering this project of national differentiation, the corporate statement found on the Maplelea Girls website reads: "Our mission is to make a difference in the lives of *Canadian* [emphasis added] girls by providing dolls and activity products that promote creative play, healthy active lifestyles, and a knowledge and pride of the country we live in" ("Mission Statement," n.d.). Through the stories of the Maplelea Girls and their products, such as camping equipment and horses, the dolls emphasize a healthy lifestyle, the leisurely pursuit of happiness, a connection to the land, and pride in being Canadian.

One doll owner noted that Maplelea Girls "are basically the Canadian version of American Girl" (SummerStudiosAG, 2012). Others see them as "this country's answer to Mattel's American Girl" (Kwan, 2012). Making comparisons between cultural products in Canada and the United States is a longstanding tradition in Canadian society and scholarship.[3] Differentiation and seduction are well known processes of identity formation (Meyer, 2008). Canadian dolls are in this sense a very compelling and desirable version of the American Girl because of the superficial difference that permits seduction. Stuart Hall explained: "You know that you are what everybody else on the globe is not. Identity is always, in that sense, a structured representation that achieves its positive only through the narrow eye of the negative" (Hall, 1997, p. 174). Drawing on this oppositional framework of identity, Maplelea Girls function as both unique, expensive playthings and as tools of specifically Canadian sense of belonging.

Maplelea Girls are posited as a platform for differentiated identification from the American Girl collection. For example, "[e]ach doll is accompanied by a 64-page *keepsake* [emphasis added] journal.…This journal imparts *subtle* [emphasis added] factual information about Canada's geography, heritage and culture. All content references are authentic, and spelling is *Canadian*" [emphasis added] ("The Maplelea System," n.d.). Each adjective offers a telling, if unstated contrast: the "keepsake journal" markets the dolls as nostalgic objects for girls to pass on to their future citizen-daughters, as opposed to less expensive, and perhaps disposable, dolls, such as the quintessential American "diva" type Barbie doll; the patriotically inclined educational content is "subtle," in opposition to the supposedly more obvious brand of American patriotism; and the Canadian spelling (such as "neighbour") only needs to be stated as distinct from American spelling ("neighbor"). While the emphasis on the difference between Canadian Maplelea Girls and American Girl dolls may seem largely perfunctory, as the similarly proportioned dolls can share clothing and accessories as well as owners, the national distinction is one of the implied motives behind the Maplelea product line.

Efforts at differentiation aside, the collections are almost identically priced; as of 2013, American Girl dolls start at $110 USD and Maplelea Girls start at $99.99 CAD (plus $9 for shipping). Thus, access to the educationally inspired alternatives to Barbie dolls—which retail starting at $11 USD—is an expensive option for consumers. Despite the sizeable cost of ownership, both the Canadian and American doll-based product lines are a commercial success, with 50,000 Maplelea Girls sold between 2003 and 2012 (Kwan, 2012) and 21 million American Girl dolls sold between 1986 and 2013 ("Fast Facts," n.d.). The two nationally based initiatives offer a fruitful point of entry for a discussion of cultivating national identity in the pre-teen girls targeted by the doll products.

American Girl dolls have been celebrated by Suzanne Rust (2004) as a positive "multicultural phenomenon" that aims to "instill values" through fun (p. 76). However, photographer Ilona Szwarc argued that

> [e]ach doll can be customized to look exactly like its owner, yet all of them really look the same. American Girl dolls offer an illusion of choice and therefore an illusion of individuality. Yet they play a crucial role for girls at the time when they are forming their identities. (Zavos, 2012)

This "illusion of choice" applies equally to the Maplelea Girls; with the key exception of the Inuit-themed doll, Saila, all of the Maplelea dolls share a face template modeled from the face of a girl from Aurora, Ontario.[4] Furthermore, if a Maplelea Girl doll becomes damaged, sending the doll to the "Maplelea Spa" will result in the delivery of an identical replacement doll for half the price of the original doll, with less discerning young doll owners none the wiser (Avonlea Traditions, 2012, p. 68). The fact that the replacement doll is identical to the original doll mirrors the superficial, skin-deep difference of the six Maplelea Girls and the 12 unnamed Maplelea Friends dolls launched in 2012. Of the 12 new dolls, six have "light skin" with a variety of hairstyles and eye colors. Of the remaining six, three have "medium-light skin," one "medium skin," one "medium-dark skin," and one "dark skin," all with brown eyes (p. 4). According to Anne duCille (1996)

> [t]he toy industry is only one of many venues where multiculturalism, posed as an answer to critical questions about inclusion, diversity, and equality, has collapsed into an additive campaign that augments but does not necessarily alter the Eurocentric *status quo.* (p. 337)

The Maplelea Girls and Maplelea Friends redeploy Canadian diversity and multiculturalism in the context of merchandise that repackages difference for the consumption of the young female market.

The reassuring package of multiculturalism and deftly marketed diversity of American Girl dolls and their attendant books and curriculum products has been critiqued at length by academics (Inness, 1998, Susina, 1999, Hade, 1999, Acosta-Alzuru & Kreshel, 2002, Marshall, 2009, Orr, 2009). While these critiques inform our work, our interest lies in the Canadian manifestation of national-identity-based doll merchandising. The uniqueness of Canadian childhood is suggested by Jacqueline Reid-Walsh and Claudia Mitchell (2009) in their call for "the recognition of the *unique* features of *Canadian* [emphasis added] childhoods" (p. 125). This scholarly emphasis on a shared experience of belonging and enacting unity and regional diversity through doll play is promoted through the Maplelea Girls collection. Indeed, Gallagher Morton (2012) described each "Maplelea Girl [as] a *unique* [emphasis added] individual" exemplifying the individuation of the dolls within the unified collection, echoing the primacy of nation-ness over nationhood (Brubaker, 1996).

In the framework of consumer culture, several Maplelea Girl doll items, available exclusively by mail order from the Canadian company, are described in a way that accentuates the Canadian-ness of the products, such as the Saila doll's qamutiik (sled) "Made of Canadian hemlock" (Avonlea Traditions, 2012, p. 52). Furthermore, the cover of the November 2012 catalogue features two dolls in maple-leaf bedecked winter wear seated on an authentic "Made in Canada" doll-sized toboggan "Made of Canadian hardwood" (p. 7). The scene was billed as a "very proud Canadian look" in a December 2012 post on the Maplelea Girls Facebook page. What, exactly, makes the dolls so *unique* and their owners so *Canadian*?

IDENTITY FORMATION THROUGH DOLL-PLAY

Alongside the "Made in Canada" toboggan, the cover of the November 2012 *Maplelea Girls Catalogue* has the word "Canadian" on it three times. Borrowing from Canada's red and white maple-leaf flag, the cover surely fulfills some Canadian Content quota, with 15 maple leaves incorporated into three logos and an additional three-and-a-half maple leaves visible on the featured red-and-white doll clothing. On the second page of the catalogue, which features a letter to parents and girls, the words "Canadian" or "Canadians" appear 12 times, "Canada" appears twice, and "Canadiana" appears once. Mentions of Canada are most prominent on the eighth page of the catalogue, where the items featured under the heading "Proud to Be Canadian" include a small Canadian flag and "Canada Outfit for Dolls" as well as a "Canada Shirt for Girls," a red-and-white maple-leaf lined "Strong and Free" doll hoodie (referencing a line from the Canadian national anthem), red-and-white maple-leaf sneakers, and a photograph of two girls posed with their dolls and three Canadian flags on the patriotic holiday Canada Day (July 1), for a total of more than 50 maple leaves on one page.

With this preponderance of maple in mind, the Maplelea Girls can be read as a celebration of the unitary Canadian state, represented by the national flag, even though the sugar maple tree can be found only in parts of Canada, and despite the fact that the Canada Day national holiday is not widely celebrated in Québec. Québec's national holiday, Saint-Jean-Baptiste Day, is celebrated on June 24, which is also the birthday of the Léonie doll, according to her journal ("The Journal...," 2008, p. 62). The overt celebration of Canada Day and the maple-leaf attire worn by the dolls and their owners, in contrast to the casual mention of Léonie's birthday as "La Fête nationale du Québec," silences difficult differences in the Canadian experience, a practice that echoes the implementation of multiculturalism, according to critics of the policy (such as Fernand Dumont, 1971, and Neil Bissoondath, 1995). The Canadian policy of multiculturalism reinscribes the normativity of White-Anglo-Canadian identity as central to the narrative of the nation-state. While tallying maple leaves may seem pedantic, the mindless repetition of a national symbol serves as an incessant reminder of the Canadian-ness of the products and consumers.[5] As Michael Billig (1995) explained, "all these unwaved flags... are providing banal reminders of nationhood: they are 'flagging' it unflaggingly" (p. 41). The remainder of the catalogue showcases the accessories available to accompany each unique Canadian Maplelea Girl doll, but the message is abundantly, redundantly clear on the front page of the product website: Maplelea is "distinctly Canadian."

Because of the emphasis on Canadian uniqueness, as well as the role of the dolls as increasingly popular objects of patriotic pedagogy, Maplelea Girls are important to consider in the context of Canadian girlhood. As duCille (1996) argued:

> More than simple instruments of pleasure and amusement, toys and games play crucial roles in helping children to determine what is valuable in and around them. As elements of the rites and rituals of childhood, dolls... assist children in the process of becoming, in the task of defining themselves in relation to the world around them. (p. 17)

As such, we are interested in how Maplelea Girls work to define "Canadian" and what Maplelea Girls help Canadian girls to become through the practices and politics of play.

The pedagogical value of the Maplelea Girls for forming Canada identities is a key marketing point. In a letter to parents on the Maplelea website, Gallagher Morton (n.d.) wrote:

> Maplelea Girls were created to be positive role models for our daughters... Through the journal that accompanies the doll, your daughter will learn not only about her Maplelea Girl, but also about our country's geography and heritage. Canada is a wonderful country and knowing more about it will help our daughters become positive, caring citizens.

The mention of "our daughters" twice and "your daughter" once is telling— the Maplelea Girl doll line asserts responsibility for communal education of "our daughters" and markets knowledge about "our country" to future citizens. The doll serves as a role model in terms of teaching Canadian identity and citizenship. The continuing growth of the Maplelea Girls product line, along with glowing parent testimonials, indicate that the "Canadian Girl-Dolls" for "Canadian Doll-Girls" are fulfilling a perceived lack in existing identity-based play and education.

How do parents and other Canadian consumers—who pride themselves on being more subtle in their patriotism than "obnoxious Americans"—respond to the nationalism inherent in the Maplelea product line? According to testimonials on the Maplelea website, parents from across Canada love the Canadian dolls, as these excerpts attest: "Bless you folks for making these dolls available to the Canadian market"; "I applaud the values of your company, making a Canadian doll for Canadian girls"; "My wife and I are very pleased with this real doll and her Canadian identity."[6] Bloggers, many of whom received free dolls to review, were similarly enamored with Maplelea: "These all-Canadian 18" vinyl dolls are simply awesome... You really can't get more Canadian then [sic] the Maplelea Girls."[7] "As a mom, I'm impressed with Maplelea Girls. Not only do they provide a high quality toy for Bridget to play with, but they also teach her about being Canadian in a fun way."[8] "I'm thrilled that there's [sic] dolls out there specifically for Canadian girls."[9] Such clichéd commentary about the dolls is useful to study precisely because of its repetitive "rhetorical dullness," which reinforces what Billig (1995) termed non-violent, taken-for-granted, insidious "banal nationalism" (p. 93). The phrases "Canadian market," "Canadian girls," "Canadian identity," "all-Canadian," "more Canadian," and "being Canadian" apply "Canadian" as an adjective endowed with unspecified, taken-for-granted meaning(s).

However, other commentators—including a blogger, a journalist, and doll researchers—challenge such assumptions about dolls and identity: "Exactly what makes a young girl growing up in Canada, Canadian?"[10] "Looking at the six Maplelea Girls in a lineup...it's clear that some stereotypes are at play. But as a whole, do they represent what it means to be Canadian? Can you define a national identity in a 46-centimetre plastic doll?"[11] "What is a Canadian doll?"[12] Reid-Walsh and Mitchell (2009) attempted to define the parameters for the Canadian-ness of a doll by considering national boundaries, the doll's place of manufacture, the nationality of the character represented by the doll, or the nationality of the doll owner. They ultimately concluded that the definition of "Canadian" is a flexible construct. This flexibility is celebrated by Canadian politicians, such as former Prime Minister Pierre Elliott Trudeau, who announced the federal policy of multiculturalism in 1971, stating: "we believe that cultural pluralism is the very essence of Canadian identity" (Trudeau, 1971). The cultural pluralism modeled by the variations in Maplelea Girls, then, embodies the essence of Canadian identity.

CANADIAN DOLLS TEACH CANADIAN GIRLS HOW TO BE CANADIAN

For those engaged in doll play before the availability of six Maplelea Girls, or for those who purchase one of the 12 unnamed dolls from the Maplelea Friends collection, naming their doll can be one of the most symbolic and important rituals for children to begin organizing and categorizing the world around them (Markman, 1989). Because the Maplelea Girls come prepackaged with a name and backstory, doll play is subverted. The adaptation and adoption process of doll ownership is important. Activities such as naming, bathing, and dressing the doll, sometimes with one's own old baby clothes, brushing the doll's hair or cutting it, taking her to the park, explaining how the family works, how big and scary the world is and how Québec is different from Canada, and introducing her to friends, positions the doll owner as the mother or role model in the world of play. The doll might not speak English unless forced to do so, meaning that the child would help her doll adapt to the new playground reality she faced. The doll is a plaything, but also a psychosocial instrument mastered by its owner. As a projection of the child's fears and desires, the doll is a medium that adults can use to learn more about the child.

The Canadian Maplelea Girls, like their historically based American Girl doll counterparts, pre-exist the contact with the child. Because the doll's journal is already half full of her own back story, the remaining fill-in-the-blank pages limit and guide the child's development process of asking questions about the world around her. Unlike adopted (if pre-named) Cabbage Patch kids that were vulnerable and included into the child's family, the owner of one of the Maplelea Girls gets a new friend that reflects what an average Canadian girl experiences in real life. According to the Canadian Museum of Civilization (CMC) (2000–2003) exhibit "Timeless Treasures: The Story of Dolls in Canada," "A doll is much more than a miniature three-dimensional representation of a person. It is something common to every region, culture and time period, and the roles it can play are limited only by the imagination." With Maplelea Girls, imaginative play is subverted to make learning about the "other" more important than learning about oneself. With their pre-existing qualities, tastes, and a complete wardrobe, Maplelea Girls have a pre-written story, a pre-assembled life, and a line of maple-leaf products available for doll and girl to wear while engaging in ostensibly Canadian activities together, such as dog-sledding (Avonlea Traditions, 2012, p. 52).

The repetition of maple leaves and Canadian activities on each page of the catalogue deliberately reinforces the notion of Canada as homeland for the dolls and their owners. As Billig (1995) argued:

> If the homeland is being rhetorically represented, then, as such, it is literally being presented again (or re-presented). The familiar patterns of the patriotic flag are being waved. Flagging, in this respect, is always a reminding, a re-presenting and, thus, a constricting of the imagination. (p. 103)

Even though the doll owner can expand the story by adding more pages to the doll's diary, the identity of the doll as Canadian is fixed. Equally important in defining the relationship of the child with her Pygmalion doll is the fact that each doll comes with an established relationship with the other Maplelea Girls. The doll owner is an afterthought to this pre-existing relationship, because "the Maplelea Girls are always sharing their adventures with each other, and with you" ("Meet the Maplelea Girls," n.d.). When playing with the Canadian Maplelea Girls, the child is put in the position of integrating with her doll's life and circle of friends. The child is assumed to be malleable and ready to be shaped into a citizen, unlike the hard plastic-faced doll.

Even with the purchase of one of the 12 unnamed Maplelea Friends, which allow girls to "create her story!" or "tell your own unique story!" in the fill-in-the-blank journal, the doll comes with maple-leaf bedecked shoes and a maple-leaf adorned shirt. Furthermore, the first few journal pages offer a map of "My Canada" above an image of Canadian Parliament, thereby re-presenting Canada and constricting the imaginative framework of play (Avonlea Traditions, 2012, p. 5). The doll owner can choose a name for the doll, but only within the framework of the doll's Canadian identity, which is constantly re-inscribed through the available clothing and journal pages. Children can dress in over-sized doll clothes to match the dolls and, through the doll's journal, become more knowledgeable Canadian citizens. The relationship prioritizes the doll as a reflection of Canada and, as celebratory customer testimonials attest, as an inspiration to become a better Canadian.

HOW THE DOLLS ARE CANADIAN

According to Donna Patrick (2010), "What is perhaps most interesting in Canada is how State processes have intervened to promote and protect different group interests, primarily by providing official language status to French in Québec and to both French and English in New Brunswick, and at the federal level through a policy of official multiculturalism" (pp. 286–301). Despite the use of more than 50 Indigenous languages and many immigrant languages in the country, the *Official Languages Act* (1969) and the *Multiculturalism Act* (1988) reframed Canada as a tolerant mosaic of cultural differences united by two official languages, French and English.

Mirroring the principles of bilingualism and multiculturalism enshrined in Canadian law, the Maplelea catalogue is available in both official languages, and the Maplelea Girls represent Canadian diversity. Indeed, the Maplelea website cites Statistics Canada as justification for selecting the heritage of the four original dolls and notes that Maplelea "plan[s]…to introduce a new Maplelea Girl character every few years… to represent more of Canada's diversity" ("Meet the Maplelea Girls," n.d.). The current selection of dolls represents some of this historical ethnic diversity:

> Léonie describes herself as having "lots of French blood, but also a little Native and some Irish." ….For Brianne who lives on a farm in Sandy Lake, Manitoba, it was very likely that she would have a Ukrainian heritage, so that's what we gave her. For Jenna who lives in Lunenburg, Nova Scotia, we gave her Scottish and German heritage, which is common in that area of Canada. For Taryn, from Banff, Alberta, we gave her Caucasian features but left out any mention of her cultural or religious background…. And for Alexi, who lives in [the Cabbagetown neighborhood of] Toronto where 42% of the population considers itself to be part of a visible minority, darker skin, hair and eye colour seemed the right thing to do. Thus, there are two dolls for which ethnic and cultural backgrounds are left open to a girl's imagination. (Maplelea FAQs, 2012a)

The agency ascribed to each doll's heritage is particularly interesting. While Léonie "describes herself" as any fiercely independent girl from Québec City would, Brianne and Jenna are given their immigrant heritage, and the ethnicity of Taryn and Alexi "are left open to a girl's imagination." This speaks to the "illusion of choice" offered by the dolls, which share the same face (albeit with slightly altered coloring) and outfits, offering superficial differences of the food, fun, and frolic variety that are the most palatable (and easily consumed) aspects of multiculturalism (Mackey, 2002).

Many Canadians celebrate the multicultural mosaic as an alternative to the melting pot metaphor more common in the United States. Multiculturalism has informed the Canadian identity since Trudeau's announcement of the Multiculturalism Policy in the Canadian House of Commons in 1971:

> No citizen or group of citizens is other than Canadian... The policy I am announcing today accepts the contention of the other cultural communities that they, too, are essential elements in Canada and deserve government assistance in order to contribute to regional and national life in ways that derive from their heritage yet are distinctively Canadian. (Trudeau, 1971)

Parroting Trudeau's phrase "distinctively Canadian," the Maplelea Girls product line highlights the importance of sharing cultural heritage and increasing awareness of cultural diversity, mimicking tenants of the Canadian imagination of self.

As Kieran Keohane (1997) wrote in *Symptoms of Canada: An Essay on Canadian Identity*, the estrangement process is the process by which integration is permitted. The rhetoric of seduction can only operate when the Otherness of the other is well established, then the union can happen—or, seen through a different lens, the predator can act and assimilation can happen (Trépanier, 2001):

> The emigrant to Canada risks estrangement from the shared life of the parent society, and the same immigrant risks misrecognition and estrangement in the new collective... By risking estranging themselves in the communities of which they are secure members, by showing their desirability for Others outside of that community, they increase their desirability to and their recognition by both their families and one another. They play for the desire of multiple Others by playing them off against one another. (Keohane, 1997, p. 90)

If multiculturalism gave an identity to the Canadian peoples as part of a mosaic, differentiated from the praxis of the melting pot of integration in the United States, the Conservative government in place in Canada since 2006 tends to redirect the country's identity towards a more stable, historically rooted narrative. After Québec lost its last referendum on sovereignty in 1995, and after Nunavut was created in 1999, Canadians in general were more welcoming to internal historical diversity, even accepting the notion of nations within the nation. The recent addition of Léonie and Saila in the Maplelea Girls collection reflects a changing paradigm in Canadian imaginary of self, accommodating the historical others as well as preserving the multicultural others.

SAMPLING CANADIAN GEOGRAPHY

When considering the Canadian Maplelea Girls, one enters into a storytelling environment that is candid about Canada's diversity and sense of regions. Canada is reframed and remapped as the representations of its diversity are named Brianne,

Alexi, Taryn, Jenna, Léonie, and Saila. Representing rural, urban, western, eastern, French-speaking, and northern parts of Canada, the dolls showcase Canada's diverse landscapes and senses of place. This template matches the official projection of Canada as a patchwork of landscapes and of peoples. The dolls duplicate the representation of Canadian space currently displayed in the Canada Hall at the Canadian Museum of Civilization, where visitors find themselves immersed in an environment portraying places such as the fisheries of the Maritimes, the classical look of Québec City, and the diverse commercial venues of Toronto.

The dolls' interests and attire reflect their regional identity. Taryn, the doll from Banff, is an environmentalist with hiking boots (Avonlea Traditions, 2012, p. 17). Léonie from Québec City has a Pioneer Québécoise costume, which is featured as both a Halloween costume and a heritage outfit (p. 25). Jenna, the red-haired doll from the Atlantic provinces (not entirely dissimilar from the famous Anne of Green Gables), wears a bucket (or fishing) hat, reflecting the stereotype of the area's fishing culture (p. 37). Alexi's fashionable denim, metro, and urban outfits reflect her multiethnic metropolitan home, Toronto (pp. 44–45). Saila's amauti (parka) and hat are made in Nunavut (p. 53). Brianne, from a farm in Manitoba, has a horse and a Stetson hat to reflect her rural western identity (p. 58).

According to the Maplelea catalogue (Avonlea Traditions, 2012) the addition of Léonie and Saila was motivated by popular demand:

> We... asked the public who the next Maplelea Girl should be... As we sorted through the submissions, we found that two strong themes emerged—you wanted a Maplelea Girl who spoke French as a first language, and a Maplelea Girl from up north. In 2008 we were delighted to present Léonie from Quebec City, and in 2011 we introduced Saila from Nunavut. (p. 38)

Although Québec and Nunavut have both been recognized as distinct nations within the Canadian state, their approachable exoticism, enshrined in the Maplelea Girls, make them likeable Canadian role models. The following case studies unpack these two recent additions to the Maplelea Girls collection to explain how accommodation and diversity function through the politics of play.

CASE STUDY: LÉONIE

> "Where in Canada should the next Maplelea Girl call home?" With a country as vast as Canada, the suggestions were understandably diverse and far-ranging. But after sorting through the mountain of suggestions.... [m]any girls, from all corners of Canada, were asking for a Maplelea Girl from Quebec. ("What do Canadian Girls Want?" 2009)

The requested doll from Québec City, named Léonie Bélanger-Leblanc, has the stereotypical attributes of a Québec girl, starting with an identifiable French first name (note the accent on the e) and a historical national costume she wears at the sugar shack, which she visits in the spring to play music and have fun.[13] This case study will progress from a historical survey to an explanation of the Québec doll as an exotic other within the Canadian multicultural framework, accompanied by a discussion of the current integration policy of Québec, known as interculturalism.[14]

Launched in 2008, the doll depicts the new Québec as seen by the ROC (Rest of Canada). Québec is no longer considered the "separatist zone" but rather the "exotic within," the place where difference is enchanting, historical, touristic, and accessible. The doll's attributes, qualities, name, and hobbies show a fairly good understanding of this renewed, approachable Québec identity. The catalogue does not insist on Québec's secularism; Léonie celebrates Christmas and has a splendid white First Communion dress in her wardrobe. In reality, few contemporary Québec girls receive the Catholic sacrament of First Communion, but the tradition may matter for girls who are learning French in immersion programs in other places in Canada. In Ontario, where many schools are still denominational, French immersion education is often paired with Catholic education.[15] In contrast, the Québec school system has been secular for more than 10 years.[16]

Léonie, which is not biblically inspired, is a name that reflects Québec's accepted secularism. According to the doll's journal (2008, p. 62), it is a "very, very old family name" emphasizing Québec's role as a historical part of Canada. Québec's historical difference, derived from a history closely tied to the aesthetic old stones of Quebec City, is emphasized by the catalogue, which tells readers that Québec City "is now over 400 years old!" (underlined in original, 2012, p. 25). Québec City is Québec's provincial "national capital" and, therefore, is seen as a *mise en abîme* of the province's aims, tastes, and landmarks, providing a stereotypically perfect miniature version of what Québec is, just as Russian nesting dolls contain smaller and smaller copies of themselves.

The doll's hyphenated last name, Bélanger-Leblanc, reflects the practices of Québec, where brides have not adopted their husband's last names since 1983.[17] Most of the children born in Québec after this date use the family names of both parents. The choice for the Québec doll's family names implies that all Quebecois are of French descent. This reflects a statistic that is largely true for Québec City and rural areas, but not for Montreal, where 20% of the population was born outside of Canada.[18] Bélanger is in fact the 13th most common surname in Québec, with Bélanger descendants stemming from two French males who settled at the time Québec City was first built out of stone (François in 1634 and Nicolas in 1655).[19] Leblanc is a typical Acadian name that dates back to 1640 in North America (Tremblay, 2004).

However, there is more than a hyphen separating the history of these early French settlers. Bélanger had to live through the sieges of Québec, France's abandonment and the definitive passage of power to the British in 1760, while the Leblanc were deported in 1755 in the Great Upheaval that would be the foundational wound of the Acadian narrative of the Acadian difference.[20] The connection between Québec and Acadia is a wishful projection of a shared francophone identity. Acadian heritage follows a narrative of distinction from Québec for historical reasons but also because of the nationalist movement in Québec that territorialized the identity to transform the state as a definer of the nation since 1960. The Léonie doll is playing the role of a Canadian bilingual francophone from Québec City, one of the most homogenous cities in Canada, where the English language ability is low and where learning English is not especially encouraged due to French language laws that mandate French language instruction through high school.

Québec's accessible exoticism is exemplified by the English-language version of the catalogue page introducing Léonie, which opens with "Bonjour!" and closes with "À plus tard" ("until later"), simple French phrases on an otherwise English page (Avonlea Traditions, 2012, p. 25). Likewise, the doll's English-language journal is interspersed with accessible French words like "Maman" (2008, p. 62). In the journal, some of the doll's listed "favourites" include: the snowy owl, Québec's avian emblem; the fleur-de-lys, the royal French symbol found on the Québec flag; and hockey. In addition to a hockey uniform, a snowboarding outfit is available for the doll. Such winter activities are stereotypically central to Québec. Québec City's Mont Sainte-Anne and Montreal's Mont Tremblant are touristic venues for many Canadians in search of a "sport and culture" getaway. To encourage family ties and an active childhood, the catalogue describes Léonie's frequent trips to the Laurentian Mountains and to visit her cousins.

Since Québec City lost its Nordiques hockey team to Colorado the year of the last referendum on Sovereignty in 1995, support for the Montreal Canadiens team is very present, especially in opposition to the Toronto Maple Leafs team. Illustrations from Roch Carrier's famous story, *Le Chandail de hockey* (*The Hockey Sweater*), were watermarked on the 5 dollar bill until Spring 2014. This exemplifies Québec's passion for hockey and for identifying their political strife with the game and its heroes, such as Maurice Richard, who could stand against his big English bosses and score goals to prove to every French Canadian that the true Canadiens could win the Stanley Cup. Despite its strong oppositional content—with the Montreal Canadiens representing Québec political aspirations and the Maple Leafs the rich Anglo-Saxon domination—the story can now be told as a make-me-smile story of a hockey lover, because hockey has been the official Canadian national sport since...1994! Just like the political history of Québec and Canada is being pacified with the creation of this dolls series, the hockey history is used as a peacemaking tool in this particular case.

Culturally, Québec is distinct from the rest of Canada because of the French language expression in art, but also because of its "European style." Léonie's extremely developed sense of fashion tells a tale of sophistication, as her talent in both guitar and flute call for simplicity and history. Unlike a piano, those instruments can travel with the girl and are well suited to sugar shack parties or folksy bonfires. The guitar and flute are prevalent in Québec's traditional and popular music, which has historically been heavily influenced by Irish music. Appropriately, Léonie has "some Irish" heritage to accompany her musical interests. The guitar, especially, leaves room for a singer to develop. This echoes Québec's summer festival and rich chansonnier music culture expressed in "the largest, city-wide, outdoor music festival in North America" (Avonlea Traditions, 2012, p. 27), and Léonie has a special outfit to attend. Despite the many differences attributed to her city of "birth" that Léonie's style of life incarnates, the term Canada is always preferred to Québec in the catalogue's wording.

Since the last referendum on Sovereignty in 1995, the most feared country-breaking event in the young History of Canada, the Canadian House of Commons has declared Québec a nation within the nation (2006). Québec has been, for a long time, associated with a plethora of rebellious ways of celebrating its distinct identity. In the past decade, this difference has become a Canadian advantage in branding communications, both internationally and domestically.[21] Indeed, how would Canada celebrate its bilingual identity without the Province of Québec, home to the vast majority of Canadian Francophones? How would all the young girls practice their immersion-school French if school and family trips were not planned to the touristic old Québec City? How would Canada rhetorically build its relationship with history without having acknowledged its roots in New France? How would one discuss Canada's complexity without analyzing the effect of the two founding nations, France and England, on its classical literature, from poems to novels to plays, and the film industry, where Québec plays a large role, representing Canada at the Cannes Film Festival and the Oscars? Léonie's bilingual diary, in French and English, is reassuring and educating, although unrealistic.

Of greatest importance in the evolution of French Canadian culture has been the sustained contact with the British, especially since the French colony was ceded to Britain in the mid-eighteenth century. Although this contact has not excluded the processes of synthesis and assimilation, Anglo-Canadian culture has generally served the role of foil and catalyst for the development in pride of an already distinct but oppressed culture. For Québec, and not for Acadia, reference with regards to cultural origins has continued to be France. Since the 1960s, Québec society underwent rapid modernization. The Québec nation has migrated from an ethnic and cultural definition to a territorial and civic one inspired by a common culture that is not Canadian, that is democratic, egalitarian, and expressed in French; a change that has crystallized the importance of the French language in the federal balance of power. If the policy of bilingualism could appease some of the fears of losing one's heritage and language, multiculturalism has not received great support in Québec. This is mainly because the political implementation intended to take the historical argument out of the picture, which resulted in reframing French Canadians "just like another ethnic group."[22] The Québec approach of immigrant integration is called "interculturalism" with a dominant culture that invites other cultures to blend in. The Léonie doll serves as an appeasing projection of French-Canadian identity while exotifying and commodifying Québec's difference.

SECOND CASE STUDY: SAILA

"When the company asked its customers where its next girl should come from, Morton said customers wanted to see a doll that represented Canada's North" (Rogers, 2011). The doll named Saila Qilavvaq is from Iqaluit, the capital city of Nunavut, a territory created in 1999 out of the existing Northwest Territories in Canada. Nunavut, widely touted as a successful modern Indigenous land claim and a victory for Inuit self-government initiatives, is the most recent territory to join Canada. In 2011, Saila became the most recent doll to join the Maplelea Girls club. As a contented, slightly smiling member of the club, the doll serves as a microcosm for Nunavut's membership in the Canadian body politic. "[P]roud of [her] Inuit heritage" (Avonlea Traditions, 2012, p. 49), Saila's outfits combine contemporary Canadian styles with traditional Inuit attire, such as her amauti (traditional parka) and Pang hat, both made in Nunavut. Likewise, her list of "favourite foods" in her journal include both muktaaq (whale skin) and pizza (2011, p. 5).

Just as Léonie's page in the English-language catalogue is interspersed with basic French, Saila's page in the English-language catalogue opens with a greeting in Inuktitut syllabics, the written form of the Inuit language, and closes with "Taima and tavvauvutit!" ("That's all and goodbye!") (Avonlea Traditions, 2012, p. 49). The English-language version of her journal offers her backstory with a sprinkling of romanized Inuktitut words, such as "kamiik" (boots) and "ulu" (an Inuit knife) (2011, pp. 5–6). Like Léonie ("pronounced 'Lay-oh'-nee," Avonlea Traditions, 2012, p. 24), Saila's full-page image in the catalogue is accompanied by a pronunciation guide ("Sigh-la," p. 48). Presumably, readers will already know how to pronounce Alexi, Taryn, Brianne, and Jenna.

An entire page of the Maplelea Girls website is devoted to explaining "The Making of Saila Qilavvaq of Nunavut: Our newest Maplelea Girl!" (n.d.). Citing "two years of extensive research," "many sources of information," and "numerous resource people," the site further explains the creation of this "interesting, authentic and positive role model." As part of the research for the doll's creation, Gallagher Morton and her family spent 10 days in Nunavut, where she interviewed local Maplelea owners and young girls. After this period of consultation, the company commissioned "our Canadian artist" to sculpt the Saila doll, making her the only Maplelea doll whose face is not based on a girl from Aurora, Ontario.

Saila is a successful and popular product. Shortly after the doll's debut, over two dozen dolls had been ordered from Nunavut and other parts of Canada. Former Nunavut Member of Parliament Nancy Karetak-Lindell emailed Gallagher Morton to express her pleasure with the doll and the Government of Nunavut planned to order the dolls for territorial day care centers (Rogers, 2011). In 2012, the doll was awarded the Canadian Toy Testing Council Children's Choice Award, largely for the superficial (and compelling) reasons that make the beautiful Maplelea Girl collection so popular:

> Black-haired Saila "lives" in Iqaluit, Nunavut, speaks Inuktitut and English, and is proud of her Inuit heritage. She has a wooden bed and beautiful bedding with attractive Arctic images, as well as a very informative keepsake journal (in three languages)... Testers like the doll's realistic look, its quality, and the quality of the beautiful clothing. (Canadian Toy Testing Council, 2011)

This Canadian fixation on Inuit or Inuit-themed products is not unique to Saila. For example, the first chapter of *Dolls of Canada: A Reference Guide* (Strahlendorf, 1990) focuses on Inuit dolls, as does the first section of the exhibition *Timeless Treasures: The Story of Dolls in Canada* (2000–2003). From very early Inuit "artifacts" to the Pang hats crafted for contemporary Maplelea Girls, Inuit crafts and Inuit-themed objects have proven quite popular throughout southern Canada. This may help to explain why a doll representing "Canada's North" was requested by popular input from Maplelea customers (Rogers, 2011).

Because of Saila's popularity, it is worth exploring some noteworthy gaps in the doll's story. First of all, in explaining Saila's last name, the journal reads: "Qilavvaq... was my grandfather's name. Inuit used to have just one name but when they started using two, he gave his to his family and chose a new one" (2011, p. 4). This brief statement ignores the socially disruptive federal policy of issuing "Eskimo identification discs" to Inuit as a means of labeling individuals (Smith, 1993). The passive phrase "they started using two [names]" overlooks the cultural difficulties associated with Project Naming, a system of designating surnames in Inuit communities that met with resistance and has since been critiqued as colonizing and patriarchal (Alia, 2007, pp. 57–59). This single example of the rapid, often destructive collision of traditional Inuit practices and centralized Canadian bureaucracy is neatly packaged in a glib explanation of Saila's names.

Secondly, Saila's journal says she was "born" at Baffin Regional Hospital, an actual hospital with two birthing rooms.[23] With dispersed settlements, sparse resources, few medical professionals, high infant mortality and suicide rates, and drastic cultural shifts, life expectancy is 6 to 11 years shorter for northern Inuit populations than the Canadian average (Oliver, Peters, & Kohen, 2012, p. 1). With a population of 6,699, Iqaluit is the largest settled Inuit community in Nunavut (Statistics Canada, 2012). Saila's birth in her home city stands in stark contrast to the experiences of most Inuit mothers and infants, who are flown from their communities to Iqaluit or Ottawa to give birth and then flown home (Purdon, 2008). Furthermore, the termination of funding for the National Aboriginal Health Organization and its subsidiaries, including Inuit Tuttarvingat (Midwifery Network), in June 2012, speaks to a larger pattern of neglect for remote, underserved communities.

The drawing of Saila's room in her journal (This is the journal, 2011) shows three beds in one room for Saila and her two sisters. This nod to the severe housing shortage and overcrowding of Inuit homes is one of the more realistic aspects of the journal, but the reality is tempered by innocent illustrations of a polar bear, inuksuit, and dog sled on the journal page, as well as the depiction of the "Arctic Fun Bedding" in the image (Avonlea Traditions, 2012, p. 54). According to *Nunatsiaq News* (Rogers, 2011) these optimistic depictions of contemporary Inuit life in Canada were derived from Gallagher Morton's time in Nunavut:

> [S]he met and spoke to several Iqaluit girls aged 10 to 13. "I was really impressed with these young girls," [Gallagher] Morton said. "They seemed to blend so easily into modern Canadian life, woven with going to camp, eating country foods and doing traditional activities. I felt like they had a foot in two worlds." So Saila was created the same way— her character speaks Inuktitut and English and sports a fleece vest, jeans and kamiks.

However, in the keepsake journal pages that accompany the new Maplelea Friends dolls, the map labeled "My Canada" does not include the northernmost portion of the country, and many of the islands that make up Nunavut (Avonlea Traditions, 2012, p. 5). This omission exemplifies the difficulty in accessing the region—as the catalogue notes "the only way you can get there is by plane" (p. 53)—which has financial implications for access to nutritious food as well as access to timely health care. Furthermore, the fact that much of Nunavut is off the Maplelea map speaks to the continuing ignorance of many Canadians about the northernmost region of "their" country. The inclusion of the Saila doll and the exclusion of much of Nunavut from the map demonstrate the broader ambivalence southern Canadians have toward northern Canada.

The doll-sized "Amazing Amauti," which retails for $56 CAD, is "made in Nunavut according to traditional design" (Avonlea Traditions, 2012, p. 53). However, Canadian art historian Michelle Bauldic (personal correspondence) offered concerns about the relatively inexpensive price of this item, as many doll-sized items crafted in Nunavut retail for well over $300 CAD and great expense is typically associated with Inuit crafts. The doll-sized Pang hat, which retails for $20 CAD, is made by the Uqqurmiut Centre for Arts and Crafts in Pangnirtung. The price for an adult-sized Pang hat made at the Uqqurmiut Centre was $75 CAD in 2009.[24] The high prices speak to the expense associated with the remote location of many fly-in communities in Nunavut, as well as their relative inaccessibility by boat during much of the year. The discrepancy between the prices of the doll clothing and other products that are made in Nunavut fails to problematize the reality of the costs associated with marginalized northern life.

It is unnecessary to list every discrepancy found in the Maplelea Girl catalogue and products. The point of these examples is to demonstrate a problematic co-optation and misleading exotification of Canadian lived experiences. Offering partial exposure to specific, rosy versions of Canadian history and contemporary life—particularly through a product with the stated goal of providing positive role models to develop knowledgeable, caring, "productive citizens" (Avonlea Traditions, 2011, p. 2)—is troublesome. Playing with the dolls is not a problem; rather, it is important to understand the partial nature of the stories presented by the doll journals and to recognize the Maplelea Girls as objects of conspicuous (Canadian) consumption. With the corporate mission "to enlighten and entertain our daughters" and their ideological emphasis on unique Canadian-ness, Maplelea Girls are oblique pedagogical tools that replace historical analysis and careful consideration of the role of the nation-state framework and capitalism in propagating inequalities in contemporary society, Canadian or otherwise ("Mission Statement," n.d.).

CONCLUSION

Billig (1995) argued that "metonymic stereotypes... impl[y] that these essential particularities... are unique: the essentials of 'our' nation, 'our country' are to be found nowhere else" (p. 102). From the byline "Canadian Dolls for Canadian Girls!" to the deliberately touted Canadian spelling ("The Maplelea System," n.d.), Maplelea Girls emphasize the unique Canadian-ness of the product line, as displayed in the company's catalogue and on-line store. The company's electronic newsletter of 26 October 2012 announced that Maplelea Girls had won the "Dr. Toy's Best Picks 2012 Children's Products Award" recognizing high standards in, among other attributes, "uniqueness" (personal correspondence). The constant flagging of the dolls as "distinctly Canadian"—through reference to the Canadian maple-leaf flag in the company name, Maplelea[f], and the preponderance of maple leaves on the company's products, including clothing for Canadian dolls and clothing for Canadian girls—reinforces the mission to teach girls to be Canadian.

Many critiques of the American Girl doll line also apply to the Canadian Maplelea Girls, including the whitewashing of multiculturalism, the token exoticism, and historical niceties that replace harsher realities in the doll's admittedly fictional stories. The expense associated with ownership of both types of dolls and their pricey accessories encourage a class-based critique of these role-model dolls. Furthermore, like American Girl dolls, Maplelea Girls and most of their accessories are made "overseas" (Avonlea Traditions, 2012, p. 2). This fact could temper claims of nation-based identification with the dolls.

Other identity-based dolls, such as Australian, British ("My London"), and Jewish ("Gali") Girl dolls also tout their national uniqueness and role in the pedagogy of identity formation.[25] This interest in identity formation, girls, and dolls bespeaks a larger interest in the future mothering of the nation. In the case of Maplelea Girls, this is made particularly explicit:

> We are confident that a Maplelea Girl doll will be a meaningful part of your daughter's childhood... When she is finished her doll-playing years she will...place...her doll and accessories in the sturdy keepsake storage box and save it to share with her own daughter some day. (Gallagher Morton, 2012)

Although "artfully partial, and selectively idealized," the dolls "represent the essence which is to be carried unamendably into the future" (Billig, 1995, p. 102). This emphasis on nostalgic preservation of dolls for anticipated future (Canadian) daughters bespeaks an ongoing interest in raising caring, responsible citizens to propagate the nation. While this advocacy of responsible citizenship through entertaining education can be read as beneficial, it is important to interrogate the role that dolls, as blatant objects of banal nationalism, play in identity formation.

The Maplelea Girls showcase how banal nationalism is at work—and play— through girlhood toys in the settler-invader colony of Canada. The dolls, particularly Léonie from Québec City and Saila from Iqaluit, demonstrate large-scale political and rhetorical concerns around the Canadian federal policy of multiculturalism reframed by a conservative ideology. The dolls demonstrate how disparate identities are accommodated in the Canadian framework through celebratory, commercially viable, and publicly sanctioned inclusivity. This interrogation of the popularity of the Canadian Maplelea Girls as objects of play and tokens of identity within the Canadian framework demonstrates that, through a subversion of role playing, the dolls teach Canadian girls what to become. Perhaps *Nunatsiaq News* says it best: "the Maplelea Girls [is] a line of Canadian dolls that aim to capture the country's different regions and cultures" ("Saila Doll Picks Up Canadian Toy Testing Council Award," 2011). Is it possible to let them go?

ACKNOWLEDGEMENTS

We would like to thank Emily Hazlett and Eva Mackey for their thoughtful feedback on drafts of this chapter. We credit: Jillian Klean Zwilling for bringing Ilona Szwarc's work to our attention; Eva Mackey for the phrase "skin deep difference;" and André Loiselle for suggesting the "ambivalence" of southern Canadians toward northern Canada.

NOTES

1. The original dolls, from Manitoba, Toronto, Banff, and Nova Scotia did not represent the first four provinces to enter Canadian Confederation in 1867 (although Nova Scotia and Ontario were represented, Québec and New Brunswick were not).
2. "Settler-invader colony" is a term used in post-colonial studies to indicate recognition of ongoing, unresolved Indigenous land claims alongside permanent settlement by immigrant communities.
3. For further consideration of Canadian cultural sovereignty in the face of overwhelming American media influences, see Bodroghkozy (2002), one of many publications on the topic.
4. The homepage of Aurora, Ontario, bills it as an affluent, "scenic," "heritage" community north of Toronto (http://www.town.aurora.on.ca/). Its location near the commercial center of Canada, Toronto, and the centrality of the Maplelea headquarters in Newmarket, Ontario, reflect the subur-banality of the product.
5. For an exploration of the effects of exposure to national symbols, see Butz, 2009.
6. "Our Customers are Saying," http://www.maplelea.com/en/for-parents/our-customers-are-saying.aspx
7. MapleLeafMommy, http://www.mapleleafmommy.com/2012/06/maplelea-girls-all-canadian-dolls-great.html
8. SimplyStacie, http://www.simplystacie.net/2012/06/maplelea-girls-review-giveaway-can/
9. FiestyFrugalAndFabulous, http://feistyfrugalandfabulous.com/2012/08/maplelea-girls-dolls-for-canadian-girls/
10 Tales Of A Ranting Ginger, http://www.talesofarantingginger.com/2012/07/maplelea-girls-review-giveaway.html
11. Kwan (2012).
12. Reid-Walsh and Mitchell (2009, p. 111).
13. La cabane à sucre (sugar shack) is the maple syrup production cabin.
14. Interculturalism as an integration policy speaks to current-day Québec society, a host society whose definition now revolves around French language as the only true vector of integration. This is ideal ground for inquiring into Quebec's identity in terms of language, its distinction from the rest of Canada, and social change, although this is not the primarily focus of this chapter.
15. Law 118 was passed in 2000 at the Quebec National Assembly following the amendment of article 93 of the Canadian Constitution in 1998 to change the denominational system into a secular one, the language of education being the sole differentiation between public schools.

16. For an in-depth exploration of these questions, see: Meunier (n.d.) «Catholicisme et laïcité au Québec,» and Meunier and Mager (2007, 2008).

17. This practice facilitates civic identification for everything from university degrees to health care.

18. For detailed statistical and qualitative information on the historical and current integration of immigrants in Montréal, see Laura-Julie Perreault and Jean-Christophe Laurence (2010), *Guide du Montréal Multiple*.

19. Éric Bédard, *Chroniques Généalogiques. Le Québec: Une Histoire de Famille.* «Les Bélanger». Originally published in a popular newspaper, *Le Journal de Montréal*, these genealogical chronicles are now accessible on-line : http://lequebecunehistoiredefamille.com/node/40761

20. The deportation of 10,000 Acadians by the British in 1755 that led some survivors to find shore in Louisiana where the Cajun identity developed.

21. For more on branding Canada, see Richard Nimijean, "The Politics of Branding in Canada: The International-Domestic Nexus and the Rethinking of Canada's Place in the World" (2006).

22. See Danic Parenteau (2008), "Interculturalisme Multiculturalisme, Bonnet Blanc, Blanc Bonnet." For the current expressions of the rejection of multiculturalism in the context of the reasonable accommodation commission, see Kathryn Chan (2008) and her reference to Danic Parenteau's ideas in "Charitable According to Whom? The Clash Between Quebec's Societal Values and the Law Governing the Registration of Charities."

23. When Qikiqtani General Hospital opened in 2007, this number increased to four birthing rooms.

24. According to their brochure, http://www.uqqurmiut.com/catalogue-retail-sheet-december-2009.pdf

25. The "uniquely Australian play doll" was launched in November 2008 (personal correspondence). The Australia Girl doll homepage plays "Waltzing Matilda," and every doll comes with "specially designed" sandals that only fit the feet of Australian Girl dolls (http://australiangirldoll.com. au/Australian). My London Girl dolls were launched in September 2011, and the logo consists of a pink and purple British flag in the shape of a heart (http://www.mylondongirl.co.uk/). Gali Girls, "Jewish dolls for Jewish Girls," launched in 2004. The now-defunct homepage featured a doll waving the flag of Israel at an Israel Day Parade in 2012 (http://www.galigirls.com/).

REFERENCES

Acosta-Alzuru, C., & Kreshel, P. J. (2002). "I'm an American Girl ... Whatever that means": Girls consuming pleasant company's American Girl identity. *Journal of Communication 52*(1), 139–161.

Alia, Valerie. (2007). *Names and Nunavut: Culture and Identity in Arctic Canada.* New York & Oxford: Berghahn Books.

Avonlea Traditions. (2011, October). *Les filles Maplelea Girls: Canadian dolls for Canadian girls! Catalog.* Ontario, Canada: Avonlea Traditions.

Avonlea Traditions. (2012, November). *Maplelea: Canadian dolls for Canadian girls. Catalog.* Ontario, Canada. Avonlea Traditions.

Billig, M. (1995). *Banal nationalism.* London, England: Sage.

Bissoondath, N. (1995). *Le marché aux illusions.* Montréal, Canada: Boréal.

Bodroghkozy, A. (2002). As Canadian as possible…: Anglo-Canadian popular culture and the American other. In H. Jenkins, T. McPherson, & J. Shattuck (Eds.), *Hop on pop: The politics and pleasures of popular culture* (pp. 566–589). Durham, NC: Duke University Press.

Brubaker, R. (1996). *Nationalism reframed: Nationhood and the national question in the new Europe.* Cambridge, England: Cambridge University Press.

Butz, D. A. (2009). National symbols as agents of psychological and social change. *Political Psychology, 30*(5), 779–804.

Canadian Toy Testing Council. (2011). *Children's Choice Awards 2012.* Retrieved from http://toy-testing.org/wp-content/uploads/2011/11/CC12Picture-ss1.pdf

Chan, K. (2008). Charitable according to whom? The clash between Quebec's societal values and the law governing the registration of charities. *Les Cahiers de Droit, 49*(2), 277–295.

DuCille, A. (1996). Toy theory: Black Barbie and the deep play of difference. In *Skin trade.* Cambridge, MA: Harvard University Press.

Dumont, F. (1971, October). L'avènement du multiculturalisme. *Le Devoir.*

Fast facts (n.d.). Retrieved from http://www.americangirl.com/corp/corporate.php?section=about&id=6

Gallagher Morton, K. (n.d.). Dear parents. Retrieved from http://www.maplelea.com/en/for-parents/dear-parents.aspx

Hade, D. (1999). Lies my children's books taught me: History meets popular culture in "The American Girls books." In R. McGillis (Ed.), *Voices of the other: Children's literature and the postcolonial context* (pp. 153–164). New York, NY: Garland.

Hall, S. (1997). The local and the global: Globalization and ethnicity. In A. McClintock, A. Mufti, & E. Shohat (Eds.), *Dangerous liaisons: Gender, nation, and postcolonial perspectives* (pp. 173–187). Minneapolis, MN: University of Minnesota Press.

Inness, S. A. (1998). "Anti-Barbies": The American Girls collection and political ideologies. In S. A. Inness (Ed.), *Delinquents and debutantes: Twentieth-century American Girls' culture* (pp. 164–183). New York, NY: NYU Press.

The journal of Léonie Bélanger-Leblanc. (2008)(pp. 61–64). http://www.maplelea.com/documents/Leonie%20Journal%204p.Eng.0001.pdf

Keohane, K. (1997). *Symptoms of Canada. An essay on Canadian identity.* Toronto, Canada: University of Toronto Press.

Kwan, A. (2012, June 28). Do these dolls perpetuate Canadian stereotypes? *Globe & Mail.* Retrieved from http://www.theglobeandmail.com/life/parenting/do-these-dolls-perpetuate-canadian-stereotypes/article4378145/

Mackey, E. (2002). *The house of difference: Cultural politics and national identity in Canada.* Toronto, Canada: University of Toronto Press.

Maplelea FAQs. (2012). What is the "ethnicity" or "cultural background" of the six characters? Retrieved from http://www.maplelea.com/en/customer-tools/common-questions.aspx

Maplelea FAQs. (2012). How did you choose the ethnic/cultural background of the Maplelea Girls? Retrieved from http://www.maplelea.com/en/customer-tools/common-questions.aspx

Maplelea Girls Facebook. (December 2012). Very proud Canadian look… Retrieved from https://www.facebook.com/Maplelea

The making of Saila Qilavvaq of Nunavut: Our newest Maplelea Girl! (n.d.). Retrieved from http://www.maplelea.com/en/for-parents/the-making-of-saila.aspx

The Maplelea system. (n.d.). Retrieved from http://www.maplelea.com/en/about-us/who-we-are/themapleleasystem.aspx

Markman, E. M. (1989). *Categorization and naming in children*. Cambridge, MA: The MIT Press.

Marshall, E. (2009). Consuming girlhood: Young women, femininities, and American Girl. *Girlhood Studies, 2*(1), 94–111.

Meet the Maplelea Girls. (n.d.). Retrieved from http://www.maplelea.com/en/fun-for-girls/Meet-the-Maplelea-Girls.aspx

Meunier, E. M. (Dir.). (n.d.). Catholicisme et laïcité au Québec. *Recherches Sociographiques, LII* (3), 201.

Meunier, E. M., & Mager, R. (Dirs.). (2007, 2008). La religion au Québec. Regards croisés sur une intrigue moderne. *Globe: Revue internationale d'Études québécoises, 10*(2), *11*(1), 1.

Meyer, P. (2008). *Principia rhetorica. Une théorie générale de l'argumentation*. Paris, France: Fayard.

Mission statement. (n.d.). Retrieved from http://www.maplelea.com/en/about-us/Mission-Statement.aspx

Nimijean, R. (2006). The politics of branding in Canada: The international-domestic nexus and the rethinking of Canada's place in the world. *Revista Mexicana de Estudios Canadienses, Verano, 011*, 66–85.

Oliver, L. N., Peters, P. A., & Kohen, D. E. (2012, September). Mortality rates among children and teenagers living in Inuit Nunangat, 1994 to 2008. *Health Reports, 23*(3), 1–6. Retrieved from http://www.statcan.gc.ca/pub/82-003-x/2012003/article/11695-eng.htm

Orr, Lisa. (2009). "Difference That Is Actually Sameness Mass-Reproduced": Barbie Joins the Princess Convergence. *Jeuness: Young People, Texts, Cultures, 1*(1), 9–30.

Parenteau, D. (2008, November–December). Interculturalisme multiculturalisme, bonnet blanc, blanc bonnet. *Action Nationale*.

Patrick, D. (2010). Canada. In J. Fishman & O. Garcia (Eds.), *Handbook of language and ethnic identity* (pp. 286–301). Oxford, England: Oxford University Press.

Perreault, L. J., & Laurence, J. C. (2010). *Guide du Montréal multiple*. Montréal: Boréal.

Purdon, H. (2008). Inuit midwives: The evolution of Inuit women's birthing practices in Northern Canada. *The Health eZine*. Retrieved from http://health.lilithezine.com/Inuit-Birthing-Practices.html

Reid-Walsh, J., & Mitchell, C. (2009). Mapping a Canadian girlhood historically through dolls and doll-play. In L. Lerner (Ed.), *Depicting Canada's Children* (pp. 109–129). Waterloo, Canada: Wilfrid Laurier Press.

Rogers, S. (2011, October 17). Saila Qilavvaq dolls make their entrance. *Nunatsiaq News*.

Rust, S. (2004, November). An American Girl tea party: Multicultural dolls escort some very special young readers to a fun event. *Black Issues Book Review, 6*(6), 76–77.

Saila doll picks up Canadian Toy Testing Council award. (2011, November 9). *Nunatsiaq News*.

Smith, D. (1993). The emergence of "Eskimo status": An examination of the Eskimo disk list system and its social consequences, 1925–1970. In N. Dyck & J. Waldram (Eds.), *Anthropology, public policy and native peoples in Canada* (pp. 41–74). Montreal, Canada: McGill-Queen's University Press.

Statistics Canada. (2012, September). Catalogue no. 82-003-XPE.

Strahlendorf, E. R. (1990). *Dolls of Canada: A reference guide*. Toronto, Canada: University of Toronto Press.

SummerStudiosAG. (2012, November 4). *New AG products vs. Maplelea* [Video file]. Retrieved from http://www.youtube.com/watch?v=HvaAQf2xHBw

Susina, J. (1999, January). American Girls collection: Barbies with a sense of history. *Children's Literature Association Quarterly, 24*(3), 130–135.

This is the journal of Saila Qilavvaq. (2011). (pp. 3–6). http://www.maplelea.com/documents/Saila%20Journal.pdf

Timeless treasures: The story of dolls in Canada [Exhibition]. (2000–2003). http://www.civilization.ca/cmc/exhibitions/hist/dolls/doint01e.shtml

Tremblay, S. (2004). Une grande famille acadienne: Les Leblanc. *Cap-aux-Diamants: La Revue d'Histoire du Québec, 77,* 50.

Trépanier, A. (2001). *Un discours à plusieurs voix, la grammaire du oui en 1995.* Ste-Foy, France: Presses de l'Université Laval.

Trudeau, P. E. (1971, October 8). Multiculturalism. Retrieved from http://www.canadahistory.com/sections/documents/Primeministers/trudeau/docs-onmulticulturalism.htm

What do Canadian girls want? Ask them! (2009, November 20). Retrieved from http://www.newswire.ca/en/story/419641/what-do-canadian-girls-want-ask-them

Zavos, Alison. (2012, April 3). Portraits of American Girls with their "American Girl" dolls. Retrieved from http://www.featureshoot.com/2012/04/portraits-of-american-girls-with-their-american-girl-dolls/#!C5wLr

Contributors

Diana Anselmo-Sequeira recently completed her dissertation on the history of American cinema and the first generation of movie-loving girls at the University of California, Irvine. Her work has been published in the *Spectator* and *Luso-Brazilian Review*, forthcoming in *Cinema Journal*, and in such anthologies as *Transnational Horror Across Visual Media* and *Princess Cultures: Mediating Girls' Identities and Imaginations*. She is also co-editor of the forthcoming *Girls' Economies: Work & Play Cultures*.

Miriam Forman-Brunell is professor of History at the University of Missouri-Kansas City. She is the author of *Made to Play House: Dolls and the Commercialization of American Girlhood* and *Babysitter: An American History*. Forman-Brunell is the editor of *The Story of Rose O'Neill: An Autobiography* and *Girlhood in America: An Encyclopedia*. She is also co-editor of *The Girls' History & Culture Readers: The Nineteenth and Twentieth Centuries* and *Princess Cultures: Mediating Girls' Identities and Imaginations*. Forman-Brunell guest edited the doll-themed issue of *Girlhood Studies: An Interdisciplinary Journal* that inspired this collection. She is also co-editor of the forthcoming, *Girls' Economies: Work & Play Cultures*.

Index

mediated
youth

Sharon R. Mazzarella
General Editor

Grounded in cultural studies, books in this series will study the cultures, artifacts, and media of children, tweens, teens, and college-aged youth. Whether studying television, popular music, fashion, sports, toys, the Internet, self-publishing, leisure, clubs, school, cultures/activities, film, dance, language, tie-in merchandising, concerts, subcultures, or other forms of popular culture, books in this series go beyond the dominant paradigm of traditional scholarship on the effects of media/culture on youth. Instead, authors endeavor to understand the complex relationship between youth and popular culture. Relevant studies would include, but are not limited to studies of how youth negotiate their way through the maze of corporately-produced mass culture; how they themselves have become cultural producers; how youth create "safe spaces" for themselves within the broader culture; the political economy of youth culture industries; the representational politics inherent in mediated coverage and portrayals of youth; and so on. Books that provide a forum for the "voices" of the young are particularly encouraged. The source of such voices can range from in-depth interviews and other ethnographic studies to textual analyses of cultural artifacts created by youth.

For further information about the series and submitting manuscripts, please contact:

SHARON R. MAZZARELLA
School of Communication Studies
James Madison University
Harrisonburg, VA 22807

To order other books in this series, please contact our Customer Service Department at:

(800) 770-LANG (within the U.S.)
(212) 647-7706 (outside the U.S.)
(212) 647-7707 FAX

Or browse online by series at WWW.PETERLANG.COM